REFERENCE BOOKS BULLETIN 2004 2005

A Compilation of Evaluations
September 2004 through August 2005

Prepared by American Library Association Reference Books Bulletin Editorial Board

Edited by Mary Ellen Quinn
Compiled by Jerry Eberle

Booklist Publications
Chicago, 2006

Copyright 1996, 2006 by the American Library Association.

Permission to quote any review in full or in part must be obtained from the Office of Rights and Permissions of the American Library Association. Permission to quote a review in full will be granted only to the publisher of the work reviewed.

Library of Congress Catalog Card Number 73-159565

International Standard Book Number 13: 978-0-8389-8412-3
International Standard Book Number 10: 0-8389-8412-6

International Standard Serial Number 8755-0962

Printed in the United States of America

Cover design by Jim Lange

Contents

iv	Preface
v	Reference Books Bulletin Editorial Board
vi	Contributing Reviewers
1	Encyclopedia Update, 2004
6	Special Features
	Reviews
24	Generalities
28	Philosophy, Psychology, Religion
32	Sociology, Anthropology, Political Science
38	Business, Economics, Resources
40	Law, Public Administration, Social Problems and Services
44	Education, Commerce, Customs
47	Language
49	Science
53	Medicine, Health Technology, Management
62	Fine Arts, Decorative Arts, Music
65	Performing Arts, Recreation
68	Literature
73	Geography, Biography
78	History
	Indexes
92	Subject Index
95	Title Index

Preface

This thirty-seventh annual compilation consists of the reviews and articles appearing in *Reference Books Bulletin* from September 2004 through August 2005. The *RBB* Editorial Board and contributing reviewers continue to provide the reliable reviews needed to navigate the changeable world of reference publishing. Their contribution to the profession is invaluable. It is a privilege to be associated with such a talented and dedicated group of individuals.

I would like to thank *RBB* editor extraordinaire Mary Ellen Quinn for her guidance and patience. Thanks are also due to Annie McCormick, editorial assistant and Jerry Eberle, former editorial assistant, and to the staffs of *Booklist* and ALA Publishing. Finally, I would like to thank my colleagues at the Chicago Public Library for their continued support.

Carolyn M. Mulac
Chair

Reference Books Bulletin Editorial Board
2006-2007

Reference Books Bulletin Editorial Board, 2004–05

Carolyn Mulac, Division Chief, General Information Services, Chicago Public Library, Chicago, Illinois, Chair.

Donald Altschiller, History Bibliographer, Mugar Memorial Library, Boston University, Boston, Massachusetts.

Barbara Bibel, Reference Librarian, Oakland Public Library, Oakland, California.

Christine Bulson, Assistant Director for Reference and Circulation Services, Milne Library, SUNY Oneonta, Oneonta, New York.

Susan Gardner, Reference/Instruction Librarian, Leavey Library, University of Southern California, Los Angeles, California.

Dona Helmer, Librarian, Anchorage School District, Alaska.

Jack O'Gorman, Reference Librarian, Roesch Library, University of Dayton, Dayton, Ohio, Chair.

Linda Loos Scarth, Reference Librarian, Busse Center Library, Mount Mercy College, Cedar Rapids, Iowa.

Diana Donner Shonrock, Science Librarian/Family and Consumer Sciences Bibliographer, Parks Library, Iowa State University, Ames, Iowa.

Shauna Yusko, Librarian, St. Monica School, Mercer Island, Washington.

Reference Books Bulletin Contributing Reviewers, 2004–05

Donald Altschiller, History Bibliographer, Mugar Memorial Library, Boston University.

Susan Awe, Director, Business and Economics, Parish Memorial Library, University of New Mexico, Albuquerque, New Mexico.

Ken Black, Director of Teaching and Learning Technology, Dominican University, River Forest, Illinois.

Barbara Bibel, Reference Librarian, Oakland Public Library, Oakland, California.

Christine Bulson, Librarian Emeritus, Milne Library, SUNY Oneonta, Oneonta, New York.

Craig Bunch, Librarian, Coldspring-Oakhurst High School Library, Coldspring, Texas.

Nancy Cannon, Reference Librarian, Milne Library, SUNY Oneonta, Oneonta, New York.

Jerry Carbone, Director, Brooks Memorial Library, Brattleboro, Vermont.

Ann E. Cohen, Assistant Division Head, Information Center, Rochester Public Library, Rochester, New York.

Sharon E. Cohen, Boynton Beach, Florida.

Harold V. Cordry, Independent scholar, Baldwin, Kansas.

Jennifer Dawson, Electronic Resources Librarian, Kanawha County Public Library, Charleston, West Virginia.

Carole C. Deily, Reference Librarian, Plano Public Library System, Plano, Texas.

John Doherty, Librarian, Arts and Humanities, Cline Library, Northern Arizona University, Flagstaff, Arizona.

Marie Ellis, Librarian IV Emeritus, University of Georgia Libraries, Athens, Georgia.

Susanna Eng, Reference/Instruction Librarian, University of Southern California, Los Angeles, California.

Stephen Fadel, Public Services Librarian, Everett Community College, Everett, Washington.

Lesley S. J. Farmer, Professor, CSU Long Beach, Long Beach, California.

Susan Gardner, Leavey Library, University of Southern California, Los Angeles, California.

Rochelle Glantz, Reviews Editor, Linworth Publishing, Santa Fe, New Mexico.

Susan Gooden, Librarian, Concord High School, Wilmington, Delaware.

Carol Sue Harless, Stone Mountain High School, Dekalb County School System, Stone Mountain, Georgia.

Nora Harris, Harris Indexing Service, Novato, California.

Dona Helmer, College Gate Elementary School, Anchorage, Alaska.

Michelle Hendley, Reference/Instruction Librarian, Milne Library, SUNY Oneonta, Oneonta, New York.

Robin Hoelle, Cybrarian, Live Oaks Career Development Center, Milford, Ohio.

Patricia M. Hogan, Administrative Librarian, Poplar Creek Public Library District, Streamwood, Illinois.

Danise Hoover, Associate Librarian for Public Services, Hunter College Library, New York, New York.

Merle Jacob, Chicago, Illinois.

Sally Sartain Jane, former Head of Adult Collection Development, Lee County Library System, Fort Myers, Florida.

Lisa N. Johnston, Associate Director/Head of Public Services, Sweet Briar College Libraries, Sweet Briar, Virginia.

Diana Kirby, Royal Palm Beach, Florida.

Jeff Kosokoff, Head of Reference Services, Lamont Library, Harvard University, Cambridge, Massachusetts.

Marlene M. Kuhl, Catonsville Library, Catonsville, Maryland.

Abbie Vestal Landry, Head of Reference Division, Watson Library, Northwestern State University, Natchitoches, Louisiana.

Jan Lewis, Interim Head of Reference, Joyner Library, East Carolina University, Greenville, North Carolina.

Art A. Lichtenstein, Director of Library, University of Central Arkansas, Conway, Arkansas.

Kathleen M. McBroom, Resource Teacher for Library Media and Automation, Dearborn Public Schools, Dearborn, Michigan.

Christopher McConnell, Librarian, Protein Design Labs, Inc., Fremont, California.

H. Robert Malinowsky, Professor and Manager of Collection Development, University of Illinois at Chicago Library, Chicago, Illinois.

Michael E. Matthews, Reference and Instruction Librarian, Northwestern Memorial Library, Natchitoches, Louisiana.

Arthur S. Meyers, Library Director, Russell Library, Middletown, Connecticut.

Carolyn M. Mulac, Information Center, Chicago Public Library, Chicago, Illinois.

Jack O'Gorman, Reference Librarian, Roesch Library, University of Dayton, Dayton, Ohio.

Kathryn C. O'Gorman, Director, Johnnie Mae Berry Library, Cincinnati State, Cincinnati, Ohio.

Maren C. Ostergard, Children's Librarian, Bellevue Regional Library, Bellevue, Washington.

Sue Polanka, Coordinator, Reference and Instruction, Roesch Library, University of Dayton, Dayton, Ohio.

Margaret Power, Reference Services Coordinator, DePaul University Library, Chicago, Illinois.

James Rettig, University Librarian, Boatwright Memorial Library, University of Richmond, Richmond, Virginia.

Linda Scarth, Reference Librarian, Busse Center Library, Mount Mercy College, Cedar Rapids, Iowa.

Diana Donner Shonrock, Science Librarian/Family and Consumer Sciences Bibliographer, Parks Library, Iowa State University, Ames, Iowa.

Esther Sinofsky, Coordinating Field Librarian, Library Services, Los Angeles Unified School District, Los Angeles, California.

Mary Ellen Snodgrass, Independent Scholar, Hickory, North Carolina.

Kathleen Stipek, Adult Services Librarian, Alachua County Library District, Gainesville, Florida.

Stephen E. Stratton, Head, Collections and Technical Services, California State University, Channel Islands, Camarillo, California.

Kaye M. Talley, Coordinator of Technical Services, Torreyson Library, University of Central Arkansas, Conway, Arkansas.

William Joseph Thomas, Instruction/Reference Librarian, Joyner Library, East Carolina University, Greenville, North Carolina.

Terri Tomchyshyn, Head of Library Information Services, CSE Library, Ottawa, Ontario.

Michael Tosko, Information Literacy Coordinator, University of Akron, Akron, Ohio.

Scottie Wallace, Managing Librarian, Downtown Reno Library, Washoe County Library System, Reno, Nevada.

Cheryl Karp Ward, East Hartford High School, Library Media Center, East Hartford, Connecticut.

Sarah Barbara Watstein, Associate University Librarian for Public Services, VCU Libraries, Virginia Commonwealth University, Richmond, Virginia.

Ann Welton, Grant Center for the Expressive Arts, Tacoma, Washington.

Shauna Yusko, Librarian, St. Monica School, Mercer Island, Washington.

Encyclopedia Update, 2004

Compton's Encyclopedia and Fact-Index	1
Encyclopedia Americana	1
Encyclopedia Americana Online	3
Encyclopedia Britannica Online	2
Encyclopedia Britannica Online School Edition	2
Grolier Online	3
Grolier Multimedia Encyclopedia	3
The New Book of Knowledge	2
The New Book of Knowledge Online	3
World Book Encyclopedia	2
World Book Online Reference Center	4

In this year's Encyclopedia Update we review four print encyclopedias: Compton's Encyclopedia and Fact-Index, Encyclopedia Americana, The New Book of Knowledge, and The World Book Encyclopedia. There is no print Encyclopaedia Britannica with a 2004 copyright; the 2005 Britannica will be out in February. We also review Encyclopaedia Britannica Online and Encyclopaedia Britannica Online School Edition; Grolier Online's Encyclopedia Americana Online, Grolier Multimedia Encyclopedia, and The New Book of Knowledge Online; and World Book Online Reference Center. Online, encyclopedias continue to morph from being souped-up versions of their print counterparts to being more robust "reference centers" with one-stop searching, a concept most fully realized in Grolier Online at this point because it has a bigger armament of resources from which to draw. Because these reference centers now offer so many different features, we have replaced our old table of basic comparative numbers with fuller summaries (p.4) of what each one offers. For a table of numbers on the print encyclopedias, see p.2.

—Susan Awe and Barbara Bibel

Compton's Encyclopedia and Fact-Index. 26v. 2004. Encyclopaedia Britannica, $699; 2–5 sets $664; 6+ sets $629 each (1-59339-180-0). 031.

Compton's continues to serve students and home users by providing basic information on a wide variety of topics related to the school curriculum and current events. Most articles are not signed. The current edition went to press on November 21, 2003, and no events that occurred after this date appear in the text. There are no new illustrations for 2004 and no new maps, although some maps have been changed. No bibliographies were updated.

This edition has 16 new articles, including *Global warming, SARS,* and *West Nile virus,* and biographies of Yo-Yo Ma, Osama bin Laden, and Britney Spears. Among the 78 revised articles are *Africa, Bridge, Korea, Plant, Race and ethnicity,* and *United States.* The accident that destroyed the space shuttle *Columbia* is mentioned in the article *Space exploration.* There is no entry for the war in Iraq, although it does show up in other entries. The Saddam Hussein entry notes the deaths of his sons. The entry for George W. Bush contains information on the war and also about some 2003 domestic matters, such as the tax-cut package approved in May. The Iraq entry mentions some 2003 events, but the bibliography has no titles published later than 1991. The bibliography in the revised article on Africa is equally also out-of-date, and the article contains little from the years after the late 1990s.

Compton's has continued the practice of putting all tables and many brief articles in its *Fact-Index* volume. The *Fact-Index* is the only place that users will find many articles and biographies (including a few popular current personalities not found in other encyclopedias), some of which deserve space in the main encyclopedia. A number of the new entries, including those for *Global warming, SARS,* and *West Nile virus,* are found here instead of in the main encyclopedia. Although some *Fact-Index* articles are fairly lengthy and include bibliographies, *Global warming* is nothing more than a short dictionary-style definition. Many of the numerous tables in the *Fact-Index* are useful, but it would make more sense to put the lists of presidential cabinet members in the articles about each president, just as the table of books of the Bible belongs in *Bible.* Asthma deserves full coverage in an article. Because it is easier to make changes to the *Fact-Index* than to the rest of the encyclopedia, a number of the *Fact-Index* entries have information that is more up-to-date than in the rest of the encyclopedia, but the division of content makes *Compton's* more difficult to use, especially for unsophisticated searchers.

Compton's is a decent basic encyclopedia suitable for home and school use, but it is not a first choice.

Encyclopedia Americana. 30v. 2004. Grolier, $999 (0-7172-0137-6). 031.

Encyclopedia Americana, known for thorough scholarly coverage, had numerous changes for 2004—adding 41 new articles, 35 rewritten articles, 75 new color photographs and 34 new black-and-white ones, and revising or adding 125 bibliographies—in addition to ongoing projects. Among the editorial programs for this edition were additions of or changes to some 350 visual arts entries; an overhaul of coverage of Canadian literature; ongoing disease article revisions; the start of a project to rework urban studies coverage; and, in science and technology, a focus on bringing military technology articles up-to-date. The more than 30 new contributors include Stephen Frederic Dale, professor of South Asian and Islamic history, Ohio State University *(Afghanistan)* and Richard T. LeGates, professor of urban studies, San Francisco State University *(City, Urban planning, Urban renewal, Zoning).*

Since the campaign against terrorism is still a major factor in current events, country articles on Iraq, Yemen, and Afghanistan were completely replaced, while issues like chemical and biological weapons and the creation of the Department of Homeland Security were also addressed. A color relief map of Afghanistan replaced a less detailed one; six maps were altered significantly, including Kurdistan and the Balkans; and a map showing the troop movements during Operation Iraqi Freedom was included in the *Persian Gulf Wars* entry, which was extensively revised. Despite that fact that the revision deadline for the 2004 edition was mid-November 2003, the December capture of Saddam Hussein is noted in both the Saddam Hussein and Iraq entries. A new entry on the confederation of Serbia and Montenegro was added, as well as an extensive update for *Athens, Greece* in anticipation of the 2004 Olympic Games. The article on *Bush, George W.* was updated and expanded in light of his role in international relations, and there is information about his falling approval ratings in the fall of 2003, as well as a projected budget deficit figure for 2004.

Entirely new entries include *Cladistics; Fibromyalgia; Schwarzenegger, Arnold; Sociobiology;* and *Williams, Venus.* In the California article, Arnold Schwarzenegger's election has been added to several tables though not to the article text.

There still is no entry on *SARS,* but in the index, users are referred to the article on *China,* which has one line about the SARS outbreak there. Several paragraphs on the *Columbia* accident have been added to *Space shuttle.* There is no entry for John Kerry.

Americana's revision program has always resulted in unevenness, and while portions of the encyclopedia march briskly along, others lag farther and farther behind. The 40-page *Motion picture,* for example, seems not have been touched in a generation. Still, in many respects, *Americana* remains a good choice for high-school, academic, and public libraries. For

Encyclopedias in Print

Name	Number of Volumes	Number of Entries	Number of Pages	Number of Illustrations	Percent of Illustrations in Full Color	Price
Compton's	26	37,000	11,000	23,000	71	$699
Encyclopedia Britannica	30	45,000	26,800	23,000	20	$999
New Book of Knowledge	21	9,243	10,576	27,850	93	$699
World Book	22	17,300	14,244	27,500	80	$859

2004, the print *Americana* has completely changed its drab covers, adding photographs, color, and easy-to-read volume numbers to its sturdy binding—a vast improvement.

The New Book of Knowledge. 21 v. 2004. Grolier, $699. (0-7172-0584-3). 031.

The New Book of Knowledge (NBK) continues to address the information needs and after-school interests of elementary- and middle-school children at their reading levels. Illustrations are found on nearly every page, and these and the large font make this encyclopedia very child friendly. Saddam Hussein's capture, the inauguration of Arnold Schwarzenegger as governor of California, the outcomes of the 2003 World Series and 2004 Superbowl XXXVIII, and the 2003 Nobel Prize winners are included in this edition. Some of these events occurred after the mid-November 2003 revision deadline. Among the 36 new entries are *Arbitration; Atheism; Eleanor of Aquitaine; Holistic medicine; Homeland Security, United States Department of; Iraq War;* and *Oriental Exclusion Acts.* With the *Europe* entry, NBK completes its revision of articles on continents. The 37 replacement articles also include *Archaeology, Oils and fats, Serbia and Montenegro,* and *Video recording.* Entries that received major revisions include *Bush, George W.; Elections; Iraq; Organization of Petroleum Exporting Countries (OPEC); Slovenia;* and *Whales.* There are 7 new maps, 459 new photographs, and 105 new pieces of color art.

NBK includes a variety of interesting features designed for its audience: "Wonder Questions," "Literary Selections," "Homework Help," "Projects and Experiments," and "Did You Know That . . ." Each volume still has its own index with blue pages, which is a nice feature for young users. A thorough, comprehensive index volume is also included with the set. Clearly organized and simply written, this encyclopedia is a real help for elementary- and middle-school teachers and students.

The World Book Encyclopedia. 22v. 2004. World Book, school and library price $859; 2-5 sets $839; 6+ sets $809 each (0-7166-0104-4). 031.

Designed to meet the research needs of students in elementary through high school, *World Book* is also a good general encyclopedia for adults. It is current, accessible, easy to use, and well illustrated. The 2004 print edition has 88 new articles. They include *Angiogenesis, Bullying, Factory farming, Identity theft, Macular degeneration, Money laundering, Obesity, Palestinian Authority, Statin,* and *Wal-Mart Stores, Inc.* Judy Dench, Bill Frist, and Annika Sorenstam are a few of the people covered in new biographical entries. *Alzheimer's disease; Arafat, Yasir; Halley's Comet; Marijuana;* and *Tofu* are among the 174 articles that have been extensively revised or rewritten. Another 2,200 articles were partially revised. More than 220 maps were added or changed, and there are 350 new illustrations. Revisions were made to 315 bibliographies. Some 155 new contributors provided fresh entries or revised existing ones.

World Book "makes revisions in every field of knowledge or activity whenever developments make it appropriate to do so." It generally scores high in providing current information, and there are few examples of topics that are left to languish while others are brought up-to-date. Changes related to the war in Iraq are evident in many entries, including *Terrorism* and the entries on George W. Bush and Saddam Hussein. *Iraq* includes references to the July 2003 deaths of Saddam Hussein's sons. A new entry, *Persian Gulf War of 2003,* gives the number of deaths of coalition soldiers (300) as of September 2003. New entries on SARS and the West Nile virus reflect recent health concerns. The space shuttle *Columbia* has an index entry, and the accident that destroyed it is covered in two paragraphs added to the article on *Space exploration.* There is an entry on John Kerry although it has not been updated since his election to the Senate in 1985. Since *World Book* begins printing in October of the year prior to the year of the copyright, it sometimes misses late-in-the-year developments, such as the December capture of Saddam Hussein. In a few cases editors were able to anticipate changes and include some postdeadline events, such as the results of the California governor recall election. The index is detailed and easy to use, and includes page numbers for illustrations and maps. The research guide is useful for students who need help organizing a project.

Offering high-quality, current, accurate information in an attractive package, *World Book* continues to be a first choice for libraries, schools, and homes.

Online Encyclopedias

Encyclopaedia Britannica Online. [Internet database]. Encyclopaedia Britannica, pricing from $295 [http:// www.britannica.com]. (Last accessed July 31, 2004).

Encyclopaedia Britannica Online School Edition. Encyclopaedia Britannica, pricing from $295 [http:// www.britannica.com]. (Last accessed July 31, 2004).

Encyclopaedia Britannica Online (EB Online) bundles Encyclopaedia Britannica, The Britannica Student Encyclopedia (for middle school and up), The Britannica Elementary Encyclopedia (for elementary school and up), The Britannica Concise Encyclopedia, Britannica Internet Guide, and video and media. Users can enter a word, phrase, or question to search all of these databases at the same time, or singly, or in any combination using check boxes. Encyclopaedia Britannica Online School Edition (BOLSE) is a similar product that provides a K–12 audience with most of the same content, but some of its features are different. It has a different splash page, for example, and a database of magazine articles appropriate for school users.

In both products, several browse features are available including Subject Browse, Article Browse (a traditional alphabetical listing of encyclopedia entries), and Time Line Browse. EB Online also has a Year in Review Browse. It would be nice if users could search within an area that they are browsing (for example, if searches could be limited by subject area or year). A search on Iraq in EB Online yields 100 hits from Encyclopedia Britannica, the first half of which are occurrences of the term in the Iraq entry. There are another 100 hits from Britannica Student Encyclopedia (100 seems to be the standard upper limit), and 63 Internet sites. In BOLSE, an additional 47 results are retrieved from Britannica Elementary Encyclopedia. In all cases, the Iraq article is current through Saddam Hussein's capture; more current information can be found in links to magazine articles and Web sites. Articles in all four encyclopedias on President Bush are current through spring 2003. When searching Kerry, John Forbes, the only relevant article returned is Presidency of the United States of America, which mentions John Kerry as a candidate who opted to forgo federal matching funds for the primaries and caucuses.

Examples of new articles added to EB Online over the past year are Computer crime, GPS, Nanotechnology, SARS, and Yo-Yo Ma. The SARS article covers events through June 2003. Replaced or significantly revised articles include Electronics, Genetics, and Vietnam War. There are 60 minutes of new video. The Year in Review feature details events year by year for the past 10 years, through 2003. Also available are the Merriam-Webster Collegiate Dictionary and Thesaurus or, in BOLSE, the Merriam-Webster Student Dictionary and Thesaurus, and users can double click on any word in the encyclopedia for a pop-up definition. A new atlas with more maps, hyperlinks, and country statistics and profile data has recently been added.

Britannica's suite of online databases offers a great deal of content at different reading levels. It is easy to expand a search by selecting additional databases and to switch from one database to another. Content is well organized, appearing in large, readable fonts, and hyperlinks to relevant related articles are apparent. Libraries wanting online access to Britannica content will be generally well served by either EB Online or BOLSE. Britannica is working on making the sites accessible in accordance with Section 508 of the Rehabilitation Act.

Grolier Online. [Internet database]. Grolier, pricing starting at $415 for a combination of two or more databases [http://go.Grolier.com]. (Last accessed July 30, 2004).

Three encyclopedias—*Encyclopedia Americana, Grolier Multimedia Encyclopedia,* and *The New Book of Knowledge*—form the core of *Grolier Online*. Although each is aimed at a different audience, all are cross-searchable. The other databases that compose *Grolier Online* are *America the Beautiful, Encyclopedia of American Studies, Lands and Peoples, La Nueva encyclopedia Cumbre en línea,* and *The New Book of Popular Science*. A free database, *The American Presidency,* covers all the candidates and will keep users current on the 2004 campaigns and election. When we checked this site on July 30, it had information that had been added on July 29.

Encyclopedia Americana Online.

Targeted to high-school and college students, *Encyclopedia Americana Online* (*EA Online*) is well-organized, reliable, frequently updated, and user-friendly. The attractive splash page has changed minimally from last year and leads the user to four modules: Browse, Journal, Editors' Picks, and Profiles. Browse is an easy-to-use subject search. In a basic search, content can be searched by Article Titles (the default) or Full Text or full text within Americana Journal, *EA Online*'s weekly update feature. Advanced Search uses a "Query Builder" that allows users to select search categories from a variety of menus. Searchers can also choose to browse within broad subject areas.

EA Online's advantages over its print counterpart in terms of currency are significant. When *SARS* is searched, there is a link to the article on *Pneumonia,* where two paragraphs briefly describe last year's outbreak. *Afghanistan* ends at the same point as the article in the print set—the *loya jirga* in June 2002—but the online version has a more extensive and more current bibliography via a link with WorldCat, as well as links to 2004 magazine articles and Americana Journal entries. Although Article Titles is the default search, the user does not necessarily have to know the exact article title to perform a successful search as long as a term appears somewhere in the title or there is a cross-reference (for example, from *SARS* to *Pneumonia*). In the case of *Bush, George W.,* however, an Article Title search yields no results— users must search *Bush, George* and then select *Bush, George Walker*. A nice feature of the entry, not found in the corresponding entry in the print set, is a listing of Bush's cabinet members and other officials of his administration. The article on John Kerry is quite thorough, with two current bibliographic citations. Search terms are not always highlighted, but searchers can use the Find feature on their browsers to locate terms within an article.

Maps are readable and print quickly and easily. Most Web links are relevant and current. The links to WorldCat for further reading lists and EBSCO for periodical articles based on the search terms are very useful. Among the new or replacement articles not appearing in the print set are *Attack aircraft; Child, Julia; Draft riots; Federal Emergency Management Agency; Guggenheim, Peggy; Monopoly; Vampire; Wooster, College of;* and *World Trade Organization*. Numerous articles received major revisions in the database over the past year, including biographies of scientific, popular culture, and sports figures, as well as entries for animals, countries, cities, diseases, musical instruments, and organizations. The ADA-compliant text-only option functions well and is easy to turn on and off. Media added to this encyclopedia would make it more appealing to students.

Grolier Multimedia Encyclopedia

Grolier Multimedia Encyclopedia (GME) is aimed at students from the elementary grades through college, as well as adults. Although it derives from Grolier's *Academic American Encyclopedia* (1980–1998), it has no print counterpart. Text is complemented by videos, animations, and sound. Users can search by Full Text or by Titles or browse by subject category. Advanced Search allows search terms to be combined. Recent enhancements include a text-only version and a search mechanism that retrieves results for both articles and media.

Searching *Bush, George W.* yields 193 items, including his biography, a Fact Box link, pictures, and related places and people. Search terms are printed in red, which will help users locate them. It would be nice if the search engine retained the search terms in case the user would like to modify or slightly change the search string. Searching *Summer Olympics* brings up the article on *Athens, Greece,* which mentions that the games will be held there in 2004. The table of contents for longer articles provides many access points.

Unlike *EA Online,* the default *GME* search is full text rather than title, so more results are returned. The *Kerry, John Forbes* entry is shorter than that in *EA Online* but has good hyperlinks to relevant related topics. Overall, content is well organized, and the interface is clear and simple, with tabs across the top for Web links, Periodicals, and Print/E-mail. Hyperlinks within the articles are useful to narrow a term-paper topic or to broaden the scope of a search. The "How-to-Cite-this-Article" feature teaches users to cite references, and the media, such as 150 national anthems, lend another dimension to learning.

The New Book of Knowledge Online

The opening page of *The New Book of Knowledge Online* (*NBK Online*) has a bright, colorful appearance with lots of charming graphics. *NBK Online* offers youngsters a broad overview of appropriate topics with additional resources that have been added to make learning interesting and entertaining. The search box at the top of the screen is easy to locate and use. A quick search on *Bush, George W.* locates 130 items, with the first one being a lengthy, current encyclopedia article on the president. Buttons on the top right of the screen link users to Print/Email, Web Links, and Magazines. A persistent side panel contains links to all the *NBK Online* features plus Alphabetical and Subject Browse, Help, and About buttons. The Advanced Search allows users to specify up to three terms and uses Boolean operators. In Advanced Search, users can also choose to search article titles or full text, limit searches to NBK News (a nice feature that presents interesting kid-friendly news stories) or encyclopedia images, and search within broad subject categories. Searching is quick and results are very relevant. A search on *Columbia accident* results in 18 documents, with the first being *Space shuttles,* an encyclopedia article; and the second "The Columbia Tragedy: A Special Report (02/10/03)" from NBK News. A search on *Kerry, John Forbes* returns two documents; the first, "Massachusetts Profiles," presents a one-paragraph entry for Kerry and indicates he was a front-runner after the first rounds of primaries in early 2004 in the Democratic presidential nomination. A search on *vegetarianism* returns 21 documents, with the first a very thorough encyclopedia article. Within articles, search terms are easy to find, since they are highlighted in red.

NBK Online's "Web Feat!" and other features will entertain youngsters for hours. Scholastic News offers links to pages about Games and Quizzes; Movies, TV, and Music; and Sports—especially fun for preteens and teens. Well suited for young users, this reference source will provide information needed for school reports and answer questions to satisfy the curiosity of young minds on a wide variety of topics. And it's easy and fun to use. A text-only version is new for 2004.

World Book Online Reference Center. [Internet database]. World Book, pricing from $445 [http://www.worldbook.com]. (Last accessed July 30, 2004).

The new home page for *World Book Online Reference Center* (WBORC) is sleek and uncluttered. WBORC now complies with the Americans with Disabilities Act and section 508 of the Rehabilitation Act, so users may adjust the font and the type size as needed. The encyclopedia contains the complete text of the print edition and the *World Book Dictionary*, as well as 8,500 articles created for the electronic version and 13,000 Back in Time articles from past yearbooks. In addition, there is an atlas and access to a British English version of *World Book* and to *Enciclopedia Estudiantil Hallazgos*, a Spanish-language encyclopedia for elementary-school students. The site is also rich in media.

Users may access the content from a search box at the top of the page. They can browse by broad subject area or media type or use the basic or advanced keyword search functions. One must click on Site Contents to get to the browse mode, which is not exactly intuitive. The Advanced Search mode allows Boolean operators, limits (article text, title word, atlas, media type, etc.), and truncation.

Articles added in the past year include biographies of all Nobel Prize winners and all current U.S. senators, current news topics (*Business Ethics, Hamas, Obesity*) and biographies of celebrities and political leaders such as Cecilia Bartoli, Howard Dean, and Eminem. More than 170 articles were revised or rewritten, including *Gaza Strip, Narcolepsy, Silica gel,* and *Singapore*. John Kerry's biography has been updated, stating that he "will almost certainly receive the 2004 Democratic nomination for President of the United States." The article on space exploration has information about the *Columbia* disaster with a picture of the crew. Coverage of vegetarianism includes a special report on planning a healthy vegetarian diet. The entry on Iran contains a sentence about the earthquake in Bam under recent developments in the history section. Saddam Hussein's biography notes his capture, and Howard Dean's includes his unsuccessful race for the presidential nomination. Arnold Schwarzenegger is listed as governor of California. A Boolean search for information about drug use among athletes using the terms *sports* and *drugs* produced odd results. The first two citations were for articles on *Television* and *AIDS,* in which both terms appear. The third, *Olympic Games,* had some information at the end. The searcher can choose whether to have search terms highlighted in the text.

Special features in WBORC include Surf the Ages, a set of 100 Web sites from different historical periods. Back in Time allows users to see articles about important events in earlier *World Book* editions. Behind the Headlines links users to articles that provide background for current events. *World Book Research Libraries,* requiring a separate subscription, offers two collections of primary sources in American history and political science and law.

WBORC is very current. Features such as Behind the Headlines are revised daily, and new and revised articles are added monthly. Web links are validated on a continuous basis. The new site design is easier to navigate, and it makes all of the features available from anywhere in the site. Articles download faster, too. The print capability now allows users to print specific sections of an article, which saves ink and paper. These improvements plus the broad range of content at several different reading levels make WBORC an excellent resource for school and public libraries.

Online Encyclopedia Summary

Encyclopaedia Britannica

Core encyclopedias

Encyclopaedia Britannica
The Britannica Elementary Encyclopedia
The Britannica Student Encyclopedia
The Britannica Concise Encyclopedia
- 125,000 articles in all four encyclopedias
- Approximately 3,000 video clips, 334 animations, 158 sounds
- 23,296 illustrations, 3,006 maps
- More than 165,000 Internet links

Additional database features

- Britannica Spotlights: the Spotlight Archive currently includes 19 separate feature sites.
- *Encyclopaedia Britannica*'s Year in Review: details events year by year for the past 10 years
- Interactive time lines
- *Merriam Webster Collegiate Dictionary and Thesaurus* (*Britannica Student Encyclopedia* uses *Merriam-Webster Student Dictionary and Thesaurus*)
- Periodicals: full text of more than 300 journals from EBSCO
- Teacher Resources and more than 400 learning materials, activity guides, and worksheets (included in B*ritannica Online Student Encyclopedia* only)
- Biography of the Day and This Day in History

Update schedule: site content is updated every two-four weeks, with more frequent updates as needed. Home page content changes daily.
Pricing: starts at $295 per school and is based on enrollment. District-wide, statewide, and consortium pricing also available.
Contact: 800-621-3900; contact@eb.com

Grolier Online

Core encyclopedias

Encyclopedia Americana Online
- 45,000 encyclopedia articles
- 6,175 illustrations
- 1,415 maps
- Updated quarterly
- Americana Journal (50,000 current events items, updated weekly)
- Editor's Picks (introductions to research topics, updated weekly)
- Profiles (1,500 frequently consulted biographies)
- Approximately 100,000 periodical articles from 830 journals, under license from EBSCO Content Solutions
- ADA-compliant (W3C level AA and Section 508) version

Grolier Multimedia Encyclopedia
- 39,800 entries
- 7,550 illustrations
- 896 maps
- 18 videos, 151 panoramas, 33 animations, 28 interactive cutaways, 256 sounds
- Updated monthly
- GME News (updated weekly)
- Today Is (historical events, updated daily)
- Other features: Brain Jam, Research Starters, Timeline, Event Planner, Quizzes and Games
- Approximately 100,000 periodical articles from 830 journals, under license from EBSCO Content Solutions
- ADA-compliant (W3C level AA and Section 508) version

The New Book of Knowledge Online
- 9,243 articles
- 6,364 illustrations
- 721 maps
- 165 videos, 22 sounds, 25 animations
- Updated quarterly
- NBK News (updated weekly)
- Homework Help
- Other features: Question of the Day, World History Time Line, Spotlight (features selected topics), Web Feat! (games, puzzles, etc.), Teachers' Guide
- Approximately 2,500 age-appropriate periodical articles from 200 journals, under license from EBSCO Content Solutions
- ADA-compliant (W3C level AA and Section 508) version

Additional encyclopedias available on Grolier Online

America the Beautiful
Encyclopedia of American Studies
Lands and Peoples
The New Book of Popular Science
La Nueva encyclopedia Cumbre en línea

Additional cross-database features

- American Heritage dictionaries
- Global Search
- Grolier Online Atlas
- Grolier Internet Index: links to more than 47,000 sites

Pricing: Grolier Online is sold in a variety of bundled packages. Stand-alone encyclopedias are not sold. Pricing starts at $415 for the smallest schools.
Contact: http://go.grolier.com

World Book Online Reference Center

Core encyclopedia

World Book Encyclopedia
- All of the articles from World Book plus 8,500 articles specially created for World Book Online Reference Center (WBORC)
- 11,000 illustrations
- 1,500 maps
- approximately 45 animations, 70 videos, 10,000 sounds (including 9,000 pronunciations of difficult and unfamiliar words), 114 360-degree photographs
- 7,000 Internet links

Additional database features

- Back in Time: approximately 13,000 historic articles from past *World Book* annuals
- Behind the Headlines
- *Enciclopedia Estudiantil Hallazgos* (Spanish-language edition of *The World Book Student Discovery Encyclopedia*)
- Parent Resources
- Periodical articles: EBSCO Content Solutions provides a selection of articles published in the last three years
- Special Reports: nearly 500 in-depth feature articles
- Student Resources
- Surf the Ages: imaginary news sites from the past
- Teacher Resources
- Through the Year: articles, activities, and quizzes that teach facts about each month of the year
- Today in History
- What's Happening: special events taking place in the current month
- The World Book Dictionary

Update schedule: monthly; some features updated daily
Pricing: starts at $445 for a small school. This includes remote access for students at home and the Spanish-language encyclopedia.
Contact: 800-975-3250; http://www.worldbook.com

Special Features

Another Look At . . .
    Annals of America 6
    Grove Art Online 7
A Century of Books
    The Changing Face of Reference..7
    The Changing Face of Reference, Continued 8
    Complete Library of Reference 8
    They Might Have Been Top of the List 8
From the RBB Archive
    Not So Fast..9
    From the RBB Archive 9
    History of Ideas 10
    Hidden History 10
    Oxford Dictionary of Quotes 12
    Stopgap Measures 12
Focus Reviews
    An Undertaking of Exceptional Magnitude 12
    The Way We Lived Then...13
Reference on the Web
    Alone Together 14
    Countdown to November..14
    Outstanding Art and Architecture Online 15
Other Featrues
    Atlas and Dictionary Update, 2005 15
    Children's Reference Sources..16
    Did You Hear about the Reference Book That . . . ?..18
    Read-Alikes: Exploring Exploration 18
    Reference Book in Spanish for Children and Adolescents 19
    Reference Book in Spanish for Children and Adolescents 19
    Reference Sources on the Presidency and the Presidential Elections 20
    Some Key Reference Works for Genealogists 21
    Twenty Best Bets for Student Researchers 22

Another look at . . .

Annals of America

Annals of America. 22v. 2003. illus. index. Encyclopaedia Britannica, dist. by World Book, $529 (0-85229-960-5). 973.

World Book is now the distributor for Encyclopaedia Britannica's *Annals of America*. The current edition is the first new edition since 1987.

Annals contains more than 2,500 documents and 5,000 black-and-white photographs. Coverage begins in 1493 with "Christopher Columbus: Discovery of the New World," taken from his letters. Volume 22 is new and extends the set to 2001 with an article on September 11 and its aftermath, taken from *Encyclopaedia Britannica 2001 Year in Review*. Each volume begins with a chronology for the time span it covers, and each entry begins with a brief introduction that provides some context. In some cases, documents have been excerpted and slightly modernized. A volume-by-volume list of contents and an index that lists authors and their selected documents can be found in volume 22.

Annals has not been altered so much as added to. The first edition was published under the guidance of Mortimer Adler, and volumes 1–18 reflect a typically Adlerian plan to present "all the great American documents." Each of these volumes closes with an index of authors, including brief biographical summaries. Subsequent volumes strive to present material that is representative rather than "great"—newspaper and magazine articles, official reports, and the like. The author index found in volumes 1–18 has been replaced in later volumes by a subject index, but subject indexing is not cumulative for these volumes, and there is no subject indexing at all for volumes 1–18.

In 1972, we recommended *Annals* for secondary-school libraries and public libraries, "particularly those serving students where the use of primary materials is emphasized in American history courses." We also recommended it for academic libraries where, although many of the documents might be already be at hand, "the convenience of having such a handy compilation available is obvious." Now, of course, many of the documents that are collected in *Annals* are available on the Web, at sites like Amdocs [http://www.ukans.edu/carrie/docs/amdocs_index.html] and http://www.ourdocuments.gov. Because of the wider availability of historical documents, *Annals* is not a necessary purchase, but it still offers a convenient way to add these materials to the reference collection.

—**Mary Ellen Quinn**

Grove Art Online

Grove Art Online. [Internet database]. Grove, call for subscription information. [http://www.groveart.com]. (Last accessed September 14, 2004).

Since 1998 Grove (now part of Oxford University Press) has offered *Grove Art Online* (GAO) as a complement to its 34-volume *Dictionary of Art* (1996), the 1996 Dartmouth Medal recipient.

In 1999 RBB praised GAO as "crisp, elegant, and easy to negotiate." Oxford has kept the site clear and intuitive while adding features that expand the usefulness of the online version as a stand-alone reference source as well an update to the print edition. The GAO's "What's New" page indicates that 190 articles and 100 bibliographies have been updated this quarter and provides links to articles added or updated since 1996 in African, Chinese, Classical, Northern Renaissance, Twentieth Century, and Latin American and Caribbean art.

Access to Images

One of the biggest changes in GAO since our last review is access to many more images. Color images of excellent quality are now available through hyperlinks within 500 of the most frequently viewed articles, including 1 image for *Art nouveau,* 3 for *William Blake,* 6 for *Botticelli,* and 12 for *Athens.* Among the images linked through articles are frequently requested works, such as Botticelli's *Primavera* and *Birth of Venus,* Bosch's *Garden of Earthly Delights,* and—of interest to *Da Vinci Code* fans—Leonardo's *Mona Lisa* and *Virgin of the Rocks.* The hyperlinks can be hard to find, but the images can also be retrieved by clicking on an Illustrations button at the top of the article.

Another way to retrieve images is by opening Image Search on the home page (or Image Links at the article level) and clicking on either Art Image Links or Art Image Collections. Art Image Links provides access to more than 40,000 images from museum and gallery Web sites (up from around 10,000 in 1998). Art Image Collections offers two collections that further expand the visual material available to users. The Bridgeman Art Library includes 100,000 images, from prehistoric to contemporary art. Art Resource, begun as a teaching collection by a Columbia University art professor, includes 90,000 images. Both collections offer keyword as well as artist and location searches, making them valuable for students who want to find paintings of knights in armor, hunting scenes, or other themes. Free registration enables users to save images in a "lightbox" for later reference.

Results

Results for many searches were excellent. A search of Art Resource on the keyword *Viking* retrieved 173 artifacts, including several important Gotland picture stones. Another keyword search in Art Resource on *luncheon grass* retrieved three images of Édouard Manet's shocking 1863 painting *Déjeuner sur l'herbe* under its English name, *Luncheon on the Grass.* It also retrieved paintings with the same title by Eugene Boudin, Claude Monet, and Pablo Picasso. The same search in Bridgeman retrieved the Manet and two Monets. Other searches produced disappointing results. Searches of the Art Resource collection for performance artist Laurie Anderson and photographers Robert Mapplethorpe and Andres Serrano resulted in the message, "this artist does not exist." Copyright restrictions contribute to availability of art images on the Web. As both the Bridgeman Art Library and Art Resource grow, so will GAO users' access to images.

GAO's images remain static at a time when the Web is becoming increasingly interactive. Searches of GAO's online biographies under the classifications "video artist" and "performance artist" retrieved 57 and 87 entries, respectively, including Matthew Barney. The article on Matthew Barney has two photographs of installations at the San Francisco Museum of Modern Art from his controversial "Cremaster Cycle." Neither Art Resource nor the Bridgeman Art Library has images of Barney's works. However, Web-savvy searchers will discover Barney's interactive Web site, including video clips, at http://www.cremaster.com. Users seeking examples of specific artists' work may want to bookmark Artcyclopedia [http://Default_XREF_styleREFwww.artcyclopedia.com] as a supplement to GAO. Artcyclopedia does not offer GAO's scholarly articles or sophisticated searches, but it does have images and links to Web pages of artists such as Barney.

Refined Searches

Explore, a feature new to GAO this September, enables progressively refined article searches. Users select terms from Art and Art Forms, Geography, People, Styles and Cultures, or Time Periods. For example, a user selecting *medieval art* under Styles and Cultures retrieves 1,795 articles. Adding *Spain* to the search narrows the articles to 153, and adding *books and manuscripts* under Art and Art Forms results in 14 articles. This search missed a discussion of Mozarabic *Beatus* manuscripts within the article on *Mozarabic decorative arts* and an image of the Morgan *Beatus* linked from the article on *Apocalypse: Manuscript.* Explore is fun to use, but a full-text Boolean search on GAO's Advanced Search page retrieved more relevant articles on medieval Spanish manuscripts.

In 1999 the Board noted that GAO "does not yet exploit the Web format as much as it could." It has expanded its access to images, but users should know that there are many other sources available on the Web, ranging from Google image searches to artists' own Web pages. GAO is highly recommended for public, academic, and senior-high-school libraries for what it continues to do best—offer increasingly flexible access to up-to-date scholarly articles.

—Christine Whittington

A Century of Books

The Changing Face of Reference
by Mary Ellen Quinn

Everyone who works with reference materials is familiar with the changes that new technologies have wrought on the way we do reference and the way reference materials are published. The delivery of so much information via the Web, making some of us question whether there is even a point to print reference collections anymore, is the most obvious change. But for this, *Reference Books Bulletin*'s seventy-fifth anniversary year, we've been spending some time looking at past issues, and we've seen that RBB's pages have also recorded changes that are more subtle.

When RBB began as *Subscription Books Bulletin* in 1930, a big chunk of what could be called reference publishing seemed designed primarily to provide something educational and self-improving to homes and even some libraries and schools that were stuck out in the middle of nowhere and couldn't afford to buy many books. These publications ranged from compilations of extracts of children's books, intended for children who had no regular access to good literature, to "courses of study" for business or civil engineering and from single-volume collections of facts designed especially for farm homes having no other reference material to multivolume sets, often sold by subscription, with titles like *New Larned History for Ready Reference, Reading and Research: The Actual Words of the World's Best Historians, Biographers and Specialists; A Complete System of History for All Uses, Extending to all Countries and Subjects and Representing the Better and Newer Literature of History*, which we reviewed in July 1930. It's easy to laugh now at some of these more grandiose-sounding publications, but the late Victorian zeal for collecting and systematizing that resulted in many overly ambitious projects also gave us some of our most enduring reference monuments, such as the *Oxford English Dictionary* and the *Dictionary of National Biography.*

Along with our reviews, *Subscription Books Bulletin* dished out advice that still applies today. An article called "Reference Books for Children: Some Considerations on Selection" in the July 1941 issue states that "the prospective buyer of a reference set should have clearly in mind the purpose he hopes to be able to fulfill through the ownership of such a work." This article also notes a shift toward a more customer-driven approach in reference publishing: "Changing educational aims and methods reflected in changed demands upon libraries react in turn upon the editorial policies of publishers." In World War II–era issues of *Subscription Books Bulletin,* we see another shift. Besides the use of thinner paper dictated by a wartime economy, there is a growing emphasis on reference materials related to current events. Some of the realities faced by librarians who were trying to supply their patrons with topical resources were summarized in an article in the January 1942 issue on atlases: "Although world events have brought the atlas into its own, they have also added new complications to the already vexing question of selection, preservation and duplication of this costly part of the reference collection. Few libraries want to spend freely on these volumes at present. However, the added need for geographical information is placing unusual strain upon this group of books. In addition, many places mentioned in the news are off the beaten track of small maps, and only the large expensive atlases are sufficiently detailed to include these remote spots. Many of these costly volumes are printed abroad, and in the face of world conditions probably can no longer be replaced." As inexpensive substitutes, we recommended clipping maps from newspapers and magazine.

In the next few issues of RBB, we will be looking at more changes as reflected in our reviews over the years.

The Changing Face of Reference, Continued
by Mary Ellen Quinn

In our last issue, we wrote about *Reference Books Bulletin* from its inception as *Subscription Books Bulletin* in 1930 through the World War II era. Now we take a look at the period from after the war to the arrival of electronic media.

Although *Subscription Books Bulletin* was founded as a consumer advisory resource, in the 1940s the *Subscription Books Bulletin* Committee determined that it was being used primarily by librarians as a selection tool. In a 1955 editorial marking *Subscription Books Bulletin*'s 25th anniversary, the committee wrote: "In early years the *Bulletin* was much concerned with trade practices; recent years have brought a decrease in the proportion of editorial attention to selling methods and an increase in articles on the content of reference works." This change in emphasis led to the merger with *Booklist* in 1956 and to a name change to *Subscription and Reference Books Bulletin* in 1969.

Beginning in the 1970s, we evaluated around 350 titles a year, a big jump from our earlier yearly average of just 27 books, but still just a sampling. Although it's risky to make generalizations about reference publishing based on our reviews, if we can judge by that sampling, the new generation of librarians saw more reference titles of a very practical kind—indexes, bibliographies, and other helpful tools designed to point the way to other information. Gone was the "complete library" approach so common in earlier reference publishing. Our priorities give a hint of what was considered most useful for our audience at the time:

1. general English-language encyclopedias
2. general fact-finding sources such as unabridged dictionaries, biographical reference works, atlases and gazetteers, directories, yearbooks, and statistical compendia. General bibliographical reference sources and periodical indexes follow in priority, and references confined to a single subject are given least precedence in assigning a review.

Nowadays, many of these types of works are all but dead in print form, thanks in large part to the Internet. Reflecting the increasingly specialized nature of scholarly research, a big chunk of what we now review are the "references confined to a single subject" that were once ranked so low on our priority list.

Although general encyclopedias and a few other items were still being sold door-to-door, by the 1980s the *Subscription* part of our name had become an anachronism, and we became *Reference Books Bulletin* in 1983. In the same year, we published our first review of a resource available through an online service. In our next issue, which is *Booklist*'s Spring Electronic Media Showcase, we'll take a look at reviewing in the electronic age.

Complete Library of Reference
by Mary Ellen Quinn

In RBB's very early years, most of the materials available for us to evaluate were frequently of a kind that claimed to offer the universe of knowledge between covers. A typical title was one we reviewed in 1930: *New World Wide Cyclopedia: A complete library of reference; superbly and profusely illustrated with hundreds of subjects in full color; monotone and text-cuts, with a valuable appendix of often-sought-for facts in almost every department of human knowledge, a chronological history of the world, showing the most important events in history from the earliest times, and the most comprehensive narratives of the world war briefly noted day-by-day*. Although the hyperbole seems quaint to us today, we have embraced a new ideal of information access that is even loftier, made possible by advances in electronic publishing.

Since we published our first database review on April 15, 1984 (for an electronic version of *Academic American Encyclopedia* available through dial-up services such as CompuServe and Dow Jones News/Retrieval), RBB has provided a snapshot of how electronic reference publishing has evolved. In the early 1990s, our reviews, especially of encyclopedias, read like a catalog of technologies that would soon be on their way to the electronic publishing graveyard: laser disc, Data Discman, CDTV, CD-1, Tandy VIS, not to mention CD-ROM. In 1993 *Compton's* was available in 10 different versions (one of them online) to accommodate all the different hardware and operating systems. In June 1987, we published our first review of a CD-ROM, *Books in Print*, noting that CD-ROM had an advantage over online databases because it was not reliant on telecommunication networks to access remote databases, so costly connect-time charges inherent in online searching are eliminated. On the other hand, "initial expenditures for CD-ROM-based software and compatible hardware can be prohibitive." That same year, our review of the *Oxford English Dictionary* on CD-ROM complained about having to wait 15 to 20 minutes for some searches to be completed.

In our 1990 review of World Book's *Information Finder* CD-ROM, we said "the program has much to recommend it and is not merely, as some critics have labeled the new electronic products, 'an electronic page turner'." While *Information Finder* offered only text, *Compton's MultiMedia Encyclopedia*, which we enthusiastically reviewed in the same year, was the first to incorporate illustrations and sound. Various other reference publishers jumped on the CD-ROM bandwagon during the 1990s, not always with good results or for good reasons. In some reviews, our frustration comes through: "Why does every CD-ROM developer have to come up with its own set of icons, buttons, etc.?" This new publishing activity did have one unforeseen effect: in our 1992 review of Bowker's *Library Reference Plus,* we commented that "publications we all thought were excellent in print form are shown to be riddled with inconsistencies that can make them difficult to search when put online."

Britannica Online, which we reviewed in our December 15, 1994, issue, was the first appearance of a major multivolume encyclopedia available through the Internet, and also broke new ground by providing links from the encyclopedia to other Internet sources. As the 1990s progressed, the Internet became the avenue of choice for electronic publishing, and the number of CD-ROMs, with their inherent limitations, dwindled—we stopped reviewing them in 1999. Since then, reference publishers have adopted a variety of approaches to publishing online, ranging from giant databases of databases to individual titles in e-book form.

Despite a few clouds, the horizons of the online environment appear to be limitless, and massive digitization projects such as the one recently announced by Google will push the boundaries even further. We are moving in the direction of a "complete library of reference" on a scale no one could have imagined when we published our first reviews.

They Might Have Been Top of the List
by Mary Ellen Quinn

Although January has been Top of the List time for *Booklist* since 1992, RBB came late to the party, adding reference books to the Editor's Choice and Top of the List lineup beginning in 1996. We decided to use the opportunity of our 75th anniversary to pay homage to a handful of reference works that might have earned top honors, starting in 1930, our first year of publication.

1930

Although in later years we made it a policy not to recommend a set until it was complete, we based our 1930 review of *Macmillan's Encyclopedia of the Social Sciences* on the first volume alone. We wrote, "This undertaking is planned and executed by American and foreign scholars of such distinction, its field is so broad, it is in every way so monumental, so scholarly and so interesting, that we recommend it to all the larger libraries and reference rooms." Despite its age, this classic work has never been entirely supplanted, and it remains an important resource for its historical perspective. *International Encyclopedia of the Social Sciences,* which Macmillan published in 1968, was meant to complement, not supersede it.

1940

In 1940 we recommended Scribner's *Dictionary of American History* for "its broad scope, its value as a 'quick reference' tool, its timeliness and the authentic, simple and clear manner in which its material is presented." A revision was published in 1976 to coincide with America's bicentennial. The third edition appeared in 2003.

1952

We said of Columbia University Press' *Columbia Lippincott Gazetteer of the World,* "It contains more varied, accurate, up-to-date geographical information than can be found in any other single reference volume, and in this respect can compete with multivolume encyclopedias." A long-awaited new edition, *The Columbia Gazetteer of the World,* was published in 1998.

1968

Like so many other reference titles from our past, *International Encyclopedia of the Social Sciences* had a long and tortuous review history. This history actually began in 1964, when we received a preliminary table of contents and directory of contributors, items that triggered six years' worth of painstaking records. In keeping with our old practice of review-by-committee, the publisher was asked in 1968 to send nine sets (at 17 volumes each), which were mailed to nine different reviewers. A year later the process began of gathering up all the sets and returning them, which was apparently our policy at the time. There ensued another year of missing volumes, missing sets, post-office and insurance claims, and three sets held captive by reviewers who refused to give them up. Our 6,000-word review (more than 20 times our current average) was published June 1, 1969, but the file on *International Encyclopedia of the Social Sciences* wasn't closed until May 1970.

1982

Work on *The New Grove Dictionary of Music and Musicians* began in 1969 and was completed in 1982. It was originally conceived as a sixth edition of Grove's *Dictionary of Music and Musicians* but became a totally new work. In our 1982 review we said, "We can rejoice in *New Grove 1*. A danger in using it is that of being lured away from the pursuit of a particular bit of information by something seen in passing. Who can resist a trombone-playing angel, the Bach family tree, the fascinatingly illustrated discussion of embouchure, a Pahouin mvet, or an article on bells, or even on education in music?" We also noted, "It is perhaps not too soon to think ahead to *New Grove 2*. Will it be a multivolume set or only a database?"—an unusually prescient thing to ask back then. The answer, when *New Grove 2* appeared in 2000, was both.

1990

Volumes of Scribner's *Dictionary of the Middle Ages* started coming off the press in 1982, culminating with the thirteenth volume, the index, in 1990. We called the set "an admirable effort" and noted that our examination of later volumes "confirms the early predictions of its usefulness." One of the goals of the dictionary was to "transcend geographic and disciplinary boundaries," reflecting a trend in academic research that has only accelerated in the last decade or so. A supplemental volume published in 2004 [RBB Je 1 & 15 04] goes farther in incorporating a global and interdisciplinary approach and also adds topics such as ecology, gender, race, and sexuality, which the larger set generally ignored.

1992

Our review of Macmillan's *Encyclopedia of Sociology* described it as "the first comprehensive encyclopedia of the sprawling discipline of sociology ever successfully ventured in America" and "a momentous publishing event for the discipline." It was a successor to but not a replacement for *International Encyclopedia of the Social Sciences* (1968), just as that work was a successor to but not a replacement for 1930's *Encyclopedia of the Social Sciences*. Each set reflects different approaches and perspectives of a new generation, and the older sets retain historical value even as the disciplines they cover evolve.

1995

It would have been adventurous to choose *Britannica Online* as Top of the List for a year when such titles as Scribner's *Civilizations of the Ancient Near East* and Macmillan's *Encyclopedia of Bioethics* were published, but we like to think we would have been that forward-looking. We said in our review that Britannica was "carving a new path of electronic access" by marking "the first appearance of a major multivolume encyclopedia available through the Internet." Although we were frustrated by slowness and by the lack of any illustrations except for tables, flags, and maps, we called *Britannica Online* "an easy-to-use system that bodes well for information delivered in this format."

From the RBB Archive

by Mary Ellen Quinn

"Although all encyclopedias are imperfect, all encyclopedias are not imperfect in the same way or to the same degree." (*Reference and Subscription Books Bulletin,* March 15, 1969).

In recognition of RBB's 75th anniversary, we will be featuring material from our archive to provide a snapshot of reference reviewing over the years. Here we've excerpted some past encyclopedia reviews to tie in with our annual Encyclopedia Update.

On *Encyclopedia Americana*

The essential criticism of Americana is that revision is unequal and seemingly haphazard within the limits adopted. Librarians will regret that means could not be found to bring up to date certain material, such as the article on Medicine, recent progress in, which remains as in the issue of 1927 . . . and many bibliographies which hold over from 1918–1920. Pronounced inequalities in the age of information often introduce an element of uncertainty which the reader must consider. Like criticisms of course could be applied in some degree to probably any partial revision of an encyclopedia. (*Subscription Books Bulletin,* October 1936)

On *Encyclopaedia Britannica*

For the moment it can be said that as a reference work which uses a new design for the organization and presentation of knowledge the fifteenth edition of *Encyclopaedia Britannica* will be found, at least by some readers, to be difficult to use and by most, hard to get accustomed to. (*Reference and Subscription Books Bulletin*, June 1, 1975)

On *World Book*

The editors of *World Book* state that they have "developed policies and style guidelines to avoid sexist language or assumptions," and numerous examples of this can be found. The article once called *Prehistoric Man* is now *Prehistoric People. Manpower* is now cross-referenced to *Labor Force.* The articles on the military services refer to men and women members and include pictures of both. The article on sewing, which in 1973 opened with the sentence, "Sewing is a useful occupation that many girls enjoy learning," now begins with a definition and goes on to say that many people enjoy it. (*Reference and Subscription Books Bulletin,* May 1, 1979)

On *Compton's Multimedia Encyclopedia*

An exciting CD-ROM concept that will appeal to all young people, *Compton's Multimedia Encyclopedia* integrates sound, pictures, animation, and text. *Compton's Encyclopedia* was first published in 1922 as a home and school reference work pledged "to stimulate the imagination, to provide the inquiring mind with accurate information told in an interesting style, and thus lead into broader fields of knowledge." Sixty-eight years later this purpose is still evident but in a more stimulating, innovative format that couldn't have been imagined even five years ago. CD-ROM technology appeals to different learning styles, fosters different ways of thinking, provides introductory experiences with new technology, and is just plain fun." (*Reference Books Bulletin,* June 15, 1990)

Not So Fast

by Mary Ellen Quinn

Many librarians will remember (and maybe some still use) the sturdy old wooden furniture that was designed to hold catalog cards. One of these still occupies a corner of the RBB office, and, since the *Booklist* database only goes back to 1992, it's where the record of most of RBB's long history resides. Every single title we reviewed, or considered for review, is meticulously documented on three-by-five-inch index cards, from the moment it arrived in the RBB office until the moment its file was closed.

The further back one goes, the more detail appears on the cards, providing a glimpse into working habits that now seem both quaint and mind-numbing. What's also striking is the more relaxed idea about timeliness—the review process could drag on for years. Take our somewhat spotty reviewing history of *Grove's Dictionary of Music and Musicians,* which starts with a 1940 supplement to the fourth edition. We did our first review of the full *Grove's* in its fifth edition, published in 1954. Here is the chronology, as typed on index cards by diligent staffers, of what was a relatively straightforward review process.

- 1-19-54 Answered letter from Mr. Kenneth M. MacMurdoe, Sales Manager, St. Martin's Press, which was forwarded to this office from Mr. Ransom L. Richardson, Editor of *ALA Bulletin*. Informed Mr. MacMurdoe that his request for a new review of this publication is being brought to the attention of the SBC for reconsideration.
- 6-23-54 Title for Consideration to Chairman.
- 2-7-55 Title approved for review. Assigned to Northam.
- 2-23-55 Letter assignment to Northam. Letter to publisher requesting review copies.
- 3-7-55 Chairman rec'd review set.
- 3-7-55 Northam rec'd review set.
- 3-8-55 Headquarters rec'd review set.
- 4-26-55 Northam returned review set.
- JULY 1955 SBB - - is recommended.
- 8-26-55 Chairman returned review set.
- 9-12-55 Hdqs. returned review set.

Other phases of our history with Grove's were more murky. On a card typed in 1961, we find the following cryptic notes, indicating both a bad-apple reviewer and an absence of any sense of urgency. These notes refer to a supplementary volume.

- 6/29/61 Assigned to reviewer
- 12/7/61 Follow-up on receipt of review
- 7/14/62 2nd follow-up for review
- 11/18/62 3rd follow-up for review
- 2/6/63 review dropped

The next time Grove's appears in the files, it's in the form of a 10-volume paperback version of the fifth edition, published in 1970 and assigned to a reviewer we'll call Hall. We've retained all typos that appear on the index cards.

- 10/7/70 Hall called. He is at a standstill. He would not at this time recommend Grove's for 5 reasons. Its 16 years later. He has reservations about the good recommendation the Committee gave Grove's in 1955. He thinks perhaps the Committee's review at the time was not written by a music person, and I confirmed that fact by referring to our files. The review was written by a univ. reference librarian. 42% of the contributors are dead. The Harvard Dictionary and Baker's supercedes Grove's and they are also cheaper. Musicoloically Grove's is biased. It has a definite British bias, and the paperback binding at $60 is not practicable. He said he could have gone ahead and written a bland note without referring to the poor quality of the material. Asked if he would be willing to give Grove's a full dress review. He would not commit himself but said he would follow whatever instructions I and Mrs. Bartling gave him. I promised to be back with him as soon as I had talked with her.
- 10/9/70 Informed Hall that I talked with Bartling briefly about his findings. She thinks we had best steer clear of what might develop into a problem for the Committee by saying nothing about the paperback ed.

More than a decade passed before we broke our silence. *The New Grove Dictionary of Music and Musicians* arrived in the RBB office on July 1, 1980, and was "highly recommended" in a review published in May 1982—almost two years later.

Besides what they tell us about a more leisurely approach toward publishing reviews, some of the notes on our index cards hint at larger dramas—disgruntled publishers, reviewers whose lives are in turmoil, overworked staff. These things still occur, but events move too fast now for us to take the time to record them in the painstaking detail found in our old catalog card file.

History of Ideas

by Mary Ellen Quinn

The first edition of *New Dictionary of the History of Ideas*, called *Dictionary of the History of Ideas: Studies of Selected Pivotal Ideas,* appeared in 1973. Here is an excerpted version of our extremely detailed, 1,200-word review, which was published October 1, 1974. (For our review of *New Dictionary of the History of Ideas,* see opposite page.)

It is rare to come upon a work that is so satisfying as is the *Dictionary of the History of Ideas.* Grandly conceived and executed, impressive in its coverage and authority, the books are eminently readable. One might quibble about some of the omissions, but it is altogether an unusual production, a kind of encyclopedia of intellectual history, and an excellent representation of the discipline that has come to be known as the History of Ideas.

The editors and contributors are a galaxy of scholars, many quite famous. Names on the editorial board like George Boas, Felix Gilbert, and Ernest Nagel are known to almost everyone with a liberal arts background; and Philip P. Wiener, editor in chief, as editor also of the prestigious *Journal of the History of Ideas,* is in a position to know the scholars in the field and their strengths. Almost all of the contributors are non-American experts in their fields; they range from Tehran west to Tokyo and include experts from Edinburgh, Jerusalem, Warsaw, Toulouse, Uppsala, Pisa, Geneva, and many other centers of learning.

While the articles are arranged alphabetically, there is an "Analytical Table of Contents" that organizes the contents into seven categories, thus "discovering important relationships which might otherwise have been overlooked." One can see that the topics are broad, covering large ideas, and that the scope of even a small category among the seven is grand. Any reading in the *Dictionary* reveals that it is interesting, and the qualifications of the contributors promise superior authority.

Not the least important aspect of each article is its extensive bibliography. There is considerable unevenness in this area, some bibliographies being annotated, others not, and some separating primary from secondary sources, others not. But the contributors seem to have taken the bibliographical assignment seriously and done at least a good job, often a distinguished one.

The *Dictionary* does not deal with facts or static descriptions; it deals with concepts and change. In its interdisciplinary coverage of many topics in the history of ideas, it both breaks new ground and summarizes old knowledge in a novel way. It is recommended to libraries because of its authority, uniqueness of approach, and readability.

Hidden History

by Mary Ellen Quinn

For our 75th anniversary, we've spent quite a bit of time going through the old RBB files. It's a bit like rummaging around in grandmother's attic, where, amidst all the empty Ball jars and bundles of *National Geographic,* there are occasional glimpses into a real personal history. One gets the most sense of personality from records for RBB's first 50 years, in which every step in the review process, however small, is painstakingly documented. Today we like to congratulate ourselves for being efficient, but something was lost when editorial staff adopted a more streamlined approach and when computers became a part of the everyday routine.

What I think of as the baroque period of RBB (or RSBR, for *Reference and Subscription Books Review,* as it was called) falls during the 1960s and 1970s, when the records were kept by someone whose admirable attention to detail is matched by a penchant for elaboration. Though it's hard to embellish simple facts such as "1/12/66 Ack. receipt of 2 sets returned by Sanders," again and again the files provide completely superfluous information that reminds us of the human dimension behind each one of our reviews. Typical is the record for a dog encyclopedia for which we sought a reviewer in 1971:

```
12/7/71 Carpenter cannot.
12/7/71 Bruner will do the review if no xx one more capable
volunteers.
12/8/71 Green is a "cat" person
12/9/71 Martin is a lover of dogs, but knows very little
about them officially. She is xx willing to undertake revie
12/9/71 Briscoe informs that Dr. & Mrs. Martin Manger, one
of the chemistry professors and his wife, have agreed to x
work with her on the review. They have a number of dogs
and participate regularly in dog shows throughout the coun-
try
12/30/71 Sent follow up for books
12/30/71 Tell Briscoe we hope to forward the books to her
shortly.
```

The more complex the transaction, the more efflorescent the account. For example, there is the case of a publisher we'll call Jones, who first surfaces in 1962 when a set of his encyclopedias is given an unfavorable review: "Jones was at headquarters this week with many complaints for the Assoc. about the review. He has cancelled advertising contracts and says that in the future he intends to put all his money into producing better books rather than in wining and dining librarians." In 1964 Jones turns up with another encyclopedia, which is assigned to a Miss Healey for review. It's late summer, and Miss Healey is about to go on vacation. We've culled the highlights from our record for the review, which fills 16 index cards, front and back.

- 8/24/64: Call from Gertrude Rice at Mr. Jones' office. They wanted to send encyclopedia to Healey even tho she is on vacation—wanted us to call Healey and charge call to them—or call Providence and find out where she was as Mr. Jones has a persistent impression she wanted the books while on vacation. Jones was talking to the Rice person on the side. From the way they talked it seemed they want to contact Healey on their own so they could send the books as they are ready.
- 8/24/64: Healey's assistant was pushed until she finally gave her address. Jones put in a long-distance person-to-person call to Maine. Healey wasn't there because there was a death in the family the same day and she had to leave. Her mother has rheumatoid arthritis and was alone and could not get to the phone. No operator was given. Healey said to tell Jones not to call her again.
- 9/4/64: Jones is at his wit's end to get the review of the set published before the end of the year. He hopes that the present reviewer will not take the destructive attitude that the reviewer of his previous encyclopedia took.
- 9/4/64: Told Jones that we would appreciate it if he would not contact committee members personally. The copy of a letter from Healey attached demonstrated what tragedy of errors it has caused her. Told Jones not to attempt to apologize to her.
- 9/8/64: Jones called in abject contrition for upsetting Healey on her vacation. He didn't know quite what to do. We reminded him that we had written a letter to Healey indicating no matter how sorry he was, he was advised not to attempt to apologize to her.

Meanwhile, the review engine grinds on. Then there's this, which almost makes us feel sorry for Mr. Jones.

- 4/3/65: The review is a miserable failure.
- 8/23/65: Healey sending the revision.
- 9/23/65: We do not have the nucleus of a publishable review. No hope for it from the present reviewer.
- 9/29/65: Inform Jones that review has been dropped and we will wait for the 1966 edition.
- 9/29/65: Review assigned to Strale.
- 3/16/67: Jones called to find out if review was nearing publication.
- 5/8/67: Inform Jones that the review has been dropped and we will wait for the 1968 edition.

It wasn't only publishers who sometimes stirred up a tempest. Reviewers could create drama, too. Take the case of a reviewer named Scott who was assigned the seven-volume *London Bibliography of the Social Sciences*.

- 5/5/72: Scott volunteered to do review.
- 8/21/73: Memo to Mrs. Elizabeth Scott regarding her inability to complete her assignment. Inform that if she wishes to resign she should write a letter.
- 11/30/73: Letter from Colin Forbes regarding Committee's inability to publish a review of the title. He adds that he met Mrs. Scott who expressed an interest in reviewing the books for ALA. "I very much hope a review may eventually appear this time."
- 12/3/73: Write Forbes and explain that Scott is no longer an RSBR Committee member—that she accepted this assignment as an ordinary person without the Committee's approval. Cc: to [committee chair] Matthews who replies—Damn!
- 1/4/74: Letter from Forbes who was distressed by letter concerning Scott. He asked if she submitted a review to the Committee, would it be not considered? He explains importance of review by ALA and asks what can be done.
- 1/14/74: Scott writes Forbes regarding her "uncooperative member" status on RSBR Committee. "I would like to clarify the statement that when I talked to you at a library association meeting I assumed I was still under the Committee's direction."
- 1/14/74: Letter from Scott with cc of 1/14 letter to Forbes. "The attached letter to Forbes is self-explanatory, and I suppose that what I have to say in my defense sounds very flimsy. But, I shall write you anyhow, so that you don't 'treat me tersly,' as Mr. Forbes suggested. I remember that I received a letter from you shortly after the ALA convention in Las Vegas . . ." She goes on to explain how she lost the letter, is understaffed, and will probably be let go. "If we are still on speaking terms at midwinter please let me know where I should ship the volumes."
- 1/16/74: Write to Forbes. Suggests that he can ask Mrs. Matthews to consider the title for review—since she is Chairperson the decision is hers alone. "I must reiterate that the committee is not involved with Mrs. Scott. She was a failure as a member and never prepared any of the assigned work that was given to her. Our relationship with her has ceased, because of her lack of past performance."
- 1/29/74: Letter from Forbes apologizing for offending with his recent correspondence with Scott. He admits he doesn't know how Committee operates and would like to begin again, leaving the Scott misunderstanding aside.
- 4/16/74: Review dropped.

Nothing better illustrates the difference between the style of the 1960s and 1970s and the more minimalist approach adopted in later years than the records for the dog encyclopedia mentioned above and a later version published in 1995. Here is our documentation for the latter:

```
The International Encyclopedia of Dogs. Ed. by Anne
Rogers Clark and Andrew H. Brace. Howell, 1995.
496p. illus. index. $49.95 (0-87605-624-9). DDC:
636.7. Dogs

Reviewed by: Landry
Pub. date: April 15, 1996
MS revised:
```

Now, in the digital age, even the most starkly furnished index cards are superfluous. What we have is data, but no more glimpses into the hidden human history of RBB.

Oxford Dictionary of Quotes

by Mary Ellen Quinn

In our 75 years of reviewing we've developed much more than a nodding acquaintance with certain long-lived reference works. To complement our review of the sixth edition of *Oxford Dictionary of Quotations*, here is a condensed version of our review of the first edition, which appeared in the April 1942 *Subscription Books Bulletin* (as we were formerly called).

The arrangement of quotations is alphabetical by author. The Book of Common Prayer (14 pages of quotations) and the Bible (29 pages of quotations) come after this alphabetical arrangement, followed immediately by the Anonymous and Miscellaneous entries, the latter including ballads, nursery rhymes and one page of quotations from *Punch*. After this come the Latin and Greek sections and the foreign quotations (which are again arranged alphabetically by author in each of the languages represented). A short section of Addenda follows. Thus there are at least eight alphabetical arrangements. Arrangement of quotations by subject groups in a single alphabet would have afforded an easier and more natural approach.

The index by keyword occupies approximately one-third of the total bulk of the book. It is divided into two parts, the first indexing all the quotations in English. The second part contains vernacular indexes for the Latin, Greek, French, Italian, Spanish, and German sections. The arrangement of the keyword index in several sections of language makes the search for a quotation a slow process. The index reference is to page and column only. Location of the desired item could have been facilitated by numbering the quotations in each column or on each page.

In the main text under each author the arrangement of the extracts is alphabetical according to the title of the poem or work from which the quotation is taken. No information as to the author's occupation or nationality is given. Forty-four authors have no identification other than their names. There is no uniformity in the notation of author's birth and death. No indication is given of the death of some authors, mostly American. The date of Walt Whitman's birth is questioned though the *Dictionary of American Biography* gives it definitely as May 31, 1819.

In the section A–Aldrich the work has but one author entry not included in Bartlett's *Familiar Quotations* whereas in the same section Bartlett has 19 author entries not included in the *Oxford*, among them Franklin Pierce Adams, Henry Adams, John Adams, George Ade, Conrad Aiken, and Louisa May Alcott. American users will note the omission of many quotations considered familiar in this country. For library reference purposes the arrangement of both text and indexes in several alphabets decreases the value of the volume. The *Oxford Dictionary of Quotations* is recommended only for large libraries, as an additional source.

Stopgap Measures

by Mary Ellen Quinn

For at least as long as RBB has been reviewing atlases, it has been a challenge for libraries to keep the atlas collection up-to-date. The problem became especially acute during World War II, when a burgeoning demand for geographical information collided with dwindling availability, especially of the larger and more detailed atlases printed abroad. In our January 1942 issue we published an article called "Atlases" that addressed both the need to help library patrons locate places in the news and the necessity of preserving the existing atlas collection until the wartime barriers to publishing, shipping, and communication came down again. Here are some excerpts:

Those who are using maps widely are looking about for inexpensive substitutes which will serve as a stop-gap. Clippings from daily and weekly publications of national importance form the most obvious ephemeral supply. These maps are purely regional in most cases, but together they would soon form a complete picture of the shifting centers of world upheaval.

In an effort to find what authority lay behind maps sketched by newspaper staff artists, a visit was made to a paper famous for its international news. The library atlas cases in the building were nearly empty; the reporters had borrowed for use in the foreign staff room all the best volumes published in past years. In addition they had made an atlas of their own which was particularly interesting. They had gathered, with the aid of the librarian, the best separate maps they could find for countries as they came into the news. These were mounted in loose-leaf volumes with tough reinforced board covers. Each had its own table of contents and each map was numbered for rapid reference. Where size permitted, the maps were pasted to the page to save their edges. When their spread was too great for this, creases were reinforced and the map was left partially folded. The completed volumes were each about the proportions of a commercial atlas.

The volumes included a large number of maps saved from the *National Geographic Magazine*. Some were obviously collected from steamship companies, national railway systems, or oil companies. Others were printed in foreign countries, or by foreign governments, as ordnance maps, or mining surveys. A large one of South America, issued by the American Geographical Society of New York, had been especially valuable for locating towns in boundary disputes. The reporters had also included maps clipped from other American newspapers where they supplemented existing materials. The care with which the volumes had been compiled was evidence of the reporters' efforts to get accurate information.

The volumes presented a scrappy appearance, but the motley collection was so obviously made for a specific purpose and temporary use, that this point could be ignored. The maps themselves were more compact than if they had been stored in separate drawers or folders. The fundamental plan might be practical in libraries lacking large volumes, or wishing to save expensive ones.

In consulting various authorities teaching subjects involving the use of atlases, it was discovered that maps as they were in 1938 seem more useful for reference than those which attempt to follow the shifting boundaries. Students in school and college are taught to make the necessary adjustments and to sketch on outline maps the cumulated changes of which they read. One specialist commented on the increased need for topographical maps in interpreting the news, as so many movements are comprehensible only in terms of the terrain itself.

These comments by educators, and similar statements by map publishers partially answer the question of those who have asked if atlases now on hand should be considered outmoded. Actually the exact location of boundaries remains a point over which statesmen and cartographers can ponder. Until there is a general world peace treaty each country will continue to recognize all international boundaries as its own government sees fit. Those using atlases, meanwhile, will work out for themselves each evening to what extent the battle lines of the day have shifted the potential world frontiers.

Focus Reviews

"An Undertaking of Exceptional Magnitude"

Oxford Dictionary of National Biography. 60v. Ed. by H. C. G. Matthew and Brian Harrison. 2004. illus. index. Oxford, $13,000 (0-19-861411-X). 920.

Oxford Dictionary of National Biography. [Internet database]. Oxford, contact for pricing [http://www.oxforddnb.com]. (Last accessed November 19, 2004.)

This classic of British collective biography, called "an undertaking of exceptional magnitude" by Sidney Lee, its second editor, was first published between 1885 and 1900. Ten-year supplements were issued through the 1980s, and five-year supplements through the 1990s. Half the original set was written by only 34 contributors. The supplements were written by a wider range of people, often based on "personal acquaintance." The original set gave women short shrift, along with people in trade and commerce, and Victorian sensibilities meant that certain topics were taboo.

To be included among the 50,000 entries in the *Oxford Dictionary of National Biography* (ODNB), subjects must have died by the end of 2000. No one was dropped, but 70 percent of the old essays (all those on prime ministers, for instance) were replaced, and the rest were revised. More than 16,000 entries treat people who were not included in the original DNB. The scope spans 2,400 years and includes mythical figures like Robin Hood and Piltdown Man. Some people are treated in group entries. Ten percent of the entries are for women. All traces of Victorian propriety are gone: now Oscar Wilde is described as homosexual, and artist Eric Gill's unorthodox sex life is described in detail. As in the original set, the writing is clear and often witty. The ODNB is aimed at the general reader, as well as the scholar, and contains many figures from popular culture: Barbara Cartland, Benny Hill, and Sid Vicious, for example.

What does *national* in the title mean? The set includes those who were born or died in Britain (including Ireland), as well as people "noteworthy in the history of the British Isles, and their overseas connections." This net is cast in the broadest possible way. Many people from the former British Empire, such as Malawi's president Hastings Banda and Australian novelist Patrick White, are included. There appear to be some inconsistencies in coverage: American Jimi Hendrix is here (because he died in Britain) but not Jamaican Bob Marley. Coverage of 500 people from colonial America is a useful addition, and it is interesting to see them described from a British point of view.

Each entry begins with birth and death dates and a tag describing what the person was known for (e.g., "cotton spinner," "cricketer," or a marquess who is simply labeled "wastrel"). While the average biography is about 1,000 words long, some entries are as long as 37,000 words. Entries conclude with a section called "References," which contains often-extensive bibliographies (called "Sources"), a list of archives holding the subject's papers, sources of likenesses, and, sometimes, "wealth at death." Ten thousand entries are illustrated with portraits: in the print set they are all in black and white, but online some are in color.

The print set has no list of entries nor any indexes, except a volume that lists all the contributors with a list of the entries they wrote. No institutional affiliations are given for contributors, more than 1,000 of whom are from the U.S.

Researchers looking for biographies by anything other than personal name will need to use the online version, with its powerful searching capabilities. In addition to a Quick Search by name or full-text keyword, there are three basic ways to find information online: Browse, Themes, and Search. Browse lets the user scan the entries alphabetically by name or by year of birth or death. Themes Search offers two features. Ready Reference has lists of prime ministers, archbishops of Canterbury, Nobel Prize winners, Olympic title holders, and others. Feature essays focus on topics such as medical biography and Disraeli's 2004 bicentenary.

The Search function is extremely sophisticated, with five ways to search: People, Full Text, References, Contributors, and Images. Wild cards can be used in most fields. People Search can be modified by sex, religion, field of interest, dates, places, and the presence of an image in the entry. One can find all the Jewish women in the ODNB or all the men who lived in the nineteenth century whose field of interest was travel and exploration in Africa. The Fields of Interest filter has 25 broad categories, from Agriculture to Travel and Exploration, which can then be divided into subfields and sub-subfields. The full list is so long that it can be slow to load.

Full Text Search uses Boolean limiters and can be limited to a particular part of entries, such as place or organization names. In References Search, one can search Sources, Archives, Likenesses, and Wealth at Death. Using Contributors Search results in a list of all entries by an individual, just as in the print set. Images can be searched by artist, dates, location, and credit.

In a results list, each entry name is followed by birth and death dates, the descriptive tag, and an icon if there is a portrait. Within an entry, it is possible to highlight any word or phrase and do a quick search in the whole database. Long entries have clickable lists of subheads. There are links to entries in the original DNB and entries in *American National Biography* (Oxford, 2000), assuming the institution subscribes to *ANB Online*.

The online context-sensitive help is useful, but most users will need some direction to take advantage of all the database's features. According to Oxford, the online version will be updated three times per year, and the print set "periodically."

The *Oxford Dictionary of National Biography* is fascinating reading and will prove useful to researchers in many disciplines. The online version provides extremely powerful tools for searching. The ODNB is an important purchase for most academic libraries and very large public libraries. Libraries that can only afford one version of this mammoth compilation should consider subscribing to the online one.

—Sandy Whiteley

The Way We Lived Then

★**Greenwood Daily Life Online.** [Internet database]. 2004. Greenwood, pricing from $595 [http://www.dailylife.greenwood.com].
★**The Greenwood Encyclopedia of Daily Life:** A Tour through History from Ancient Times to the Present. 6v. Ed. by Joyce E. Salisbury and others. 2004. 3,000p. bibliogs. illus. index. Greenwood, $599.95 (0-313- 32541-3). 390.

History is messy." Joyce Salisbury, the general editor, makes this observation in her introduction to *The Greenwood Encyclopedia of Daily Life*. Despite her claim, this ambitious and accessible resource intended for a general audience provides an amazingly organized overview of the minutia that has shaped everyday life from antiquity through the present day. These myriad details represent the common experiences that are essential to a thorough understanding of history and the development of civilizations but are too often glossed over or relegated to footnote status in many standard works. In recognition of the importance of this type of data, the editors have devised an organizational structure, equally effective in both the print and online versions, that provides multiple access points.

In the print version the first level is chronological, with each of the volumes covering a distinct time period: *The Ancient World, The Medieval World, 15th and 16th Centuries, 17th and 18th Centuries, 19th Century,* and *The Modern World*. However, relatively few cultures fit neatly into these chronological divisions, and the flow of daily life tends to transcend political and historic boundaries. Correspondingly, the editors have divided each volume into seven major categories: "Domestic Life," "Economic Life," "Intellectual Life," "Material Life," "Political Life," "Recreational Life," and "Religious Life." Following overview essays, these categories are further divided into subcategories, some of which address topics that are common to all periods, such as "Marriage," and some of which address topics unique to a period, such as "Peasants, Serfs and Slaves" in the "Political Life" section in *The Medieval World*. Information is further refined through culture-specific examples. For instance, "Peasants, Serfs and Slaves" has separate discussions of Europe, the Vikings, China, and the Islamic world. A "concept compass" that charts these divisions appears in the margin of almost every page. The set index, which is 77 pages long and included in each volume, is an essential tool in pulling together all the information on a particular concept or culture.

The text assumes a fairly mature audience; there are frank discussions of sexual practices, birth control, infanticide, medical procedures, and so on. Text is set off by subheadings and accompanied by black-and-white illustrations, boxed informational inserts called "Snapshots," and quotes. Most major entries are followed by suggested Web sites or sources for further research. A particularly helpful feature is a selection of primary sources that concludes each volume. These documents have been judiciously chosen to complement and further define text material. Some selections have been excerpted from readily accessible and well-known documents, such as the *Egyptian Book of the Dead* or Machiavelli's *The Prince*. Others come from more obscure sources, such as an eyewitness account of an eighteenth-century peasant uprising in Japan or the first 12 articles of the 1936 Soviet Constitution.

The online version, which incorporates the print version as well as material from the 27 volumes in Greenwood's Daily Life through History series, is equally detailed and well organized and features an exceptionally accessible interface. The welcome screen offers several ways to access information. A Quick Search box allows researchers to type in a specific term. Advanced Search options help refine queries through standard Boolean operators and to limit searches by era, subject, or region. Researchers can also choose to "Browse by Time Period" (eras that correspond to the print volumes); "Browse by Subject" (seven broad categories—"Domestic Life," "Economic Life," etc.); or "Browse by Region" (a map of the world highlights various continents). A browse search takes users into graphic-rich, uncluttered pages that nicely integrate search types. For example, clicking on the continent of Africa yields a screen that lists 10 entries on domestic life, 18 on intellectual life, 23 on material life, and so on, as well as options for browsing Africa by time period, browsing another region, or entering a new search.

On the results screen, entries are organized under four tabs—encyclopedia articles, book chapters, primary documents, and images. The default sort is the number of times a term appears in an entry, but results can also be sorted by topic, region, or time period. Actual entry pages feature illustrations with complete captions and links to related resources (entries, chronologies, images, maps, lesson plans, and "Tours through Time," the "Snapshots" of the print version). External links, Web sites that have been evaluated for their accuracy and authenticity, are also provided. Currently the database includes 701 sites, with plans for continuing monitoring and expansion. An additional user-friendly feature is the "View Page Citation" link, which pulls up a complete article citation, perfect for copying and pasting. Entries that are chapters from books in the Daily Life series include a table of contents for the entire book. Despite the wealth of search options, screens are visually appealing and easy to navigate and offer running search histories. Clear and detailed help screens and "Tips and Tricks" provide examples and clarify the search process. There is also a "User's Manual" that can be downloaded as a pdf file.

Daily Life provides a level of detail and ease of access that users will appreciate. Whether using the print or the online version, researchers can find in-depth information about a specific civilization, follow the development of particular social phenomena through history, or dip in for ready-reference-type facts and statistics. Although in general the print version offers less detail than Gale's World Eras series, its structure facilitates cross-cultural comparisons, and the online version greatly expands the content base. *Greenwood Daily Life Online* and *The Greenwood Encyclopedia of Daily Life* are highly recommended for high-school, academic, and large public libraries. Special pricing is available for combination purchases.

—Kathleen McBroom

Reference on the Web

Alone Together

by Keir Graff

Television has long been decried as an isolating influence. The medium's detractors would have us believe that, each evening, Americans shun all social intercourse to sit alone in their rooms, communing with make-believe friends in TV land. Personally, I believe the effects of the idiot box are much more complicated, leading to . . . wait, I lost my train of thought. Anyway, TV does often help its adherents find common cause, whether in righteous struggle (consider the clamor after Janet Jackson's nipple greeted football fans at last year's Super Bowl) or hard-won triumph (a campaign of loyal *Farscape* fans prompted network executives to bring back the canceled sf show).

In between galvanizing events, TV fans love to get together online and share the everyday miracles that occur on their favorite shows. To accompany our starred review of the *Encyclopedia of Television* (see p.994), we examine two sites that help them do just that. (All sites last visited December 16, 2004.)

TV Tome. [http://www.tvtome.com/].

This ambitious site hopes eventually to become "the greatest TV episode and actor guide ever." From IMDB to Wikipedia, the model of user-created content, vetted and edited by other users, has been well established, and the folks behind TV Tome are using this approach to good effect. The heart of the database is comprised of guides to individual shows (2,300 complete and more than 3,400 partially complete, according to the site's developers). When complete, guides feature general information such as show introductions (short explanations of the concept); broadcast histories (date, time, and channel); show formats; lists of actors, creators, and crew; news updates about the show; and DVD releases of older episodes. In-depth information includes episode lists, episode guides, "Goofs and Nitpicks" guides, episode reviews, and forums where fans can debate the fine points of *The Surreal Life* or simply ask, "Whatever happened to Brian Benben?"

Design of the site is functional and clean. Users navigate either by a simple search feature or well-organized browsing. There are extensive hyperlinks for the people involved with the shows; clicking a name brings up a page listing all the person's other entries in TV Tome. There's a startling amount of information here, especially as talk shows are included. Anyone wondering what David Spade did before hawking credit cards will, after exhausting *Just Shoot Me* and *Saturday Night Live*, note his many appearances as a talk-show guest. The episode lists for nightly shows like *Late Show with David Letterman* are jaw-dropping.

TV Tome has entries not just for popular new shows (the various *CSI* franchises) and classic oldies (*The Dick Van Dyke Show*) but also cult cable fare (*Curb Your Enthusiasm*) and the quickly canceled (*The Brian Benben Show*). British shows (*The Black Adder, Coupling*) are included, too. Perhaps the most entertaining portion of the site, however, is the list of shows in development. Just reading these august working titles—*Gaydar* (VH1), *Naked Hotel* (ABC), *Untitled David Arquette Project* (WB)—should have TV fans reaching for the remote—and clicking the *off* button.

Like any user-created project, TV Tome has its shortcomings, but it's worth tuning in, at least as a starting point.

The Classic TV Database. [http://www.classic-tv.com/].

Much more modest in scope than TV Tome, the Classic TV Database provides quick snapshots of mostly older shows. The creators' definition of *classic* may be debatable (*Friends* makes a certain amount of sense, but are we so culturally impoverished that *Doogie Howser, M.D.*, qualifies?), but the four 1950s-era shows cited (*The Adventures of Ozzie and Harriet, I Love Lucy, Leave It to Beaver,* and *The Lone Ranger*) certainly qualify. Each entry consists of a brief summary, a cast list, and a broadcast history. A store and banner ads make this a more commercial and cluttered venture, but if you were lying awake at night trying to remember the date *Hogan's Heroes* first aired (September 17, 1965), you can find it here.

A helpful tip: turn the volume on your computer down while searching the Classic TV Database, as the cheesy MIDI renditions of the theme songs will leave you longing for the good old days of silent film.

Countdown to November

by Linda Scarth

These political Web sites are nice to have handy any time, but they are especially good to bookmark in a presidential election year.

Registering to Vote

Registering to vote has never been easier for those with Web access. No matter one's politics or interests, there are ways to find voter registration information and forms.

Federal Election Commission: National Mail Voter Registration Form. [http://www.fec.gov/votregis/vr.htm].

The FEC has an information page with a link to the form for voter registration by mail. It may be used to register out-of-town visitors and when conducting voter-registration drives and is available in English or Spanish.

League of Women Voters: Voter Information. [http://www.lwv.org/voter/register.html].

The LWV is a grass-roots organization for the dissemination of information on public policies, elections, and the democratic process. The site provides links and online information on registering to vote and finding out about local candidates. It is a well-designed and easily navigated site.

Rock the Vote. [http://www.rockthevote.com/].

Aimed at young people, Rock the Vote was begun in 1990 as a nonprofit, nonpartisan organization concerned with freedom of speech and artistic expression. A link to voter registration information figures prominently on its home page.

Your Vote Matters: Register to Vote. [https://www.workingforchange.com/vote/].

Another organization that encourages participation in the democratic process by voter registration is WorkingForChange. Like all of the others, it also encourages viewers to become active in the causes it supports.

The two major parties have links on these pages to voter registration information.

Democratic National Committee: Register to Vote. [https://electionimpact.votenet.com/dnc/].

Republican National Committee: Register to Vote. [http://www.gopteamleader.com/register/index.asp].

Major Parties and Candidates

The major parties and their candidates have sites that are highly partisan, as expected, and brimming with information. The site maps, quick links, and menus found on these sites are worth exploring to learn more about platforms, ideologies, and strategies in the 2004 presidential election.

Democratic National Committee. [http://www.democrats.org].
Senator John Kerry. [http://www.johnkerry.com].
Republican National Committee. [http://www.rnc.org/gopinfo].
President George W. Bush. [http://www.georgebush.com].

The Electoral College and Voter Information

National Archives and Records Administration (NARA): Federal Register: U.S. Electoral College. [http://www.archives.gov/federal_register/electoral_college/].

NARA has built a site to explain this little-understood feature of the U.S. electoral system. There is general information on how the Electoral College works, important dates, past election results, links to state Electoral College information, and more. It provides an important civics lesson.

Project Vote Smart. [http://www.vote-smart.org/].

This highly respected site provides the American public with unbiased and accurate information about campaigns, candidates, issues, and elections. PVS was begun in 1992 by a group of national leaders, including Gerald Ford and Jimmy Carter, to "uphold the ideal of democracy" for a well-informed electorate.

Outstanding Art and Architecture Online

by Craig Bunch

Included here are many of my favorite online art and architecture resources, ranging in scope from the vast to the narrowly focused. All have significant (if not entirely) free content. I have resisted the urge to include individual museum or artist sites in favor of portals linking to the great and the too-little-known alike.

Archives of American Art. [http://archivesofamericanart.si.edu].
Online exhibits, hundreds of oral history transcripts, online reference assistance, finding aids, and more on American art.

Art & Design Associations on the World Wide Web. [http://web.uflib.ufl.edu/artsorg/].
Links to more than 560 art, architecture, design, and related association Web sites, arranged by subject.

Art History Resources on the Web. [http://witcombe.sbc.edu/ARTHLinks.html].
Vast, well-organized selection of links to Web sites covering all of art history. Maintained by Chris Witcombe of Sweet Briar College.

Art Information. [http://americanart.si.edu/art_info/index.cfm].
"Ask Joan of Art" online reference feature, Smithsonian American Art Museum collection search with selected images, Inventories of American Painting and Sculpture, Pre-1877 Art Exhibition Catalogue Index, a guide to Researching Your Art, and more.

Art on the Web. [http://www.bc.edu/bc_org/avp/cas/fnart/Artweb_frames.html].
More than 1,200 well-organized links to visual arts (including, especially, architecture) Web resources. Maintained by Jeffery Howe of Boston College.

Artcyclopedia. [http://www.artcyclopedia.com].
Free access to some 125,000 images by 8,000 artists, and free articles on many. Excellent museum directory. Fee-based links to *Artprice.com* auction results and to *Highbeam Research* articles.

ArtLex Art Dictionary. [http://www.artlex.com].
Definitions of more than 3,600 terms, supporting images, pronunciations, quotations, cross-referencing, and related Web links.

Artnet. [http://www.artnet.com].
Free online magazine featuring articles, news, book and exhibition reviews, and more. Free links to museums and to images of more than 90,000 artworks for sale in galleries. Links to other fee-based services.

ArtsJournal.com: The Daily Digest of Arts, Culture & Ideas. [http://www.artsjournal.com].
Daily summaries of and full-text links to significant arts stories selected from a wide range of international English-language sources, fully archived and keyword searchable. A great place for the art lover to start the day.

AskART. [http://askart.com].
Specializes in American art. Free features include museum and gallery directories, searches of "about 32,000 American artists" for their inclusion in these museums and galleries, special features, and an art glossary. Paid services include auction results and more extensive image results.

The British Library. [http://www.bl.uk/cgi-bin/print.cgi?url=/collections/wider/artwebsite.html].
Directory and links to selected art and architecture Web sites, arranged by topic.

International Directory of Art Libraries. [http://artlibrary.vassar.edu/ifla-idal//].
Vital statistics, contact information, and date of latest update for each of some 3,000 libraries and (in many cases) links to their Web sites.

The Pritzker Architecture Prize. [http://www.pritzkerprize.com].
Biographical information, photo gallery of works, Pritzker Jury's citation to the laureate, architect's essay, and more for each winner of architecture's most prestigious award, 1979 to the present.

UNESCO World Heritage Centre. [http://whc.unesco.org].
Features photos and data documenting each of the 788 sites on the World Heritage List as of July 2004.

Virtual Library Museums Pages: A Distributed Directory of On-line Museums. [http://vlmp.museophile.com].
The most extensive Web directory of museums worldwide, with links to their Web sites. As of August 31, 2004, linked to 1,348 U.S. and 770 Japanese museums, to cite just two countries.

Yahoo! Arts and Humanities. [http://www.yahoo.com/Arts].
Well-organized portal to artists; art history; museums, galleries, and centers; design arts (including architecture); and much more.

Other Features

Atlas and Dictionary Update, 2005

by Mary Ellen Quinn

The atlases and dictionaries listed here are ones we've seen since our last Atlas and Dictionary Update, in the May 15, 2004, issue. Some of the annotations are excerpts of reviews previously published in RBB; others are brief notes on new editions.

For our full World Atlas and Dictionary Update and Children's Atlas and Dictionary Update go to the *Booklist* Web site at http://www.ala.org/booklist. Click on Special Lists and Features and then on Reference.

How often should atlases and dictionaries be replaced? The atlas collection needs regular updating and weeding, since geographic changes make older editions inaccurate. However, the past 12 months have been fairly uneventful in terms of changes to country names and boundaries, so adding an atlas this year is not essential as long as your collection has at least one atlas published in 2004. If only one new atlas can be considered, it should be the eighth edition of the *National Geographic Atlas of the World*.

Since changes to the language don't necessarily render older words and forms obsolete, dictionaries don't become superannuated as quickly as atlases do. At the adult level and at the upper levels of children's dictionaries, it's important to have at least one title on hand that contains newer words and reflects current usage. Librarians serving middle- and high-school students should take particular note of the new editions of the *Merriam-Webster's Intermediate Dictionary* and *Merriam-Webster's School Dictionary*.

Atlases

Atlas of the World. 12th ed. 2004. 448p. Oxford, $80 (0-19-522147-8).

Oxford updates its flagship atlas every year. Additions for 2005 include a geographical glossary and tables showing the populations of the world's largest cities. New high-speed rail links in France and South Korea, the full extent of the Trans-Siberian highway, and interstate and state highway maps throughout North America are now shown.

Hammond World Travel Atlas. 2004. 413p. Hammond, $65 (0-8437-1982-6).

Hammond bills this medium-sized atlas as a source of geographic knowledge as well as a travel guide. The 300-plus pages of maps are of good quality but are littered with more than 100 types of color-coded "pictograms," which are icons identifying features and attractions. The index contains about 100,000 entries with pictograms and page and grid locators.

Illustrated World Atlas. 2004. 399p. Reader's Digest, $49.95 (0-7621-0536-4).

Reader's Digest has published a new medium-sized atlas with maps from European Map Graphics Ltd. Previous Reader's Digest atlases have used Rand McNally or Bartholomew maps. The atlas has 200 pages of maps and a gazetteer of 80,000 place-names. The first 50-plus pages are devoted to weather, migration, resources, communication, and other global topics. The maps are arranged by continent, beginning with Australasia and going west to Europe, Africa, and the Americas. Classic atlases, such as Oxford's *Atlas of the World*, begin with Europe, and some atlases now put the Americas first. No specific city maps are included—city maps are a feature found in some but not all medium-sized atlases.

The Kingfisher Children's Atlas. 2004. 80p. Kingfisher, $14.95 (0-7534-5774-1).

This atlas is designed for a younger audience (grades two through five) than *The Kingfisher Student Atlas* (2003). An introductory section on using maps is followed by maps arranged by continent. Like several other atlases for the age group, this one has simplified maps that are dotted with picture symbols, some representing industries but most depicting animals. Maps for each country or group of countries are accompanied by fact boxes listing largest cities, longest rivers, etc.

National Geographic Atlas of the World. 8th ed. 2004. 416p. National Geographic, $165 (0-7922-7543-8).

The National Geographic Society is celebrating its ninetieth year of mapmaking with the eighth edition of this major, comprehensive atlas. Among the changes are a new "Cities" section—with maps, fact boxes, and photographs of 51 world cities—which replaces useful city-map sections for each continent (which had many more maps of smaller cities) in the seventh edition. The heart of the atlas, the maps of continents and countries, shows great cartography, the strength of the NGS. As in previous editions, the Americas are first, proceeding eastward around the globe. The editors admit that North America is given additional coverage since the primary readership is from the U.S. and Canada. Maps are not as colorful as those in other atlases, but the number of place-names is impressive, rivaling the *Times Atlas of the World* (10th ed., Crown, 1999).

National Geographic United States Atlas for Young Explorers. 2004. 176p. National Geographic, $24.95 (0-7922-6981-0).

Like its sister atlas, *National Geographic World Atlas for Young Explorers* (2003), this atlas for ages 8 through 12 features strong introductory material, including a transportation map and a special city map for Washington, D.C. Large, easy-to-read state maps are organized by region and complemented by fact boxes. Small icons are used to indicate industries, crops, and other aspects of the economy. For each region, there is a physical map and a two-page spread of color photos.

Dictionaries

Merriam-Webster's Intermediate Dictionary. 2004. Merriam-Webster, $17.95 (0-87779-579-7).

Merriam-Webster's School Dictionary. 2004. Merriam-Webster, $18.95 (0-87779-580-0).

Merriam-Webster has revised both its *Intermediate* (for grades 5–8) and its *School* (for grades 9–11) dictionaries to reflect the eleventh edition of *Merriam-Webster's Collegiate Dictionary* (2003). Meanings are listed in historical order (one of the features that makes the Merriam-Webster line unique), and many definitions go into some detail about word histories and origins. They may also include usage notes and illustrations, etymologies, and synonym paragraphs.

Children's Reference Sources
by Maren Ostergard and Shauna Yusko

Perhaps you have the task of opening a new library (school or public) that will serve students in kindergarten through fifth grade. Or maybe you have inherited a children's reference collection that has not been updated since the 1980s. If money is no object in your quest to provide exemplary reference materials for younger students, we are envious. However, if you are on a budget like the rest of us, here are some suggestions for a core reference collection for elementary students.

Resources are divided by Dewey decimal classification, omitting the 100s as this is generally not a core area for K–5 students. In addition, print publications on certain topics have been omitted where subscription databases are better suited to the reference needs of younger researchers (biography, poetry, and art, just to name a few). Contact your state library, local public library, or school district to find out about cost-effective ways to subscribe.

Of course, each library will have its own unique requirements, including annual assignments and topics of local interest. Also, it is important to realize that, when considering cost, many of these items will be onetime purchases, while others should be updated frequently.

000s

For an outstanding single-volume encyclopedia geared to younger students, purchase the *Scholastic Children's Encyclopedia* (2004). This highly user-friendly tool is a great starting place for curious young researchers and browsers alike. More than 600 entries are arranged alphabetically and are illustrated with more than 2,000 photographs, diagrams, charts, time lines, and maps. A "For Further Reference" section contains several useful resources, among them maps of the world, the U.S., and Native American nations; a countries table with names, flags, capitals, and populations; and a table of the 50 states with state flags, postal abbreviations, nicknames, capitals, years of admission, and populations. Other core purchases include *A to Zoo: Subject Access to Children's Picture Books* (Greenwood, 2001); Kathleen O'Dean's *Great Books about Things Kids Love: More Than 750 Recommended Books for Children 3 to 14* (Ballantine, 2001); and to add interest and credibility to your reference collection (at least in the student's eyes), pick up the latest *Guinness Book of World Records* (2004).

200s

Although many religion reference titles are geared to older students, if you have a need for a single-volume resource on world religions, consider *Encyclopedia of World Religions* (Usborne, 2004). This title explores the beliefs, history, and customs of all the major world religions, as well as many less well-known faiths, past and present. With full-color photographs, maps, and a time line, the volume provides plenty of information without being overwhelming. It also includes links to Internet sources.

The *DK Illustrated Dictionary of Mythology* (1998) is organized by geographic region and includes 500 key characters in world mythology. The brief entries and full-color artwork make this resource a starting place for reports and for students needing visuals.

300s

If endangered species are on the list of assignments, consider *Endangered Species* (UXL, 2003). Entries are two or three pages and discuss the biology, habitat, current distribution, history, and conservation measures for each species. All entries include a fact box and locator map, and most include a full-color photograph. Although it is geared to slightly older students, the short entries make this set usable for fourth grade and up, with some librarian, teacher, or parent assistance.

Two must-have resources for any librarian working with teachers and students are a folktale collection such as *Twenty Tellable Tales* (Wilson, 1986), by Margaret Read MacDonald, and a *Chase's Calendar of Events* (McGraw-Hill, 2004).

400s

A good children's dictionary is a must, and the *Scholastic Children's Dictionary* (2002) is clearly laid out and easier to use for readers at the younger end of the age range than are similar dictionaries. The pronunciation guide uses letter sounds instead of symbols, definitions include homophones and sample sentences, and illustrations are labeled in detail. This updated tool adds almost 200 words (*cell phone*, *DVD*, *rap*) to prior editions and includes a useful reference section.

500s

Children's science reference materials abound and could easily be the focus of an entire article. However, if forced to choose, here are some resources that we could not live without.

Science dictionaries such as *The American Heritage Children's Science Dictionary* (Houghton, 2003) or *The Ultimate Visual Dictionary of Science* (DK, 1998) are nice, general introductions to the language of science.

There are a number of excellent animal encyclopedia sets, but if you have to choose one, start with *Wildlife and Plants of the World* (Marshall Cavendish, 1999). This 17-volume set contains information on more than 300 species of animals, as well as plants, microorganisms, and biomes. For a single-volume source, try *The Kingfisher Illustrated Animal Encyclopedia* (2000).

No reference collection would be complete without something on science experiments. *Science Experiments Index for Young People* (Libraries Unlimited, 2001) is the premier resource for tracking down science activities for classroom use, science fairs, or just plain fun. Thousands of experiments are organized by subject area and project, with a brief description of the project and a reference to the book and page number where the experiment is printed.

If money were no object, some other valuable resources, all by Marshall Cavendish, are *Aquatic Life of the World* (2000), *Encyclopedia of Mammals* (1997), *Endangered Wildlife and Plants of the World* (2001), and *Insects and Spiders of the World* (2003).

600s

School and public libraries meeting the needs of elementary students would be well served by *Sick! Diseases and Disorders, Injuries and Infections* (UXL, 2000). This comprehensive source is accessible for younger students yet still contains enough information to meet the needs of older students. It offers thorough coverage of more than 140 maladies, including causes, symptoms, diagnoses, tests, treatments, and prognoses.

Encyclopedia of the Human Body (DK, 2002) provides detailed descriptions of all the major systems of the human body, as well as how each body part works. Typical DK format makes this an appealing and highly browsable resource that teachers will appreciate also.

Another useful title is *The Multicultural Cookbook for Students* (Oryx, 1993). Although somewhat outdated, it still has valuable information and contains 337 recipes from 122 countries. The recipes are arranged geographically by the seven continents or regions. Each of the seven sections begins with a description of the continent or region and provides general information on the types of recipes offered.

Also useful is The New Book of Popular Science (Grolier, 2003), which can be found either as a print resource or as an online database [http://www.go.grolier.com].

700s

Although elementary students require information on music and the arts, there is little published in the area of reference that is appropriate or well reviewed. This is one instance where young researchers would be better served by either online sites or subscription databases, such as *Grove Art Online* [http://www.groveart.com/].

Although intended for ages 12 and up, *History of Art for Young People* (Prentice Hall, 2003), which offers a comprehensive introduction to Western art, might be used by younger students as well.

The Kingfisher Young People's Book of Music (1999) has one-page articles on any number of musical subjects, including the periods, instruments, genres, music of different lands, and short composer biographies. It offers a solid introduction to music.

Children's Jukebox: A Subject Guide to Musical Recordings and Programming Ideas for Songsters Ages One to Twelve (ALA, 1995) is a key resource for any librarian serving children. This convenient text covers about 2,400 children's songs organized by 50 popular themes, for example, color, emotion, and transportation. In addition, hello and good-bye songs each receive individual coverage. Each entry includes song summary, appropriate age and grade level, distribution information, and tips for using the songs in a classroom or library setting.

800s

Although *Bartlett's Familiar Quotations* (Little, Brown, 2002) is a well-known source for quotations, *Quotations for Kids* (Millbrook, 1999) is much better suited to the needs of students. This appealing compilation offers more than 2,000 quotations, arranged alphabetically by topic. It is easy to use and includes quotations from the Bible, works of children's literature, songs, and more. Each quotation includes an author, title, and, when appropriate, character speaking. The book concludes with a topical index and an author index.

Currently in its fifth edition, the *Read Aloud Handbook* (Penguin, 2001) by Jim Trelease belongs in every library. The first half of this essential resource provides information on the how and why of reading aloud. It concludes with an annotated bibliography of more than 1,000 titles for children arranged by theme, including wordless books, predictable books, and reference books. Educators will find chapters on sustained silent reading and television especially useful.

The Children's Literature Dictionary (Neal-Schuman, 2002) is geared to librarians and teachers working with students and examines 325 terms relating to children's literature. Entries include suggested activities for reinforcing understanding and retention of concepts.

900s

Although many student reference needs are in the areas of geography and history, building a collection can be daunting because of price and the fact that geography books may require frequent updates. A number of history reference titles are not suited to a core collection because of their narrow scope. Also, there is abundant information to be found for free on the Internet or on fee-based databases. However, one single-volume world-history source to contemplate is the recently updated *Kingfisher History Encyclopedia* (2004). For U.S. history, *A History of the U.S.* (Oxford, 2004) offers extensive coverage with an engaging text.

State Names, Seals, Flags, and Symbols: A Historical Guide (Greenwood, 2001) is an authoritative resource offering facts and figures about states and territories. Such facts include names and nicknames, mottoes, flowers, trees, birds, songs, and more. The third edition has new chapters on state and territory universities, governors, and professional sports teams. Other coverage includes postage stamps, fairs and festivals, legal holidays and special observances, and license plates.

Another excellent reference tool is *Lands and Peoples* (Grolier, 2004). Here, children will find current statistical, geographical, and economic information on the people, languages, cultures, and histories of every country around the globe. The final volume of the set includes general statistical information as well. There is also a fee-based online version [http://www.go.grolier.com].

Encyclopedia of Native American Tribes (UXL, 1999) studies 80 tribes arranged by 10 geographical areas. Various aspects of the groups are covered, including history, religion, language, government, economy, daily life, arts, customs, current issues, and notable individuals.

Every library should include an atlas. One atlas that is especially useful for students is *Goode's World Atlas* (Rand McNally, 2004). Although the maps contained in this text may not be as detailed as other resources, it more than compensates with its thematic section maps, which feature population density, precipitation, vegetation, language spoken, energy use, tectonic plates, temperatures and landforms, and more. For the very youngest students, consider *National Geographic's Beginner's World Atlas* (1999).

It is vital to provide a practical, interesting, and sound reference collection that meets the needs of students. By teaching them early, and often, that the library (and the librarian) is an excellent resource, they will naturally look to us when they have information needs in middle and high school and beyond. In a future issue, we will present a core reference collection for young adults.

Did You Hear about the Reference Book That . . . ?

by Donald Altschiller

Of the making of arcane reference books, there is no end. No, that profound observation does not appear in the Book of Ecclesiastes. Nevertheless, it may ring a responsive chord among many reference librarians. Like a philatelist who searches for the odd-shaped or strangely themed postage stamp, I love finding unusual and offbeat reference works. Of course, quirkiness may be in the eye of the librarian. But surely, even the most seasoned reference librarian may take some special delight in the following titles.

Women Serial and Mass Murderers: A Worldwide Reference, 1580 through 1990. By Kerry Segrave. McFarland, 1992.

Gender disparity, unfortunately, still exists in many vocations and jobs. But, as this unique reference book amply documents, one can feel at least some partial comfort that serial murder is not only confined to those with XY chromosomes.

Show Me the Good Parts: The Reader's Guide to Sex in Literature. By Robert George Reisner. Citadel, 1964.

The dust jacket immediately, er, arouses your interest. "The book grew out of the author's experience as a librarian. Patrons would frequently request books that contained what they euphemistically described as 'romantic episodes.' Mr. Reisner was eventually inspired to compile an index to assist such readers."

What a brilliant idea! And what a diligent librarian! Alphabetically arranged by topic (*Adultery, Exhibitionism, Masochism, Promiscuity,* and *Zoophilia,* to name only a few), this 340-page work contains annotated citations to these "romantic episodes"—and Mr. Reisner helpfully provides the specific page references to the "good parts"! Who said bibliographies are boring?

A dictionary of onomatopoeic sounds, tones and noises in English and Spanish, including those of animals, man, nature, machinery and musical instruments, together with some that are not imitative or echoic = Un diccionario de las voces, sonidos, y tonos onomatopeyicas en ingles y español, incluye las de animals, hombre, naturaleza, maquinaria e instrumentos musicales, junto con algunas que no son verdaderamente ni imitativas ni ecoicas. By Donald R. Kloe. B. Ethridge, 1977.

As the mass media serving the Hispanic-American community grows at an exponential rate, it is indeed gratifying that there is at least one print reference work informing the reader that there are Spanish and English for many different sounds. "Glug-glug," for example, the sound of a liquid being poured from a bottle—is the noise Anglos hear; Spanish speakers, however, hear this sound as "glu-glu."

Lights! Catalogue of Worldwide Matchbox Labels with the Word 'Light' in the Title. By Raymond W. Norris. British Matchbox Label and Booklet Society, 1983.

There will always be an England! (Hat tip: *Bizarre Books*, by Russell Ash and Brian Lake, for this citation.)

Who's Who on the Postage Stamps of Ecuador. By Albert F. Kunze. Pan American Union. 1953.

A man comes to the reference desk and sheepishly says, "I have a pretty strange question." You immediately reassure him that there are "no" strange questions.

He reaches into his briefcase and pulls out a loose-leaf binder. He opens up the binder and says, "I have these postage stamps and I want to find biographical information about the person depicted on each one."

"From what country?" the librarian expectantly asks. "Ecuador," the man quietly notes.

"Hmm. I have just the right reference book for you . . ."

Read-alikes: Exploring Exploration

by Mary Ellen Quinn

Many libraries ramped up their collections on explorers for the 1992 recognition of Columbus' voyages, and even now, when we think *explorers*, we might think first of men of the Age of Discovery, such as Columbus and Magellan. But in the curriculum, and consequently in reference works, *exploration* is defined more broadly. Marshall Cavendish's *Explorers and Exploration*, which we review opposite, joins a bevy of sources in which an explorer is anyone who makes a journey of discovery, whether the journey takes him or her to the court of Kublai Khan, to the Galapagos on *HMS Beagle*, or to outer space. For libraries that need to freshen their collections in this area, here is a list of titles we've reviewed since 1993.

For Schools

Explorers: From Ancient Times to the Space Age. 3v. Ed. by John Logan Allen and others. 1999. Macmillan $370 (0-02-864893-5).

Three introductory essays are followed by alphabetically arranged profiles of 333 men and women.

Explorers and Discoverers from Alexander the Great to Sally Ride. 7v. 1994. UXL, $350 (1-4144-0480-8).

An *A–Z* arrangement makes it easy to find information on the 200 or so individual explorers included.

The Grolier Student Library of Explorers and Exploration. 10v. 1997. Grolier, $299 (0-7172-9135-9).

Each volume concentrates on a specific region or aspect of discovery. The many pictures, photographs, and sidebars provide visual appeal.

For High Schools and General Collections

Encyclopedia of Exploration. 2v. 2004. Facts On File, $200 (0-8160-4678-6).

Volume 1, *The Explorers,* presents more than 950 biographical entries. More than 260 topical entries are found in volume 2, *Places, Technologies, and Cultural Trends.*

Encyclopedia of the Lewis and Clark Expedition. By Elen Woodger and Brandon Toropov. 2003. Facts On File, $65 (0-8160-4781-2).

Even though it is fairly specialized, high current interest in the topic makes this volume appropriate for general collections.

The Encyclopedia of Women's Travel and Exploration. By Patricia Netzley. 2001. Oryx, $65 (1-57356-238-6).

Covers women explorers, tourists, mountain climbers, writers, geographers, anthropologists, archaeologists, missionaries, and more. There are also entries for continents, travel guides, clothing, transportation, and other topics.

Explorers. 2v. 1998. Salem, $95 (0-89356-970-4).

Compiles 78 biographies from several titles in Salem's Great Lives from History series and adds nine new essays.

Explorers and Discoverers of the World. Ed. by Daniel B. Baker. 1993. Gale, $120 (0-8103-5421-7).

More than 300 explorers and discoverers are profiled. Biographies range in length from one-half to three pages, many with portraits or maps and all with bibliographies.

Web Sites (last accessed April 27, 2005)

Discoverers Web. [http://www.win.tue.nl/~engels/discovery].

Discovery and Exploration. [http://lcweb2.loc.gov/ammem/gmdhtml/dsxphome.html].

Society for the History of Discoveries. [http://www.sochistdisc.org/].

Reference Books in Spanish for Children and Adolescents

by Isabel Schon

Atlases

Atlas visual Océano de botánica (Océano Visual Atlas: Botany). 2004. 84p. Editorial Océano, paper, $10.95 (84-494-1279-X).

Gr. 9–adult. Like the other 11 titles in this series designed for high-school students, this is not a simple overview; rather it is a comprehensive survey of plant life, including the characteristic features and biology of plant habitats around the world. Numerous color maps, charts, and diagrams and a detailed text describe the plant world—from tropical rain forests to aquatic vegetation. Unfortunately, the atlas does not include an index.

Mi primer atlas (My First Atlas). By Elizabeth Dalby. Tr. by Pilar Dunster. 2004. 64p. EDC Publishing, $12.95 (0-7460-6392-X).

Gr. 3–5. Full-color maps, drawings, and photographs, and clear captions and informative sidebars, along with brief text, introduce readers to the geography of the world and unique customs and traditions worldwide. From a Mayan temple, to the Amazonian forest, to the Himalaya Mountains in Asia, to the Sahara Desert in Africa, this is an enticing primer to maps and the world. Cyber-enthusiasts will appreciate the publisher's numerous Web links to sites with supplemental information.

Biographical Dictionary

Quién es quién en la ciencia (Who Is Who in the Sciences). By Giorgio Dragoni and others. Tr. by Juan Vivanco and others. 2v. 2004. Acento, $49.99 (v.1: 84-483-0781-X; v.2: 84-483-0780-1).

Gr. 9–adult. Originally published in Italy, this dictionary includes biographical entries of outstanding world scientists and a description of their principal achievements. From one-paragraph entries (for example, *Abbe, Ernst*) to six pages devoted to *Einstein, Albert*, this is a panoramic view of recognized scientists and their theories or contributions. The lack of illustrations of any kind limits its use to serious students.

Dictionaries

Diccionario enciclopédico, 2004 (Encyclopedic Dictionary, 2004). 2003. 1,826p. Larousse, $38 (970-22-0920-X).

Gr. 7–adult. Divided in two parts, a dictionary of the Spanish language and biographical and geographic entries, this encyclopedic dictionary with more than 90,000 entries and 5,000 color illustrations, charts, and maps will be most useful to those who can afford only one reference source in Spanish. With information up to 2003 and just as attractively designed as its predecessors (including the same limitations—e.g., four pages devoted to Spain, two to the U.S.), users will appreciate the wide coverage, neologisms, and Latin Americanisms. Although some readers may object to the small font, most will appreciate the conciseness.

Diccionario general de la lengua española (General Dictionary of the Spanish Language). 2005. 1,455p. Edebé, $22.95 (84-236-7134-8).

Gr. 8–adult. With more than 30,000 entries and a clear, easy-to-read format and design, this is a good basic Spanish-language dictionary. Contemporary speakers will appreciate the inclusion of current neologisms such as *chat, e-mail, móvil*, and *videoteléfono* as well as colloquial expressions. Also useful are the grammar notes and sidebars as well as the informative appendixes that include such topics as common language errors and the use of computer spell-checkers. One caveat: most examples consider only Peninsular Spanish usage.

Redes: Diccionario combinatorio del español contemporáneo (Webs: Integrative Dictionary of Contemporary Spanish). By Ignacio Bosque. 2004. 1,839p. SM, $29.95 (84-675-0276-2).

Gr. 9–adult. The purpose of this dictionary is not to define words nor to offer a selection of synonyms but, rather, to explain how words are combined in Spanish and the context in which they are used. Serious students of the language will appreciate the numerous examples of current unusual and idiosyncratic words and phrases and how these are combined to determine meaning.

Refranero mexicano (Mexican Proverbs). By Herón Pérez Martínez. 2004. 458p. Fondo de Cultura Económica, paper, $13.95 (968-16-7070-1).

Gr. 9–adult. Arranged in alphabetical order, this scholarly compendium of proverbs that originated in Mexico or came from other countries but are now in widespread use in Mexico is a dream come true for students of proverbs. From short sayings that express basic truths such as *lo caido, caido*, to practical precepts such as *negocio platicado, negocio no arreglado*, students will find thoughtful explanations, well-organized themes, variants, and grammatical structures that clarify meaning.

Encyclopedia

Enciclopedia hispánica (Hispanic Encyclopedia). 18v. 2005. Barsa Planeta; dist. by World Book, $1,399 (1-56409-070-1).

Gr. 8–adult. Long considered one of the best general encyclopedias in the Spanish language, this set includes a 14-volume *Macropedia* with more that 5,000 generic and specific topics arranged in alphabetical order, a two-volume *Micropedia* with basic information on 34,000 entries, a *Temapedia* with 40 general essays that classify knowledge, and a *Datapedia* that presents information in tables and charts. With 380 new articles, excellent color photos, charts, maps, and drawings as well as updated information up to 2004, this is indeed a must-have Spanish-language encyclopedia.

Distributors

Lectorum [http://www.lectorum.com].
Mariuccia Iaconi Book Imports [http://www.mibibook.com].

Reference Books in Spanish for Children and Adolescents

by Isabel Schon

Atlas

Atlas del mundo. (Peters Atlas of the World). By Arno Peters. 2002. 231p. Ediciones Vicens-Vives, $25.95 (84-316-6538-6).

Gr. 9–adult. Originally published by HarperCollins, this atlas includes 43 double-page physical maps of the world; 246 thematic maps with such topics as world culture and information, health, and sports; and a most complete index.

Bilingual Dictionaries

Everest Cumbre diccionario español-inglés. (English-Spanish Dictionary). 2003. 911p. Editorial Everest, paper, $13.95 (84-241-1236-9).

Gr. 8–adult. More than 60,000 words are included in this handy dictionary with easy-to-understand definitions. Learners of either language will especially appreciate the phonetic transcriptions following each entry as well as the explanatory notes and examples of usage. It also includes a table highlighting British and American English usages.

The Oxford Spanish Dictionary: Spanish-English/English- Spanish. (Gran diccionario Oxford: Español-inglés/Inglés-español). 3d ed. 2003. 1,979p. Oxford, $49.95 (0-19- 860475-0).

Gr. 8–adult. The third edition of this well- designed dictionary will satisfy the needs of users of Spanish and English from both sides of the Atlantic. The introduction guides readers to more than 300,000 words and phrases and 500,000 translations, including recent terms; a useful writing guide with more than 70 sample letters; and easy- to-understand labels, phrases, and cross-references. Serious students of both languages will especially appreciate the clear regional labels indicating whether a word or expression is restricted to particular areas of the English-speaking or Spanish-speaking worlds.

Dictionaries

Diccionario Anaya de la lengua. (Anaya's Language Dictionary). 2002. 1,195p. Grupo Anaya, $47.95 (84-8332-245-5).

Gr. 7–12. Especially designed for students, this Spanish- language dictionary includes more than 34,000 entries. Users will appreciate the clear, easy-to-read format and design. Also valuable to students are the appendixes, which include straightforward spelling and grammar rules.

Diccionario de argot español. (Dictionary of Spanish Slang). By José María Iglesias. 2003. 196p. Alianza Editorial, paper, $9.95 (84-206-5531-7).

Gr. 8–adult. With more than 4,000 entries, this handy dictionary includes frequently used words and expressions that vary from standard Spanish. Divided into two sections—slang to standard Spanish and standard Spanish to slang—the dictionary provides users with examples of language used in casual, informal, and playful speech. Definitely not for purists, this is Spanish "slanguage" at its best.

Diccionario de uso del español de América y España. (Usage Dictionary of the Spanish Language of America and Spain). 2002. 2,022p. SPES Editorial, $23.95 (84-8332-349-4).

Gr. 8–adult. This dictionary, especially designed for contemporary Spanish speakers from the Americas and Spain, includes more than 53,000 entries and 112,000 meanings as well as numerous examples, regional new words, notes, and clear labels indicating usage.

Diccionario esencial lengua española. (Essential Spanish Language Dictionary). 2002. 870p. Vox/SPES Editorial, paper, $10.95 (84-8332-248-X).

Gr. 7–adult. The purpose of this dictionary is to provide as many words and meanings as possible in a concise, easy-to-use format. It has more than 26,000 entries with simple definitions reflecting Peninsular Spanish usage.

Diccionario para la enseñanza de la lengua española: Español para extranjeros. (Dictionary for the Teaching of the Spanish Language: Spanish for Foreigners). 2000. 1,248p. Vox/SPES Editorial, paper, $16.95 (84-8332- 111-4).

Gr. 7–adult. This dictionary includes more than 22,000 entries selected for frequency of usage. Students of the language will especially appreciate the syllabication and pronunciation of words, which are seldom given in Spanish-language dictionaries. In addition, it notes special difficulties for students of Spanish as a second language.

El pequeño Larousse, 2003. (The Small Larousse, 2003). 2002. 1,824p. SPES Editorial, $39.95 (84-8332-280-3).

Gr. 7–adult. Like its predecessors, this encyclopedic dictionary with more than 85,000 entries, 5,000 color illustrations, and 320 maps and charts is most useful to those who can't afford a Spanish encyclopedia. Especially noteworthy are the current scientific and technical terms, numerous lexical and encyclopedic entries from Hispanic America, and the clear (albeit small) typography and color photos and drawings.

Encyclopedias

Everest enciclopedia básica del estudiante. (Everest Basic Student's Encyclopedia). 12v. 2002. 1,147p. Editorial Everest; dist. by Gale, $262.67 (84-241-1849-9).

Gr. 4–7. Especially designed for students, this simply written, attractive encyclopedia includes more than 1,300 easy-to-understand entries and 5,000 color photographs, drawings, maps, and charts. The only caveat is that, like other encyclopedias published in Europe, it includes more European than American or Latin American content. Nonetheless, the lack of recent children's encyclopedias in the Spanish language makes this a welcome addition to any school or library.

La enciclopedia de los deportes. (Junior Sports Encyclopedia). By Donna Vekteris and Francis Magnenot. Tr. by Jimena Licitra and others. 2002. 224p. Ediciones SM, $33.95 (84-348-8866-1).

Gr. 6–10. Basic information about more than 100 sports is included in this large-format encyclopedia. It explains how each sport is played and what special equipment is required. Computer-generated illustrations, which show athletes as they perform a sequence of movements, add further to its informational and recreational values.

Handbooks

Religiones del mundo. (World Religions). 2002. 395p. Editorial Oceano; dist. by Gale, $55.95 (84-494-2195-0).

Gr. 9–adult. Offering a wide panorama of religious ideas and beliefs throughout the history of humankind, this volume has well-organized chapters and excellent color photos, artistic reproductions, charts, chronologies, and maps describing the evolution of religion from primitive cults to rites of passage in the modern world.

Diccionario de literatura universal. (Dictionary of World Literature). 2003. 1,152p. Editorial Océano, $150 (84-494-2435-6).

Gr. 9–adult. More than 2,000 authors from around the world are included in this comprehensive survey of more than 20 centuries of literature from ancient times to contemporary authors. Arranged in alphabetical order with special emphasis on authors from Spain and Latin America, it also offers informative overviews of literary movements as well as specific Latin American countries. Color and black-and-white photos, interesting critical sidebars, a chronological author index, and an interactive CD-ROM add further to its usefulness.

Reference Sources on the Presidency and Presidential Elections
by Donald Altschiller and Jack O'Gorman

I can tell you this. No man who ever held the office of President would congratulate a friend on obtaining it. Make no mistake about it, the four most miserable years of my life were my four years in the Presidency.
—*President John Quincy Adams*

The perennial race for the U.S. presidency has been aptly called "The Endless Campaign." The news media has already begun speculating about the possible candidates for the White House in 2008. In the meantime, Americans are now subjected to 24-hour television and radio coverage and also saturation print reporting about the presidential race of 2004. Fortunately, for library users who might want to learn more about the broader historical, cultural, and political aspects of the U.S. presidential election, comprehensive and informative reference sources are on hand. The following recent and classic reference titles would work in any library serving patrons at the high-school level and up.

The Almanac of American Politics 2004. Ed. by Michael Barone and Richard E. Cohen. 2003. 1,837p. National Journal, paper, $59.95 (0-89234-106-8).

Besides the presidential election, one-third of the U.S. Senate is up for grabs, as are all 435 seats in the U.S. House of Representatives. This work contains biographical information about governors, representatives and senators. Entries include biographical information and group ratings (such as those from the ACLU or American Conservative Union). It also lists congressional leadership and congressional committee memberships.

American First Ladies. Ed. by Robert P. Watson. 2001. 439p. Salem, $135 (0-89356-070-2).

Containing 44 biographical essays, this nicely illustrated volume also includes narrative essays on the different roles of the First Lady as well as a useful annotated bibliography.

American Presidential Campaigns and Elections. 3v. By William G. Shade and Ballard C. Campbell. 2003. 1,137p. Sharpe, $325 (0-7656-8042-2).

Following some overview essays, there is an analysis of every presidential election from 1789 to 2000. Each election chapter offers a description of the issues, conventions, campaigns, and election results; a chronology; a sidebar focusing on an interesting aspect of the election; a vote analysis in chart and map form; a bibliography; and a collection of between five and seven documents.

Congressional Quarterly's Desk Reference on the Presidency: Over 500 Answers to Frequently Asked Questions. By Bruce Wetterau. 2000. 311p. CQ, $43.95 (1-56802-589-0).

Part of the well-regarded CQ Desk Reference series, this work contains a wide variety of questions and answers on all aspects of presidential history, powers and duties, the nomination, and campaign and election, to name only some topics. An excellent index provides easy and quick access to the contents.

CQ Voting and Elections Collection. [Internet database]. CQ, for pricing call 800-834-9020, ext. 1906. [http://www.cqpress.com].

CQ Press has a new database that contains election information for students and researchers. It is organized into six categories: Presidential Elections, Congressional Elections, Gubernatorial Elections, Campaigns and Elections, Political Parties, and Voters and Demographics. In-depth features include candidate and office histories, studies of incumbents, party control of districts, and more. This product will support class work in campaigns and elections for AP high-school and university political science courses.

Encyclopedia of Presidential Campaigns, Slogans, Issues, and Platforms. By Robert North Roberts and Scott Hammond. 2004. 432p. Greenwood. $75 (0-313-31973-1).

This reference provides a different slant on presidential elections. Part 1 describes the elections from 1789 to 2000, including cross-references to campaign issues. Part 2 describes key figures, events, and slogans from various presidential campaigns.

The Encyclopedia of the Republican Party; The Encyclopedia of the Democratic Party. 4v. Ed. by George Thomas Kurian and Jeffrey D. Schultz. 1996. Sharpe, $399 (1-56324-729-1).
Supplement to The Encyclopedia of the Democratic Party;
Supplement to The Encyclopedia of the Republican Party. 2v. Ed. by George Thomas Kurian. 2001. Sharpe, $199 (0-7656-8031-9).

Through its parallel two-party structure, this encyclopedia covers the positions, the history, the people, and the platforms of the Republican and Democratic parties. It also presents biographies of presidents, vice presidents, losing presidential candidates, and speakers of the house. Issues such as abortion and foreign policy are discussed from both sides of the political spectrum.

Facts about the Presidents. 7th ed. By Joseph Nathan Kane and others. 2001. 721p. Wilson, $120 (0-8242-1007-7).

This updated edition of the classic presidential fact book— originally compiled by the late Kane, an incomparable researcher"—provides everything you ever wanted to know about our presidents and possibly more, for example, presidents who married on their birthdays and the age of presidents at the death of their mothers.

The Fathers of American Presidents: From Augustine Washington to William Blythe and Roger Clinton. By Jeff C. Young. 2003. 255p. McFarland. $39.95 (0-7864-1699-8).

This title contains brief biographies of presidential fathers, who, in some cases, guided their sons to greatness or, in others, ignored the careers of their successful offspring.

The Presidency A to Z. 3d ed. By Michael Nelson. 2003. 603p. CQ, $36.95 (1-56802-803-2).

Providing easy-to-understand information, this source covers both the presidents and the office of the presidency, including overviews of executive powers, administrations, and elections. Brief biographies of presidents, vice presidents, and influential First Ladies are also presented.

Presidential Elections, 1789–2000. 2002. 256p. CQ, paper, $39.95 (1-56802-790-7).

A handy volume offering a chronology of presidential elections as well as information on primaries, popular votes, the Electoral College, and electoral votes from 1789 to 2000. It concludes with biographies of presidential and vice-presidential candidates.

Vital Statistics on the Presidency: Washington to Clinton. Rev. ed. By Lyn Ragsdale. 1998. 464p. CQ, $50.95 (1-56802-393-6).

A superb source. Besides the standard election statistics, this work provides a wide range of useful information, including the dates and descriptions of major presidential speeches, polling data, and the rankings of presidents by historians, to list only a few examples.

Some Key Reference Works for Genealogists

by Evva Benson, Mark E. Gardner, Russell S. Lynch, and Raymond S. Wright III

The following bibliography was compiled by librarians at the Family History Library in Salt Lake City, Utah. The list focuses upon works that will meet the research needs of most persons searching for ancestors in U.S. libraries. Some of the largest European immigrant descendant groups in the U.S. are also represented. Emphasis was given to reference works that would provide access to resources that document family members' lives. No research handbooks are listed because library users can find research guidance on almost any ethnic group or geographic area at the free site FamilySearch.org [http://www.familysearch.org]. This site also provides access to a large genealogical database with about a billion entries as well as access to the catalog of the largest genealogical library in the world, the Family History Library in Salt Lake City, Utah. The free Web site Cyndi's List of Genealogy Sites on the Internet [http://www.cyndislist.com] is a gateway to almost every genealogy Web site in the world. A subscription Web site that provides access to the Web's largest set of genealogical databases is Ancestry.com [http://www.ancestry.com].

United States

The American Census Handbook. By Thomas Jay Kemp. 2002. 128p. Rowman & Littlefield, $90 (0-8420-2924-9); paper, $29.95 (0-8420-2925-7).

Describes how to use the census schedules for 1790–1920 to determine a family's residence and identify the members in the household.

Ancestry's Redbook: American State, County and Town Sources. Rev. ed. Ed. by Alice Eichholz. 1992. 858p. MyFamily.com, $49.95 (0-916489-47-7).

Describes record sources available for each state and county.

Commercial Atlas and Marketing Guide. 135th ed. 2v. 2004. Rand McNally, $327.85 (0-528-8151-56).

The most commonly used atlas to determine the location of ancestral hometowns, with detailed maps of all states.

The Genealogist's Address Book. 4th ed. By Elizabeth Petty Bentley. 1998. 832p. Genealogical Publishing, paper, $39.95 (0-8063-1580-6).

Contains addresses and contact information for federal, state, and local government agencies as well as nongovernment organizations like historical, genealogical, hereditary, lineage, and patriotic societies. A section is devoted to ethnic and religious organizations and research centers.

Guide to Genealogical Research in the National Archives of the United States. 3rd ed. Ed. by Anne Bruner Eales and Robert M. Kvasnicka. 2000. 411p. National Archives and Records Administration, $39 (1-880875-21-7).

Details the rich record collections at the U.S. National Archives and explains how to access microfilmed copies of federal records.

International Vital Records Handbook. 4th ed. By Thomas Jay Kemp. 2000. 603p. Genealogical Publishing, paper, $34.95 (0-8063-1655-1).

Lists addresses of federal and state agencies that provide copies of birth, marriage, divorce, and death records. Contact information for registration offices in other countries is also included.

Land and Property Research in the United States. By E. Wade Hone. 1997. 517p. MyFamily.com, $49.95 (0-916489-68-X).

Describes the types of land records created on the local, state, and federal levels and explains how to obtain them.

Map Guide to the U.S. Federal Censuses, 1790–1920. By William Thorndale and William Dollarhide. 1995. 420p. Genealogical Publishing, paper, $49.95 (0-8063-1188-6).

Shows the state and county boundaries for a particular census year.

The New A to Zax: A Comprehensive Genealogical Dictionary for Genealogists and Historians. 3rd ed. By Barbara Jean Evans. 1995. 300p. Hearthside, paper, $14.95 (0-945231-02-4).

Defines many terms and abbreviations found in genealogical resources.

The Source: A Guidebook of American Genealogy. Rev. ed. Ed. by Loretta Dennis Szucs and Sandra Hargreaves Luebking. 1997. 834p. MyFamily.com, $44.95 (0-916489-67-1).

Describes the major record types in the U.S. and how to use them to find ancestors.

U.S. Military Records: A Guide to Federal and State Sources, Colonial America to the Present. By James C. Neagles. 1994. 441p. MyFamily.com, $39.95 (0-916489-55-8).

Describes the types of U.S. military records and how they help in family history research.

Europe

Ancestors in German Archives: A Guide to Family History Sources. By Raymond S. Wright III and others. 2004. 1,189p. Genealogical Publishing, $85 (0-8063-1747-7).

Covers most of the federal, state, and local archives of Germany. See review on p.684.

Avotaynu Guide to Jewish Genealogy. Ed. by Sallyann Amdur Sack and Gary Mokotoff. 2004. 624p. Avotaynu, $85 (1-886223-16-5).

Describes the history of Jewish settlement in each country covered and details which records are available in each country and how to obtain them.

Following the Paper Trail: A Multilingual Translation Guide. By Jonathan D. Shea and William F. Hoffmann. 1994. 241p. Avotaynu, $29 (0-9626373-4-3).

Provides examples of documents in 13 European languages—including Latin—commonly used by genealogists, along with instructions for translating the documents into English.

General Alphabetical Index to the Townlands and Towns, Parishes and Baronies of Ireland Based on the Census of Ireland for the Year 1851. Repr. 2000. 968p. Genealogical Publishing, $50 (0-8063-1052-9).

Aids researchers in determining where ancestral hometowns are located.

German-English Genealogical Dictionary. Repr. By Ernest Thode. 2003. 286p. Genealogical Publishing, $29.95 (0-8063-1342-0).

Defines terms and abbreviations encountered in original and published German-language resources.

Irish Records: Sources for Family and Local History. Rev. ed. By James Ryan. 1997. MyFamily.com, $49.95 (0-916489-76-0).

Describes the various records created in Ireland and where they are found today.

A New Genealogical Atlas of Ireland. 2d ed. By Brian Mitchell. 2002. 175p. Genealogical Publishing, $20 (0-806316-84-5).

Shows county boundaries and boundaries of Roman Catholic, Methodist, Presbyterian, and Church of Ireland jurisdictions. Barony boundaries, jurisdictions of probate districts, and poor law unions are also shown.

Tracing Your Ancestors in the Public Record Office. 6th ed. By Amanda Bevan. 2002. 416p. Public Record Office, paper, $24.94 (1-903365-34-1).

The definitive guide to genealogical sources in the National Archives of the United Kingdom.

Twenty Best Bets for Student Researchers

by Mary Ellen Quinn

As the new school year gets under way, our annual "Best Bets" list features titles we reviewed in the past 12 months that are targeted for students from the elementary- through high-school levels.

The American Heritage Children's Science Dictionary. 2003. 280p. Houghton, $17.95 (0-618-35401-8).

More than 2,500 entries provide the kinds of definitions students in grades four through six need in areas of science such as astronomy, biology, and physics as well as topics like weather and computer technology.

American Presidents in World History. 5v. 2003. Greenwood, $200 (0-313-32564-2).

Arranged chronologically from George Washington to George W. Bush, this set for grades five and up proffers a unique view of U.S. and world history. Instead of the usual biography or administration highlights, it examines each president's actions and policies from a global perspective.

Career Discovery Encyclopedia. 8v. 5th ed. 2003. Ferguson, $175 (0-89434-275-4).

In its latest edition, this career resource continues to provide fresh and very basic information for upper-elementary and middle-school students. Around 70 of the more than 650 entries are new, and other entries have been revised.

The Civil War. 10v. 2004. Grolier, $309 (0-7172-5883-1).

This set intended for students in grades five through nine features detailed articles that address significant individuals, battles, events, and conditions of the American Civil War. Colorful graphics appear on every page and include archival photographs, political cartoons, maps, broadsides, and other vintage illustrations.

Encyclopedia of Life Sciences. 13v. 2d ed. 2003. 1,872p. Marshall Cavendish, $459.95 (0-7614-7442-0).

It was time for an update of the first edition, which appeared in 1996. Among the 78 new entries are biographies of 23 scientists. Multiple indexes make it easy to pinpoint information. The target audience is grades seven and up.

Encyclopedia of the Aquatic World. 11v. 2003. 1,582p. Marshall Cavendish, $459.95 (0-7614-7418-8).

More than 70 articles cover the mammals, fish, birds, amphibians, reptiles, crustaceans, plants, algae, and microorganisms that inhabit aquatic environments as well as their symbiotic relationship with humans. Over 1,500 illustrations are included to enhance learning and encourage browsing by students in junior high and high school.

Exploring Ancient Civilizations. 11v. 2003. 880p. Marshall Cavendish, $329.95 (0-7614-7456-0).

This lavishly illustrated encyclopedia for grades five and up covers the time period between 6,500 B.C.E. and 500 C.E., the span beginning with the development of writing and agriculture and concluding with the fall of the Roman Empire. The final volume contains several thematic indexes, along with other reference aids.

Exploring Technology. 11v. 2003. 880p. Marshall Cavendish, $329.95 (0-7614-7406-4).

There are few available resources on technology for middle readers. Agriculture and food, engineering and construction, medicine, transportation, and the history of invention are just some of the areas covered here. The colorful and eye-catching presentation should appeal to an upper- elementary and middle-school audience.

Fashion, Costume, and Culture: Clothing, Headwear, Body Decoration, and Footwear through the Ages. 5v. By Sara Pendergast and Tom Pendergast. 2004. 1,040p. UXL, $275 (0-7876-5417-5).

From the furry hides probably worn by Neanderthals to designer jeans, this set intended for middle-schoolers surveys how people have covered and adorned themselves through the ages and around the world. Notable for its organization, breadth of coverage, and attractive design, it will likely have appeal beyond its targeted audience.

Great World Writers: Twentieth Century. 13v. Ed. by Patrick M. O'Neil. 2003. 1,848p. Marshall Cavendish, $459.95 (0-7614-7468-4).

Following *Great American Writers of the Twentieth Century* (2002), these volumes survey the lives and works of 93 distinguished authors from 42 countries beyond the U.S. Imaginatively designed and profusely illustrated, the set is intended to attract and hold the attention of a young adult audience.

Grolier Student Encyclopedia. 17v. 2004. 1,088p. Grolier, $249 (0-7172-5865-3).

Substantive reference sources for students in primary grades are hard to find. In this one, more than 700 one- to two-page entries provide a solid introduction to general topics, with plenty of aids to help students in grades three to six develop research and report-writing skills.

How It Works: Science and Technology. 20v. 3d. ed. 2003. Marshall Cavendish, $499.95 (0-7614-7314-9).

More than 800 articles and 2,800 illustrations explain the technologies of modern life in a well-indexed set designed for students at the junior-high-school level and up. Some of the topics in this new edition pertain to recent developments in biotechnology, computers, and microelectronics.

Industrial Revolution Reference Library. 3v. 2003. UXL, $159 (0-7876-6512-6).

Like other sets in the UXL history series for middle school through high school, each volume in this offering—*Almanac, Biographies,* and *Primary Sources*—can be purchased separately. The set covers the first, English phase of the Industrial Revolution (1750–1850) as well as the second phase (1850–1940), which occurred mainly in continental Europe and the U.S.

The Kingfisher Geography Encyclopedia. By Clive Gifford. 2003. 488p. Kingfisher, $39.95 (0-7534-5591-9).

Superior illustrations will draw students to this volume. Directed to grades four through eight, it offers entries that cover each country's geography, industries and products, people, history and government, and characteristics that make it interesting or unique.

The Newest Americans. 5v. 2003. Greenwood, $200 (0-313-32553-7).

This set for grades 6 through 12 looks at 34 national groups that, according to the U.S. Bureau of Immigration, represent the largest number of immigrants to the U.S. since 1965. Chapters provide background information about each country of origin and then examine immigrants' lives in America.

The Renaissance: An Encyclopedia for Students. 4v. Ed. by Paul F. Grendler. 2003. 970p. Scribner, $395 (0-684-31281-6).

Another stylish and thoughtful adaptation of a larger Scribner set, in this case, *Encyclopedia of the Renaissance* (1999). More than 450 entries have been rewritten for a middle- through high-school audience.

Scholastic Dinosaurs A to Z: The Ultimate Dinosaur Encyclopedia. By Don Lessem. 2003. 224p. Scholastic, $22.95 (0-439-16591-1).

Libraries can never have too many dinosaur books. Here, striking illustrations and thorough and engaging explanations combine to address most of the questions kids have about dinosaurs. The text should be accessible to elementary-school readers.

Scholastic Visual Sports Encyclopedia. 2003. 224p. Scholastic, $19.95 (0-439-31721-5).

This encyclopedia for ages nine and up is designed to explain the rules and the equipment used for approximately 100 sports. Text is very brief, but detailed drawings help the reader understand the rules or finer points.

World Book's Celebrations and Rituals around the World. 11v. 2003. World Book, $249 (0-7166-5019-3).

Designed to meet the needs of students in grades four and up researching multicultural holidays and customs, this set features double-page spreads jammed with color illustrations and photographs. Each volume offers a geographic tour based on a different theme, such as weddings, winter, or welcoming the new year.

World of Animals: Birds. 10v. By Ron Hume. 2003. Grolier, $419 (0-7172-5731-2).

The second cluster of the five-set World of Animals collection (following Mammals) covers more than 250 characteristic species of birds. Vivid photographs and illustrations contribute to the volumes' appeal. The designated audience is students at the upper-elementary through high-school levels

Reviews

Generalities

Encyclopedia of Cryptozoology: A Global Guide to Hidden Animals and Their Pursuers. By Michael Newton. 2005. 576p. illus. index. McFarland, $95 (0-7864-2036-7). 001.944.

The continuing search for Nessie, Bigfoot, sea serpents, and other mysterious creatures, or *cryptids,* is a fascinating subject. The discovery of living coelacanths, long believed extinct, fuels the imagination that other creatures, such as dinosaurs, may still walk the earth. This encyclopedia presents the latest information on sightings and hoaxes.

Concentrating on plausible creatures, not paranormal entities such as ghosts, the volume consists of 2,744 alphabetically arranged entries describing 1,583 creatures as well as places, people, and more. Two essays on *Cryptotourism* and *Hoaxes* are included. Some entries are accompanied by small black-and-white illustrations and photographs. Longer entries on *Alien big cats, Nessie,* and *Octopus (giant)* provide much information on these mysteries, describing sightings with dates and locations and giving possible explanations. The author is careful to not offer opinions of the validity of sightings but does refer to documented evidence calling them into question, as with recent sightings of the extinct *Passenger pigeon.* This is the opposite story from the *Eastern cougar,* where numerous sightings are forcing a reconsideration of their extinction. Each article ends with a list of sources with complete citations for those titles not included in the bibliography and short citations for those that are included. A glossary, six appendixes (a time line, a filmography, Internet links, and more), a bibliography, and an index complete the work.

Cryptozoology is treated in several other books. *Cryptozoology A to Z: The Encyclopedia of Loch Monsters, Sasquatch, Chupacabras, and Other Authentic Mysteries of Nature* (Simon & Schuster, 1999) provides an overview with approximately 100 entries. *Mysterious Creatures: A Guide to Cryptozoology* (ABC-CLIO, 2003) has half the entries (1,125 compared to 2,744) of the *Encyclopedia of Cryptozoology* and is arranged more as a field guide. The depth of coverage in the current work makes it an excellent purchase for academic, high-school, and public libraries whose patrons are interested in this subject. —*Abbie Landry*

Encyclopedia of Evaluation. Ed. by Sandra Mathison. 2004. 481p. illus. index. Sage, $150 (0-7619-2609-7). 001.4.

Emphasis in this work is on "the components that make evaluation a *practice, profession,* and *discipline.*" The audience is defined as "practitioners, theorists, and the public." The helpful readers' guide provides an overview of the types of information included. Concepts (*Accountability, Peer review, Subjectivity*); ethics and standards (*Impartiality, Informed consent*); approaches and models (*Accreditation, Multicultural evaluation*); organizations (*ERIC Clearinghouse on Assessment and Evaluation, National Institutes of Health*); and qualitative and quantitative methods (*Checklists, Matrix sampling*) are some of the areas that are covered. The more than 600 entries vary from a single paragraph to several pages in length, and many are accompanied by one or more suggested further-reading citations.

As explained in the preface, most of the literature on evaluation comes from the U.S., and the U.S. has a history of strong government support for evaluation. Nevertheless, the encyclopedia attempts to present an international perspective. Scattered throughout are boxes labeled "Evaluation Practice around the World" that describe a problem or issue in a specific country, such as Germany or Spain. One puzzling feature of the work is the more than 120 brief biographies of researchers and practitioners, a number of whom are also contributors. The profiles mostly describe career paths, and although of interest to fellow practitioners, they offer little to the general user looking for explanations and definitions.

The encyclopedia will be most useful in academic libraries and institutions with evaluation programs, though large public libraries should consider it. —*Linda Scarth*

Berkshire Encyclopedia of Human-Computer Interaction. 2v. Ed. by William Sims Bainbridge. 2004. 958p. illus. index. Berkshire, $295 (0-9743091-2-5). 004.

This encyclopedia, edited by the deputy director of the National Science Foundation's Division of Information and Intelligent Systems, compiles 186 articles on the maturing field of human-computer interaction (HCI). Topics cover applications (e.g., *Classrooms, Law enforcement, Telecommuting*), computer hardware (*Keyboard, Liquid crystal displays, Mouse*), fields of study (*Ergonomics, Sociology and HCI*), methods (*Gesture recognition, Icons, Natural-language processing*), societal issues (*Cybersex, Workforce*), and other subjects (*Arpanet, Mosaic, Website design*).

Article length averages 3–5 pages, with some longer articles, such as the 10-page *History of HCI.* Many entries are divided with boldface subheadings, enabling users to quickly identify main elements.

Names of article authors appear at the end of each article, usually followed by a list of *see also* references and a list of additional readings. Readings consist of books, articles, and Internet sites. Figures, tables, and photos are clear and aid understanding. Fifty-eight short sidebar entries provide added perspective within select articles. For example, the article *Education in HCI* includes a sidebar titled "A Personal Story—Bringing HCI into the 'Real World.'"

Both volumes include an alphabetical list of entries at the front and a set index in the back. Volume 1 also contains a list of sidebars and a list of all articles arranged under 10 general categories. The largest category, "Methods," has 35 articles. Appendixes include a combined list of further readings and an annotated list of HCI-related fiction and nonfiction books, works, films, TV and radio programs, and music. A glossary is also included but, at two pages, is perhaps too short.

This resource provides unique content not found in conventional encyclopedias on computers such as the *Encyclopedia of Computer Science and Technology* (Facts on File, 2003). Somewhat advanced for high-school users, it should be useful in academic and larger public libraries. —*Stephen Fadel*

Local and Regional Government Information: How to Find It, How to Use It. Ed. by Mary Martin. 2005. 239p. index. Greenwood, $65 (1-57356-412-5). 015.73.

This well-designed research guide will be a welcome addition to the reference collections of librarians, students, and citizen researchers. Editor Martin manages to pack a ton of information into a compact and readable text. Clear chapter and section divisions and a commonsense writing style make it a pleasure to use.

The first 2 of 19 chapters provide context for the chapters that follow. Chapter 1, "Access to Local Government Information," introduces access barriers, freedom of information, privacy laws, and alternate sources of information. Chapter 2, "Forms of Local Government Structure," explains municipal, county, and regional governments. Subsequent chapters cover the use of archives, general indexes, and administrative sources and explain in detail how to find local information about health, crime, transportation, education, small business, and much more.

Chapter 11, "Finding Information on Crime and Criminals," is typical as to arrangement, layout, and design. Directly under the chapter title is a handy list sof major topics and major resources covered in the chapter. Following this list is a concise introduction to the subject of crime and individual sections on each of the topics and resources listed at the beginning of the chapter. Throughout the volume, all sources are clearly cited and easily identifiable within the text.

A reference guide that is both informative and pleasurable to read is a rare bird, especially when the subject is on the dry side. Researchers using *Local and Regional Government Information* will be happy to find that it is one of those rare birds. It is also a steal at $65. Highly recommended for any library serving folks who seek government information at the local and regional level. —*Art Lichtenstein*

The Arthurian Annals: The Tradition in English from 1250 to 2000. 2v. By Daniel P. Nastali and Phillip C. Boardman. 2004. 1,216p. indexes. Oxford, $450 (0-19-515437-1). 016.39.

This is an impressive feat of bibliographic scholarship listing more than 11,000 works that make use of the Arthurian legends. It shows, at a glance, the virtual explosion of such works in the twentieth century; while coverage of the literature of 1250–1899 takes less than 200 pages, more than 600 pages are required to document the literature of 1900–2000.

Volume 1 is arranged chronologically and lists those works considered by scholars to be "in the province of Arthurian studies," in other words, works that are about the tradition, legend, and myth of King Arthur and his knights, the Round Table, Camelot, and the Holy Grail. Most of the entries are primary texts, ranging from Chaucer's "The Wife of Bath's Tale" (a retelling of the Gawain and Loathly Lady story) to, more recently,

Marion Bradley's *Mists of Avalon* (1982) and Stephen R. Lawhead's *Arthur* (1989). Among the works that are included are reprints and retellings of classic texts, translations into English, and, for more recent years, sound recordings, comic books, films, television programs, and computer games. Secondary criticism is listed very selectively.

The entries are arranged by year and then, within the year, alphabetically by author. Bibliographic information is followed by a brief description of the work. The primary entry for each work also includes a publication history. Each year's listings conclude with cross-references that are meant "to complete the picture of Arthurian production for that year."

Volume 2 is essentially an index to volume 1. There are eight indexes for people, titles, characters, and more, each referring back to volume 1 by year only, rather than by page number. This unfortunately perpetuates the only weakness of the work: lack of accessibility. The arrangement of volume 1 encourages little else but browsing; a lack of page references in volume 2 does not provide any relief. Nevertheless, *The Arthurian Annals* is a worthy addition to research collections in academic and large public libraries. —*John Doherty*

Early American Imprints, 1639–1800. [Online database]. Readex, pricing from $14,000 [http://www.readex.com]. (Last accessed September 7, 2004).

Charles Evans' seminal *American Bibliography* needs little introduction for most librarians. A one-person effort (later supplemented) from the man who was ALA's second member (behind Melvil Dewey) that ultimately covered the bibliographic record of the U.S. from 1639 until 1800, Evans' work was *the* place to turn for bibliographic information from early America before more organized efforts from the Library of Congress' *National Union Catalog* all but superseded it. Several years after publication was complete, the American Antiquarian Society teamed up with Readex to publish microcards and, later, microfiche editions of copies of the nonserial texts in Evans' work

Readex and AAS now make available the latest iteration of the works in Evans: full-image reproductions of extant copies of the titles, with additional titles included in Roger Bristol's *Supplement to Evans' American Bibliography*, searchable by keyword within the text. Rather than peering at microfiche readers, subscribers to this edition will be treated to downloadable PDF, TIFF, and GIF versions of the images. The work is the first of four projected digital series from Readex, joining *Series II* of *Early American Imprints (Shaw–Shoemaker, 1801–1819)*, *Early American Newspapers (1690–1876)*, and the *U.S. Congressional Serial Set (1817–1980) with American State Papers (1789–1838)*. The present series is almost complete, with content through *American Bibliography* document number 49,786 (published in 1798) at the date of last access. All products will feature a common interface.

Early American Imprints opens with a basic search screen with searchable fields for citation text, all text, title, subject, genres, author, place of publication, publisher, document number, and year. This screen also has tabs that link to listings of works by Genre, Subject, Author, History of Printing, Place of Publication, and Language. Each screen then provides additional categories to select to retrieve relevant listings; the Genre screen, for example, is broken down by subheadings such as Almanacs, Hymnals, and Spellers.

An Advanced Search option allows one to combine fields, expand a search to all text, and limit a search by date. The thorough Help screens will be particularly necessary for users to consult when it comes to dealing with the "long S character," which the OCR technology that was used when scanning the documents could not differentiate from the letter *f*. The Help screen correctly recommends using the single character wildcard when searching for terms with the letter *s*. In addition, one must be aware of alternate spellings (Delaware/Delaware).

Once a list of citations is retrieved, the user can go directly to a specific work and view the full citation, the first page of the work, or the pages in which a search term is found. A clickable Table of Contents flags each page number containing the term. The user can also enter terms in a search box to Search Within This Imprint. Individual citations feature hyperlinked subject headings so that related entries can be retrieved.

Page numbers, when clicked, are viewed immediately on the screen and can be magnified. Individual pages can be right-clicked and saved as GIF files. In addition, links on the page prompt the user to save the page as PDF or TIFF file. Every citation screen also has a View Imprint link that will open the first page of the document as an image. The user can then navigate through the entire document or download specific pages. Though an entire work can be downloaded, one is limited to a maximum of 25 pages per download. This maximum is not entirely unwarranted: downloading 25-page segments of one work averaged more than 7 MB per download for this reviewer.

A wise searcher will do several combinations of searches. In a number of sample searches terms were not found even though they were present, presumably because of inaccuracies of the OCR indexing. Still, the positives far outweigh any negatives in this fine effort. Full-text searching with images of these works gives scholars unprecedented access to a collection of documents key to U.S. history. The tabbed searches provided on the main screen will more than suffice for most researchers, since major topics likely to be researched, such as *Boston Massacre, 1770*, or *Tea Tax (American Colonies)*, can be retrieved there. With the covered works ranging from the noteworthy (*The Federalist*) to the everyday (a recipe for carrot pudding, among other dishes, in Amelia Simmons' 1800 work *American Cookery*), researchers will be able to find items of interest that could previously be found only by scouring through screens of microfiche images. Pricing varies by size of institution, ranging from $14,000 for small colleges with 1,000 students to $107,500 for Ph.D.-granting universities. Depending on the size of the school, this is actually less than the microfiche version, which ranges from $24,505 to $61,570. Academic institutions with a strong research interest in the literary or historical period in question should seriously consider this source. —*Ken Black*

Guide to the Gothic III: An Annotated Bibliography of Criticism, 1993–2003. 2v. By Frederick S. Frank. 2004. 1,427p. index. Scarecrow, $200 (0-8108-5101-6). 016.8093.

From a revered expert comes a third volume of inclusive bibliography of scholarly criticism, which adds 1,600 annotations to the 4,000 entries compiled in the first two volumes: *Guide to the Gothic: An Annotated Bibliography of Criticism* (1984) and *Guide to the Gothic: An Annotated Bibliography of Criticism, 1983–1993* (1995). The set's principal divisions are for British, American, and "Other National Gothics," with individual author sections under each.

Frank is skilled at elucidating the best in critical commentary by summarizing the point of departure that makes each source valuable to an analysis of Gothic literature. Annotations are clear and unpedantic; organization suits the needs of teachers, students, researchers, and librarians. Of particular interest in *Guide to the Gothic III* is commentary on blue books, Gothic film, Canadian Gothicists, and miscellaneous topics, including Satanism and the Wandering Jew. Coverage of world Gothic shortchanges adherents of such best-selling authors as Isabel Allende, Marie-Claire Blais, Peter Carey, Laura Esquivel, and Janet Frame, all of whom have Gothic elements in their work. A valuable addition to Frank's summations would be an appendix of themes such as alchemy, *danse macabre*, dreams, madness and psychological anomalies, and gay and urban Gothic. Recommended for large public and college and university libraries. —*Mary Ellen Snodgrass*

The Holocaust Film Sourcebook. 2v. Ed. by Caroline Joan (Kay) Picart. 2004. 991p. index. illus. Praeger, $249.95 (0-275-97850-8). 016.79143.

Editor Picart has created a comprehensive annotated listing of international films related to the Holocaust. The two volumes are divided by type of film covered. Volume 1 deals with fiction, for the most part feature or television films from various countries. Volume 2 contains two separate listings, one for documentaries and one for propaganda films. Volume 1 also contains a list of resources including archives of Holocaust films, film databases, film indexes, and sources for purchase of scripts. Each volume is indexed separately. Since there are several Hollywood fiction films, such as *Casablanca*, included in the propaganda film section, a set index of film titles would have been helpful.

Entries are arranged alphabetically by the film's original title, no matter the language, with its English translation in parentheses. Information provided in each entry generally includes country of production, date, genre, running time, production company and producers, cast and crew (including historical figures who appear in documentaries), inspiration (for example, the book on which a film is based), plot summary, primary sources (such as scripts and posters), and selected secondary sources. Picart has listed films even when much of the information normally included is unavailable, so that the reader will at least know that the film existed. Black-and-white stills from the films are scattered throughout both volumes. Several "Spotlight Essays" offer analyses of either a particular film or a theme related to one or more films.

As with any listing of this type, users may argue for or against the inclusion or placement of certain titles. However, it would be hard to find any film that has not been included. The set will be extremely useful in an academic or special library that supports either a film studies or Holocaust studies program. Its value as a collection development tool is enhanced by information on where to obtain these films. —*Rochelle Glantz*

Popular Series Fiction for Middle School and Teen Readers: A Reading and Selection Guide. By Rebecca L. Thomas and Catherine Barr. 2005. 514p. indexes. Libraries Unlimited, $50 (1-59158-202-4). 016.823008.

This is the book that many of us have been waiting for or wishing we had time to write. It is a companion to *Popular Series Fiction for K–6 Readers* (2004), and both evolved from *Reading in Series* (Bowker, 1999). For this volume, a list of series books was compiled using standard selection tools such as *Booklist* and Web sites such as Amazon.com and Teenreads.com. The authors define a series as "books with a consistent theme, setting, or group of characters." Additionally, a series "needed three or more books" (an exception was made for developing series) and an age range of grades 6 through 12. Focus is on books still in print or widely available in many library collections.

The entries begin with the series title, usually the one designated by the author or publisher. Some series are known by an unofficial title, and those are cross-referenced. For example Junior Jedi Knights is referenced to Star Wars Junior Jedi Knights. The author, publisher, grade level, genre, and accelerated-reader designation follow. The annotation is about a paragraph long and tries to encompass the most important plot, theme, and character elements. This is followed by a list of book titles and publication dates in chronological order—current to 2005—capturing *Drowned Wednesday* from Garth Nix's Keys to the Kingdom series, for example.

Several indexes support the series listings: an index by author with series name(s) in parentheses, by book title with series name, and by genre or subject with age level. Additional tools are lists of series for boys, for girls, for reluctant readers, and developing series. None of these lists has page numbers, only series titles.

Although the annotations give the important information, there is rarely an indication of style or of comparable series that readers might also like. Graphic novels are included, but the fact that a series belongs to the graphic-novel genre is not indicated in the series information and is rarely mentioned in the annotation. However, there is a list of graphic novels in the "Genre/Subject Index" (though *CLAMP School Detectives* is missing).

Despite its few flaws, this is an excellent tool for school and public librarians who work with teen and tween readers. It should be in every school and public library. —*Robin Hoelle*

Reference Sources in History: An Introductory Guide. 2d ed. Ed. by Ronald H. Fritze and others. 2004. 334p. index. ABC-CLIO, $85 (0-87436-883-9). 016.909.

First published in 1990, this second edition contains entries on 930 reference works, making it almost one-third larger than its predecessor. The content is still organized in 14 chapters by topic, format, and country. The chapters cover bibliographies, historical statistics, biographies, dictionaries, encyclopedias, and atlases, to give only a few examples. Each entry is helpfully numbered and includes useful bibliographical information and an evaluative annotation and frequently provides references to related works not listed in the volume. The index provides personal name and title access. Especially noteworthy are the listings of core journals and the extensive coverage of Web sites, databases, and CD-ROMs.

The editors are to be commended for mining the huge historical reference literature and compiling this compact and superbly researched guide. Nicely designed with easy-to-read type, this unique and updated work is highly recommended for both reference and acquisition librarians in public and academic libraries. The chapter on bibliographies lists *Reference Books Bulletin* as "one of the premier sources of reference reviews in the United States." Even if the editors hadn't offered this trenchant and wise observation, the volume is still outstanding! —*Donald Altschiller*

Ancestors in German Archives: A Guide to Family History Sources. By Raymond S. Wright III and others. 2004. 1,189p. indexes. Genealogical Publishing, $85 (0-8063-1747-7). 016.929.

According to the 2000 census, nearly 43 million Americans—about 15 percent of respondents—claim to have German ancestry, making them the largest ethnic group in the U.S. People who are serious about exploring their German roots will find that sooner or later they need to turn to German archives, and this book was designed to help. It is one result of the German Immigrant Ancestors Project launched at Brigham Young University in 1996 to survey and catalog all the relevant public and private records in the Federal Republic of Germany. Information was collected from questionnaires sent to German archivists.

Following an introductory chapter are two chapters that describe German government and religious archives, the two most common record repositories. Each of the remaining chapters covers a German state. The state chapters are divided into sections for state, city and regional, church, and family archives, with an additional section for other archives for which a Web site was found or questionnaire was returned. Within each section, archives are organized alphabetically by the name of the city in which they are located. The listing for each archive provides contact information (including Web sites and e-mail addresses when available) and summaries of the jurisdiction of each archive; what kinds of records it contains (for example, emigration records, military records, civil registration records); and how the records are organized. More than 2,000 archives are listed. Eighteen simple line maps help pinpoint locations. The volume concludes with an index of archives (by city) and an index of localities.

Researchers will find this well-organized guide to be very helpful in sorting through the maze of German records. It belongs in all libraries holding large genealogy collections or serving an interest in German heritage. —*Mary Ellen Quinn*

International Government Information and Country Information: A Subject Guide. By Andrea M. Morrison and Barbara J. Mann. 2004. 298p. index. Greenwood, $65 (1-57356-479-6). 025.04.

Part of the series How to Find It, How to Use It, this work aims to "introduce the wide variety of international information resources that are available on a given subject, from such sources as international governmental organizations (IGOs), national governments, organizations, universities, and commercial publishers." The types of materials that are covered include electronic resources, serials, monographic series, and individual book titles.

The authors have divided the work into two parts. The first part lists resources related to particular government organizations such as the UN, the League of Nations, the European Union, and the Organization of American States. Part 2 contains 21 subject chapters, including "Agriculture and Food," "Communication," and "Environment." Each chapter contains an overview that explains the chapter's breakdown and layout. Before individual descriptions of sources, there is a listing of sources discussed. Most of the entries contain a summary and a detailed description. Cross-references guide readers to full descriptions if a resource is listed in more than one place. Each chapter contains notes for further information or explanation. The volume concludes with two appendixes, one explaining selected acronyms for international organizations and the other listing selected international organization Web sites. There is also a detailed index.

Although there are other works about government information, such as *Government Information on the Internet* (Bernan, 2003) and *U.S. Government on the Web: Getting the Information You Need* (Libraries Unlimited, 2003), this one covers various kinds of materials and has an international focus. With its overviews and detailed descriptions of resources, the work would be a worthy addition to public and academic libraries. —*Jennifer Dawson*

Encyclopedia of the Library of Congress: For Congress, the Nation, & the World. Ed. by John Y. Cole and Jane Aikin. 2005. 569p. illus. index. Bernan, $125 (0-89059-971-8). 027.573.

The largest library in the world merits its own reference work, and this encyclopedia offers much interesting and useful information. Although the editors acknowledge that it is not comprehensive, the volume does contain almost 100 pieces written by Library of Congress subject specialists. Fourteen essays cover topics such as "American Literature and the Library of Congress." Shorter, alphabetically arranged articles, among them *Lincolniana, Main Reading Room, Overseas operations, Preservation and conservation,* and *Reference and Research Services,* provide an impressive amount of material on major collections, functions, and administrative units. In addition, the volume includes biographies of all 13 Librarians of Congress and statistics from 1801 to 2003 detailing the growth of the library collection and also the congressional budget appropriations.

A handsomely produced volume printed on coated paper, this work features many black-and-white and some color photographs. It concludes with a useful bibliography and a nicely detailed index. Recommended for academic libraries and major public libraries. —*Donald Altschiller*

Kids InfoBits. [Online database]. 2004. Gale, pricing from $595 [http://www.gale.com]. (Last accessed September 7, 2004).

Originally Gale's *Kid's Edition, Kids InfoBits* offers students in grades K–5 a much more user-friendly interface to children's and general interest periodicals, reference materials, and newspaper articles. Not surprisingly, the list of sources relies heavily on Gale's children's imprints, such as Blackbirch Press and UXL, although articles from the sixth edition of *The Columbia Encyclopedia* (2000) are also part of the mix. A sampling of the periodical titles includes *Cobblestone, Current Science, Jack & Jill, National Geographic for Kids,* and *Ranger Rick.*

On the home page, cartoonlike icons represent 12 content areas, among them Animals, Geography, Stories and Literature, History and Social Studies, Transportation, Health, and Sports. Students can click on an icon to perform a Topic Tree Search, which offers three levels of subject terms. For example, clicking on Animals leads to icons for topics such as Mammals, Bird, Bugs and Worms, and Dinosaurs and Other Extinct Animals. Clicking on Dinosaurs and Other Extinct Animals leads to topics such as Trilobites and Saber-Toothed Tigers. This is an excellent way to introduce students to the idea of narrowing a research topic down. A "breadcrumb trail" along the top of the page keeps track of the search. Results are displayed in standard Gale format, with documents grouped by type on tabbed pages: Reference; Magazines; Newspapers; Maps, Flags & Seals; Charts & Graphs; and Images. The results include title, source, and reading level ("easy" or "more difficult") and are arranged alphabetically except for magazine and newspaper articles, which are arranged in reverse chronological order.

To perform other kinds of searches, the user can enter terms in a search box (Subject Guide Search) or click on the Advanced Search button. Subject Guide Search provides a list of indexed subject terms including *see* links. Advanced Search mirrors the standard Gale conventions. Pull-down menus allow users to select desired Boolean operators; choose an index type (Title/Header, Source, Author, Subject, Full Text, Document Number, Document Type, Date of Publication, and Reading Level); and limit searches by date, document type, reading level, document number, and number of results per page.

A My Backpack feature enables users to add documents to a file in order to create a bibliography or search list. The file lasts only for the one session; there is no way to save it for future use. Dictionary allows a search for any term in *Merriam-Webster's Elementary Dictionary.* InfoMarks saves a page location and allows for the bookmarking of URLs for future reference or copying to an e-mail or a Web page and also allows for the creation of a predefined search. The Teacher Toolbox offers tips on topics such as doing research and writing a report.

Kids InfoBits does an excellent job of preparing elementary-grade students to research other Gale databases and, by extension, databases in general. The multitude of tips available via Help offers great starting points for lesson planning. The selection of magazines and newspapers includes titles not otherwise accessible to many students. Libraries working with students in grades K–5 will want to consider a subscription to this database. —*Esther Sinofsky*

The Kingfisher Children's Encyclopedia. Rev. ed. 2004. 480p. illus. index. Kingfisher, $24.95 (0-7534-5767-9). 031.

This graphically rich encyclopedia is being marketed as an all-purpose reference for the home. Its 300-plus articles are arranged in alphabetical order and address standard school-report topics (civil rights, genetics, etc.) as well as popular subjects such as forensic science and dinosaurs. Aimed at students in mid-elementary grades through middle school, the volume has many user-friendly features. Each article begins with a one-sentence definition followed by neatly compartmentalized paragraphs set off by subheadings. More than 2,000 full-color illustrations, photographs, and cross sections, accompanied by detailed captions, add visual interest. Every article receives at least one full page of coverage, with the longest selections spanning four pages. *See also* references direct researchers to related topics, as does an index of more than 3,500 terms. The alphabetical entries are followed by a 12-page ready-reference "Factfinder" section offering statistics, lists, and rankings. Four pages are devoted to brief biographies. The section concludes with a one-page summation of highlights of the twentieth century.

The first edition was published in 1998, and this second edition claims to be "revised and updated." The "Factfinder" section includes one sentence on the 2001 terrorist attacks in the U.S. and a brief reference to the 2003 *Columbia* space-shuttle disaster. A few articles reflect twenty-first-century events: the 2001 overthrow of the Taliban, the UN 2003 Security Council deliberations on Iraq and subsequent American-led coalition attacks, and the doping scandals of the 2000 Olympics. The Olympics article incorrectly identifies Mark Spitz as holding the record for the most medals won by an athlete during one Olympics. Other articles, notably *Computer, Internet,* and *Space exploration,* have not been expanded beyond 1998.

Equally effective for schoolwork or leisure browsing, this title offers introductory material suitable for novice researchers. It also provides significant value for a modest price. Homes, schools, and public libraries that don't already own a one-volume reference, such as the more comprehensive *Scholastic Children's Encyclopedia* [RBB O 15 04], may want to consider this visually enticing, accessible work. —*Kathleen McBroom*

La nueva encyclopedia cumbre. [Online database]. Grolier, pricing starts at $415 in combination with other Grolier Online databases [http://go.grolier.com]. (Last accessed January 3, 2005).

The newest version of Grolier's online -Spanish-language encyclopedia has both current information and useful features. It is ADA compliant and has help available in both English and Spanish so that librarians and teachers who do not know the language can assist Spanish-speaking users. The new version also has *Aula de Español,* a site for students of Spanish with 350 readings at the beginner and intermediate levels, illustrated vocabulary pages, grammar, thematic maps, menus and recipes, and calendars of holidays observed in the Hispanic world.

The encyclopedia is easy to use. The home-page menu includes both basic (*Buscar*) and advanced (*Búsqueda avanzada*) search modes and an atlas. New features include subject browsing (*Consultar categorías*), chronologies (*Cronologías*), teacher resources (*Recursos para profesores*), and current events (*Actualidades*). Revised monthly, the current events are taken from Spanish-language periodicals. There are also links to newspapers from all over Latin America and Spain.

The 18,000 articles and associated media—fact boxes, graphs, charts, maps, and sounds—are revisions from the 1999 edition of *Cumbre* and translations of material from the *Grolier Multimedia Encyclopedia* as well as other revised and compiled materials. The *Cronologías* feature offers a series of time lines and graphic chronologies of world history. The 7,000 illustrations include photographs, artwork, and country flags. The only sound files are 200 national anthems. The atlas now has maps with hyperlinks to related articles and thematic maps of Spanish-speaking regions. There are both Spanish and English Web links, with those in Spanish listed first. Oddly, there are no links to MedlinePlus, which has -Spanish-language information.

The basic search allows options for keyword, full text, or article title. The advanced mode offers the use of Boolean operators and truncation. A pull-down menu of Spanish characters allows users to import them into the search box, a useful enhancement. All articles have a table of contents at the beginning and citation information at the end. Users may print or e-mail an entire article or sections of it.

The encyclopedia's strength is its coverage of the Spanish-speaking world. *La nueva enciclopedia cumbre,* available as part of a Grolier Online subscription, is an excellent resource for school and public libraries that serve Spanish speakers. —*Barbara Bibel*

Scholastic Children's Encyclopedia. 2004. 710p. illus. index. maps. Scholastic, $19.95 (0-439-43816-0). 031.

A great starting place for curious young researchers and browsers alike, this reference tool explains topics in sufficient but not overwhelming detail for students ages 9–12. More than 600 entries are arranged alphabetically and range in length from one-half page to just over four pages. Entries are illustrated with more than 2,000 photographs, diagrams, charts, time lines, and maps. Longer entries include subheadings that divide text into easy-to-read sections. An introductory sentence or two follows entry headings and provides a brief definition or overview of the subject. Country and region entries have maps that show key geographical features, capitals, and major cities. "Key Facts" boxes give facts and figures about continents, regions, countries, and planets. Population figures are based on the 2000 U.S. census, 2001 Canadian census, or mid-2000 United Nations estimates.

"Did You Know?" boxes highlight interesting information (most Communist flags were red to represent the blood shed by workers in their struggle), while "Amazing Facts!" boxes showcase facts about the natural world and modern technology (the longest known cave stretches over 330 miles in the Mammoth system in Kentucky; the gray kangaroo can cover a distance of up to 30 feet in a single hop). *See also* references direct students to appropriate or related entries. A concluding "For Further Reference" section contains several useful resources, including maps of the world, the U.S., and Native American Nations; a time zone map; a countries table with names, flags, capitals, and population; a table of the 50 states with state flags, postal abbreviations, nicknames, capitals, years of admission, and population; and a U.S. presidents table including party affiliations, terms of office, vice presidents, and "Did You Know?" facts. A plant and animal classification chart, measurement calculations and conversions, and an index conclude the reference section. Libraries serving younger students will want multiple copies of this highly usable and user-friendly tool. —*Shauna Yusko*

My First Britannica. 13v. 2004. 1,288p. glossaries. illus. index. maps. Britannica, $249 (1-59339-017-3). 032.

The 12 main volumes of this work are designed to engage children ages 7 to 11 who are interested in developing their background knowledge on broad topics like technology, people and culture, places, and science. Each volume is devoted to a specific area of study, for example, *The Arts, People in History,* and *Mammals*. Entire volumes are devoted to Africa, the Americas, and Europe, but Asia, Australia, and New Zealand share a single volume. Coverage is representative rather then comprehensive. For example, the "Literature" section in *The Arts* volume has entries for nine writers, among them Basho, Emily Dickinson, and Wole Soyinka.

The style is chatty and informative, and the 525 topical articles are longer than those in many introductory encyclopedias. Each article in each approximately 100-page volume covers two pages, one page of text and one large, generally attractive color illustration or photograph. The "Search Light" feature contained in each article helps focus the user's attention on an important fact, and the "Learn More" feature provides access to information on the topic in other volumes. Each volume has its own table of contents and glossary, and some volumes contain stories as well as articles. Volume 5, *Folklore and Religions,* has the added bonus of stories from sources as varied as the Kalilah wa Dimnah, Korea, Australia, and Nigeria, and Inuit, Cherokee, Mayan, and ancient Greek cultures, but it does not contain any source notes. Volume 13 offers maps and a glossary as well as an integrated index.

Essentially this work is designed for browsing and not arranged for library reference. Its thematic arrangement makes it difficult to find those quick answers one normally associates with reference work. Nevertheless, it does contain information that would be useful to young readers. Public and school libraries with large collections may want to purchase this for their circulating collections. For the same audience, the alphabetically arranged *Grolier Student Encyclopedia* [RBB My 15 04] offers a more encyclopedic treatment. —*Dona Helmer*

Oxford Dictionary of Quotations. 6th ed. Ed. by Elizabeth Knowles. 2004. 1,140p. Oxford, $50 (0-19-860720-2). 082.

Samuel Johnson once observed that "Every quotation contributes something to the stability or enlargement of the language." And since every book of quotations certainly contributes to the enlargement of the reference collection, why add another?

This is no ordinary book of quotations. As one would expect from the publishers of the *Oxford English Dictionary,* this work is thoroughly cross-referenced, packed with special features, and, most importantly for a collection of quotations, provides citations and context for each entry. Among the special features set off in boxes throughout the text are lists of epitaphs, catchphrases, borrowed titles, misquotations, opening lines, last words, and film lines and titles. The keyword index is exhaustive.

Since its first edition, in 1941, the *Oxford Dictionary of Quotations* has offered a wide array of quotations, succeeding in preserving the wisdom of the ages as well as presenting the latest catchphrases and sound bites. The fifth edition (1999) restored sections devoted to proverbs and nursery rhymes that had been cut from an earlier edition; these sections remain. That edition had paid particular attention to the sacred texts of several world religions, and those passages are also enshrined in this new edition. A comparison of this edition with its predecessor found that although George Abbott, Beryl Bainbridge, Lord Bancroft, Antonio Callado, Salvador Dali, Newton Gingrich, Ice Cube, Barry Scheck, Emma Thompson, and Raquel Welch have been dropped, Elizabeth David, Amelia Earhart, Carly Fiorina, -Penelope Fitzgerald, Indira Gandhi, Bill Gates, Frank Gehry, Rudolph Giuliani, David Hare, Eddie Izzard, Frida Kahlo, Donna Karan, -Estée Lauder, Alison Lurie, Thurgood Marshall, Georgia O'Keefe, Vladimir Putin, J. K. Rowling, Ernest Shackleton, Ariel Sharon, and Sam Walton have been added.

Large collections will want to add this edition to the previous ones on their shelves; smaller collections should consider it as a way to add depth to their quotation holdings. —*Carolyn Mulac*

Oxford Digital Reference Shelf. [Internet database]. Oxford, contact for pricing [http://www.oxfordonline.com/digitalreference]. (Last accessed May 3, 2005).

Not to be confused with other Oxford online products, the *Oxford Digital Reference Shelf* is the search interface for one-time-purchase Oxford e-books. Titles available at the time of this review included seven from history, for example, *Encyclopedia of the Enlightenment,* (2002), plus the *Encyclopedia of Evolution* (2002), the *Encyclopedia of Global Change* (2001), the *International Encyclopedia of Dance* (1998), the *Oxford Encyclopedia of Food and Drink in America* (2004), and the *Oxford Encyclopedia of Theatre and Performance* (2003). More titles will be added in the future.

With a simpler interface than ABC-CLIO's *eBooks* and the *Gale Virtual Reference Library, Oxford Digital Reference Shelf* provides a single text search box. For two or more words, AND is the implied default. Boolean command searching is not available. Neither is an advanced search screen. Instead, searching follows a behind-the-scenes four-step search process. First, entry titles are searched. Then, if no matches are found, the search automatically proceeds to full text, then to an OR search, and finally to a search of similar words. The inability to browse full-article title lists and topical-article title lists, tools often found at the beginning of Oxford print reference resources, will frustrate some users and librarians.

Entering *beer* in the search box of the *Oxford Encyclopedia of Food and Drink in America* retrieved nine articles. The first sentence or two of an article accompanies each entry listing. The results screen includes two drop-down selection boxes—Results per Page (10, 25, 50, 75, 100) and Order Results (By Relevance or Alphabetically). A Widen Your Search Button (full-text search) is also included.

No additional plug-ins are required to view full text. Articles integrate illustrations within the text, displaying good quality, large pictures. Unfortunately, no illustrations were found in the e-versions of the *International Encyclopedia of Dance* and the *Oxford Encyclopedia of Theatre and Performance*.

On the full-text screen, features include a linked list of adjacent articles (5 before and 5 after), linked terms within the text, linked *see also* references, links to exterior Internet sites, and the option to link bibliographic references to the library's online catalog. In addition, users reading full-text articles can highlight words within the text and then search the e-book on the word or phrase by clicking a button labeled Cross-Reference. Material can be e-mailed, downloaded, or printed.

Purchasers can choose to buy just the print edition of a title, just the electronic version, or both the print and electronic versions. E-book prices are based on 110 percent of the print price. Bundled prices are based on 100 percent of the e-book price plus 50 percent of the print price. Size of user population determines corporate, government, college, and university prices. Purchasers can either host on-site or have Oxford host for a maintenance fee (e.g., one year–$40/title).

Those considering purchase will need to judge each title on its own merits. Students, instructors, and others will love the opportunity for off-site access to high-quality content. Could use minor tweaks. Still, highly recommended. —*Stephen Fadel*

Philosophy, Psychology, Religion

The Oxford Companion to the Mind. 2d ed. Ed. by Richard L. Gregory. 2005. 1,004p.illus. index. Oxford, $75 (0-19-866224-6). 128.

It has been almost 20 years since *The Oxford Companion to the Mind* was first published, and scholars and practitioners in psychology and cognitive science would no doubt agree that there has been tremendous progress in these fields in the intervening years. Neuropsychologist Gregory, who also edited the first edition, has assembled an ambitious reference with more than 1,000 entries on every aspect of brain and mind science. A distinguished lineup of contributors picks up the gauntlet and succeeds in capturing what it is we know about the human mind. *Anxiety* and *Artificial intelligence, Depression* and *Dreaming, Face-to-face communication* and *Feedback and feedforward, Metaphor* and *Metaphysics,* and *Time-gap memory* and *Truth*—such pairings demonstrate the reach of this reference, which ranges across neuroscience, philosophy, and psychology.

In his preface, Gregory notes that "this book sets out to be a friendly companion to the mind." Is this indeed a "friendly companion"? Cross-references between entries are limited, and the bibliographies appended to entries provide readers with very little to go on in terms of further reading or research. Moreover, the subject at hand, the mind, is complex and, frankly, dense. But although the work may be lacking in friendliness, it succeeds in other ways. There is no question but that it is unparalleled in its ambition, scope, and the overall quality of its entries; as such it succeeds in offering professionals, students, and general adult readers a unique resource.

In recent years, a number of reference sources in psychology have been published. Large public and academic libraries that have resources such as the *Encyclopedia of Human Intelligence* (Macmillan, 1994), the two-volume *Encyclopedia of Human Emotions* (Macmillan, 1999), or the in-depth, four-volume *Encyclopedia of Cognitive Science* (2003), not to mention Oxford's other recent ventures in this arena—*A Dictionary of Psychology* (2001) and the eight-volume *Encyclopedia of Psychology* (2000)—will still want to add this guide to their shelves. —*Sarah Watstein*

Popular Psychology: An Encyclopedia. By Luis A. Cordón. 2005. 274p. illus. index. Greenwood, $75 (0-313-32457-3). 150.

The 120 or so entries in this volume cover a wide range of topics, including, for example, *Alien abduction, Birth order, Insanity defense, Mad cow disease, Multiple personality disorder, Parenting styles,* and *Satanic ritual abuse.* Also represented are individuals such as Carl Jung and Dr. Phil. The goal is "to try to counteract the tide of misleading information about the field of psychology with a concise guide to some things that the well-informed student of psychology and the interested general public ought to know."

The length of each entry varies from just a few lines to nine or more pages (for *Memory*), and there are a few black-and-white illustrations scattered throughout. Nearly all entries include a limited "Further Reading" list, generally offering both supporting and critical sources. Following the A–Z entries is an annotated bibliography that includes Web sites.

The book cover states readers will "want to consult this work to understand what is good in the popular presentation of psychology and what is unworthy of serious attention." That may well be too expansive a goal as some topics that could have been valuable for both students and lay readers appear to be missing. Two specific contemporary topics that have apparently not been included are transpersonal psychology and tissue memory. Another curiously missing topic is counseling. In the entry *Psychiatry,* there is a relatively straightforward discussion of the difference in practice between psychiatrists and clinical psychologists. There is, however, no mention of counseling psychologists, though this discipline is licensed by most of the individual states and is also certified nationally in the U.S.

Popular Psychology is easy to read, easy to browse, and would be of value in public and undergraduate libraries that have limited information on this topic. It would also be appropriate in high-school libraries, where it could be used as a basic reference for class-based study. —*Scottie Wallace*

Psychology Basics. 2v. Rev. ed. Ed. by Nancy A. Piotrowski. 2004. 1,008p. illus. index. Salem, $104 (1-58765-199-8). 150.

The 127 essays here, averaging seven pages each, appeared originally in *Magill's Encyclopedia of Social Science: Psychology* (2003). All bibliographies have, according to the publisher, been updated; accordingly, one will find some books and articles dated 2004 among the annotated reading lists. An earlier edition of *Psychology Basics* (1998) was drawn from *Survey of Social Science: Psychology* (1993). Each clearly written essay and its accompanying matter provide a basic overview of the topic and guides to further study, both within and beyond these two volumes.

Essays address historical and contemporary issues, all major theoretical approaches, and topics ranging from psychological aspects of daily life to the varieties of abnormal behavior. In each entry, the type of psychology, field(s) of study, a brief abstract (which often contains a definition), and a list of key concepts precede the essay. The essay itself is subdivided into more discrete topics and followed by well-annotated sources for further study and a list of *see also* references. All entries are signed by contributors, who are almost entirely from American colleges and universities.

Other features add to the ease of use and reference value. Concluding volume 2 are a glossary, capsule biographies of prominent psychologists, an annotated Web-site directory, and a thorough index, with main entries in boldface. Black-and-white illustrations include diagrams and photographs of psychologists. A very helpful feature is the inclusion of *DSM-IV-TR* (*Diagnostic and Statistical Manual of Mental Disorders*) criteria for relevant entries, such as *Mental retardation, Phobias,* and *Substance use disorders.*

Highly recommended for high-school, public, and academic libraries not already owning *Magill's Encyclopedia of Social Science: Psychology* (2003). —*Craig Bunch*

Ethics. 2d. ed. Ed. by John K. Roth. 3v. 2004. 1,685p. illus. index. Salem, $331 (1-58765-170-X). 170.

In today's social and moral climate, few topics are more in need of clarification and discussion than ethics. The fact that there are a number of reference sources on the topic is an indication of demonstrated interest. Now, Salem offers a major revision of one of these sources, first published in 1994, which purports in its introductory material to address the ethical dilemmas of the twenty-first century with an emphasis on applied ethics.

The revised edition is greatly expanded (1,685 pages compared to 961) and covers topics that are of recent interest, such as *Child soldiers, Downsizing, Family values,* and *Napster.* More than 200 of the entries are new, and many of the original 817 entries have been revised. There is an increase in visually attractive material (photographs, maps, charts, and informational sidebars), all of which give the volume a more modern appearance. One particularly useful feature of the first edition remains: each entry begins with explanatory material. For a term, the entry begins with the definition, the type of ethics that it most relates to, and a brief statement of the significance. An individual who is the subject of any entry is given a brief identification, birth and death dates, type of ethics he or she is connected with, and a statement of significance. Appendixes provide a glossary, a list of Nobel Peace Prize winners, a time line, and more. Entries are indexed by category, person, and subject.

Other titles, such as Academic Press' four-volume *Encyclopedia of Applied Ethics* (1998), Routledge's three-volume *Encyclopedia of Ethics* (2001), and Facts On File's one-volume *Encyclopedia of Ethics* (1999), all have relatively current information and are reputable sources. It is difficult to compare these on a side-by-side basis since each seems to have a different level of user in mind and a different approach to what aspects of ethics to discuss. The Salem encyclopedia is more student than scholar oriented, with an accessible format, fairly short articles, and visual appeal. It may not be essential for libraries owning all the above-mentioned sources, but if the previous edition has been useful, this excellent revision should definitely be considered. Its relatively reasonable price should appeal to high-school, public, and academic libraries alike. —*Danise Hoover*

Holy People of the World. 3v. Ed. by Phyllis G. Jestice. 2004. 999p. illus. index. ABC-CLIO, $285 (1-57607-355-6); E-book, $310 (1-85109-649-3). 200.

The theme of this work "is that most effective intermediary between heaven and earth: the holy human being who has a foot in both realms." More than 1,000 of the 1,183 entries are biographical sketches of men and women from a variety of religious traditions, including African religions, Amerindian religions, Bahaism, Buddhism, Christianity, Hinduism, Islam, Judaism, Shinto, and Sikhism. There are also survey articles that address aspects of holy people across religious traditions. For example, *Attributes of holy people* discusses special marks or signs various traditions have regarded as proof of an individual's holiness, while *Intermediaries* shows the place of the holy person as mediator between the divine and the rest of humankind. Other entries describe activities or lifestyles commonly associated with holy people (e.g., *Meditation and holy people, Hermits*). Still others treat the intersection of holy people with such topics as aesthetics, gender, politics, suffering, and violence. While it may be no surprise to find entries for various Christian saints or the current Dalai Lama, entries for Nelson Mandela and the last Romanovs demonstrate how different cultures approach holiness in different ways.

The alphabetically arranged entries were written by a team of international scholars, are signed, and conclude with *see* references and suggestions for further reading. The set contains some black-and-white illustrations.

The editor admits that the coverage of holy people among various religious traditions is uneven, explaining this in more detail in her preface. In the end, "what this encyclopedia offers is very much a sampler pack of holy folk from around the world," an admission that may well be instructive to libraries considering purchasing the work. Large academic or research libraries with rich reference collections in biography and religion will not find too much new here. Libraries lacking such resources and in need of biographical information in this area may find this sampler filling in many a gap. —*Christopher McConnell*

Gods, Goddesses, and Mythology. 11v. 2004. 1,584p. illus. indexes. Marshall Cavendish, $459.95 (0-7614-7559-1). 201.

In this latest addition to the substantial reference literature on mythology, more than 300 alphabetically arranged entries cover deities and mythological beings from around the world, although over half of the articles feature Greek and Roman entities. Ten of the 11 volumes focus on mythological characters and themes. Signed entries range from one to eight pages, summarizing the mythological story, contextualizing its importance, and providing the main sources of information. Frequent sidebar information supplements the main text, such as a description of Cheiron accompanying the entry on Achilles. Briefly captioned color art reproductions and photographs festoon nearly every page. Cross-references to related articles end most of the entries.

Twenty-eight entries focus on people and cultures; while largely dealing with Western classical civilizations, they do include Asian, Oceanic, and American regions. (It should be noted that Africa is confined to sub-Saharan areas; a separate article deals with Egypt, but the rest of North Africa is ignored.) These articles (usually eight pages in length) cover traditional and modern religions and beliefs and list the major deities for the regions. Thirty-eight articles focus on groups (e.g., *Devils, Priests and priestesses*) or themes (e.g., *Animals, Dual-ism, Rites of passage*). Usually the treatment is cross-cultural, with a clear effort to address non-European cultures.

Each volume has its own index, and volume 11 contains a cumulative index as well as six other brief thematic indexes, a list of major pantheons by major cultural region, a few deity family trees, and a glossary. Two bibliographies, one for general readers and another for younger readers, are arranged by region and suggest further reading. The titles that are listed tend to be general interest works rather than definitive scholarly volumes.

Resources from other publishers, such as ABC-CLIO's World Mythology series, cover non-Western mythologies in greater depth. Still, this set should attract readers because of its high visual content, manageable amount of information per entry, and cross-cultural thematic articles. Recommended for high-school and public libraries. —*Lesley Farmer*

Shamanism: An Encyclopedia of World Beliefs, Practices, and Culture. 2v. Ed. by Mariko Namba Walter and Eva Jane Neumann Fridman. 2004. 1,055p. illus. index. ABC-CLIO, $185 (1-57607-645-8); e-book, $200 (1-57607-801-9). 201.

Shamanism is, arguably, the oldest form of religious experience, and the least understood. Almost every religious tradition has shamans, although they may be called prophets, healers, mystics, or miracle workers. The broad definition of *shamanism* used for this encyclopedia is "a religious belief system in which the shaman is a specialist in the knowledge required to make a connection to the world of the spirits in order to bring about benefits for the other members of the community."

Volume 1 contains 55 *A–Z* entries on "General Themes in World Shamanism." These include *Demonic possession and exorcism, Fire and hearth, Initiation, Music in world shamanism,* and *Offerings and sacrifice in shamanism,* among others. Following the general entries, volume 1 has sections on North America, Central and South America, and Europe. Volume 2 looks at Eurasia, Korea and Japan, China, South Asia and Tibet, Southeast Asia, Australia and Oceania, and Africa. Within each of these sections, an introduction is followed by between 6 (for Australia and Oceania) and 27 (for Eurasia) articles on various aspects of shamanism among the cultures of the region. Every article is signed and has a bibliography as well as *see also* references. The articles vary in size from less than a page to several pages. There are many black-and-white photographs (one of Zora Neale Hurston as a Voudou dancer) and drawings. The last volume has a complete and extensive bibliography, which includes numerous titles in languages other than English; a list of contributors and their credentials; and an index. The index is key to finding information in the regional sections. Unfortunately, the index is only in the second volume and does not indicate which volume a particular page number is in, which will be inconvenient.

The fascinating text debates the validity of older theories of shamanism as they relate to newer and more inclusive theories. It investigates the practice from prehistoric times to the present. It is a fascinating, scholarly work, rather than one written for a popular audience. Academic libraries in institutions with religious curricula will want at least one copy. Larger public libraries will need this, too. —*Robin Hoelle*

Dictionary of Gods and Goddesses. 2d. ed. By Michael Jordan. 2004. 402p. index. Facts On File, $45 (0-8160-5923-3). 202.

Although Greek and Roman gods and goddesses have been well covered in reference books, few resources try to encompass a complete worldview. Basing his compilation on standard religious reference books, including specialized titles for lesser-known sects, the author of this volume lists more than 2,500 deities from Sumerian, Egyptian, Australian Aboriginal, Akkadian-Babylonian, Hindu, Hittite-Hurrian, Greek, Hebrew, Mayan, Celtic, and Buddhist religions, among others. He focuses on names that readers would be likely to encounter in iconographic and mythological texts. The second edition corrects the underrepresentation of Pacific Islander cultures of the first edition (*Encyclopedia of the Gods*, 1993) and expands the bibliography to include new religious reference titles. Cross-references have been increased, and a comprehensive index facilitates research access.

The main body of the work consists of alphabetically arranged entries listed under the most common form of the deity. Principal gods and goddesses (e.g., *Istar, Thor, Zeus*) are indicated by entry headings in all-capital letters and are given a lengthier treatment (a half to a full page) noting origin, known period of worship, synonyms, center of cult, art references, literary sources, description, and importance. Other entries are generally one to two paragraphs in length. The six-page bibliography is divided geographically and by major religion. Besides listing all the deities alphabetically, the index categorizes deities by culture and function (e.g., *fire, messengers*).

Coverage is impressive; few other reference works include the Western Semitic local goddess of healing Thatmanitu, the Phrygian river god Sangarios, the Lithuanian corn goddess Gabjauai, the Polynesian creator god Quat, or the Aztec minor fertility goddess Matlalcueye. This volume is a solid consolidation of information and is recommended for high-school, public, and academic libraries. —*Lesley Farmer*

Encyclopedia of Religious Rites, Rituals, and Festivals. Ed. by Frank A. Salamone. 2004. 487p. bibliogs. illus. index. Routledge, $150 (0-415-94180-6). 203.

Whether it's the Ghost Festival in China or a Good Friday procession among Christians, "ritual is often the most visible manifestation of religion and the one that first comes to the attention of outside observers." Rituals, however, are not only to be found among the world's religious traditions. Societies have secular rituals, although many of them have their roots in religion and belief. Employing an anthropological approach and drawing upon scholars from a variety of disciplines, this encyclopedia consists of 130 alphabetically arranged entries on rituals, both religious and secular. Each is signed by its author and concludes with a nice supplemental bibliography. There are illustrations throughout.

Entries treat concepts applicable to rituals of many religious traditions, such as *Asceticism, Divination, Ecstatic worship,* or *Prayer,* citing specific examples of how they are employed. Some entries are surveys for types of rituals (e.g., *Agricultural rituals, Food and rituals, Naming rituals*), but, again, tradition-specific information is included. The major rituals of the world's largest religious traditions are described in entries for *Buddhism, Hinduism, Islam, Judaism, Shinto,* and *Taoism.* Christianity is treated in multiple entries, such as *Catholicism, Orthodoxy, Pentecostalism, and Protestantism.* Finally, there are entries for specific rituals (e.g., *Day of the Dead, Passover,* and *Ramadan*).

Noteworthy is the inclusion of rituals and religious traditions less well known than the aforementioned. For example, there are two survey articles on Africa (i.e., *Africa, Central* and *Africa, West*) along with entries on the *Azande, Yoruba,* and *Zulu.* A description of the *Naven ceremony* of the Iatmul tribe of New Guinea, along with entries for *Australian Aboriginal, Melanesia, and Micronesia,* and treatment of *Vodun* in Haiti and a survey of *Afro-Caribbean* rituals, all demonstrate the volume's inclusiveness.

The encyclopedia contains an interesting combination of religious and anthropological information. But an in-depth anthropological survey article on a topic such as marriage rituals would be difficult enough to keep to a manageable length without the addition of tradition-specific information. Readers should be aware that the work will serve, at best, as a cursory introduction to topics. Nevertheless, academic and large public libraries may want to consider acquiring it. —*Christopher McConnell*

Encyclopedia of Christian Theology. 3v. Ed. by Jean-Yves Lacoste. 2004. index. 1,928p. Routledge, $495 (1-57958-250-8). 230.

The *Encyclopedia of Christian Theology* is an English translation of the *Dictionnaire critique de théologie* (PUF, 1998) with some additions and modifications to the French original. A densely academic work, its nearly 500 entries on doctrines, events, theories, schools of thought, and individuals are alphabetically arranged and conclude with excellent supplemental bibliographies and *see* references. The editor opted against many shorter, dictionary-like entries in favor of fewer, lengthier essays. Consequently, use of the detailed index is necessary. For example, there is no separate entry for the medieval thinker William of Ockham. Rather, he is included in the essay *Nominalism* and several others.

Theology is here narrowly defined for purposes of what topics to include. "Attention is concentrated on such matters as Trinitarian theology, Christology, the Incarnation, the Redemption," etc. This is evidenced in lengthy entries for *Christ/Christology, God, Holy Spirit,* and *Incarnation*. Other core issues for Christian theology include *Faith, Hope, Love,* and *Peace*. Entries are very good at tracing differences among Roman Catholic, Protestant, Anglican, Lutheran, and Orthodox thought, thereby providing the reader with a variety of Christian responses to theological issues even though the work as a whole is rooted in the Roman Catholic tradition. Its importance notwithstanding, Christian teaching about many social issues is not covered for the most part, although the entries for *Abortion, Property,* and *Race* provide interesting glimpses. Entries often conclude with "a speculative section . . . pointing to tasks remaining to be accomplished and directions in which theological discussion appears to be moving." Many readers may be unused to finding such reflection in an encyclopedia or may find an encyclopedia an altogether inappropriate venue for it.

Although the *Encyclopedia of Christian Theology* does a great service in making a fine work of scholarship available to the Anglophone world, the excellent supplemental bibliographies are generally to very specialized works, the majority in languages other than English. Moreover, the critical approach to the subject matter is continental in general, French in particular. With these caveats in mind, the work is highly recommended for large academic and theological libraries. —*Christopher McConnell*

Handbook of Classical Mythology. By William Hansen. 2004. 394p. bibliogs. glossary. illus. index. ABC-CLIO, $75 (1-57607-226-6); e-book, $80 (1-85109-634-5). 292.1.

In this title in the publisher's Handbooks of World Mythology series, *classical* refers to Greek and Roman civilizations (a slightly Eurocentric perspective). The author is a university professor of classical studies and folklore and has written other books on the topic. He cites about five pages of books and articles and provides a list of "Annotated Print and Nonprint Resources."

The first third of the volume is an extensive essay on basic concepts and "chronology" of the myth stories, concluding with general Greek and Roman notions about the nature of the world and its mythological characters. The author also discusses how classical Greeks and Romans regarded mythology: some literally, some allegorically, and some as fantasy. The majority of the volume consists of individual entries on deities, themes, and concepts. Deities, the main emphasis, are inconsistently listed under Greek or Roman nomenclature (e.g., *Greek Apollon, Roman Satyrs*). Entries range from a page (e.g., *Titans, Nectar*) to nine pages (e.g., *Divine guilds*); most entries are two to three pages in length. Each entry starts with a definition and then provides a narrative description of the main associated stories, citing the source of information. About a quarter of the entries include black-and-white drawings that appear to be based on ancient artworks. Cross-references and suggested readings end each entry.

In addition to the lists of references and resources, the reader will find a four-page glossary of terms that are used throughout the text. The detailed index includes various aspects of the deities; for instance, under *Athena* are references to her birth, judgment, craftsmanship, transformation, and relationship with other characters.

This volume combines a traditional reference tool and a textbook. Although it does not appear to break new ground, it is a convenient way to package information about Greek and Roman mythology, particularly as part of a mythology series. Recommended for libraries that serve the apparent audience of college- bound high-schoolers and university students. —*Lesley Farmer*

The JPS Guide to Jewish Traditions. By Ronald L. Eisenberg. 2004. 806p. index. Jewish Publication Society, $40 (0-8276-0760-1). 296.4.

The ongoing debate about the growing role of religion in American life raises another important issue: the urgent need to understand the beliefs and practices of each of the many religions in our multicultural society. This highly informative work covers the major elements of Jewish life, including life-cycle events (birth, bar and bat mitzvah, marriage, divorce, parenting, and death), the Sabbath and holidays, the synagogue, prayer, and the Bible and Jewish literature, among many other topics. In addition, the volume surveys a variety of other fascinating issues, including popular superstitions, attitudes toward specific foods and animals, the Israeli flag, and conversion to Judaism. Informative sidebars scattered throughout the book provide more specific information on a variety of Jewish practices and customs; a "Notes" section offers useful bibliographical references from each chapter to other pertinent works. The book concludes with a long bibliography, a list of weekly and holiday Torah readings, and an excellent keyword index.

Although *Seasons of Our Joy: A Handbook of Jewish Festivals* (Bantam, 1982) is more graphically pleasing, *The JPS Guide to Jewish Traditions* is a much more comprehensive work. The author has done a masterful job in distilling the major beliefs and practices of a 3,000-year-old religion into lively and informative prose and in creating an accessible, essential reference work. Highly recommended. —*Donald Altschiller*

The Student's Encyclopedia of Judaism. Ed. by Geoffrey Wigoder. 2004. 390p. bibliog. glossary. illus. index. New York Univ., $39.95 (0-8147-4275-0). 296.

This resource focuses on the Jewish religion itself: its history, practices, and people; Orthodox, Conservative, and Reform movements; the customs, traditions, and prayers of daily life, the Sabbath, and holidays; and brief biographies of leading biblical and rabbinical figures. Although it draws material from the *New Encyclopedia of Judaism* (2002), the information has been rewritten for its intended audience of students in grades 7–12, as well as their families. The list of contributors and their affiliations includes such familiar names as Marc D. Angel and Yehuda Bauer. Editor in chief Wigoder was editor in chief of the *Encyclopedia Judaica*.

The more than 900 alphabetically arranged entries range in length from a brief paragraph to two pages. Many entries are under their Hebrew term *(Tallit, Tefillin)* with cross-references to and from their English counterparts. This should pose no problem for Jews familiar with the religious terminology but may frustrate other users. Topics such as Israel and the Holocaust are discussed in terms of religion, not as the usual history lesson. Black-and-white illustrations with four sets of color inserts, summaries of biblical books, texts of prayers, sayings of the sages, and similar sidebars highlight the entries. Most biblical translations are based on the Jewish Publication Society of America version. Entries do not provide any pronunciation help, nor are they signed.

This title fills a niche for the teen audience. It offers quick reference and a starting point for research, as well as browsing pleasure. Given the price, school and public libraries can't go wrong by adding it to their religion collections. College libraries may also find it appropriate for their undergraduates. The publisher is also marketing it as a family purchase or for bar and bat mitzvahs and Hanukkah. —*Esther Sinofksy*

African Mythology A to Z. By Patricia Ann Lynch. 2004. 137p. bibliog. illus. index. Facts On File, $35 (0-8160-4892-4). 299.6.
Celtic Mythology A to Z. By Gienna Matson. 2004. 114p. bibliog. illus. index. Facts On File, $35 (0-8160-4890-8). 299.
Native American Mythology A to Z. By Patricia Ann Lynch. 2004. 130p. bibliog. illus. index. Facts On File, $35 (0-8160-4891-6). 398.2.
South and Meso-American Mythology A to Z. By Ann Bingham. 2004. 142p. bibliog. illus. index. Facts On File, $35 (0-8160-4889-4). 299.8.

These volumes are part of the Mythology A to Z series from Facts On File. Each volume has a similar format: an introduction includes a history of the culture(s), an explanation of the book, and a pronunciation guide, followed by a time line and a map. The main text is an alphabetical listing of names, places, and ideas important to the mythology of the culture. The definitions are mostly brief—a single paragraph—although some are as lengthy as a page. Many black-and-white illustrations, mostly of artifacts, enhance the text. Each volume includes a good bibliography with Internet addresses.

The series is designed for young people in junior high and high school, and it is appropriate for younger children who are better readers or interested in mythology. Except in the Celtic volume there is not much storytelling since the volumes are intended to be encyclopedias rather than collections of stories. They will help students to make connections between mythological characters and images and compare similarities between cultures. The indexes are constructed to help make those connections, too. Multiculturalism and world history are an integral part of most school curricula, and this series fits both of these themes.

Although the pronunciation guides in the introductions are excellent, a young audience also needs pronunciations at appropriate entry headings. It is difficult to remember strange pronunciations or to flip to the front of the book to figure out how to say foreign names. It seem a disservice to the Native American, Meso- American, and African cultures to lump so many of their mythologies into such a few pages. Another disservice is the use of some English translations as main entries in the Native American volume, with *see* references from the Native American terms. Although this is explained in the introduction, it reinforces attitudes of cultural superiority.

That being said, these titles are an excellent introduction to the mythologies of these cultures and should be in most public and school libraries. —*Robin Hoelle*

Handbook of Inca Mythology. By Paul R. Steele. 2004. 319p. illus. index. ABC-CLIO, $75 (1-57607-354-8); e-book, $80 (1-85109-621-3). 299.8.

Another entry in ABC-CLIO's Handbooks of World Mythology series, with an introduction and overview followed by an *A–Z* "Encyclopedia of Mythic Narratives, Themes, and Concepts." Despite a note on orthography—modern spellings versus older spellings—both varieties are used within articles (e.g., Tiahuanaco and Tiwanaku), not always consistently. Andean myths, rather than exclusively Inca myths, are included, since the Incas co-opted the mythology of conquered peoples into their own. The nearly 70 encyclopedia entries mostly cover individual gods, demons, and heroes, but there are also entries for *Coca, Colors, Felines, Mountains,* and other topics that are an important part of Andean tradition.

Illustrations include black-and-white photographs and reproductions of title pages of early printed books and manuscripts. Each article has cross-references and readings. There are an annotated list of print and nonprint resources and a separate bibliography as well as a glossary and a separate pronunciation guide and index. The index does not include both older and modern spellings.

This work would probably be most useful in academic libraries with Andean studies or folklore and mythology collections. Larger public libraries with extensive folklore and mythology collections may also want to consider it. The Handbooks of World Mythology series also includes titles on Arab, Celtic, classical, Egyptian, Hindu, Japanese, Mesoamerican, Native American, Norse, and Polynesian mythology. —*Kathleen Stipek*

Sociology, Anthropology, Political Science

Encyclopedia of Social Theory. Ed. by George Ritzer. 2v. 2004. 982p. index. Sage, $350 (0-7619-2611-9). 301.

Myriad areas of specialization pertinent to social theory are covered in this set, among them macrosociological and microbehaviorist theories, cultural theory, Marxist theory, feminist theory, and national traditions (e.g., American, British, French, and German social theory). Readers interested in better understanding key concepts, theorists, schools, or texts in these areas will not be disappointed. Qualified scholars from 14 countries provide 300-plus entries ranging from 400 to 6,000 words. Examples of entry headings include *Annales school; Consumer culture; Globalization; Imperialism; Marx, Karl; Queer theory; Social Darwinism;* and *Revolution.* Entries conclude with a brief listing of further readings and a set of cross-references. A "Chronology of Social Theory," a "Master Bibliography," and an index conclude the set; the chronology and bibliography provide significant added value.

Balanced coverage of historical and contemporary social theory, as well as of the areas of specialization pertinent to social theory, is one of the hallmarks of this set. Also notable is the consistently high quality of the scholarship and general accessibility of the entries. The set is, to date, without direct competition, and there is much to recommend it to advanced social-science students, including undergraduates with a more scholarly inclination or those with theoretical interests, as well as researchers and scholars.

This carefully focused work will be a useful complement to standard sociology reference sources that provide broad coverage of the social sciences or social thought in general. It should prove a welcome addition to academic and large public library collections. —*Sarah Watstein*

Encyclopedia of American Social Movements. 4v. Ed. by Immanuel Ness. 2004. 1,750p. illus. indexes. Sharpe, $399 (0-7656-8045-9). 303.48.

This is the first major reference work to convey social conflicts in U.S. history that mainstream accounts usually gloss over—the struggles waged by ordinary people against power. The 152 contributors are mainly from American universities, and the editor is at Brooklyn College, City University of New York. The encyclopedia is organized according to 16 movements, among them the antislavery, civil rights, women's, labor, and environmental movements. After an introductory overview, each section contains from 5 to more than 30 articles that correspond to time periods (e.g., "Religious Movements, 1730s–1830s" in the chapter "Religious, Utopian, and Health Movements") or subject (for example, "Eugenics Movement" and "Prohibition and Repeal" in the chapter "Moral Reform Movements").

The writing is lively, accurate, and balanced. As a result of interrelationships in the movements, and probably the plan of organization for the work, there is some duplication. A history of the Knights of Labor can be found in both the "Knights of Labor" and the "Labor Movement, 1877–1919" sections of the "Labor Movement" chapter. As with any reference work, readers may quibble about some editorial decisions. For example, the only individual woman who is given full-article treatment in the "Women's Movement" chapter is Matilda Joslyn Gage. African American and Latino mutual aid societies are described but not ones begun by European or Asian immigrants.

A bibliography at the end of each of the articles and a 54-page bibliography at the end of the work direct users to further resources. Each volume has cumulative general and biographical indexes. Photos appear in most articles, as do sidebars that generally highlight a prominent person or a pertinent document. The work is current, including, for example, a June 2003 decision by the Supreme Court.

Some similar information can be found scattered across other works, but this title provides a unique context and will fill a need for easily accessible information in public and academic libraries. —*Arthur Meyers*

Public Opinion and Polling around the World: A Historical Encyclopedia. 2v. Ed. by John G. Geer. 2004. 897p. index. ABC-CLIO, $185 (1-57607-911-2); E-book, $200 (1-57607-912-0). 303.3.

Although the literature about public opinion polling is extensive, there is surprisingly little reference material on this widely discussed topic. This work fills a serious gap in the literature. The first volume covers the U.S. and contains a wide range of essays surveying polling in different eras in American history, followed by *A–Z* entries examining public opinion on 33 issues such as *Abortion, Foreign policy,* and *Women presidential candidates.* A third section includes information on major pollsters and polling organizations along with some informative essays on Internet surveys, exit polls, and other aspects of polling. The second volume covers international polling, surveying countries as diverse as Israel, Kyrgyzstan, Thailand, and Uruguay, among many others. The entries in volume 2 are very helpful for students and researchers, providing hard-to-find material in one source.

Most useful are the bibliographic references at the end of each entry in both volumes. Polling graphs and charts appear frequently in the two volumes and enhance the reader's understanding of the text. The concluding bibliography of print and nonprint resources would have been more useful if arranged topically, instead of alphabetically. This unique encyclopedia is an outstanding reference source for both major metropolitan public libraries and academic institutions. —*Donald Altschiller*

Terrorism: A Guide to Events and Documents. By Michael Kronenwetter. illus. index. 2004. 298p. Greenwood, $55 (0-313-32578-2). 303.6.

Reference works on terrorism and extremist groups have proliferated over the past several years. This one offers a general survey in seven chapters, ranging from the philosophy of terror and the historical and global background of the subject to case studies (a 1906 U.S. lynching, the 1972 Olympics massacre, the resurgence of the Ku Klux Klan in the twentieth century, and 9/11). Content is based on recent secondary sources and many Web sites (accessed March and April 2004). The chapter on terrorist groups has *A–Z* descriptions of approximately 35 groups, including lesser-known organizations such as the Gray Wolves of Turkey and the Red Hand Defenders of Northern Ireland. Following the chapters are a 54- page chronology from 1831 through 2003 and a selection of documents including Osama Bin Laden statements, UN positions, and speeches by President Bush. A bibliography at the end of each chapter and a selected general bibliography enable the student to research further. The index is accurate, the writing is lively and clear (such as in the chapter on weapons of mass destruction), and black-and-white photos enhance the book.

Encyclopedia of Terrorism (Facts On File, 2002) provides an *A–Z* approach, with the focus on post–World War II events. *Encyclopedia of World Terrorism* (Sharpe, 2003) is a global and historical work looking especially at the contemporary period. Although lacking the depth of these resources, the current work will be useful for secondary students and the general public seeking an accessible overview as well as highlights of the subject. It is recommended for high-school and public libraries. Libraries with more extensive resources may want to consider it for circulation rather than reference. —*Arthur Meyers*

Encyclopedia of Genocide and Crimes against Humanity. 3v. Ed. by Dinah L. Shelton. 2004. 1,458p. illus. index. Macmillan, $345 (0-02-865847-7). 304.66303.

This outstanding comprehensive sourcebook of the worst in human behavior throughout history also includes instances of some of the best responses. It is aimed at the adult general reader but will be valuable for both specialists and older students studying the destruction of a people. The editor and contributors are broadly representative of academic experts around the world, and some of them have had extensive involvement with the subject.

The 350 signed, well-documented entries, varying from 500 to 5,000 words, as appropriate, are arranged alphabetically. The topics comprise the diverse aspects of crimes against humanity—acts and consequences, cultural memory and representation, international institutions and laws. Each article is well written, balanced (such as the entry on the Sabra and Shatila Palestinian refugee camps), and includes *see also* references and a bibliography. The set covers judicial decisions and events as recent as mid-2004. There is some overlap (for example, in treating different aspects of the crimes in the Balkans), but each entry is fresh and shows careful editing.

Every continent and likely every people have had their share of the crimes, and while the impact of the Nazi Holocaust drives much of the work, the editorial team has cast its net wide, encompassing, for example, less-known crimes against the Beothuk people in Newfoundland and Labrador. Birth and death dates of persons and specific dates of the crimes are given. Entries cover ancient and modern genocides, *Perpetrators* and *Victims, Incitement* and *Resistance, Denial* and *Documentation,* international tribunals and national trials, and cultural aspects, such as the ways in which genocide intersects with music and dance. The work includes separate two-page entries on the atrocities at Carthage, Srebrenica, and Wounded Knee as well as concise biographies for individuals ranging from Klaus Barbie, chief of the gestapo in France, to Louise Arbor, chief prosecutor for the International Tribune for the Former Yugoslavia. Concluding the set are a glossary, an excellent filmography, 190 pages of primary sources (historical and international texts and judicial decisions), and an accurate index, which is supplemented by a topical list of entries. Black-and-white photos convey some of the horror of what humanity has wrought. The layout of this very accessible work is noteworthy.

The *Encyclopedia of Genocide* (ABC-CLIO, 1999) emphasizes the Nazi Holocaust and does not aim to cover the entire history and range of genocides. The new work has twice the number of pages and is larger in physical size. It will be the standard resource for many years. —*Arthur Meyers*

U.S. Immigration and Migration Reference Library. 5v. By Sonia Benson. 2004. bibliogs. glossaries. illus. indexes. maps. UXL, $250 (0-7876-7565-2); e-book, contact for pricing (0-7876-9331-6). 304.8.

This set covers immigration—why people moved, how they were received, and how they lived or live in the U.S. Some cultural traditions and current trends are also examined. The set is divided into three parts—a two-volume *Almanac, Biographies* in two volumes, and one volume of *Primary Sources.* There is also a separate cumulative index. Each volume opens with an introduction, time line, "Words to Know," and research ideas and ends with a bibliography and subject index. Sidebars, black-and-white photos, and explanatory subheadings help make the content attractive and inviting for students in middle school and up.

The most useful part of the set is the *Almanac,* a "comprehensive overview of groups of people who have immigrated to the U.S.," starting with pre-Columbian migrations and ending with the post– World War II "third wave." In addition to chapters on groups coming from other countries, there are also chapters on internal migration—the westward movement, forced migrations of the Navajo and others, Japanese American internment, and urbanization. A list of "Words to Know" and a bibliography of books, periodicals, and Web sites are included in each chapter.

Although *Primary Sources* has only 18 documents, there is quite a range of sources. Included are excerpts from laws, first-person accounts, proposed legislation, judicial decisions, and a controversial Mark Twain essay, "Concerning the Jews." Each offers an introduction to the author and the document, things to remember while reading, and interesting related facts. Unfamiliar words and phrases are defined in sidebars in page margins. The *Biography* volumes cover 50 people "who were involved or influential in U.S. immigration or immigrants who became successful." This is a highly selective and representative rather than a comprehensive list. The inclusion of the Statue of Liberty as a biographical entry seems odd.

There are a few other minor faults in the set. Pronunciation is rarely given for names or words, and some defined terms seem obvious *(new world).* The cumulative index is adequate for finding individual names or national groups but has no career fields (astronauts, teachers, scientists). Overall, however, the set is well done and will be used by students doing research at many levels (a must for History Day) as well as teachers and librarians looking for background material. —*Susan Gooden*

The Asian Databook. 2004. 2,274p. Grey House, $150 (1-59237-044-6). 305.

This first edition of *The Asian Databook* uses the same format as the publisher's *Hispanic Databook* and takes a detailed look at the growing Asian population in the U.S. It presents statistical data for the 50 states plus the District of Columbia, 907 counties and county equivalents (all those with a population of over 49,999), and 874 cities and municipalities (those with a population of over 9,999 or having an Asian population that is higher than the national average of 3.61 percent). Twenty-three Asian, native Hawaiian, and other Pacific Islander groups are covered. Data were derived from the U.S. Bureau of the Census, Census of Population and Housing, 2000: Summary File 4 for these population groups.

The first section contains statistical tables for 14 topics, including population, age, language spoken at home, education, income, home ownership, and more. The tables themselves are arranged alphabetically by state, then by county, then by place-name. The second section contains rankings, and only the top 75 places are listed for each data element. The ranking tables provide users with ways to determine population characteristics and see trends. An additional feature is the "City Finder List," an alphabetical list of cities intended to help users who don't know the county or state in which a city is located. *The Asian Databook CD-ROM,* available at no additional charge, contains the same topics as the book but covers thousands more places—all states, counties, and cities with Asian populations.

This useful resource will help those searching for demographics data and market research or relocation information. The depth of the information on the CD-ROM will be especially useful for market research. Accurate and clearly laid out, the publication is recommended for large public library and research collections. —*Susan Awe*

Encyclopedia of Latino Popular Culture. 2v. Ed. by Cordelia Candelaria and others. 2004. 780p. illus. index. Greenwood, $175 (0-313-32215-5). 305.868.

As popular culture continues to grow as a recognized academic area, works such as this one are increasingly important. The 500 entries, which range in length from one half to seven pages, cover topics such as Christina Aguilera, Alex Rodriguez, Olvera Street in L.A., and the Chupacabra, the Puerto Rican answer to the Loch Ness Monster and Bigfoot. Lengthier entries are reserved for wider subjects, such as *Family, Film,* and *Race.* Candelaria and the other editors are professors in the Department of Chicana and Chicano Studies at Arizona State University, Tempe.

The encyclopedia begins with an introduction to the study of Latino popular culture, which is helpful for those who know little about the subject. The work focuses predominantly on Mexican American, Puerto Rican, and Cuban American culture within the U.S. It covers a wide variety of topics, and beyond an alphabetical list of entries, there are several lists that sort entries by subject and, for individuals, by field of endeavor and country of origin or heritage. The work also includes a chronology and a general index. The articles have cross-references, are signed, and, where applicable, include a list of further readings. The bibliography at the end of the second volume is subdivided by general subject area. Some entries are enhanced with black-and-white photographs.

This encyclopedia fills a gap in the area of Latino studies. Other resources, such as *Pop Culture Latin America! Media, Arts, and Lifestyle*, focus on Central or South America, while this work covers Latino culture within the U.S. It works as an academic reference tool but is written so that it would be just as useful for those interested in reading about these topics for pure enjoyment. Recommended for high-school, undergraduate, and public libraries. —*Susanna Eng*

Encyclopedia of the World's Minorities. Ed. by Carl Skutsch. 3v. 2005. 1,413p. index. Routledge, $495 (1-57958-392-X). 305.8.

As the global political situation becomes increasingly complex, it is ever more essential to understand the distinctive interests and groups that are affected by any major decision. *Encyclopedia of the World's Minorities* makes a timely and important contribution to the information required for an intelligent understanding of the world today.

The preface speaks of the uncertainty about what precisely a minority is but notes that the meaning of the term does not really matter. The work has an *A–Z* format and is organized into four entry types: topics, nations, groups, and biographies. Seventy-five entries discuss basic concepts or provide background, for example, *Apartheid, Imperialism, Model minority, Slavery*. There are 173 nation entries, 251 essays concerning minority groups, and 62 biographies, most of them covering people such as Mahatma Gandhi and Rigoberta Menchú, who "have articulated the larger interests of minority peoples."

Overall, this seems to be a well-researched and well-presented reference source. The contributors come from all over the world, and most have academic credentials. Each article is signed and is followed by a bibliography. The set does a fine job of offering coverage to a wide range of ethnic groups, some very small indeed, and in maintaining a nonpolitical, nonjudgmental tone.

One element of the scope of this encyclopedia is worthy of mention. Although most of the nation entries treat countries from the Third World, some cover major industrial nations: the U.K., France, Canada, Germany, etc. France, for example, is discussed in terms of the history of ethnic groups within that country. In a separate article, the French are discussed as minorities in other nations. Just two entries, *Chinese Americans* and *Japanese Americans*, deal specifically with U.S. groups. There are no entries for the U.S. as a country or for Americans in other countries.

There is little in the literature to compare with this title. Most other sources in this area cover ethnic groups from more of an anthropological point of view, rather than from the geopolitical one used here. The *World Directory of Minorities* (Minority Rights, 1997) can be seen as similar but has nowhere near the scope of this encyclopedia. All academic and large public libraries that can afford this should buy it. —*Danise Hoover*

Women in Early America: Struggle, Survival, and Freedom in a New World. By Dorothy A. Mays. 2004. 495p. illus. index. ABC-CLIO, $95 (1-85109-429-6); E-book, $100 (1-85109-434-2). 305.4.

Intended "for pre-collegiate as well as college-level researchers," this cross-disciplinary encyclopedia makes available the research on women in America from 1607 to 1812. Approximately 175 entries cover groups (*Aging women, Quaker women, Milliners and seamstresses*); activities (*Gardening, Quilting, Travel*); and various other topics, such as *Childbirth, Housing, Religion*, and *Witchcraft*. Around a quarter of the entries are biographical. In part because of the chronological limits, emphasis is on the eastern part of the territory that became the U.S. and on women of European descent. Nevertheless, there are entries for African American and Native American women, among them Sally Hemmings, Pocahontas, and Phillis Wheatley, as well as for broader topics such as *African American women and the American Revolution* and *Indian women and leadership*. African American and Native American women are also represented in entries such as *Diet* and *Interracial marriage*. A number of entries shed light on unexpected topics, such as depression and personal hygiene.

Entries generally range in length from one to seven pages, and each includes a list of further readings. Numerous black-and-white illustrations and informative sidebars (for example, "Did Puritans Really Use Scarlet Letters?" and "Eighteenth-Century Cough Medicine") complement the text. The *A–Z* entries are followed by two appendixes, one describing common household chores of the period and the other containing 10 primary documents. The bibliography, organized into broad categories and annotated, is an extremely useful resource, listing historical fiction and online databases as well as primary and secondary sources. Navigational aids include -cross-references, a "Topic Finder" that lists entries by category, and a robust index.

Though there is some overlap with other resources, especially in the biographical entries, the value of this work lies in the particular context it provides. It would be an excellent addition to academic and larger public libraries. —*Mary Ellen Quinn*

Women in the Middle Ages: An Encyclopedia. Ed. by Katharina M. Wilson and Nadia Margolis. 2004. 997p. illus. index. Greenwood, $199.95 (0-313-33016-6). 305.4.

Current scholarship holds that the medieval period was a better time for women than the Renaissance. To demonstrate "women's multidimensional uniqueness" during the Middle Ages, more than 130 international contributors have helped create this encyclopedia, which spans the third to the fifteenth centuries.

More than 300 entries are meant to provide "as broad a sampling as possible of medieval women's diverse culture." Entries are generally between 1 and 10 pages in length, and most are biographical, treating women from Eleanor of Aquitaine and Hildegard of Bingen to the less popularly known mystic Marguerite Porete and humanist Maddalena Scrovegni. Figures of legend, such as Morgan Le Fay and Pope Joan, are included, as are women such as troubadour Almuc de Castlenau, for whom very little documentation exists. Interspersed among the biographies are topical entries such as *Dowry; Embroidery; Hagiography (female saints);* and *Music, women composers and musicians*. Entries that extend the work outside the European sphere include *Aztec warrior women; Fatimid Egypt, women in;* and *Murasaki, Shikibu*. Each entry concludes with a bibliography of primary and secondary sources; some of these are extensive. Many of the contributors discuss the available records as well as the current scholarship on their subjects, and readers will learn as much about the challenges of research as about the women and topics represented here.

A "Guide to Related Topics," repeated in both volumes, groups entries under broad categories. Volume 2 contains a short general bibliography. Black-and-white illustrations, though not numerous, are handsomely reproduced and enhance the text.

Some similar ground is covered by the single-author *Encyclopedia of Women in the Middle Ages* (McFarland, 2001), but in this earlier title biographical entries are usually shorter, and topical entries place more emphasis on everyday life. The McFarland title also has extensive genealogical charts. More scholarly, though still very readable, *Women in the Middle Ages: An Encyclopedia* is recommended for academic and large public libraries. —*Mary Ellen Quinn*

Working Americans, 1880–2005: Volume 6: Women at Work. By Scott Derks. 2005. 483p. illus. index. Grey House, $145 (1-59237-063-2). 305.5.

The sixth title in the Working Americans 1880–2005 series continues the publisher's innovative approach to employment history. This volume surveys the milieu of 33 individuals in 19 states and 5 other locales, including Panama and occupied Japan. Jobs range from farmer and student to midwife, photographer, and judge. Included among the profiles of full-time workers are World War I volunteer Livia Sedgwick and Ellen Watson, an activist protesting the Vietnam War. The text presents an array of social, ethical, and economic variables. Illustrations from catalogs and advertisements, media squibs, cartoons, and posters add life and humanity.

The writing style is unremarkable and handicapped by broad generalizations lacking documentation. The book needed a firmer editorial hand, especially to supervise illustration selection and layout and to maintain focus on working women in sidebars. Of particular annoyance are either paltry captions—"Joanne Binzen loves being creative," "The beauty of New Mexico is a constant delight," "Many community events are available for people of Aiken"—or no information to identify or explain inclusion of illustrations.

Additional titles in the Working Americans, 1880–2005 series include *The Working Class* (2000), *The Middle Class* (2000), *The Upper Class*

(2001), *Their Children* (2002), and *At War* (2003). *Women at Work* is recommended for libraries where these other titles are part of the collection. —*Mary Ellen Snodgrass*

The Antebellum Period. By James M. Volo and Dorothy Denneen Volo. 2004. 401p. illus. index. Greenwood, $49.95 (0-313-32518-9). 973.6.

The Gilded Age. By Joel Shrock. 2004. 313p. illus. index. Greenwood, $49.95 (0-313-32204-X). 306.

Greenwood continues its American Popular Culture Through History series with two new volumes. *The Antebellum Period* deals with popular culture from about 1788–1865, while *The Gilded Age* focuses on 1875–1900, the time between Reconstruction and the Spanish-American War.

Each follows the same format as the preceding volumes in the series. The works are split up into standard chapters covering topics such as "The World of Youth," "Fashion," "Food," and "Leisure Activities." Chapters range from about 15–30 pages in length. The volumes also include a time line of the pertinent era, an index, suggested further reading, and a page detailing some of the costs (in dollar value) of living in that age. Each also contains a few black-and-white pictures per chapter. Unfortunately, as was the case in previous volumes, the pictures are slightly dark, and the captions add little to the content of the books.

Both volumes fit in well with the series, and continue to provide a fascinating look into the pop culture side of history. While learning about government, great leaders, and war is obviously crucial to the study of history, learning about the everyday life of the regular man and woman is just as important in gaining a holistic view of the past. Greenwood excels at looking at history this way; this series is an excellent companion to its *Greenwood Encyclopedia of Daily Life* [RBB S 1 04]. These two new easy-to-read and informative volumes, alone or as parts of the entire series, are recommended for high-school, undergraduate, and public libraries. They could just as well be placed in the circulating collection as in reference.—*Susanna Eng*

Discovering World Cultures: The Middle East. 5v. 2004. bibliogs. glossaries. illus. index. maps. Greenwood, $200 (0-313-32922-2). 306.

This middle-school set profiles the 16 countries that lie in the geographic region between the Mediterranean Sea and India, the editors' definition of the Middle East. Each country (Bahrain, Cyprus, Egypt, Iran, Iraq, Israel, Jordan, Kuwait, Lebanon, Oman, Qatar, Saudi Arabia, Syria, Turkey, the United Arab Emirates, and Yemen) is covered in a multipage chapter providing detailed information on ethnic groups, land and resources, history, economy, religion, everyday life, holidays, and the arts. These sections may be subdivided into specific topics (for example, "Business and Industry" and "Media and Communications" under "Economy"). For each country, a "Fast Facts" box contains basic data (capital, population, life expectancy, currency, exports, etc.). Other sidebars and inserts that cover topics ranging from trivial cultural insights to minibiographies of notable residents to brief essays on historic and political events appear on almost every page. Occasional black-and-white photographs with detailed captions further complement the text.

Each volume begins with a common introduction that succinctly addresses the region's shared historic, political, and religious background. Several pages are devoted to the Middle East as the "Birthplace of the World's Religions." The introduction provides coverage on Islam (basic beliefs, denominations, scripture, and major observances). Judaism is covered in-depth in the chapter on Israel, and Christianity in the chapter on Cyprus, the first nation alphabetically with a sizable Christian population. The introduction also addresses basic conventions concerning courtesy and customs. Each volume ends with a comprehensive index and a volume-specific glossary and bibliography consisting primarily of Web sites, with limited print sources.

Information is current through 2003 (the capture of Saddam Hussein). The political and social scene in the Middle East will continue to evolve. However, readers in need of a source of solid, unbiased information will be well served by this resource. Accessible to students in middle school and up, and specifically designed to coordinate with typical research assignments, this set is highly recommended for school and public libraries. —*Kathleen McBroom*

Encyclopedia of Contemporary Chinese Culture. Ed. by Edward L. Davis. 2005. 786p. index. Routledge, $210 (0-415-24129-4). 306.0951.

The astounding pace of change in China presents a daunting obstacle to any attempt to present an overview of its contemporary culture. The easier of his two preliminary tasks, notes editor Davis, was to justify 1979 as a starting point for "contemporary" China. This date coincides roughly with the beginning of the post-Mao, post–Cultural Revolution, or "reform era," which continues to the present. The more difficult task, for purposes of this encyclopedia, was to define *Chinese*. Davis's decision was to focus on the People's Republic of China while still including "long entries on aspects of the culture of Taiwan, Hong Kong, and Singapore" and shorter ones on native Chinese cultural producers who now live abroad.

Entries range from a long paragraph (*Literary awards, Recreational associations,* the actress *Pan Hong*) to several pages (*Cars and taxis, Cinema in Taiwan, Tiananmen Square*). More than 200 contributors have provided nearly 1,200 articles on architecture, education, ethnic identity, food and drink, language, performing arts, political culture, religion, sports, and more. The literally hundreds of entries for individuals begin with year and place of birth and, if appropriate, year of death. Many entries are followed by *see also* references and a list of -English-language sources for further reading. Some Web sites and non-English-language sources are also cited. Main entry terms within other entries are boldfaced, as are page numbers of main entries in the thorough index.

Writers were encouraged, beyond simply stating the basic facts, "to analyze, to make judgments, and even to editorialize." Thus, for instance, contributor Lionel M. Jensen writes eloquently on the joyful and tragic history of Tiananmen Square and its evolution into the planned site of beach volleyball in the 2008 Olympics. Highly recommended for the reference sections of academic and larger public libraries, and a pleasure for the curious to dip into at random. —*Craig Bunch*

The Encyclopedia of Death and Dying. By Dana K. Cassell and others. 2005. 369p. index. Facts On File, $75 (0-8160-5376-6). 306.9.

This encyclopedia provides well-written definitions of terms and concepts surrounding issues of life and death. It also includes very practical and sometimes quirky information (one of the 13 appendixes is a four-page table of the odds of death from various causes; another is a record of U.S. war deaths). There is also a guide to end-of-life care at home. The more than 560 entries define terms related to culture, economics, history, legislation, medicine, religion, and sociology. Examples include *Burial at sea, Condolence letters, Day of the Dead, Fraud in the funeral industry, Hospice, Oregon Death with Dignity Act, Séance, Suicide,* and *Victorian mourning dress*. Each entry concludes with bibliographic references. A classified bibliography lists articles, books, and videos.

Other widely held works with similar names —*Macmillan Encyclopedia of Death and Dying* (2002) and *Encyclopedia of Death and Dying* (Routledge, 2002)—support and augment each other because of differences in treatment and scope. This new work fills an important niche, explaining a wide variety of terms with clarity and precision. An example is the definition of *Wrongful death,* credited to *FindLaw for the Public* online, which explains legal criteria and personal behavior. The Macmillan encyclopedia only mentions the term in its entry on *Rock music,* with no definition. In fact, there is surprisingly little overlap between the title under review and other works. Using entries related to death and music as an example, while the Macmillan encyclopedia has entries on classical music, the Auschwitz orchestra, death motifs, masses for the dead, and the Orpheus myth, the Facts On File volume has entries on *Dirge, Jazz funeral, Music therapy for the dying,* and *Taps*. The subject of death is much too large for one author or group of authors. There is much to be learned from all the mentioned works.

The straightforward, factual approach toward this highly emotional topic is well presented. The subtle differences in terms and jargon are carefully explained. This is a valuable encyclopedia, highly recommended to public and academic libraries. —*Linda Scarth*

Pop Culture Latin America! Media, Arts, and Lifestyle. By Lisa Shaw and Stephanie Dennison. 2005. 404p. illus. index. ABC-CLIO, $85 (1-85109-504-7); e-book, $90 (1-85109-509-8). 306.

Part of the publisher's Popular Culture in the Contemporary World series, this book is intended as an overview of popular culture in Latin America since the 1940s. However, 404 pages are not enough to provide a good one. French-speaking areas on the continent and in the Caribbean are ignored, as are English- and Dutch-speaking areas. Shaw and Dennison (University of Leeds, England) and three additional contributors provide more of a random sampling than a complete survey. The chapters cover popular music, social movements and politics, sports, theater, travel and tourism, literature, mass media, cinema, religion, and more.

The arrangement within chapters is topical, with sections on specific topics such as *Soccer* and *Tango* arranged in no logical order. Without the index, it would be difficult to locate topics, and not all of them appear in the index. Some topics are covered in detail, but there are some significant and surprising omissions. For example, there is no mention of *narcocorridos* (Mexican songs celebrating lords of the drug trade) in the music chapter. Many topics, such as Brazil's pop star Xuxa and Mexico's upscale shopping district of Polanco, are discussed in political terms. The contributors clearly favor neither U.S. nor European influences, except for socialism and Marxism.

Each topical section has its own cross-references and bibliography. There are a glossary and a separate bibliography at the end of the volume and a chronology at the start. The book is illustrated with black-and-white photographs.

This is not a necessary purchase for public libraries except those with exhaustive Latin American collections. Academic libraries with Latin American collections may wish to consider it. —*Kathleen Stipek*

Science, Technology, and Society. Ed. by Sal Restivo. 2005. 728p. index. Oxford, $150 (0-19-514193-8). 306.4.

Emphasizing an interdisciplinary and international coverage of the functions and effects of science and technology in society and culture, this volume contains more than 130 A–Z signed articles written by major scholars and experts from academic and scientific institutions and institutes worldwide. Its goals are "summarizing basic tenets in the field" of ST&S (Science, Technology, and Society) and "providing a concise and coherent overview of the achievements in this field."

The entries fit broadly into three major areas: medicine and society, science and society, and technology and society. Entries cover such topics as *Brain and mind science*, *Gender and globalization*, *Rain forests,* and *Robots and society*. Each article is accompanied by a bibliography. Other features include extensive cross-referencing throughout, a directory of contributors, and a topical index. Articles generally range in length from 1 to 2 pages up to 6 or 8 pages. The longest, *Science in history,* is almost 60 pages and has nine subentries offering a global view. The introduction suggests that readers would include high-school students as well as professional researchers; the readership level of the entries appears to vary widely from very elementary to expert. Except for one or two tables of data, the volume contains no illustrations.

There are several other reference works treating this fairly new field of study. Many of the 900 entries in *The Facts On File Encyclopedia of Science, Technology, and Society* (1999) are focused less on theory than on practicalities, covering specific topics such as airbags and eyeglasses. UXL's *Science, Technology, and Society* (2002) is designed for a younger audience. The Oxford title is recommended for those libraries with a specific need in this area and for general undergraduate reference collections. —*Diana Shonrock*

Sport in American Culture: From Ali to X-Games. Ed. by Joyce D. Duncan. 2004. 479p. illus. index. ABC-CLIO, $95 (1-57607-024-7); e-book, $100 (1-85109-559-4). 306.4.

This volume does not attempt to duplicate what other sport reference guidebooks do: it is not a fact-based, statistical, biographical encyclopedia. What *Sport in American Culture* does is provide in its 400 entries long essays written by 200-plus contributors on the impact that sports have had on the cultural life of America. The alphabetically arranged entries cover sports heroes; commercial enterprises, such as the sports apparel industry; gender and civil rights issues; gambling and other scandals; children in sports; and sports in literature and film, to name just a few of the topics. Entries for individual types of sports, such as basketball and bicycling, and for individuals, such as Hank Aaron and Lance Armstrong, focus on demonstrating how "sport reflects the larger culture in unique and important ways."

Entries contain bibliographies as well as *see also* references. A number of illustrations and photographs help support the information provided in the essays and make this resource more accessible to younger readers. A 20-page bibliography and a detailed name and subject index complete the volume. Not all of the information in the book is up-to-date. For example, the entry on Marge Schott's death in March 2004 apparently occurred too late to be included.

Since the strength of this particular encyclopedia is its emphasis on the relationship between sports and American culture, it is unique among sports reference sources and is a recommended purchase for public library reference or academic library collections. It would also be useful in high-school libraries with large sports collections. —*Jerry Carbone*

Encyclopedia of Modern Worldwide Extremists and Extremist Groups. By Stephen E. Atkins. 2004. 404p. bibliogs. illus. index. Greenwood, $75 (0-313-32485-9). 320.53.

This work complements the author's valuable *Encyclopedia of Modern American Extremists and Extremist Groups* (Greenwood, 2002). Focusing on post-1945, with 85 percent of the information coming from the period since 1980, the 285 entries encompass people and organizations on every continent, many not widely known, such as the neo- Nazi Australian Civil Liberties Union. Yasir Arafat is given one and one-half pages and Osama Bin Laden three and one-half pages. Among other entries are *Holocaust denial; Irish Republican Army; Pot, Pol; Reid, Richard; Sandinista National Liberation Front;* and *September 11.*

The arrangement is alphabetical, with *see* and *see also* references and suggested readings leading the reader further. The information is accurate, clearly written, and relatively current (for example, there is coverage of the subway bombing in Moscow in February 2004. It is also objective and balanced, as in the discussion of the effect of the intifada on Palestinian society.

The list of entries, the 10-page chronology, photos, an extensive bibliography, and an index enhance the value of the work. There is some overlap with *The Encyclopedia of World Terrorism: 1996–2002* (Sharpe, 2003), which continues an earlier large work and includes useful documents in volume 2. *Encyclopedia of Terrorism* (Facts On File, 2002) is an accessible resource for secondary-school and public libraries, but the title under review will be useful for a broader audience, including academic libraries. Although individual entries can be researched through the Internet, *Encyclopedia of Modern Worldwide Extremists and Extremist Groups* shows the value of examining the global scourge in a single source. —*Arthur Meyers*

The Uniting States: The Story of Statehood for the Fifty United States. 3v. Ed. by Benjamin F. Shearer. 2004. 1,434p. index. Greenwood, $225 (0-313-32703-3). 320.473.

This work demonstrates how varied the states are in their history, geography, economics, politics, and demographics—and how amazing it is that they came together as a nation and function as one, in spite of significant differences. The focus is on the situations and political motivations that propelled each colony or territory into full-fledged statehood, whether it was in the eighteenth, nineteenth, or twentieth century. The set will help its readers comprehend that some colonies (North Carolina, for example) were more reluctant than others to join the new Union; some territories (Utah, for one) were less welcome than others into the expanding nation; and internal issues in each area made for interesting compromises over issues like taxation, native populations, natural resources, banking, and citizens' rights.

Following editor Shearer's introductory chapter, which gives an overview from British colonization to the addition of Alaska and Hawaii, there are 50 signed articles covering the evolution of each of the states up to its admission. Most of the contributors hold PhDs in history. Each entry is about 25 pages long and includes footnotes, a bibliography, and a summary chart that lists the state's location, territorial developments in chronological order, its capital(s), and the origin of the state name. Nearly 40 black-and-white maps enhance the story of the growth of the nation. Conveniently, the full complement of maps appears in each of the three volumes. Two appendixes, found in volume 3, provide listings of admission dates. One is arranged chronologically; the other is arranged alphabetically by state.

Earlier works that cover this aspect of U.S. history, such as D. W. Meinig's three-volume *The Shaping of America* (Yale, 1986) and Oscar and Lilian Handlins' four-volume *Liberty in America* (Harper, 1986– 94), are perhaps more readable as a whole, but this new reference work treats each state individually and makes it easy to compare their development. The length of the essays and their scholarly approach make this set suitable for academic and research libraries and large public libraries. —*Sally Jane*

The Encyclopedia of Civil Liberties in America. 3v. Ed. by David Schultz and John R. Vile. 2005. 1,141p. illus. index. Sharpe, $299 (0-7656-8063-7). 323.

This reference set contains more than 700 alphabetically arranged entries on terms, historical documents and events, constitutional provisions, individuals, and associations that have been important in the struggle for civil liberties. It is intended to complement *The Encyclopedia of Civil Rights in America,* published in 1998. Editors Schultz and Vile are professors at Hamline University and Middle Tennessee State University, respectively, and are joined here by some 200 academic contributors.

The entries are short, a page or two in length, and end with suggestions for further reading. The "Topic Finder" in volume 1 indicates the range of coverage—there are entries grouped under "Academic Freedom and Education," "Campaign Contributions," "Criminal Procedures," "Laws," "Justices of the U.S. Supreme Court," "Property Rights," and "Wartime and Terrorism," to name just a few broad topics. Among the timely entries one will find are *Airport searches, DNA testing, Electronic eavesdropping, Hate crimes, Police brutality, Sexual harassment,* and *Ten Commandments: Posting.* Numerous entries cover people, from John Locke to Ethel and Julius Rosenberg to John Ashcroft, who have helped frame the debate about civil liberties in one way or another. Cross-references are found throughout the encyclopedia. The lengthy introduction discusses the history of American civil liberties from its roots to the twenty-first century. In addition to the "Topic Finder," the first volume contains a case index. Appendixes at the end of the third volume include a few primary documents, a chronology of important civil liberties milestones from 1215 to 2004, and an extensive bibliography. Some entries are accompanied by black-and-white illustrations.

No other reference source truly duplicates this set, which is recommended for high-school and undergraduate collections and public libraries as good introductory material. —*Diana D. Shonrock*

American Statesmen: Secretaries of State from John Jay to Colin Powell. Ed. by Edward S. Mihalkanin. 2004. 600p. index. Greenwood, $99.95 (0-313-30828-4). 327.73.

Although the role of the office has changed over the years, the secretary of state has always been a critical member of the president's cabinet. This volume, edited by a political scientist, provides information about the persons who have defined U.S. foreign policy, the issues they faced, and the impact they have had.

The articles are alphabetically arranged and range in length from 2 to 20 pages. Each signed entry includes important dates in the subject's life, significant background information (such as education, influences, and preservice career), expressed ideas about foreign policy, circumstances related to appointment, relations with the president and with Congress, major issues during service, postservice career, and a general assessment.

A bibliographical essay at the end of each article directs the reader to primary and secondary sources. A chronological list shows dates of service for each secretary of state as well as the administrations under which they functioned. An index allows linking specific treaties to individual secretaries of state and some cross-referencing of long-standing issues, such as nullification and slavery.

Much of the information can be found in other biographical dictionaries, such as *The Secretaries of State: Portraits and Biographical Sketches* (USGPO, 1978) and *Biographical Directory of the United States Executive Branch, 1774–1989* (Greenwood, 1990). But this volume pulls it all together, updates it, and offers current perspective on the lives and contributions of these important persons. Recommended for public and academic libraries. —*Sally Jane*

Encyclopedia of Cold War Espionage, Spies, and Secret Operations. By Richard C. S. Trahair. 2004. 472p. index. Greenwood, $75 (0-313-31955-3). 327.12.

This intriguing encyclopedia looks at key players in cold war espionage activities, reviews their activities during the cold war period, and explains what occurred because of those activities. Daniel Ellsberg, Alger Hiss, Christine Keeler, Joseph McCarthy, Lee Harvey Oswald, and Ethel and Julius Rosenberg are among those who are treated. Though most of the approximately 300 key entries cover individuals, some examine events and operations.

The author's definition of *cold war* is broad and includes more than the standard "U.S. versus Soviet Union" perspective. The encyclopedia's scope encompasses spies and operations prior to World War II and beyond the fall of the Berlin Wall and collapse of the Soviet Union. The reader will find information dealing with more than 40 countries. Trahair also pursues some aspects of fictional espionage, in entries such as *Bond, James* and *Le Carré, John*. Most of the entries include short citations of sources, helpful starting points for more in-depth research. The volume also contains a list of entries sorted by general subject, a glossary, and a cold war chronology.

A quibble is that very few cryptographers are included. Herbert Yardley's work in the U.S., as the creator of the American code-breaking agency, could have been noted. Yardley was disgraced in

U.S. spy circles after the publication of his book *The Black Chamber*. He worked in Canada during the early cold war years and helped Canada develop its cypher skills.

A solid piece of work, the encyclopedia would be a good choice for the public library where there is interest in this subject area. Colleges and universities with programs in modern history, government policy, and security and intelligence will find it a good introductory source. —*Terri Tomshychyn*

Encyclopedia of Cuban–United States Relations. By Thomas M. Leonard. 2004. 282p. appendixes. bibliog. index. maps. McFarland, $75 (0-7864-1521-5). 327.7291073.

From *Adams, John Quincy* to *Zayas, Alfredo,* this encyclopedia covers the long history of relations between Cuba and the U.S., the good, the bad, and the ugly. Entries include biographies, political and social policies, and events. They range in size from one paragraph (*Caracas Pact; Finley, Carlos; Hemingway, Ernest*) to several pages (*Carter, Jimmy; Guantánamo Naval Base; International Conferences of American States; Slavery; Sugar Acts*). The author is a professor and director of the International Studies Program at the University of North Florida in Jacksonville, Florida.

Entries are in alphabetical order. Names are entered in the Spanish form with *see* references from the English form (*Castro, Fidel* see *Castro Ruz, Fidel*). Most entries include *see also* references. The writing is clear, concise, and easy to understand by most readers. The statements are objective and factual; there is little bias evident in the text. The information is current through the George W. Bush administration. Illustrations are limited to a few well-placed maps. Four appendixes supplement the main texts: a chronology, lists of Internet sites and audiovisual materials, and a bibliography, which is divided into reference works, surveys, and books that cover specific time periods. In each appendix, annotations of a sentence or two are very helpful. The index is quite thorough.

Because of the brevity of this volume and the quality of the entries, it is an excellent starting place for research and information. It should be purchased as a companion to resources such as *Encyclopedia of Cuba: People, History, Culture* [RBB O 1 03] and *Encyclopedia of Latin American History and Culture* (Scribner, 1996), which present more cultural information. This volume's focus on political relations makes it useful for colleges and for high schools that have Advanced Placement government or history programs. —*Robin Hoelle*

Encyclopedia of Intelligence and Counterintelligence. 2v. Ed. by Rodney P. Carlisle. 2005. 750p. Sharpe, $199 (0-7656-8068-8). 327.12.

Here is a look at how intelligence and counterintelligence activities have helped shape world events, primarily in a historical context but also in contemporary times.

In a straightforward alphabetical arrangement, the encyclopedia presents more than 420 entries on people, places, and organizations. All the standard stuff is here, including information on the various types of intelligence gathering—HUMINT, SIGINT, MASINT. Readers will also learn about methods and tools for gathering intelligence, from early historical codes to satellite collection methods. Of most interest are the entries for selected U.S. presidents and the intelligence issues of their administrations. Country entries discuss the development, strength, and power of intelligence organizations in countries from Afghanistan to Zaire. These are all useful introductory articles to get a researcher started. The more than 420 entries range in length from a half column in a two-column page to several pages. Articles are signed by their contributors and include *see also* references and a bibliography of resources. Because there are multiple contributors, the writing style varies, and in some cases, such as *Canada,* an awkward style creates ambiguities.

Prior to the entries is an alphabetical list of articles. A classified list would also have been useful. Also preceding the A–Z portion of the volume is a "Timeline of Intelligence" from 1294 B.C.E. to the present. Readers not familiar with events may be puzzled by some of the references here. For example, the term "Family Jewels" is used in the entry for 1973–1975, but there is no entry for *Family Jewels* in the index that would point to additional information. Following the A–Z section is a "Resource Guide" listing books, articles, and Internet sites and an appendix with extracts from *The 9/11 Commission Report.*

This is an introductory work. Polishing in the next edition will help clear up some of the ambiguities in this edition. Of use in public libraries where this topic is of interest and in those academic institutions where course work on intelligence security and policy is taught. —*Terri Tomchyshyn*

CQ Voting and Elections Collection. [Internet database]. CQ, pricing from $600 [http://www.cqpress.com]. (Last accessed September 10, 2004).

It is refreshing to find election information with no hype, mudslinging, or political spin. This database is a wealth of facts, figures, definitions, and descriptions of the history of voting and electoral practices in the U.S. It is a repository of information for political aficionados, community activists, journalists, and Trivial Pursuit players as well as interested citizens and students.

Content, which includes bibliographies, biographies, case summaries, election analyses and returns, reports, encyclopedia entries, tables and charts, maps, and primary source material, is organized into six areas: Presidential Elections, Congressional Elections, Gubernatorial Elections, Campaigns and Elections, Political Parties, and Voters and Demographics. The user can do a keyword search across all areas or within any one area. All areas can also be browsed by topic. An Advanced Search form, available for Presidential Elections, Congressional Elections, and Gubernatorial Elections, allows users to use Boolean operators and limit searches by office, type of election (e.g., primary or general), year, state, and document type. Results can be displayed in either an abbreviated form (title only) or with the documents' first 50 words. For each record in the results list, the user is shown title, document type, event date, and relevancy. Relevancy is the default sort, but results can be resorted by title, document type, or date. Documents open in a separate window with a prominent "Learn More About" box providing links to related material. Novice users may find some features, such as the up-and-down arrows that re-sort results, confusing, and Help is not as thorough as one might wish.

The left-hand navigator bar offers sophisticated options for researching voting trends. Users can view electoral histories for particular candidates or offices, track incumbency and competition in decisive races, and follow party control, seats that changed parties, and party switches as well as third-party candidates and special elections. All of this information is delivered in the form of customizable tables. The navigator bar also provides links to maps, bibliographies, encyclopedia entries, a calendar and chronology, and lists of definitions and sources. There are good sets of Web links on campaign finances, political parties, political analysis, voter education, and more.

The database is a treasure trove of information on topics such as who changed parties or how people fared in special elections. John Quincy Adams changed parties three times. George Clinton ran for U.S. president three times (1789, 1792, 1796) with an "unknown" party and once (1808) as an Independent Democratic Republican. There have been 498 political parties that have fielded candidates since 1789. The volume of documents related to elections is impressive. Even less populous states like Nevada and Iowa have 620 and 954 documents, respectively, mentioning the state names.

The database is built from many other CQ resources and is a great way to answer specific questions from a wide range of input data. Academic and public libraries with many political reference questions will find this a useful addition. —*Linda Scarth*

Business, Economics, Resources

Encyclopedia of Capitalism. 3v. Ed. by Syed B. Hussain. 2004. 1,115p. appendixes. bibliogs. glossary. illus. index. Facts On File, $225 (0-8160-5224-7). 330.

Intended for grades nine and up, the approximately 727 entries in this encyclopedia fit under the categories of countries (97 entries); companies (95 entries, e.g., *General Electric, Nestlé*); biographies (164 entries, e.g., *Gorbachev, Mikhail; Washington, George*); and economic terms and theories (190 entries, e.g., *Keynesian economics, Say's Law*), with the remaining entries split among organizations (*World Trade Organization*), industries (*Mining*), events (*American Revolution*), and other topics tied to capitalism. All articles are signed and include a bibliography. Article length varies from one-quarter page to six pages, with longer articles leaning toward covering economic terms and theories.

The attempt to view subjects within a "capitalist paradigm" works well with most entries. For example, the article on the Bank of England not only provides a history of the bank, including reforms of the 1990s, but also describes the changing role of central banks within capitalist economies. On the other hand, some articles on companies provide little more than a company profile, with article references pointing to a company's Web page and *Hoover's Online* [http://www.hooversonline.com], neglecting articles and books.

Added features include a time line in volume 1, beginning in 400 B.C.E. ("Ancient market practices in Greece and Rome") and ending in 2002 ("Euro replaces currency of 12 European nations"). Adjacent to each time-line entry, volume and page numbers point to more information. All three volumes include a title list of articles and a list of 124 contributors with affiliations. Volume 3 contains a glossary; a resource guide (suggested books, journals, magazines, newspapers, and Internet sites); and two lengthy appendixes filled with charts and tables—"International Trade by Region" and "International Trade by Sector." Volume 3 also provides an index with main entries in bold. The index is the only place the reader will find *see also* references tying related entries together. More than 70 black-and-white photos accompany the text, but some, such as a person peering intently at a computer monitor, seem unnecessary.

The scholarly set of Palgrave dictionaries, including the dated *New Palgrave: A Dictionary of Economics* (Macmillan, 1987), cover some of the same ground. The *Encyclopedia of Capitalism* is suited for larger academic and public library collections. —*Stephen Fadel*

Affirmative Action: An Encyclopedia. 2v. Ed. by James A. Beckman. 2004. 1,074p. appendixes. bibliogs. illus. index. Greenwood, $175 (1-57356-519-9). 331.13.

This title's stated purpose is "to provide an overview of current scholarship on topics related to affirmative action and impacting a diverse array of disciplines, such as law, political science, history, and sociology." The editor is a professor of law and justice at the University of Tampa. This encyclopedia is particularly noteworthy because it explores a very topical and highly contentious issue.

Following an excellent introductory essay describing the development of the notion of affirmative action, the text contains approximately 500 alphabetically arranged entries, most of which are signed. The articles range from a few paragraphs to several pages. Articles conclude with suggestions for further reading and cross- references. The encyclopedia also contains a bibliography of current books on affirmative action.

This reference work brings together an impressive variety of information spanning the period from the end of the Civil War to the Supreme Court decisions handed down in June 2003 relating to the University of Michigan's admissions policies. Coverage includes related laws, court cases, program recipients, sociological and legal theories, key individuals and organizations, employment, and education. The work also examines affirmative action in other nations, such as Australia, Canada, India, and South Africa. The main text is complemented by a number of useful features, among them a time line of key events that have influenced affirmative action and the full text of the Supreme Court's decisions involving the University of Michigan.

This is a comprehensive resource that effectively and objectively discusses a complex and controversial topic. Separate articles outline arguments in favor of and against affirmative action. In addition, the work contains profiles of individuals on both sides of the debate. More in-depth than *Affirmative Action: A Reference Handbook* (ABC-Clio, 1999), *Encyclopedia of Affirmative Action* is recommended for academic libraries and large public libraries. —*Michelle Hendley*

Teen Guides to Environmental Science. 5v. By John Mongillo. 2004. 720p. illus. index. Greenwood, $249.95 (0-313-32183-3). 333.72.

Although this set for middle- and high-school students should be popular, it could have been better. In thematically arranged volumes, the author presents a great deal of information on the environment. The volumes are titled *Earth Systems and Ecology, Resources and Energy, People and Their Environments, Human Impact on the Environment,* and *Creating a Sustainable Society.* The approach is interdisciplinary, covering ecological, economic, and social topics. Some of the material is excerpted from author Mongillo's

Encyclopedia of Environmental Science (2000) and *Environmental Activists* (2001), also published by Greenwood.

Every volume includes the same four appendixes ("Environmental Timeline, 1620–2004," "Endangered Species by State," "Websites by Classification," and "Environmental Organizations") and a set index. Indexing is spotty; users looking in the index for information on Toyota's hybrid car will find the description and photograph in volume 5 but not the identical photograph and the diagram in volume 2. At the end of each chapter is a glossary, a selection of student activities, and lists of books and Web sites. More than 500 black-and-white images are included, with some drawings and time lines created specifically for this set. However, photos are often very dark or unclear, and the volumes have an overall drab appearance that won't recommend them to the target audience.

On the plus side, it's nice to have social and economic factors included in a work on the environment. The set is intended to align with National Geography Standards and National Science Education Standards as well as standards from the North American Association for Environmental Education, making it a good choice for school and curriculum-oriented public libraries. —*Susan Gooden*

Encyclopedia of American Women in Business: From Colonial Times to the Present. By Carol H. Krismann. 2005. 692p. index. Greenwood, $175 (0-313-32757-2). 338.092.

More than 425 entries, most of them biographical, comprise this resource. The women who are covered range from Lady Deborah Moody (1586–1659), who founded and planned the colonial settlement of Gravesend on Long Island, to Louise Kitchen (1969–), who was Enron's chief operating officer. Selection is limited to women in profit-making enterprises and generally excludes government officials and women who are known mainly as artists. The remaining 100 or so entries deal with topics such as *Automobile industry, Latina businesswomen, Mommy track, Sexual harassment,* and *Telecommuting.*

The biographical entries provide a few personal details, but emphasis is on professional accomplishments. Most are brief, although a few, such as those for Barbara Proctor and Oprah Winfrey, cover more than two pages. All entries conclude with short further reading lists of books, articles, and Web sites, which can be found with fuller citations in the 50-page general bibliography. Other content includes a chronology; *Fortune* magazine's list of the 50 most powerful American businesswomen, 1998–2003; and lists of businesswomen who are covered in the encyclopedia organized by ethnic heritage, historical period, and profession. We found no entry for colonial printer Dinah Nuthead, even though she appears in the "Businesswomen by Historical Period" appendix.

There is some overlap with other reference sources that treat women in business, among them *A to Z of American Women Business Leaders and Entrepreneurs* (Facts On File, 2002) and *Historical Encyclopedia of American Women Entrepreneurs* (Greenwood, 2000). *Encyclopedia of American Women in Business: From Colonial Times to the Present* covers more than twice as many women as either of these, is more up-to-date, and adds depth to its treatment by combining biographies with topical entries. Smaller collections that own one or both of the older titles may not need to acquire the current work, but it belongs in academic and larger public libraries, especially where there is an emphasis on business or women's studies. —*Mary Ellen Quinn*

Industry Research Using the Economic Census: How to Find It, How to Use It. By Jennifer C. Boettcher and Leonard M. Gaines. 2004. 305p. illus. index. Greenwood, $85 (1-57356-351-X). 338.0973.

The U.S. Economic Census contains data essential to understanding the U.S. economy and determining its current health. It can also help users recognize trends in different industries, target marketing and sales, and understand key economic indicators. This handbook explains "the Census concepts, methods, terminology, and data sources" and also explains how to locate needed census data.

The six chapters in part 1, "Understanding the Economic Census," cover its history, procedures, terminology, reports, and more. Part 2, "Selected Industries," highlights agriculture, transportation and warehousing, manufacturing, wholesale, retail, and other sectors. In each of these chapters, Boettcher and Gaines define the industry, then discuss its changing nature, how it is covered in the Economic Census, how the data are made available, and how the data are used. They also give information on other data sources that provide current information in between census years. Tables at the end of each industry chapter compare NAICS codes and text with SIC codes and text. Appendixes contain sample questionnaires and lists of regional federal depository libraries, State Data Center and Business and Industry Data Center lead agencies, and Census Bureau regional offices. A thorough index, including authors, titles, agencies, symbols, and other important terms and concepts, facilitates access.

This practical guide to finding and using the multitude of data in the Economic Census will be useful in public and academic libraries, and special business collections will definitely want to purchase it. —*Susan Awe*

International Directory of Business Biographies. 4v. Ed. by Neil Schlager. 2004. 1,981p. illus. indexes. St. James, $425 (1-55862-554-2). 338.092.

The purpose of this set is to provide a biographical overview of the executives of the "world's biggest and most influential companies," including those businesses on *Fortune* magazine's Fortune 500 and Global 500 lists. Over 90 individuals, mostly independent scholars, journalists, and writers, contributed entries.

More than 600 entries are arranged in alphabetical order by each business leader's surname. The essays range in length from two to four pages and contain factual information, such as birth date and education, and an evaluative summary of the subject's career, management style, and impact on his or her company. Entries are signed and cross-referenced to relevant company reports in the *International Directory of Company Histories* (St. James, 1988–). A list of sources, including books, articles, and Web sites, completes each entry. A name index aids access to the main text. In addition to the name index, the encyclopedia includes company and industry, geographic, and nationality indexes.

The executives who are covered come from a wide range of enterprises. There are entries for the CEOs of very large publicly owned companies, such as H. Lee Scott Jr., of Wal-Mart Stores Inc., and John Browne, of Britain's BP, as well as for famous personalities who head private companies, such as Oprah Winfrey. More than 40 nationalities are represented, with approximately 60 percent of the entries devoted to Americans. There is good coverage of women and minority executives.

Well written and balanced, the *Directory* provides a very good starting point for research on major business executives worldwide and is recommended for academic, corporate, and large public libraries, particularly if they already hold *International Directory of Company Histories.* —*Michelle Hendley*

The Value of a Dollar: Prices and Incomes in the United States, 1860–2004. 3d ed. 2004. 600p. index. Grey House, $135 (1-59237-074-8). 338.5.

Want to know what a guy had to pay for a ticket to the Tunney-versus-Dempsey heavyweight title fight in 1926? What a family had to pay for a Toastmaster Automatic pop-up toaster that same year? Perhaps you're wondering what a Sears Roly Poly combed-cotton baby gown cost in 1941, what a pound of sugar cost in 1960, how much the Szechuan seafood salad sold for at the Shun Lee Restaurant, New York City, in 1988. This engaging statistical summary presents the history of the American people through the prices they paid for a wide variety of products and services. The first section is organized into six chapters covering 20-year periods and then into subchapters covering 5-year spans. Each subchapter presents a chronology of mostly economic events; tables showing typical wages and incomes, expenditures, and investment yields; a representative "food basket" comparing prices in different cities; prices on items from alcoholic beverages to travel; and more. Following these summaries is a new section called "Pricing Trends," which tracks changes in the costs of goods and services in various categories and also show values compared to today's dollar.

The precise source of the data is often included in the tables and charts. The tables are stylishly designed, with lots of white space between numbers and an occasional historical snapshot or advertising reproduction. The index is not especially detailed, and there are some errors in the running heads.

The Value of a Dollar will interest students of social history, fiction writers needing easy access to precise historical detail, business historians, and older folks nostalgic for those days gone by when you could buy your smokes for a penny apiece. This is a recommended title for academic libraries, larger public libraries, and any library serving people interested in understanding history through the eyes of everyday consumers. —*Art Lichtenstein*

Law, Public Administration, Social Problems and Services

Poverty in the United States: An Encyclopedia of History, Politics, and Policy. 2v. Ed. by Gwendolyn Mink and Alice O'Connor. 2004. 895p. illus. index. ABC-CLIO, $185 (1-57607-597-4); E-book, $200 (1-57607-608-3). 339.4.

The history of poverty in the U.S. includes many aspects of the American past; it also includes the diverse experiences of many people. These volumes contain more than 300 entries on issues, events, debates, concepts, social and political movements, legislation, and more as they relate to poverty and social welfare. Examples include *Adolescent pregnancy, African American migration, Feminization of poverty, Food stamps, Immigration policy, Salvation Army, Social Security Act of 1935,* and *Work ethic.* Also covered are important texts, such as Jane Addams' *Twenty Years at Hull House* and John Steinbeck's *The Grapes of Wrath.*

Volume 1 opens with a 50-page essay that surveys poverty "as part of the broad sweep of American history," from the colonial period to the present. The alphabetically arranged entries that follow range in size from very short to 10 pages. Each concludes with cross-references and suggestions for further reading. Scattered throughout the text are excerpts from key documents, such as speeches, congressional testimony, and court decisions. Although there are no biographical entries, people such as Addams and Steinbeck, along with Grace Abbott, Cesar Chavez, Daniel Patrick Moynihan, Jacob Riis, and others, appear as headings, with *see* references to entries for works they authored or programs or movements they helped create. One individual who is missed is Dorothy Day, although she is discussed at some length in the *Catholic Worker Movement* entry.

It is difficult to encompass such a large topic in so few entries, and readers are bound to find omissions. However, this encyclopedia is a good entry point to more in-depth study and as such is recommended for academic and large public libraries. —*Diana Shonrock*

Landmark Supreme Court Cases: The Most Influential Decisions of the Supreme Court of the United States. By Gary Hartman and others. 2004. 594p. appendixes. bibliogs. glossary. index. Facts On File, $65 (0-8160-2452-9). 347.73.

Although other works, such as The Oxford Guide to U.S. Supreme Court Decisions (Oxford, 1999), Encyclopedia of the U.S. Supreme Court (Salem, 2000), and Supreme Court Compendium: Data, Decisions, and Developments (CQ Press, 2003), provide information on landmark cases, this one succinctly describes the backgrounds of more than 350 "most important" cases and offers insight into their significance and effects on American life. The authors give no criteria for selecting these particular cases, but all seem significant in their impact.

The cases are arranged alphabetically under 15 subject categories such as "Abortion," "Freedom of Religion," "Jurisdiction," and one catch-all category, "Additional Cases." The latter includes cases that addressed the death penalty, eminent domain, blue laws, and trials of captured enemies by military tribunal, to name a few. Each entry features the case title, legal citation, year of decision, key issues, history, summary of the arguments, aftermath, significance, and related cases. Most entries are no more than two pages long. There is a detailed index that enables users to find specific cases or topics. A 13-page glossary includes the expected legal terms and a few technological terms, such as CD-ROM, database, and microfiche. Recommended readings at the end of each entry, a list of sources by case, and a brief bibliography direct the reader to other works.

This source should be useful to anyone wanting to study the development and impact of the U.S. Supreme Court and to anyone who wants to understand the significance of those few cases (approximately 150 of the 7,000 filed each year) that make it through the selection process and are heard there. Readers can grasp the Court's evolving power by using the chronologically arranged table (although it oddly skips from 1989 to 2003 even though this work includes some cases from the intervening years). They can also see attitudinal changes in the Court by studying the various cases under each subject heading. Recommended for academic, public, and high-school libraries. —*Sally Jane*

The U.S. Legal System. 2v Ed. by Timothy L. Hall. 2004. 797p. bibliog. glossary. illus. indexes. 797p. Salem, $104 (1-58765-189-0). 349.73.

Most of the articles in this resource intended to help laypersons understand legal matters originally appeared in *American Justice* (1996), *Magill's Legal Guide* (1999), or *Encyclopedia of the U.S. Supreme Court* (2000). They have been updated as necessary, and all the bibliographies have been updated.

The 256 alphabetically arranged essays range in length from 250 to 3,000 words and focus on the basic concepts and processes our legal system uses rather than the contents of laws and cases. Each begins with a concise definition and places the topic in context by showing its development and significance. Occasional sidebars, tables, and charts simplify some of the information. Longer articles are signed and end with suggested readings.

Five appendixes include a bibliography and an extensive glossary along with contact information (including late 2003 Web sites) for state bar associations, and other legal resources (government agencies, research centers, and so on), and an annotated list of legal assistance organizations. Content is indexed by broad category, court case, and subject.

This is not a do-it-yourself handbook for would-be pro se lawyers. For example, the entry *Criminal records* alludes to expungement but does not tell how to accomplish that, and *Annotated codes* defines what they are but does not walk the reader through accessing that information the way a paralegal's manual would. It is a useful tool for learning how to deal with, for example, the advantages of a nolo contendere plea and spelling out what information is privileged.

Libraries already holding the older sources mentioned above will need to determine whether they require updates. Libraries that already own *Gale Encyclopedia of Everyday Law* (2002) can pass on this unless their clientele needs a simpler source. —*Sally Jane*

West's Encyclopedia of American Law. 13v. 2d. ed. Ed. by Shirelle Phelps. 2004. illus. indexes. Gale, $1,095 (0-7876-6367-0); E-book, contact Gale for pricing (0-7876-9373-1). 349.73.

The new edition of this standard legal reference is a worthy successor to the original. The encyclopedia contains a comprehensive overview of American law, covering historical and current terms, concepts, events, movements, cases, and significant persons. New cases, events, and trends have been thoroughly integrated into existing entries. Some, such as *Absentee voting, Jurisdiction,* and *Terrorism,* have been substantially rewritten, while many others, such as *Abington School District v. Schempp, Abortion,* and *Judge advocate* have new content appended. Omissions from the first edition have been corrected, with new entries for Ralph David Abernathy, Bella Abzug, the *Amistad* mutiny, and the "abuse excuse" as well as for George W. Bush, Tom Ridge, and Kenneth Starr, of recent import. Of the more than 5,000 entries, 2,000 have been revised and 630 are new. Even the photographs have been updated—different photographs are often used, even when article content is the same.

How were several hundred entries added and others lengthened while only one volume was added to the size of the set? The greatest change seems to be a sharp decline in the number of photographs, tables, and charts. Color has also been eliminated. Nonetheless, the set still contains numerous illustrations that enrich the text and help show the effects the legal system has on individuals. Other changes include the use of italics for the definitions that begin each entry on a legal term, making these easy to distinguish, and the addition of further readings to a majority of main entries. Useful features in both editions include "In Focus" essays on controversial issues, time lines for all biographical entries that show important moments in the subject's life as well as important historical events, a dictionary of legal terms, an index of cases, and a general index. An appendix volume has been helpfully renamed *Primary Documents* and contains the text of speeches, legislation, and historic legal documents ranging from the Magna Carta to the Treaty with Sioux Nation. The "Milestones in the Law" features, which have the text of landmark cases, briefs, and related documents, have been gathered into another appendix volume. This beautifully edited encyclopedia is highly recommended for high-school, community college, public, and undergraduate libraries. —*Jan Lewis*

Encyclopedia of Federal Agencies and Commissions. By Kathleen Thompson Hill and Gerald N. Hill. 2004. 504p. bibliog. charts. index. Facts On File, $95 (0-8160-4843-6). 351.73.

The purpose of this encyclopedia is to be a "single source that shows the public how to navigate through the complexities" of the U.S. government. Both authors, who teach U.S. politics and have written several other books on politics and law, have achieved their goal.

The volume's arrangement corresponds to the government's structure, with chapters on "Executive Branch," "Independent Entities and Commissions," "Quasi-official Agencies," "Legislative Branch," and "Judicial Branch and Federal Court System." By far the largest section is devoted to the executive branch. A brief history of the White House is followed by a description of each office (e.g., Office of the Vice President, National Security Council, United States Trade Representative). A discussion of the cabinet is followed by brief histories, descriptions, and contact information for each department and its activities, programs, and services. Organizational charts are included for each department.

The chapters that follow provide the same type of information as found in the executive branch entries. Examples of the 100 independent entities and commissions explored are Amtrak, the Central Intelligence Agency, NASA, and the Smithsonian Institution. Three entries—*Legal Services Corporation, National Institute of Justice,* and *U.S. Institute of Peace*—comprise the section on quasi-official agencies. Congress and the governmental agencies it supervises (e.g., General Accounting Office, Government Printing Office) are covered in the section on the legislative branch. Introduced by a description of the authority and jurisdiction of the federal court system, the section on the judicial branch and federal court system briefly describes the Supreme Court, the U.S. Court of Appeals, and the U.S. District Courts. The last pages of the encyclopedia contain the Constitution of the United States, introduced by a short essay, a brief bibliography, and an index.

Each entry is well written, and the encyclopedia is easy to use. Targeted to grades nine and up, this encyclopedia will be a good addition to high-school, college, and public libraries. —*Kaye Talley*

Empires at War: A Chronological Encyclopedia from Sumer to the Persian Empire. 3v. By Richard A. Gabriel. 2005. 1,136p. illus. index. Greenwood, $225 (0-313-33215-0). 355.

This encyclopedia deals with the sometimes epic wars waged by empires from 4000 B.C.E to 1453 C.E. Chapter length ranges from around 13 to more than 60 pages, with the longest belonging to the Persian Empire's wars with Alexander the Great and the Carthaginian Empire's wars with Rome. Other chapters cover, for example, the Vikings, the Arab Conquest, and lesser-known empires such as the Mitanni. Gabriel, a former professor at the U.S. Army War College, has written other books on warfare for Greenwood, including *The Great Battles of Antiquity* (1994) and *The Military History of Ancient Israel* (1993).

The work begins with an introductory chapter that sets the stage and concludes with a chapter that summarizes the evolution from medieval to modern warfare. The 29 intervening chapters are in chronological order, by beginning date of the empire. Each chapter has sections on background, specific battles and armies, commanders, and "Lessons of War," encompassing strategy and tactics. Each chapter ends with a further reading list, but there is no comprehensive bibliography at the end of the work. Coverage is global and includes non-Western empires such as those of Japan and Korea. There is also a chapter dedicated to three empires from the Americas and their warfare: the Aztecs, the Incas, and the Mayas. Each volume contains more than 100 maps, illustrations, and figures, though some of the maps are small and somewhat difficult to read.

A glossary would have been helpful for some of the terms included. So would separate name and place indexes and perhaps a brief chronology or time line. Nonetheless, this is a very comprehensive work that delivers the content. Many reference works deal with battles of antiquity or with the great empires of the world, but this encyclopedia manages to combine these concepts with ease and makes for captivating reading. Recommended for anyone interested in the history of warfare and for undergraduate and large public libraries. —*Susanna Eng*

Encyclopedia of Wars. 3v. By Charles Phillips and Alan Axelrod. 2005. 1,502p. illus. index. Facts On File, $300 (0-8160-2851-6). 355.

Targeted especially to students and teachers of history, this set on wars will also be of interest to the general public. The work focuses on details of the fighting as well as on the social and political contexts of the time of each war. Arranged alphabetically (from *Abbasid Revolution* to *Zulu War*), the more than 1,800 entries cover the rather obscure to the more well-known wars from classical times to present day, circa 8,000 B.C.E. (*Jericho, Fall of*) to 2003 (*United States–Iraq War*).

Each entry includes a list of belligerents, statement of the causes, date of the declaration of war, numbers (where known) of those bearing arms and the casualties suffered, a summary of the outcome, and names and dates of treaties or documents (if any) ending the conflict. A narrative discussion capsulizes the social and political context of the period, the major battles and events of the war, and the wider significance of the conflict. The discussions range from half a page for the Afghan revolt of 699–701 to 40-plus pages for World War II, with slight emphasis given to North American conflicts. Cross-references point to related entries and from common alternate names of conflicts. Suggestions for further reading close out the entries.

Volume 1 includes a list of entries and a list of the more than 60 maps that are scattered throughout the set, and volume 3 includes a chronological listing of wars, a selected bibliography, and an index. Treatment of larger conflicts is segmented. For example, World War II is discussed in a series of entries, including *Historical background, Outbreak and early German conquests, Africa and the Mediterranean, Atlantic front, China-Burma-India Theater, Greece and the Balkans, Italian front, Pacific, Russian front,* and *Western front.*

The authors, history professors who worked on this encyclopedia for 10 years, have produced a very readable and apparently well-researched book that both scholars and history buffs will enjoy. As with other Facts On File reference books, this set is easy to use and well designed. This would be an excellent purchase for high-school, college, and public libraries. —*Kaye Talley*

On the Trail of the Buffalo Soldier 2: New and Revised Biographies of African Americans in the U.S. Army, 1866–1917. By Irene Schubert and Frank N. Schubert. 2004. 502p. index. Scarecrow/SR, $150 (0-8420-5079-5). 355.

The term *buffalo soldiers* refers to the four African American army regiments that served from the Civil War through World War I. The authors have compiled information from military records, books, military and civilian periodicals, letters, journals, family records, and Internet databases on every soldier who served in these regiments. This second edition includes all the information from the first edition (1995) plus new material that has been contributed by readers or gathered from new publications. There are more than 3,000 entries.

Entries are in alphabetical order by last name (spellings are standardized, but variations are used within entries and are cross-referenced), followed by last rank attained and military organization. This is followed by biographical data with sources and dates. Material that appeared in the first edition is marked. Entries vary in length. Most are one or two lines, many are a paragraph, and a few are one or two pages long.

A good bibliography is divided into type of source: books, articles, government documents, unpublished manuscripts and documents, military records, and electronic sources. There are two appendixes: "Battles Involving Buffalo Soldiers and Western Indians, 1867–1890," and "Buffalo Soldier Recipients of the Certificate of Merit, 1881–1914." The index is rather complicated, using several typefaces to distinguish kinds of entries. A separate index for geographical names and features might have been helpful to the user.

This book is recommended for genealogical collections, African American history collections, and other specialized collections in public and academic libraries. —*Robin Hoelle*

The Victorians at War, 1815–1914: An Encyclopedia of British Military History. 2004. 405p. illus. index. ABC-CLIO, $95 (1-57607-925-2); e-book, $100 (1-57607-926-0). 355.

This volume using recent research offers a summary of the wars, campaigns, battles, and leaders of the British army in the British Imperial Century. The 350 entries, arranged *A–Z* with cross-references and bibliographic references, center on events, people, and places. The introduction describes the years of conflict, the makeup of the army, the imperialist drive, the use of the army to control the colonial empire, and the ideology for war.

Numerous maps illustrate the different theaters of war, but there are no photographs or drawings to depict persons. The volume concludes with several appendixes: a chronology, a list of British army commanders in chief, chiefs of general staff and chiefs of the imperial general staff, a list of Indian army commanders in chief; and a note on currency. A bibliography of selected articles and books and an index complete the volume.

Besides covering specific individuals, such as Field Marshall Kitchener, or conflicts, such as the Afghan wars, the volume includes a variety of peripheral topics, such as *Military music; Photographers, war;* and *Women and the army.* A series of entries on *Military medicine, British army* provides insight into nineteenth-century standards for hospitals, sanitation, and more. Series on *Officers, British army* and *Officers, Indian army* make it easy to compare such topics as pay, social background, training, and retirement.

This is a very easy-to-use and highly readable book. It could supplement history collections as well as strengthen the reference sections on the Victorian era and on the British Empire. It would be a good purchase for academic and large public library collections, satisfying both the informal researcher and the serious student. —*Patricia Hogan*

Weapons of Mass Destruction: An Encyclopedia of Worldwide Policy, Technology, and History. 2v. Ed. by Eric A. Croddy and James J. Wirtz. 2004. 601p. illus. index. ABC-CLIO, $185 (1-85109-490-3); e-book, $200 (1-85109-495-4). 358.

According to the U.S. Code Title 50, "War and National Defense," the term *weapon of mass destruction* means "any weapon or device that is intended, or has the capability, to cause death or serious bodily injury to a significant number of people through the release, dissemination, or impact of toxic or poisonous chemicals or their precursors; a disease organism; radiation or radioactivity." Eighty-two contributors have amassed an impressive amount of historical and current information pertaining to weapons of mass destruction (WMD) in these volumes. Volume 1 covers "Chemical and Biological Weapons," and volume 2 covers "Nuclear Weapons." Each volume has its own bibliography, but the index in each volume is cumulative. Illustrations are good, though limited in number.

More than 500 alphabetically arranged and signed articles cover all aspects of WMD from definitions of terms such as *Kiloton, Novichok,* and *Payload* to such topics as *Korean War, National Strategic Target List,* and *Pugwash Conferences.* The articles are well written for general adult readers. Of particular interest are the excerpts from various treaties that discuss WMD or related destructive activities. Volume 1 is extremely detailed in describing all of the chemical and biological substances that could be part of WMD and what the consequences would be if each substance were used.

No other reference source covers such a wide array of topics related to WMD. It will dispel many myths but will also draw attention to the lethal consequences of WMD. In today's world climate of unrest and terrorism, this is a highly recommended resource that will be of great interest to public and academic libraries. —*H. Robert Malinowsky*

Encyclopedia of Social Welfare History in North America. Ed. by John M. Herrick and Paul H. Stuart. 2005. 534p. index. Sage, $150 (0-7619-2584-8). 361.97.

Here is a reference work that provides readers with information about the history of social welfare in the U.S., Canada, and Mexico. According to the preface, the purpose of the encyclopedia is to give users basic information about how these three nations have dealt with social welfare issues, some shared and some unique, and "to describe important events, developments, and the lives and work of some key contributors." *Social welfare* is defined broadly to include areas of education, informal mutual assistance, development of the profession of social work, and both voluntary charitable activities and government-supported public welfare. Editors Herrick and Stuart are social work professors at Michigan State University and the University of Alabama, respectively; they are joined by more than 160 contributors.

The 180 entries generally vary in length from one to just over four pages and include suggestions for further reading and, in some cases, collections of primary materials and "Current Comment," which consists of lists of documents produced during the time described in the entry. Appendixes at the end of the book include a good chronology of social welfare events in each country, followed by a master bibliography and a well-constructed index with cross-references.

This encyclopedia has information in common with another recently published work, ABC-CLIO's *Poverty in the United States: An Encyclopedia of History, Politics and Policy* (2004). There is also some overlap with another Sage publication, *The Handbook of Social Welfare Management* (2000). One unique strength of the title under review is its multinational perspective. Many topics, among them *Food assistance policy, Philanthropy,* and *Social Security,* are treated in separate entries for each country, making it easy to both focus on a particular country's social welfare history and draw comparisons. The "Reader's Guide" is also helpful in identifying entries associated with a specific nation, since it groups entries under *Canada, Mexico,* and *United States,* among other categories.

Although the quality of this encyclopedia is generally quite good, the issue for libraries is whether they can continue to justify the purchase of very specialized print encyclopedias. Recommended for those academic and public library collections where there is a specific need for basic information related to the history of social welfare in North America. —*Diana Shonrock*

Philanthropy in America: A Comprehensive Historical Encyclopedia. 3v. Ed. by Dwight F. Burlingame. 2004. 886p. illus. index. ABC-CLIO, $285 (1-57607-860-4); E-book, $310 (1-57607- 861-2). 361.7.

The editor, who is the associate executive director at Indiana University's Center on Philanthropy, gives in his preface what the essence of American philanthropy is: "very much a story about the interests of others as well as self-interests." This work shows the tension between interests of others and self-interests in donating money to influence society. Its 250 entries in volumes 1 and 2, the work of scholars in various disciplines, cover the people, events, organizations, and ideas of American philanthropy and are supplemented by the 75 diverse primary source documents that comprise volume 3.

The A–Z entries include a number of biographical profiles for, among others, Jane Addams, Robert Brookings, Cesar Chavez, Dorothy Day, Henry Ford, and Bill Gates. Concepts and ideas are covered as well in entries such as *E-philanthropy, Fundraising, Grantmaking, Reciprocity,* and *Social capital.* Major philanthropic organizations are also discussed, with information on their missions and practices. All entries are signed and have bibliographies, which can be used for further references. The subtitle denotes that the encyclopedia is historical, and it does provide a historical context to philanthropy with discussions of traditions around the world and how American philanthropy has developed from these roots. For example, *Law of charity* talks about the institutionalization of charity beginning in fourteenth-century England and how English systems were adopted by the American colonies.

The entries are supported by a glossary of philanthropic terms and a time line of key events. The documents in volume 3 are chronologically arranged from selections from Aristotle' writings to the summary of a position on a 2003 Supreme Court case involving the regulation of charitable solicitation.

This book is an important addition to the growing field of philanthropic studies and fills a gap in the area. It complements *Notable American Philanthropists: Biographies of Giving and Volunteering* (Oryx, 2002) and is recommended for academic and large public library collections. —*Jerry Carbone*

Encyclopedia of Homelessness. 2v. Ed. by David Levinson. 2004. 886p. appendixes. bibliogs. illus. index. Sage, $295 (0-7619-2751-4). 362.5.

Although there is nothing new about homelessness, the coverage of the topic in this encyclopedia is indeed new. According to the introduction, its goal is to "summarize our knowledge of homelessness including describing the patterns of homelessness, focusing on the recent situation in America and a sampling of homelessness around the world." Most of the contributors are affiliated with either academic institutions or social service agencies, and major researchers in the field of homeless studies, including Ellen Bassuk, cofounder of the National Center on Family Homelessness; Martha Burt, director of the Social Services Program at the Urban Institute; and Gretchen Noll, deputy director of programs at the National Network for Youth, make up the editorial board.

The alphabetically arranged entries include articles about homelessness in eight major U.S. cities and 30 cities and nations around the world. As outlined in the "Reader's Guide" in volume 1, causes of homelessness, historical aspects, housing, policy, health and lifestyle issues, and service systems are among the broad topics covered. Examples of entry headings include *Abeyance theory, Child care, Gentrification, HIV and AIDS, Images of homelessness in contemporary documentary film, Low-income housing, Marginality, Panhandling, Safe havens,* and *Salvation Army.* Ranging in length from one to four pages, entries provide cross-references and lists of further reading. Additional resources are offered in the several appendixes, which take up most of volume 2: a bibliography of autobiographical and fictional accounts of homelessness, a filmography on homelessness, a directory of street newspapers, 23 documents related to the history of homelessness, and a "Master Bibliography." The index, more than 50 pages long, includes extensive cross-references.

There have been a variety of publications on homelessness in the last five years, but no other up-to-date publication is as comprehensive as this encyclopedia. The price tag may be too steep for some, but the set is highly recommended for libraries where homelessness is an issue, for all undergraduate collections as an awareness tool, and as a great broad introduction to the issues of homelessness in today's societies. —*Diana Shonrock*

Encyclopedia of Rape. Ed. by Merril D. Smith. 2004. 336p. index. Greenwood, $75 (0-313-32922-2). 362.883.

Rape has been considered a crime and significant cultural event since ancient times, cited as far back as the Code of Hammurabi. It is part of mythology, the Bible, and current ethnic wars. In many cultures even today, the aggrieved party is the father or husband rather than the victimized woman, but its victims can be men as well as women and children. It is, as the introduction to this volume states, "much more than the actual physical act."

For this volume, 79 contributors drawn mainly from academia have produced 186 entries, all with suggested readings, that examine the topic of rape from as many aspects as possible: legal, historical, and social, to name a few. Most of the entries are a page in length or more and have a decided American focus, though entries such as *Comfort women, Genocide,* and *War crimes* approach the issue from a more global perspective. There are several biographical entries for leading feminists, legal scholars, and rape victims, such as the *Central Park jogger.* Each of the current date-rape drugs also has an entry.

The volume begins with a "Chronology of Selected Rape-Related Events," an alphabetical list of all the entries, and a topical list of entries. Extensive cross-references and an index help with access. A "Resource Guide" lists important books, Web sites, organizations, and films. The entries themselves maintain an informative and dispassionate tone despite the highly charged nature of the information provided. This timely and useful—though disturbing—volume should have a place in all libraries concerned with women's and criminal justice issues. —*Danise Hoover*

Encyclopedia of Law Enforcement. 3v. Ed. by Larry E. Sullivan. 2005. 1,410p. index. Sage, $295 (0-7619-2649-6). 363.2.

Edited by the chief librarian and associate dean at John Jay College of Criminal Justice and professor of criminal justice at City University of New York, *Encyclopedia of Law Enforcement* provides a thorough overview of law enforcement in the U.S. and around the world. According to the introduction, the public's view of policing is significantly influenced by the popular media, which oversimplifies police work; therefore, there is "an urgent need for providing students and the general interested public balanced information on what law enforcement does, with all of its ramifications." The encyclopedia's aim "is to survey the entire field of law enforcement and to be as comprehensive as possible."

The more than 550 alphabetically arranged entries were written by 300 law enforcement scholars and practitioners. Entries are signed and include a list of recommended readings and cross-references. The work is well organized into three volumes. Volume 1 is dedicated to issues related to law enforcement at the state and local levels, and volume 2 focuses on the federal level. Volume 3 examines policing in the international arena, covering approximately 160 countries. As indicated in the topical "Reader's Guide," the text covers an extensive range of broad subject areas, including "Civilian/Private Involvement," "Federal Agencies/Organizations," "International Law Enforcement," "Personnel Issues," and "Police Procedures." Examples of specific entries include *Affirmative action in policing, AMBER Alert, America's Most Wanted, Federal Bureau of Investigation,* and *INTERPOL.* Controversial issues are not ignored, and there are entries on topics such as *Civil rights violations by police; Police misconduct;* and *Profiling, racial.* In addition to the main text, each volume has its own extensive bibliography of scholarly, news, government, and Internet sources. An appendix in volume 2 contains articles on policing issues for 1989–2003 from the *Law Enforcement News.* Each volume has a comprehensive "Master Index."

The *Encyclopedia of Law Enforcement* is a valuable contribution to the field of criminal justice. It is accessible to students and general readers and should be particularly useful for correcting misconceptions about police work. It is recommended for academic and large public libraries. —*Michelle Hendley*

Exploring Gun Use in America. 4v. 2004. 576p. illus. index. Greenwood, $160 (0-313-32897-8). 363.33.

Guns are a hot topic today and one for which statistics get used and abused freely by debaters on both sides of the gun-control issue. This excellent set should find a home in every school and public library. It is unbiased, with a wealth of statistics on almost every page.

Each volume looks at a particular aspect of guns. The first volume, on the Second Amendment, covers the background of the amendment from British law through the Revolution and the writing of the amendment. It also examines militia in America; the National Rifle Association; gun-control legislation; the Bureau of Alcohol, Tobacco, and Firearms; and specific court cases. Volume 2 examines the firearms industry. Volume 3 is titled *Children and Guns.* Some of the issues tackled here are hunting, accidents, safety, gangs, and school violence. The last volume discusses public opinion, with a particular focus on political and legislative activity.

Many excellent photographs support the text. Although there are some charts and graphs, most of the statistical information is contained in the text itself. Boxes labeled "Fast Fact" are liberally placed throughout the volumes. Each volume has a bibliography, a glossary, a list of Internet sites, and an index to the set.

Many young adults are fascinated by guns and have strong convictions about the gun issue. This set will help them find information to use for classroom debates and persuasive essays. The text is concise and readable, and the authors have been fair in their treatment of all the arguments for and against guns. Because there are no footnotes, it may be difficult to find the exact sources for the numbers used in the text. A separate section with charts and graphs would be important to include in future editions, especially since interpretation of charts and graphs is a skill in most state standards. Libraries will want a circulating copy of this set as well as a reference copy. —*Robin Hoelle*

The American Dictionary of Criminal Justice: Key Terms and Major Court Cases. 3d ed. By Dean John Champion. 2005. 513p. indexes. Scarecrow, $57.95 (0-8108-5406-6). 364.

Written by a criminal justice professor at Texas A&M University, this resource defines or identifies key terms and persons in criminology and the justice system and summarizes the most recent and pertinent U.S. Supreme Court cases. The goal is to bring together in an updated single work information that undergraduate students need in their research. The publisher notes that 5,000 terms, concepts, and names are included in this edition as well as 125 new Court cases.

The first part of the volume is the "Dictionary of Terms." Entries are short, and the writing is clear and succinct. Included are a number of separate entries on gangs and juveniles and many national justice organizations. *Community policing* is defined, and *Zylon* protective armor is identified along with the modern technology of *Geographical profiling* and the nonlethal *TASER* weapon. Individuals ranging from criminologists like Eleanor and Sheldon Glueck to criminals like Unabomber Theodore Kaczynski are included. It is not clear why some non-American terms, such as *Cut-purse,* are defined.

The second part of the work, "U.S. Supreme Court Cases," covers mainly the past few decades in an *A–Z* format by case name. The author's objectivity when writing on controversial cases is notable. Cross-references from entries in this section to entries in the dictionary enable users to move easily to short definitions of pertinent terms.

The helpful indexes and appendixes include an index of cases by topic, a list of doctoral programs in criminal justice, a topical listing of Internet sites, and addresses of probation and parole agencies.

This is a fine, current, reasonably priced resource, accomplishing what it sets out to do. Although it will be especially useful in academic libraries, public libraries needing a one-volume work on criminal justice will also find it valuable. —*Arthur S. Meyers*

Crime and Punishment in America Reference Library. 4v. Ed. by Sarah Hermsen. 2004. illus. indexes. UXL, $215 (0-7876-9162-3). 364.973.

Many middle- and senior-high-school students are intrigued by true crime stories, and this set puts lots of useful introductory information in their hands. The modern criminal justice system of the U.S. is traced in three parts (four volumes plus a separate softbound index). The longest and most comprehensive section, *Almanac,* is 25 chapters in two volumes. It covers topics such as the development of the American justice system; types of crime (violent, property, white collar, organized, environmental); the court system; juvenile and military justice; and the effects of race and ethnicity.

Volume 3, *Biography,* contains alphabetically arranged profiles of 26 individuals. Deciding which authors to include is always a tough call, but this volume is disappointing. Although it covers major figures such as J. Edgar Hoover, Timothy McVeigh, Ernest Miranda, and Earl Warren, it also includes authors Charles Dickens and Truman Capote and reformer Jane Addams, who could have been dropped in favor of people more closely connected to the set's main themes.

Volume 4, *Primary Sources,* has excerpts from 18 interviews and documents, thematically and somewhat chronologically arranged. Examples include the Magna Carta, "The Plea of Clarence Darrow," the RICO Act, and "The Al-Qaeda Training Manual." In addition to the excerpts, entries are supplemented by helpful material such as definitions of words used.

The set is up-to-date, with information on the AMBER Alert and the Kobe Bryant, Michael Jackson, and Scott Peterson cases. References are listed in each chapter and at the end of each volume under "Where to Learn More" (many of the cited books are from 2004). Numerous photos and political cartoons illustrate the text, but some will add little to a reader's understanding (for example, inmates making whips in a description of Madison and the Constitution). Indexing is adequate; Cherry Hill Prison is described in *Primary Sources* but not indexed there.

Nothing quite comparable exists for middle- and senior-high-school libraries. This will be used by students for research and personal interest and by teachers for background information and classroom activities. —*Susan Gooden*

Encyclopedia of Criminology. 3v. Ed. by Richard A. Wright and J. Mitchell Miller. 2004. 1,900p. index. Routledge, $495 (1-57958-387-3). 364.

Routledge's encyclopedic offering for the discipline of criminology is a worthy addition to the field. Through more than 525 signed essays written by scholars and experts, the encyclopedia presents the latest research in this multidisciplinary field as well as traditional concepts, theories, and issues. It moves beyond the theoretical to address the practicalities of the criminal justice system: law enforcement, the courts, and corrections. All entries include a list of "References and Further Reading" as well as cross-references to related entries. Alphabetical and thematic lists of entries are provided as well as a comprehensive index. The thematic list identifies areas of emphasis: correlates of criminal behavior such as age, gender, and race; concepts in criminal law such as double jeopardy and self-defense; cross-cultural and global systems and trends; history of criminology and of legal and criminal justice traditions (e.g., *Ecclesiastical law and justice, Hindu legal traditions*); the justice system (*Arrest, Parole*); ways of measuring crime (*Recidivism, Uniform Crime Reports*); professional issues (*Corrections: careers; Publications in criminal law*); prominent figures; theories and types of criminal behavior; and victimization.

Encyclopedia of Criminology is the third multivolume encyclopedic work on this topic to be published in the last three years. Macmillan's *Encyclopedia of Crime and Justice* (2001) was quickly followed by Sage's *Encyclopedia of Crime and Punishment* (2002). The Sage work concentrates on the field of criminal justice, while criminology is the focus of the other two encyclopedias. While the Macmillan and Routledge sets have many similarities, the *Encyclopedia of Criminology* is unique in its biographic coverage of figures ranging from Freda Adler to J. Edgar Hoover. It also provides greater international and comparative coverage, with nearly 30 essays on crime and justice in specific countries or regions in addition to essays on topics such as international crime statistics and trends and discussion of the international context in entries such as *Appeals and post-trial motions* and *Bail: right to.* Legal traditions, measures of crime, and theories of criminal behavior each receive significantly more attention in *Encyclopedia of Criminology,* which has twice as many entries as the Macmillan work. On the other hand, entries in the Routledge work are generally of slightly shorter length and have fewer references than comparable entries in the Macmillan title.

Recommended for high-school, college and university, and public libraries, particularly those that do not have the Macmillan encyclopedia. —*Jan Lewis*

Encyclopedia of White-Collar and Corporate Crime. 2v. Ed. by Lawrence M. Salinger. 2004. 974p. illus. index. Sage, $295 (0-7619-3004-3). 364.16.

Arthur Andersen, WorldCom, Ken Lay, and Martha Stewart are just a few of the names tarnished by their involvement with white-collar crimes. Each is discussed in this work, which covers events from the 1863 passage of the False Claims Act to the indictments and trials of public figures in 2004. Along the way, it addresses white-collar crimes such as *Bribery, Check kiting,* and *Embezzlement* as well as harm caused by allegedly unethical or immoral behavior that has not been punished through the penal system (the *Challenger* disaster, the sale of the antinausea drug Bendectin, racial discrimination). Fraud of various types, from *Counterfeiting* to *Sweepstakes fraud,* constitutes a large number of the entries.

The time line included in volume 1 helps provide some historical perspective even though it does not reflect the majority of entries in the set. For example, six entries focus on political scandals, yet only one (AB-SCAM) is listed on the time line. Numerous federal statutes are included on the time line; entries helpfully place their passage in historical context and lead the reader to other entries discussing the events or abuses that led to their enactment. For example, the entry *Computer Fraud and Abuse Act* cross-references *Computer hacking, Cyberstalking,* and *Wire fraud.*

Written predominantly by active or retired academicians, the signed entries cover more than 500 individuals, corporations, places, events, crimes, and scandals. Entries on 35 countries and regions incorporate an international component into a work that is otherwise mainly centered on the U.S. Varying from a column to more than four pages in length, entries conclude with brief bibliographies, which contain references to Web sites and popular publications in addition to books and journal articles. This focus fits well with the intended audience of high-school, college, and public libraries. Appendixes include a "Resource Guide" listing selected materials for more information, a glossary, and summaries of several key laws.

This source complements Sage's more scholarly *Encyclopedia of Crime and Punishment* (2002), with very little overlap. In addition to criminal justice students, it will be of interest to students researching political science, popular culture, legal, and occupational safety issues. —*Jan Lewis*

Encyclopedia of Prisons & Correctional Facilities. 2v. Ed. by Mary Bosworth. 2005. 1,334p. illus. index. Sage, $295 (0-7619-2731-X). 365.

This encyclopedia features 400 alphabetically arranged, signed entries on the history and current state of imprisonment in America. The varied topics include prison architecture (*Cottage system, Supermax prisons*); life in prison (*Gangs, Islam in prison, Lawyer's visits*); security (*Electronic monitoring, Minimum security*); prisoner characteristics (*Drug offenders, Mothers in prison, Native American prisoners*); and technicalities of punishment (*Habeas corpus, Three-strikes legislation*), among others. Although there are entries for some other English-speaking countries, such as Australia and Canada, emphasis is on the U.S. In the introduction, the editor remarks that the high incarceration rate in the U.S. is now an indelible part of the country's collective cultural imagination.

Entries vary in length but are on average two and a half pages long, end with a list of further readings, and offer applicable cross-references and legal case citations. Text is supplemented with 23 interesting sidebars written by current prisoners and a handful of black-and-white photographs. The entries are preceded by a chronology that lists key legal cases, publications, and prison openings, beginning with the sixteenth century. There are both alphabetical and subject listings of entries. An appendix profiles every federal prison in the U.S., including location, contact information, capacity, visiting times, and recreational facilities. A general index listing people and concepts within main entries and an extensive bibliography and legal case list round out the work.

Current coverage of this topic is much needed. Similar in scope is the now-outdated *Encyclopedia of American Prisons* (Garland, 1996), which features 160 signed entries written in a slightly less-appealing textbook style. It cites the original 1966 American Correctional Association's *Manual of Correctional Standards,* for example, compared to the revised fourth edition from 2002 cited in the *Encyclopedia of Prisons & Correctional Facilities.* The current *Encyclopedia* lacks coverage at the state level found in the also dated and briefer *Dictionary of American Penology* (Greenwood, 1996), but it is more scholarly than the Facts On File *Encyclopedia of American Prisons,* from 2003, which lacks in-depth bibliographies. Recommended for larger reference collections and libraries supporting criminal justice programs. —*Susan Gardner*

Education, Commerce, Custom

Catholic Schools in the United States: An Encyclopedia. 2v. Ed. by Thomas C. Hunt and others. 2004. 793p. illus. index. Greenwood, $175 (1-57356-532-6). 371.071.

While other books have dealt exclusively with the history of Catholic schools or list the institutions, this set provides encyclopedic coverage, including mission and identity, types of institutions, major figures and associations, curriculum, administration, governance, finance, legal questions, and more. Although the encyclopedia is strong on history, it also covers current issues, such as the No Child Left Behind Act.

Preceding the *A–Z* portion are two lists of entries, one alphabetical and the other topical. A historical overview of Catholic schools in the U.S. follows, mentioning some of the main movements and controversies, such as attendance by non-Catholics. The second volume has a lengthy bibliography.

The 304 alphabetical, signed entries range in length from half a page to nine pages. Each concludes with cross-references and a bibliography. Occasional black-and-white photographs (usually from university collections) illustrate people and events. Coverage seems somewhat uneven. For instance, the entry on the Alliance for Catholic Education (a teacher-preparation organization at the University of Notre Dame, which one of the set's editors directs) is several pages in length. On the other hand, there are no entries on school librarianship or associated organizations, such as the Catholic Library Association or its publication *Catholic World*. There are no separate entries for teaching orders; instead, they are described as a whole in *Religious orders of men* and *Religious orders of women*. The entry *Diversity* focuses just on ethnic minorities, ignoring students with special needs.

Writing appears to reflect mainstream U.S. Catholic thought. Even though the work is not exhaustive or entirely well balanced, it does provide valuable one-stop information on many aspects of K–12 Catholic education as it is practiced. Recommended for academic and large public libraries. —*Lesley Farmer*

Sports Market Place Directory, 2004. Ed. by Richard Gottlieb. 2004. 1,745p. indexes. Grey House, paper, $225 (1-59237-048-9). 381.

Sports Market Place Directory has a 24-year history. Grey House is the new publisher and has produced an excellent edition. Ten chapters track 103 sports, from soccer and football to judo and yachting. Chapters include "Single Sports," "Multi Sports," "Media," "Sports Sponsors," "Agencies," "Events, Meetings, and Trade Shows," "Professional Services," "College Sports," "Manufacturers and Retailers," and "Facilities." Chapters, arranged by topic, begin with an alphabetical index of organizations, teams, or businesses. Entries include address, phone, fax, Web site, e-mail, key personnel, and detailed corporate data on more than 13,000 organizations and businesses.

The "Single Sports" and "Multi Sports" chapters provide an overview of sports teams and organizations from professional and Olympic organizations to youth clubs and Halls of Fame. The "Events, Meetings, and Trade Shows" chapter provides event dates for 2004–2005. In addition to mainstream events like the U.S. Open and the World Cup are smaller events like Skateboarding's Armageddon Cup, the Air Force Marathon, and the San Angelo Stock Show and Rodeo. "Professional Services" lists sports medicine specialists, agents, attorneys, recruiting services, and more. In "College Sports," 1,584 college associations, athletic conferences, NAIA, and NCAA organizations are described, along with colleges and universities that offer degrees in sports management. Individuals needing to purchase table-tennis balls, lacrosse goal cages, or in-line skates can browse the "Manufacturers and Retailers" chapter alphabetically, by sport, or using the brand-name index for more than 1,700 products and services. On a larger scale, the "Facilities" chapter contains the seating capacity and tenants (sports teams) of hundreds of stadiums, arenas, and tracks. Companies that support sports facilities, ranging from security, vending and concession, sound and video, ticket services, and architecture and design, are included.

Besides a cumulative entry index, Grey House offers a 280-page "Executive Index," a geographic index, and individual chapter indexes. The directory, which is also available in CD-ROM and online versions, is highly recommended for public libraries and academic libraries with sports management programs or a strong interest in athletics. —*Sue Polanka*

Encyclopedia of World Trade: From Ancient Times to the Present. Ed. by Cynthia Clark Northrup. 2005. 1,552p. illus. indexes. Sharpe, $425 (0-7656-8058-0). 382.03.

This alphabetically arranged encyclopedia is designed as a reference tool for those wishing to learn about trade in history and its impact on social and political issues in given periods. Treating the subject across time, from the ancient world to the present, the 450 topical, biographical, and broad-issue essays cover a variety of topics, from specific countries, regions, and continents to trade organizations, such as the Hanseatic League and World Trade Organization, to biographical entries for those who have influenced world commerce, such as Christopher Columbus and Peter the Great. Historical episodes that have altered the course of trade (for example, the fall of the Roman Empire) are included as well, along with lengthier essays on general topics that correlate with changing trade relations, such as *Religion* and *Warfare*.

Entries range in length from several columns to 10 pages, with areas of broader reach and applicability receiving appropriately more coverage. Each entry begins with a grey-boxed definition of the term under scrutiny and is followed by a detailed examination. The prose, written by numerous subject experts, most with college or university affiliations, is generally clear but dry. Each entry ends with a list of cross-references, and many also include short print bibliographies. The many black-and-white photographs, period reproductions, and maps are well placed and ably serve to extend the text. Volume 1 lists the contents for the entire set, as well as a "Topic Finder," which serves as a rough subject access. It also contains a list of contributors, with affiliations, and the list of maps for the entire set. All volumes contain full set indexes, and volume 4 has a comprehensive bibliography; a chronology; general, biographical, and geographical indexes; and an extensive set of primary source documents.

The set does a creditable job of addressing the most salient issues in the history of world trade and serves to highlight its importance. It is a sound addition to academic and large public library collections. —*Ann Welton*

Encyclopedia of Recorded Sound. 2v. 2d ed. Ed. by Frank Hoffmann. 2004. 1,283p. illus. index. Routledge, $275 (0-415-93835-X). 384.

This second edition is a revision of the *Encyclopedia of Recorded Sound in the United States* (1993), edited by Guy A. Marco and published by Garland. The new editor, who is also a librarian, writes in the introduction that 60 percent of the more than 3,500 entries are new, and all old entries have been revised (although some of the entries examined for this review are identical in both editions). Emphasis in the first edition was recorded sound before World War II, but in the second edition the chronological range has been extended, although focus is still on the U.S. There is information from the 1980s and 1990s, such as the merger of AOL and Time Warner. However, entries for some artists, among them Van Cliburn, Placido Domingo, and Michael Jackson, do not include current information.

Illustrations, mostly photographs of old record labels, have been added. There are some historic photos of people, including one of Béla Bartók recording folk songs in Transylvania, as well as current photos, such as one of an IPOD, accompanying the MP3 entry. Entries for record labels, performers, films, technical terms, and so on are short, but there are multiple-page entries for *Columbia (label), Disc,* and *Opera recordings,* among others. *Pseudonyms* offers a unique list of pseudonyms of recording artists. *Sound recording periodicals* lists more than 800 journals and magazines.

The second volume ends with a list of contributors and their affiliations, extensive endnotes, and an index. This is a comprehensive work on a subject that has not been covered in other reference sources. Although the price has increased from $125 to $275, academic and large public libraries with an interest in the recording industry should consider purchase. —*Christine Bulson*

Encyclopedia of Television. 4v. 2d. ed. Ed. by Horace Newcomb. 2004. 2,600p. illus. index. Routledge, $595 (1-57958-394-6). 384.55.

When the first edition of this encyclopedia was published in 1997, it was greeted by highly favorable reviews. Now, only seven years later, the second edition, again published under the auspices of the Museum of Broadcast Communications and continuing under the editorship of Newcomb, a professor at the University of Georgia, offers a significant amount of new material as well as substantial revision and updating. Providing both historical coverage and contemporary perspectives, the encyclopedia encompasses a broad spectrum of issues and topics related to the television industry.

Expanded to four volumes from the original three, this edition contains more than 1,160 entries, almost 180 of which are new. In addition, the editor indicates that approximately 500 articles have been updated and more than half of the 750 black-and-white photographs were not in the previous edition. Ranging in length from 1,000 to 7,000 words, entries are signed and include bibliographical references. The impact of technological advances on broadcasting is reflected by new articles such as *Broadband, Digital video recorder,* and *Streaming video,* while the rising influence of cable television is evidenced by the addition of more entries on specific cable networks, such as Animal Planet, Bravo, and Lifetime. Although the primary emphasis continues to be on television in major English-speaking countries, international coverage has been expanded by the inclusion of articles on countries such as Cuba, Hungary, and Turkey. Many programs overlooked by the previous edition have been added, including *Alfred Hitchcock Presents, Jeopardy!* and *20/20,* as have a number of programs introduced during the last decade, such as *Ellen, The Sopranos,* and *Survivor.* Among the individuals added are Katie Couric, Michael Landon, and Regis Philbin. Underscoring the significant role that television plays in our perceptions of political and historical events are new articles like *2000 presidential election coverage* and *Princess Diana: Death and funeral coverage.* Although information on television coverage of the terrorist attacks on September 11, 2001, and the subsequent war in Iraq has been added to several articles, separate entries offering more in-depth treatment of these two events would have been preferable.

Volume 4 includes a section identifying the more than 300 contributors and an index to the set, which, unfortunately, cites only page numbers and not volume numbers. An alphabetical list of all the articles in the encyclopedia appears at the beginning of each volume, but the set would benefit from a classified table of contents. More problematic is the issue of inconsistent currency. For instance, the articles on *Frazier* and *Friends* are both new, but while the *Friends* entry indicates that the series ended in May 2004, the article on *Frazier,* which ended at the same time, does not reflect the series' conclusion.

Scholarly but accessible, this excellent encyclopedia is the most comprehensive and up-to-date compendium on television broadcasting. Most academic and large public libraries will want to add this new edition because of its significantly expanded content. Moreover, it is essential for any library that supports a journalism program. Libraries that do not own the first edition and cannot afford to purchase this one can access the articles from the earlier version through the museum's Web site [http://www.museum.tv/archives/etv/index.html]. —*Marie Ellis*

Movieland Directory: Nearly 30,000 Addresses of Celebrity Homes, Film Locations, and Historical Sites in the Los Angeles Area, 1900–Present. By E. J. Fleming. 2004. 522p. McFarland, $75 (0-7864-1863-X). 384.

In 1903 Hollywood was a quiet, newly incorporated village where Sunday Sabbath was strictly observed, and gambling and alcohol were prohibited. The vast surrounding area, filled with canyons, mountain lions, and bears, was hardly habitable. All of that quickly changed in 1910 with the annexation of Hollywood to Los Angeles. By the end of 1913, Centaur Film Company had relocated to the West Coast. Samuel Goldwyn and Cecil B. DeMille settled in, and the making of the first Hollywood movie, *Squaw Man,* a Western, was underway.

Hollywood's history truly is movieland's history, and vice versa. In *Movieland Directory* are approximately 30,000 addresses of celebrity residences, film locations, and other historic movie-related sites in and around Hollywood, from its early days to the present, uncovered after years of exhaustive research. Regardless of neighborhood or township, the streets in Greater Los Angeles are interfiled and listed alphabetically. Many property addresses are listed more than once, depending upon the occupants. For example, 718 Hillcrest Road, Beverly Hills, was home to Don Knotts (1960s) and Barbara Stanwyck (1930s). 1041 N. Formosa Avenue, Hollywood, was the location of Hampton Studios (no date), Nero Films Inc. (1950s), and Pickford-Fairbanks Studios (1919).

Each numbered entry lists property occupants and occupations. When applicable, additional information, such as reference source, date, and former street name, is included. The index serves to connect individuals and enterprises to pertinent properties. The lengthy introduction is of utmost importance, giving meaning and interest to the entire directory. Fleming has proven that "there is history on every block, in almost every house" in Hollywood, not just at the focal points on tourist "star" maps. Interesting directory. —*Ann Cohen*

★**Encyclopedia of Clothing and Fashion.** 3v. Ed. by Valerie Steele. 2004. 1,600p. illus. index. Scribner, $395 (0-684-31395- 2). 391.

The first title in the Scribner Library of Daily Life, *Encyclopedia of Food and Culture* (2003), was well reviewed and won the 2004 Dartmouth Medal. *Encyclopedia of Clothing and Fashion* is the second title in the series and may be as successful as the first. Editor Steele has written more than 10 books in the field of fashion and culture and is founder of the journal *Fashion Theory.* Here, she works with an impressive list of contributors from universities, museums, and libraries in the U.S. and other English-speaking countries.

The 640 articles span three volumes, with the table of contents only in volume 1 and the index and a systematic outline of contents only in volume 3. Entries are arranged alphabetically, beginning with *Academic dress* and ending with *Zoran,* who is a contemporary designer of "simple" clothes. Entry length ranges from a half page for some particular items, clothing types, fibers, and techniques (*Cuff links and studs; Dress shirt; Weave, jacquard; Distressing*) to multiple pages for *Cross dressing; Dandyism; Hats, men's* and *Hats, women's; Kimono; Street style;* and *Twentieth-century fashion,* among others. Articles on designers or people who influenced fashion—for example, Richard Avedon, Manolo Blahnik, Princess Diana, Halston, and Twiggy—are a significant part of the content, as are articles with a historical slant (*China: History of dress; Fashion shows; Wedding costume*). All of the entries have a bibliography (including six references for *Polo shirt*). Many entries have sidebars of related information, such as a table of size comparisons over the years, a glossary of terms for recycled textiles, and the origin of *toosh.* Black-and-white photographs are numerous throughout the text, and each volume has a signature of color photos. It is unfortunate that there is are no cross-references between these photos and the text.

Many of the articles are entertaining as well as enlightening. In the *Lingerie* entry Dorothy Parker is quoted as saying, "Brevity is the soul of lingerie." We learn that *Grunge,* identified with alternative bands and do-it-yourself dressing, helped make recycled clothes a fashion statement. *Denim* is not a fad, we are told; it has become an "international classic."

Encyclopedia of Clothing and Fashion is an exciting and unique resource that excels in depth and range of coverage. It is highly recommended for high-school, public, and academic libraries with a clientele interested in what and why people wear what they wear. —*Christine Bulson*

Tobacco in History and Culture: An Encyclopedia. Ed. by Jordan Goodman. 2v. 2004. 700p. illus. index. Scribner, $270 (0-684-31405-3). 394.1.

The antitobacco litigation of the 1990s, culminating in the $206 billion Master Settlement Agreement, led to a lull during which this encyclopedia could be produced without fear of its being immediately overtaken by events. The editor has used the opportunity to good advantage. *Tobacco in History and Culture* contains 136 articles addressing every important aspect of the tobacco phenomenon and the controversies spawned by the revelations of the past several decades, most notably those relating to health risks and to the tobacco companies' awareness of those risks, long before the public was made aware of them. At this point, with the companies concentrating on foreign markets, this work will become outdated only in regard to the inevitable upward revisions of projected tobacco-related deaths in those markets—which include underdeveloped countries, where medical facilities are least capable of dealing with the results of tobacco use.

Entry length ranges from just over a page for *Black Patch War* (an early-twentieth-century conflict between Kentucky tobacco growers and the American Tobacco Company) and *Opium* to more than 10 pages for *Disease and mortality* and *Prohibitions.* Each entry concludes with a bibliography, and numerous terms are defined in page margins. Other features of the set include 250 well-chosen and well-reproduced black-and-white illustrations and, in both volumes, a section of color plates. Sidebars contribute additional facts and perspective.

What readers will not see is any primary source material, such as the tobacco company documents laying out marketing strategies and ways in which products could be made more addictive. The liability trials are covered only in general terms, subsumed under the broad category *Litigation,* and documents released during the trials are discussed primarily as documents, with little being said about specific contents. Still, this is an important foundational work, for which researchers can easily find supplemental sources that provide more detail. This first volume in the new Scribner Turning Points Library line is recommended for high-school, academic, and public libraries. —*Harold Cordry*

Holidays, Festivals, and Celebrations of the World. 3d. ed. Ed. by Helene Henderson. 2005. 906p. indexes. Omnigraphics, $110 (0-7808-0422-8). 394.26.

Whether one is interested in the Iditarod or Ramadan, *Holidays, Festivals, and Celebrations of the World* is the premier source of information. The third edition contains nearly 2,500 observances from the U.S. and more than 100 other nations. New content includes more than 400 brand-new entries, among them independence and national days around the world; religious holidays from the Muslim, Sikh, Jain, and Zoroastrian denominations; Native American celebrations; an expanded section on calendar systems; and a perpetual calendar.

The dictionary is arranged alphabetically by the name of the celebration and ranges from *Aban Parab*, at entry number 0001, to the *Zydeco Music Festival*, at number 2496. Entries include the name of the celebration, time period, a brief description, contact information, and sources consulted.

Changes from the previous edition include the removal of the introductory "Millennium" chapter and the "Web Sites on Holidays" appendix. The remaining appendixes have been updated. The index section also received an overhaul. There are now three indexes—chronological, special subject, and general. The chronological index has two parts, "Fixed Days and Events Index" and "Moveable Days Index," which lists entries observed according to the non-Gregorian calendar. The "Special Subject Index" is arranged in six categories—"Ancient/Pagan," "Calendar," "Folkloric," "Historic," "Sporting," and "Promotional." Finally, the general index combines four indexes from the previous edition and is arranged alphabetically by keyword and includes proper names.

Extensive introductory pages describe the scope and audience of the book, with detailed instructions for its use. This compilation continues to be recommended for all libraries. —*Sue Polanka*

The Oxford Dictionary of Proverbs. Rev. ed. Ed. by Jennifer Speake. 2004. 375p. bibliog. index. Oxford, $30 (0-19-860524-2). 398.9.

If it looks like a proverb and sounds like a proverb, it's a proverb—provided that people use it as they would a proverb. Thus, circulating like a computer virus in Britain and North America and ultimately finding their way into *The Oxford Dictionary of Proverbs* are "If life hands you lemons, make lemonade"; "Garbage in, garbage out"; "If it ain't broke, don't fix it" (attributed to Bert Lance); even "Different strokes for different folks" and nearly 40 other "new" proverbs. The stand-up comic Steven Wright earns a citation with a corollary to "The early bird catches the worm": "The early bird may get the worm, but it's the second mouse that gets the cheese."

Each entry in this update to *The Concise Oxford Dictionary of Proverbs* (3d ed., 1998) is arranged alphabetically by the first significant word and is followed, as before, by several illustrative quotations, beginning with the proverb's first documented use in written English. Editor Speake discusses the plan of the book in a brief preface, in which she also explains that, wherever possible, examples of usage have been brought up-to-date. (From the first, *The Concise Oxford Dictionary of Proverbs* was intended to focus on contemporary usage.) Following her preface is the introduction to the first edition (1982) by her former coeditor, John Simpson. Recommended for high-school, public, and undergraduate libraries. —*Harold Cordry*

Language

Encyclopedia of Linguistics. 2v. Ed. by Philipp Strazny. 2004. 1,304p. illus. index. Fitzroy Dearborn, $350 (1-57958-391-1). 410.

As the field of linguistics (the study of human speech) expands, overlaps, and uses the methods and findings of other disciplines, the reference literature needs to reflect these changes. In addition to the expected entries on linguistics as a discipline and the essays about specific languages and their characteristics, this encyclopedia covers topics such as *Information retrieval; Neurolinguistics; Second language: learning;* and *Official language selection*. The intent is to provide "an accessible overview of and introduction to the multiple facets of the study of language."

The 508 signed entries, between 1,000 and 3,000 words long, are arranged alphabetically and fall into four categories. Around 50 percent cover linguistic topics, such as *Biosemiotics, Dyslexia, Gender and language, Phonetics,* and *Time and tense*. Some 30 percent treat languages, among them *Ancient Egyptian, Igbo and Igboid languages, Japanese,* and *Yiddish*. Another 15 percent cover people, for example, Franz Boas, Noam Chomsky, and Jacob Grimm. The remaining entries cover regions. An alphabetical and a thematic list of entries at the beginning of volume 1 are useful finding aids. Illustrations are restricted to figures and tables. The introduction notes the inclusion of 12 language-distribution maps, but we could not find them.

The *International Encyclopedia of Linguistics* (2d ed., Oxford, 2003), which is the standard scholarly reference in the field, has approximately 750 entries. A less-comprehensive title, the single-volume *Linguistics Encyclopedia* (Routledge, 1991) has 150 entries.

With the number of languages spoken in the U.S. increasing, the language descriptions found here, in addition to explanations of standard linguistic terminology, make this a recommended addition to academic and large public libraries. It complements other linguistics encyclopedias that a library may already own and can be a good first purchase for those with no holdings in the area. —*Linda Scarth*

The Firefly Five Language Visual Dictionary. By Jean-Claude Corbeil and Ariane Archambault. 2005. 1,092p. illus. indexes. Firefly, $49.95 (1-55297-778-1). 413.21.

This visual dictionary employs more than 6,000 full-color pictures to illustrate a vast array of objects and their corresponding names in English, French, German, Italian, and Spanish. More than 35,000 terms are grouped into 17 broad subjects ("Animal Kingdom," "Communications and Office Automation" "Society," etc.) and range from technical terminology such as *dew point, moraine,* and *tyrannosaur* to everyday words such as *doorknob* and *waffle iron*. The authors, Corbeil, sociolinguist and specialist in comparative terminology, and Archambault, specialist in applied linguistics, address both the academic (such as heraldic symbols) and the practical (such as street signs). Terms not only include types of objects, such as the more than 20 distinct places to sit (*bar stool, bench, love seat, ottoman, sofa,* etc.) but also provide names for specific components of such objects (*apron, seat, stile,* etc.). The illustrations are crisp and extremely detailed and are printed on glossy white stock. Researchers can access terms by browsing through color-tabbed pages that indicate the different topical subsections or by consulting one of the five language-specific indexes.

The only other reference comparable to this is DK's 2002 publication, the *Five-Language Visual Dictionary*. Although the DK offering features full-color photographs, it is considerably less comprehensive, presenting 1,600 illustrations defining 10,000 terms in about 400 pages. In comparison, *Firefly* runs 1,092 pages. One drawback to the current work is its small dimensions. Pages measure about seven by eight inches, necessitating the use of a relatively small font for the definitions. This is a minor concern, however. Where else are researchers going to find a complete listing of all the elements of the periodical table in five different languages compiled in one place? Irresistible for browsers, serviceable as either a basic visual dictionary or thesaurus, and of immense value to second-language learners, this is recommended for high-school, public, and academic collections. —*Kathleen McBroom*

Canadian Oxford Dictionary. Ed. by Katherine Barber. 2d ed. 2004. 1,830p. Oxford, $59.95 (0-19-541816-6). 423.

This new edition of the well-received *Canadian Oxford Dictionary* (COD), published in 1998, includes many additions to Canadian and standard English. The preface states that more than 5,000 new words have been added, particularly in the information technology and alternative medicine fields. More than 200 new Canadian terms have also been identified and added; altogether, the dictionary defines 2,200 Canadian words and senses.

As with the previous edition, definitions are arranged so that the meaning most familiar to Canadians comes first. New to this edition are preferred word breaks and parts of speech that are written in full instead of being abbreviated. Part of the fun in a guide to Canadian English is checking the differences between standard American and Canadian pronunciations and spellings: *schedule* is pronounced *skedule* and red is a *color* on the American side of the border, but *shedule* and *colour* prevail on the Canadian side. *Chesterfield, gold eye, jam buster,* and other Canadian expressions and words will be found here, as will new words and terms known more widely, such as *supersize* and *weapon of mass destruction*. The COD also includes short entries for proper nouns and names of more than 1,400 Canadian places and 850 Canadian people as well as people and geographical locations from around the world. Like the first edition, the second concludes with several appendixes: a six-page style guide, a list of the prime ministers and governors general of Canada, weights and measures (Canada measures using the metric system), a short history of the English language, and the Arabic, Hebrew, Greek, and Russian alphabets.

The COD is a must for any U.S. library close to the Canadian border and for academic institutions with Canadian studies programs (or *programmes*). Canadian libraries will want to update their reference collections with this latest edition, which is also a worthy edition to any Canadian home reference collection. —*Terri Tomchyshyn*

Descriptionary. 3d ed. By Marc McCutcheon. 2005. 644p. index. Facts On File, $60 (0-8160-5925-X).

A small reference book with a large scope, the third edition of the *Descriptionary* succeeds, with minor disappointments. Divided into 24 topical sections, ranging from "Animals and Insects" to "Weapons," the volume aspires to provide the user with appropriate words related to certain concepts. For example, if a student wanted to know the name for "the area in the church where the congregation sits," a search in the "Religious Buildings" subsection of "Architecture" would provide the probable answer *nave*, along with other words that describe religious buildings and their many components, such as *aguilla, narthex,* and *triforium*.

The "Language" section now includes definitions of street slang, including names of drugs, words used in rap music and urban conversation, and underworld patois. The new edition also includes terms used in physics and chemistry, a significant oversight of the second edition, as well as a new section on "Furniture." Young adults and college students will appreciate the republishing of "Words and Expressions You Should Know," a section that may prove useful while writing papers or preparing for standardized tests.

Most of the text from the second edition has been lifted whole cloth and used in the new one. This is pardonable, given the invariably generic definitions of most words in the English language (a rose is a rose is a rose, after all). However, the author could have made several improvements. For example, the index does not include terms used in tables or lists, such as those for animal groups, international monetary units, geological time, medical fields, constellations, and baseball. The "Military" section lists definitions used mostly during the cold war and with the exception of *cell* and *IED* does not have common terminology related to 9/11 or the war on terror. "Computers" includes definitions of *BASIC, mainframe,* and *floppy disk* but overlooks *client/server system, Linux,* and *flash drive*. The "Language" section defines several rhetorical terms, including *litotes* and *metonymy,* but no mention is made of *periphrasis* or *synecdoche*.

One will not find comprehensiveness or uniformly detailed definitions here but will be given satisfactory answers to simple questions. The book fills an important niche in any reference collection because of its wide scope and comparatively low cost. Public libraries that cannot afford lavishly priced subject dictionaries will want to purchase a copy. Even academic libraries with extensive holdings should allow room on the ready-reference shelf for this compact tool. —*Michael Matthews*

Oxford American Writer's Thesaurus. Comp. by Christine A. Lindberg. 2004. 1,090p. Oxford, $40 (0-19-517076-8).

Any thesaurus inherently celebrates words' subtleties and shades of meaning. This new thesaurus does the same, offering more than 30,000 synonyms and 10,000 antonyms, but it also celebrates good writing. It sets that tone with Richard Goodman's spirited introductory essay, "In Search of the Exact Word," a meditation on the anguish of a writer's quest for the one word that has an effect no other can have and on the exhilaration of finding and using that word. Those themes replay in delightful variety in the "Word Notes" scattered throughout the volume and addressing 240 words including *adumbrate, clothes horse, effete, lurid,* and *pulvinate*. These brief notes, often amusing, have been written by people whose living depends upon their ability to find the right word, among them Zadie Smith, David Foster Wallace, and Simon Winchester. "Word Banks" for categories such as *bears, beers, dances, fabrics, insects,* and *teas* list specifics within each type. Another special feature, "Word Spectrums" are "chains of near-synonyms intended to show the shades of meaning available from a word to its opposite." Under *fat*, for example, one travels the spectrum of meanings from *fat* and *obese* through *shapely* and *well-proportioned* on to *cadaverous* and *thin*.

Each word note, bank, and spectrum is a lagniappe beyond the utilitarian thesaurus proper. The volume's expected purpose is carried out through the typical usage notes, notes differentiating easily confused words, illustrations of words through use in sample sentences, notation of parts of speech, and differentiation among senses of a word. It sets itself apart from competitors by offering more synonyms than the *Cambridge Thesaurus of American English* (1994) and by offering more context for meanings than the *Oxford American Thesaurus of Current English* (1999).

Those who seek the right word in a thesaurus will do well to start here. Even if they don't find that elusive mot juste, they will be able to enjoy the vignettes by writers who seem to find words effortlessly. —*James Rettig*

Oxford Rhyming Dictionary. By Clive Upton and Eben Upton. 2004. 672p. Oxford, $37.95 (0-19-280115-5).

Aspiring poets or lyricists can rejoice in the publication of this work, which lists more than 85,000 words and also includes proper nouns, names, places, and trademarked brands. The dictionary is based on the *Oxford Dictionary of Pronunciation for Current English* (2001), which was written by Clive Upton, and the rhymes reflect current British-English pronunciations.

Anyone who has tried to use a rhyming dictionary with no knowledge of phonetics has undoubtedly been frustrated by the experience. Despite directions for usage, these resources can still be quite complicated. The Oxford volume makes it much easier to find rhymes, because in lieu of phonetics, it is based on an easy-to-use index. To find a rhyme, the user needs merely to look up a word in the index and go to the numeric section indicated. There, the word will be grouped with similar-sounding words, and the reader can browse through that section to find other close rhymes. This work is so expansive that readers should expect to find most commonly used words. The authors try to keep up-to-date with current language and to that end include such words as *email* and *CD-ROM*.

This resource can be helpful to those writing poetry, songs, and jingles and also will appeal to word lovers in general. Though it is based on British-English pronunciation, American English is not so different as to render it ineffective. Recommended for all high-school, academic, and public libraries. —*Susanna Eng*

Hatchet Jobs and Hardball: The Oxford Dictionary of American Political Slang. Ed. by Grant Barrett. 2004. 320p. Oxford, $25 (0-19-517685-5).

The range of this delightful little dictionary is defined as "250 years of lively discourse," but most of the liveliness is of recent occurrence, with the entries being drawn primarily from the 1980s and 1990s, if not from the past two or three years. Even for words like *mugwump* (first example 1884) and *snollygoster* (1846), the editor has found more or less current instances of use.

Each entry contains part of speech, definition, and citations from a range of sources. Other elements that may be included are an etymology, a field label identifying the group or subculture that generally uses the term (for example, *Mil.* for military), variant forms, usage labels, cross-references, and notes. Much of the slang recorded here is indeed lively and clever. A prepared response to an opponent's anticipated assertion is a *prebuttle*. A *red-headed Eskimo* is a bill so precisely targeted that it might benefit only one specific person. A *twinkie* is someone or something that is appealing but lacking in substance. *Velcroid* applies to a person who seeks to advance by associating with a more important person. A *clothespin vote* is one that is cast unenthusiastically for a choice regarded as least objectionable. The idea is "that voters must use a clothespin to protect their noses from the supposed stench of such candidates."

By no means the least interesting part of the dictionary is the series of eight brief essays on topics (such as chads and the -gate suffix) about which Barrett felt compelled to comment at somewhat greater length than his definitions, notes, and etymologies permitted. This is a book to be read and enjoyed, not merely to be taken down from the shelf now and then and briefly consulted, and it is recommended for public and academic libraries. —*Harold Cordry*

The Cambridge Guide to English Usage. By Pam Peters. 2004. 608p. appendixes. Cambridge, $35 (0-521-62181-X).

The wry observation attributed to George Bernard Shaw that "England and America are two countries divided by a common language" finds support in *The Cambridge Guide to English Usage*. Author Peters, of Macquarie University in Australia, provides evidence that their common language also divides Canada and Australia from the other countries.

Within the *A–Z* arrangement of brief, to-the-point articles, entries on *catalogue* and *catalog, dived* and *dove, fitted* and *fit, freshman* and *fresher, titbit* and *tidbit* celebrate transatlantic differences, some rather subtle, others more pointed. Peters draws on a range of authorities for her judgments on usage. Those include large databases, such as the 140- million-word Cambridge International Corpus of American English, and other usage guides from throughout the English-speaking world. In line with the most recent of these other handbooks, as well as the irrefutable evidence of present usage, Peters takes a descriptive rather than prescriptive approach. Her analytical discussions of parts of speech, grammatical concepts and constructs, and the like explain the origins of rules but also provide contemporary and historical examples of how usage tempers some rules.

Like other manuals that explain the difference between a monologue and a soliloquy, the lack of meaningful difference between further and farther, the confused state between inquire and enquire, the divergence of salutary and salutatory from their common root, and recent introductions such as emoticons, Cambridge provides sound advice for those who want to understand the English language and use it effectively. More than other manuals, it describes the way in which some usages have a local habitation rather than global recognition.

Considering the abundance of peculiarities and challenges in English usage, *Cambridge* will strengthen even a library well stocked with other guides. It is a serious book for those serious about language. Those who also enjoy the playfulness of English will continue to appreciate the complementary *Penguin Dictionary of American English Usage and Style* (Penguin, 2000) and its sometimes witty examples. —*James Rettig*

Science

World Book's Science & Nature Guides. 12v. 2004. 960p. illus. index. World Book, $289 (0-7166-4208-5). 500.

This set provides students with an introduction to the natural sciences. Although the publisher indicates that the interest level is grades 5–10, the layout and content would most appeal to students in grades 2–5. Colorful graphics and charts appear on every two-page spread, and the layout is clean and easy-to-read. Hands-on projects and field activities are included. The volumes cover animal life (with separate volumes devoted to amphibians and reptiles, birds, butterflies, freshwater life, and mammals) as well as fossils, rocks and minerals, shells, trees, and wildflowers of the U.S. and Canada.

Each volume begins with a code for safe behavior. In *Mammals of the United States and Canada,* readers are advised to "always go collecting with a friend, and always tell an adult where you are going" as well as to "not touch nests or dens." *Mammals* starts with an introduction to mammals, followed by descriptions of the various habitats where they can be found. Next are sections on the individual habitats and the kinds of mammals that may be identified there. For woods and forests, some of the mammals profiled are the red bat, moose, and mountain beaver. Simple statistics are provided for each, such as length, food, young, and tracks. An example of the activities offered in this book is how to build a bat box. Each volume includes its own index and would serve as a stand-alone introduction to the topic. The coverage is brief. For example, in *Mammals,* species are generally covered with three to four sentences.

The final volume includes a cumulative glossary and a cumulative index. It also offers a geological time line, an explanation of the classification system, biographies of natural scientists, and lists of further reading, places to visit, and organizations for further research.

Although this set is nicely arranged and has an appealing layout, it is most appropriate for browsing and circulating collections. Students needing information for reports would be better served by works such as Marshall Cavendish's *Insects and Spiders of the World* (2002) and titles in Grolier's five-set *World of Animals* collection. —*Maren Ostergard*

e.encyclopedia science. 2004. 384p. illus. index. DK, $29.99 (0-7566-0215-7). 503.

As a follow-up to their publication *e.encyclopedia* (2003), DK and Google have joined forces again to produce an encyclopedia covering eight general areas in science: "Matter and Materials," "Forces and Energy," "Electricity and Magnetism," "Space," "Earth," "Plants," "Animals," and "Human Body."

The unique feature of this publication is that it correlates to a Web site created by Google [http://www.science.dke-encyc.com]. Each entry in the text has a keyword to enter on the Web page in order to access information from a range of previewed, child-friendly sites. The search engine on the Web site accepts only the keywords provided in the book. Information that is available from the Web links includes animations, videos, sounds, virtual tours, interactive quizzes, databases, and time lines as well as current reports. Teachers and librarians will also appreciate the pictures that can be downloaded free of charge for personal, noncommercial use.

Most of the entries in the book are one or two pages in length. They include an introductory paragraph followed by subentries that expand on the topic. Other items that may be included in an entry are data boxes, biographies, and time lines. There is a color-coded band across the bottom of each page to quickly show readers what section they are in. "Find out more" references point users to related entries.

Besides the companion Web site, one of the main attractions of this text is its eye-catching visuals. Each page features engaging color photographs as well as colorful charts and graphics. Although students would have welcomed a glossary, this is a useful research tool for the intermediate level and is recommended for school and public libraries. —*Maren Ostergard*

Biology Matters! 10v. illus. index. 2004. 800p. Grolier, $389 (0-7172-5979-X). 507.

This set presents the fundamentals of the life sciences in a clear format and is best suited for students in upper-elementary or middle school. The volumes each cover a broad topic, including *Cell Biology* (volume 2), *Plants* (volume 5), and *Evolution* (volume 9). Volumes contain between six and eight articles in 80 pages, and each could serve as a stand-alone title, introducing its subject, presenting a brief history, and covering many aspects of its current study and applications.

The set makes use of many different types of boxed areas to highlight supplemental information. For example, "Try This" boxes present simple science experiments (although the experiments are simple, some will require adult supervision). "Hot Debate" boxes discuss selected scientific topics about which there is some dispute concerning theory or practice. "Applications" boxes show how biological knowledge enhances daily life, and "Red Herring" boxes summarize failed theories. In addition to the boxed material, each article features clearly annotated illustrations. The text is large and easy to read, and the writing is straightforward and should be accessible to young adult readers. There is cross-referencing within and among the volumes.

Each volume concludes with a "More Information" section listing books and Web sites, a glossary of terms unique to that volume, and a set index. One nice touch is the Web site annotations, which indicate how the sites might best be used. There are some errors; for example, in the table of contents for every volume, "More Information" and "Glossary" are listed in the wrong order, with the wrong page numbers.

This title provides a simpler overview than Macmillan's *Biology* (2001) and would be a useful addition for public and school libraries, especially as there is little on this topic for students in grades 5–10. —*Maren Ostergard*

Science in the Ancient World: An Encyclopedia. By Russell M. Lawson. 2004. 291p. illus. index. ABC-CLIO, $85 (1-85109-534-9); e-book, $90 (1-85109-539-X). 509.3.

Appropriate for a high-school and general audience, this addition to the publisher's History of Science series describes scientific concepts in ancient societies, including the Egyptian, Babylonian, Greek, and Roman worlds until the fall of the Roman Empire. Most of the entries are about people, concepts, and locales of the Greco-Roman world. Arrangement is alphabetical, supported by good cross-references and indexing. Examples of the more than 140 entries include *Agriculture, Epicureanism, Euclid, Mesopotamia, Meteorology, Roman roads and bridges, Vesuvius,* and *Women and science.*

Entries vary in length from around half of a page to more than five pages for *Aristotle, Geography/Geodesy,* and *Psychology.* The lists of references attached to each entry includes both secondary sources and translations of primary sources. Some entries have black-and-white illustrations. The dictionary portion of the volume is followed by a chronology listing significant historical events along with the births of important individuals in the sciences and a bibliography divided into primary and secondary sources.

Arranged by broad scientific area, *Groundbreaking Scientific Experiments, Inventions, and Discoveries of the Ancient World* (Greenwood, 2004) has fewer entries though it covers a greater geographic expanse. With its accessible *A–Z* format, *Science in the Ancient World* is recommended for high-school, college, and public libraries. —*Jack O'Gorman*

Science in the Contemporary World: An Encyclopedia. By Eric G. Swedin. 2005. 397p. illus. index. ABC-CLIO, $85 (1-85109-524-1). 503.
Science in the Early Twentieth Century: An Encyclopedia. By Jacob Darwin Hamblin. 2005. 397p. illus. index. ABC-CLIO, $85 (1-85109-665-5). 509.

These two titles are part of ABC-CLIO's successful History of Science series. Previous titles include Science in the Ancient World: An Encyclopedia (2004), Science in the Enlightenment: An Encyclopedia (2003), and

The Scientific Revolution: An Encyclopedia (2001). The first of the titles under review covers developments in the scientific disciplines from 1900 to about 1950, while the second covers the end of World War II to the present day.

Entries cover scientific concepts, leaders, institutions, and disciplines. The reading level is appropriate for high-school, undergraduate, and general adult readers. Each entry has a narrative text, photos or other illustrations, and a brief bibliography; those looking for more advanced or detailed explanations, especially of scientific concepts, will need to look elsewhere. See also references are included at the end of the entries. Biographical entries in Early Twentieth Century are introduced by place and date of birth and, where pertinent, death; in Contemporary World, there are dates only. The bibliographies are short, many with only one or two items, usually books. Some Web sites are included. The photos endeavor to capture the scientists at their work or present a lively portrait. A chronology, selected general bibliography, and subject index appear at the end of each volume.

Since the emphasis is on science history, those looking for more detailed explanations of scientific theories and concepts will need to turn to more general titles, such as the classic scientific reference source, *McGraw-Hill Encyclopedia of Science and Technology* (9th ed., 2002). Information on many of the same topics discussed in the ABC-CLIO titles can be found in *The Oxford Companion to the History of Modern Science* (2003), but readers may choose the former for their approachable writing and attractive layout. They make good introductory texts to the history of science in the twentieth century and are recommended for public and academic libraries. —*Jack O'Gorman*

A to Z of Mathematicians. By Tucker McElroy. 2005. 308p. illus. indexes. Facts On File, $45 (0-8160-5338-3). 510.
A to Z of Scientists in Space and Astronomy. By Deborah Todd and Joseph A. Angelo Jr. 2005. 322p. illus. indexes. Facts On File, $45 (0-8160-4639-5). 520.

Two more titles in the Facts on File Notable Scientists series, designed to give concise information to students in grades nine and up. Both titles include information on about 140 individuals—their work, families, major achievements, and contributions to their scientific field. Entries are alphabetically arranged, run about 750 to 1,200 words, and are often accompanied by a small black-and-white photo.

Both volumes try to be representative of men and women from many countries and throughout history. With the exception of Kurt Gödel, *Mathematicians* excludes those born in the twentieth century. Among the mathematicians who are covered are Archimedes, Jakob Bernoulli, Ada Lovelace, and Srinivasa Aiyangar Ramanujan. In *Space and Astronomy*, subjects include Annie Jump Cannon, Aristotle, Galileo, Edmund Halley, and Stephen Hawking. Maria Mitchell is omitted. Cosmonaut Valentina Tereshkova has an entry, but no other cosmonauts or astronauts are represented.

In-text cross-references to other articles within each volume are done in bold type. There are lists of entries sorted by field, country of birth, country of major activity, and time period, in addition to a general index for each volume. Each volume also has a bibliography of works consulted. The *Space and Astronomy* bibliography includes many books and Web sites from the 1990s and later; that in *Mathematicians* lists mostly journal articles and books, with a short, selective list of math Web sites. "Further Reading" follows each *Mathematicians* entry (usually two to four older journal articles).

These titles are more inviting and easier to use than Isaac Asimov's trusty *Biographical Encyclopedia of Science and Technology* (rev. ed., Doubleday, 1982). They will be a useful though not essential purchase, where the other series titles are used. —*Sue Gooden*

The Universal Book of Mathematics: From Abracadabra to Zeno's Paradoxes. By David Darling. 2004. 383p. illus. index. Wiley, $40 (0-471-27047-4). 510.

Darling, who has written books about astronomy and science for young adults, has followed the successful formula found in his *Universal Book of Astronomy* (Wiley, 2004), to compile an encyclopedia of mathematical terms, concepts, and problems; short biographies of pioneering mathematicians; puzzles; diagrams; pictures; and history. Entries cover subjects ranging from the fairly simple (*Arithmetic*) to the more complex (*Cabali-Yau space*). The goal is to present "the unusual and the outrageous, the fanciful and the fantastic: a compendium of the mathematics they *didn't* teach you in school." To this end, the book treats numerous topics one would not expect to find in more academic math dictionaries—illusions, classic chess problems, the 1884 novel *Flatland,* to give a few examples.

Entries are alphabetized and thoroughly cross-referenced. Some are as brief as a single sentence (for example, *Congruent, Nonagon*), while others are a page or more (*Maze, Pi*). The writing is accessible and provides enough information to assist the reader in understanding the term being described. An impressive list of references used to compile the entries is included at the end of the volume, along with the solutions to the mathematical puzzles referred to in the text. This resource would be appropriate for high-school, public, and academic libraries and could be considered a basic tool in this subject. —*Kathryn O'Gorman*

The Firefly Encyclopedia of Astronomy. Ed. by Paul Murdin and Margaret Penston. 2004. 480p. illus. Firefly, $59.95 (1-55297-797-8). 520.

The mysteries of the universe have intrigued people for millennia. Written in nontechnical language accessible to high-school students and the general reader, this encyclopedia provides authoritative information synthesized from the research of hundreds of leading astronomers. The 1,750 alphabetically arranged entries range in length from a short paragraph to several pages.

Articles cover key concepts (*Grand Unified Theory, Quark, Superluminal motion*); astronomers (Subrahmanyan Chandrasekhar, Maria Mitchell, Isaac Newton); individual planets, stars, nebulae, and galaxies (*Andromeda Galaxy, Earth, Ganymede*); satellites, telescopes, and professional facilities (*Hubble Space Telescope, Yerkes Observatory*); history (*Rockets in astronomy*); and current research (*Dark energy and the cosmological constant, Exobiology and SETI, Neutrino astronomy*). Features on practical astronomy, written by noted amateurs and highlighted with a yellow background, provide information on topics such as *Observing artificial satellites, Widefield astrophotography, Finding and collecting meteorites,* and *Discovering novae.* Research conducted by professional astronomers is sometimes linked to the practical astronomy features, which results in an interesting combination of theory and practice. Excellent color photographs and illustrations, scattered throughout, supplement the text. Surprisingly, there is no large map to the constellations. Cross-references to related articles are available in some articles. Some entries provide further readings. There is no subject index.

The four-volume *Encyclopedia of Astronomy and Astrophysics* (2001), written for an academic and professional audience, is a far more comprehensive (and therefore more expensive) set, particularly suited for academic and special libraries. Written for a general audience, *The Firefly Encyclopedia of Astronomy* is recommended for high-school and public libraries. —*Nancy Cannon*

Encyclopedia of Physics. By Joe Rosen. 2004. 386p. illus. index. Facts On File, $75 (0-8160-4974-2). 530.

The value of a concise encyclopedia of physics is clear. Although sets like the *McGraw-Hill Encyclopedia of Science and Technology* (9th ed., 2002) are comprehensive and appropriate for many levels, they can be too large and expensive for smaller and less science-oriented collections. The present offering, written by the author of a variety of introductory and other texts about physics, looks to conciseness first and therefore sacrifices comprehensiveness.

The author is quite selective in terms of the topics covered. The more than 600 entries run from about 50 to 1,000 words and cover physical concepts, prominent physicists (modern and historical), and physics laboratories, societies, and organizations. The alphabetically arranged entries are supplemented with 11 topical essays that aim to shed some light on physics in a philosophical or practical way. These essays cover such topics as beauty, the nature of the relationship between physics and philosophy, and the desire among some physicists to find the unifying laws governing all physical concepts. The author has done a good job of presenting the material in language that will be accessible to the intended audience (high-school and college students as well as general readers). The text is supported by a good index, a decent bibliography, a chronological listing of all Nobel Laureates in physics through 2003, and a simplified periodic table of the elements. The entries are well written, accurate, and include equations where appropriate. Some 117 line diagrams illustrate concepts, and there are 71 black-and-white photos, most of them in the biographical entries.

Another one-volume resource, *The Macmillan Encyclopedia of Physics*

(1996), has 1,000 entries, although it is not as current and lacks biographical material. The Facts On File volume would add little to collections that already have a selection of more comprehensive titles but is appropriate for high-school, public, and undergraduate libraries where budget only allows for a volume that costs less than $100. —*Jeff Kosokoff*

Chemistry: Foundations and Applications. 4v. Ed. by J. J. Lagowski. 2004. 800p. bibliogs. glossary. illus. index. Macmillan, $395 (0-02-865721-7). 540.

Written at a level accessible to nonspecialists, including high-school students, college students in introductory courses, and the general public, this encyclopedia's purpose is to assist users in acquiring knowledge and understanding of chemistry. The 509 alphabetically arranged, signed articles were written by subject specialists and range from concise definitions to multiple-page overviews. Broad areas covered include analytical chemistry applications, biochemistry, biographies, elements, energy, environmental chemistry, medicine, organic chemistry, physical chemistry, reactions, states of matter, and structure. Examples of specific article titles are *Alchemy; Artificial sweeteners; Boron; Clones; Franklin, Rosalind; Isomerism; Mole concept; Nanochemistry; Rubber; Spectroscopy;* and *Zwitterions*. In addition to explaining scientific principles, this set relates chemistry to everyday life. For example, Silly Putty (a silicone- based material) is a "liquid solid," the color of hydrangeas is determined by soil acidity, and endorphins may allow marathoners' bodies to endure long races.

An 18-page glossary and 67-page subject index are included in each volume. Glossary definitions also appear in the margins next to the text. Although there are some cross- references in the articles, the index is more thorough. About 300 black-and-white illustrations and diagrams clarify the concepts under discussion. There are no color illustrations; color would have been useful to elucidate concepts such as bonding and molecular structure. Bibliographic references and related Internet resources are listed at the end of many articles. A "For Your Reference" section at the beginning of each volume provides selected metric conversions, an alphabetic table of the elements; common abbreviations, symbols and acronyms, and a periodic table of the elements.

The similar four-volume *Macmillan Encyclopedia of Chemistry* (1997), also edited by Lagowski, is aimed at a more academic audience and provides additional coverage of some topics.

Although *Chemistry: Foundations and Applications* could be improved with the inclusion of some color illustrations, the very impressive scholarly contributors make this set worthy of consideration, particularly for high-school, large public, and undergraduate libraries. —*Nancy Cannon*

A Student's Guide to Earth Science. 4v. 2004. 576p. bibliog. glossary. illus. maps. Greenwood, $160 (0-313-32901-X). 550.

This set furnishes basic information pertinent to the study of earth science. Volume 1, *Words and Terms,* presents more than 140 words and terms in three ways: definition (term meaning), sentence (term used in a sentence to provide context clues), and connection (historical or technical relationship of term to field of earth science). Should some prominent scientist be relevant to the term, a minibiographical sketch is also included. Numerous charts, maps, and graphs assist with visual explanation. In volume 2, *Important People,* 26 significant individuals—all men—are examined in biographies of two to five pages. Separate sections present briefer biographies of "Women Astronomers" (three) and "Women and Minorities in Earth Science" (three men and three women). Volume 3, *Developments and Discoveries,* probes in a short overview the history of the earth sciences, astronomy, geology, meteorology, and oceanography with coverage of those who made discoveries and how these discoveries relate to our world today. Volume 4, *Debatable Issues,* promotes critical thinking skills with nine current controversial topics, such as "Should Radioactive Waste Be Buried for Safekeeping?" and "Do Greenhouse Gases Cause Global Warming?" Each volume includes a glossary of terms, a cumulative index of the set, and a time line beginning with the Chinese record of the earliest comet sighting in 2296 B.C.E. and concluding with the discovery of a large planet in the constellation Puppis in 2003. Also noteworthy is a bibliography of books and Web sites. All materials listed are currently available or operational and provide a great springboard for more in-depth research. Black-and-white photographs are incorporated in all volumes.

Judged by the simple sentence structure and the use of pronunciation guides with key terms, this source would be best utilized in an upper-elementary (grades five and six) and a grades five through eight middle school where introductory-level earth science classes are taught. The value for the price merits consideration. —*Cheryl Ward*

Encyclopedia of Earth Science. By Timothy Kusky. 2005. 510p. illus. index. Facts On File, $75 (0-8160-4973-4). 550.

This new encyclopedia from the Facts On File Science Library offers approximately 700 alphabetically arranged entries ranging from one paragraph to a few pages and covering earth science subdisciplines (hydrology, oceanography, and so on) as well as concepts, theories and hypotheses, places, events, geological time periods, history, technology, and key individuals. Many entries have further-reading lists and cross-references. There are hundreds of black-and-white photos, drawings, charts, and maps. The illustrations are generally clear and detailed. Nineteen feature essays are scattered throughout the text. Two appendixes follow the entries, one containing a periodic table of elements, the other displaying a geologic time scale and other information.

Earth science includes weather, so there are many entries for weather terms. One of the feature essays is on tsunamis, an eerily timely topic. Several entries discuss how scientists are getting better at predicting such natural disasters as earthquakes, flash floods, avalanches, and hurricanes.

There are a few things to quibble about, causing varying levels of frustration. One omission is an entry in the text and the index for the term *bedrock,* which appears in at least two entries (*Groundwater* and *Soils*) as well as in the illustrations that accompany them. A glossary of basic terms might have been a useful addition for the nonexpert reader. However, the strengths of this work far outweigh any weaknesses. On the whole, this is a solid introduction for most high-school, academic, and public libraries. —*Robin Hoelle*

UXL Encyclopedia of Water Science. 3v. Ed. by K. Lee Lerner and Brenda Wilmoth Lerner. 2005. 510p. illus. index. UXL, $165 (0-7876-7617-9). 553.7.

Water is becoming an increasingly important topic and is the subject of many treaties and disputes. This set contains more than 100 signed entries on water science and water issues. Volume 1 has six chapters dealing with water science basics, volume 2 has five chapters dealing with the economics and uses of water, and the final volume has two chapters dealing with the environmental, legal, and political issues surrounding water. Each chapter contains numerous signed entries. For example, the chapter on the "Basics of Water Science" contains entries on biochemistry, chemistry of water, the hydrologic cycle, and the physics of water. Each entry has its own displayed glossary and gray sidebars with additional facts and also contains a list of print and Web resources for further study and research. The set is illustrated with black-and-white photographs, maps, and cycle charts. There is also a color photo section in each volume. The preponderance of gray and black and white does not provide a lot of visual interest.

The chapter arrangement makes it somewhat difficult to locate specific information. Within each chapter, entries are arranged alphabetically, and guide words are located at the bottom of each right-hand page. The individual entries in chapters have subheadings that are not arranged alphabetically, so it becomes slightly confusing as one pages through looking for topical information. A general glossary, a research and activities section, and a cumulative index to the set are included in each volume.

Macmillan's *Water: Science and Issues* (2003) covers similar ground in an A–Z format. Even though the UXL set is not quite as accessible, it does a good job of bringing information together for students and general readers and covering it in some detail. UXL is Gale's middle-school line, but the set will get maximum use in high-school, community college, and public libraries that serve patrons in high school and beyond. —*Dona Helmer*

Encyclopedia of Genetics. 2v. Rev ed. Ed. by Bryan D. Ness. 2004. 863p. bibliogs. glossary. illus. indexes. Salem, $210 (1-58765-149-1). 576.5.

Intended for the nonscientist, this welcome update to the first edition (1999) offers 64 new essays on current topics, reflecting the swift pace of discovery in the field. Of the 172 original entries, 7 have been dropped because they were no longer relevant and 26 were completely rewritten. Some 131 of the entries were revised and updated. Overall, the revised edition has increased in number of essays as well as in word length, consisting of 233 signed essays from *Aggression* to *XYY Syndrome*. This edition also features 25 new mini-essays that offer treatment of noteworthy or current subtopics appended to main entries.

Each volume starts with an alphabetical list of contents. The essays all follow a similar format. Each begins with top matter that lists "Field of Study" offering one or more subdisciplines under which the topic falls. This is followed by "Significance," which provides a definition of the topic and a summary of its importance. Next are definitions of "Key Terms." Headings break the main body of each essay into clearly defined subtopics. The articles conclude with *see also* references as well as a list of further reading. All of the individual essays' bibliographies are new or updated. About half of the essays include "Web Sites of Interest" directing users to Web sites of government agencies, professional or academic societies, support organizations, and a few relevant personal URLs. Basic black-and-white photographs and charts supplement the text.

The set concludes with several appendixes. The biographical dictionary of important geneticists, time line of major developments in genetics, glossary, and bibliography have been revised. Two new appendixes, a list of Nobel prizes for discoveries in genetics and a list of Web sites, have been added. To help users locate subjects according to area of study, a category index, a personages index, and a comprehensive subject index are included at the end of the second volume. There is no index in volume 1.

Macmillan's *Genetics* (2002) has a more appealing layout and better graphics and is more suited to the student with no background in the topic. *World of Genetics* (Gale, 2001) includes more articles (800) although they are generally shorter in length. The Salem set provides clear explanations and is recommended for college and high-school libraries as well as any public library that has a large science collection. —*Maren Ostergard*

The Encyclopedia of Animals: A Complete Visual Guide. Ed. by George McKay and others. 2004. 608p. illus. index. Univ. of California, $39.95 (0-520-24406-0). 590.3.

This lavishly illustrated chronicle of Earth's biodiversity is a visual delight. Compiled by a team of animal experts from Australia, the U.K., and the U.S., it presents an overview of animal life and behavior. The audience includes younger readers, who will enjoy the photos and illustrations, as well as adults interested in the natural world.

Following an overview on animal classification, evolution, behavior, and more, content is arranged in six taxonomic sections covering mammals, birds, reptiles, amphibians, fish, and invertebrates. Each of these sections is broken down into smaller sections that treat particular subgroups. A sample entry on bears covers two pages and includes the classification, two photos, six illustrations, a diagram of the skeletal structure, text about feeding and anatomy, and a sidebar on bear paws. A "Fact File," which relies heavily on icons, enumerates characteristics such as size, distribution, reproduction, and conservation status.

The information presented is a good start, although readers may need to turn to more comprehensive works, such as *Grzimek's Animal Life Encyclopedia* [RBB Ap 1 04], for details about a specific species. *The Simon and Schuster Encyclopedia of Animals* (1998) is very similar to the University of California volume in size, arrangement, and number of illustrations but does not include invertebrates. The reasonable price and attractive layout of *The Encyclopedia of Animals* will make it a popular choice for school, public, and academic libraries. —*Jack O'Gorman*

Encyclopedia of Animal Behavior. 3v. Ed. by Marc Bekoff. 2005. 1,274p. illus. index. Greenwood, $349.95 (0-313-32745-9). 591.5.

As a child, editor Bekoff wondered, "What is it *like* to be a dog or a cat or a mouse or an ant?" The *Encyclopedia of Animal Behavior* will be of interest to anyone who has ever been curious about the world of animals. The essays, written by scholars and researchers at a level appropriate for the general reader, cover all aspects of animal behavior and range in length from about 300 to 7,000 words. Alphabetically arranged major sections, such as *Antipredatory behavior, Learning, Reproductive behavior,* and *Social organization,* are organized into subtopics, examples of which include *Animal consciousness, Audience effect in whales, Orangutan culture, Tool use and manufacture by birds,* and *Veterinary ethics and behavior.* In addition, there are lengthy stand-alone essays (*Bats; Cephalopods; Washburn, Margaret Floy*) as well as short, more focused sidebars.

The entries are liberally sprinkled with fascinating facts that should appeal to the layperson. For example, we learn that the coyote population responds in inverse proportion to human efforts to control it, and telepathy has been documented in animals, including a dog that could sense the arrival of his human companion. Entries are accompanied by cross-references and lists of further readings, most of which are scholarly.

Black-and-white photographs and illustrations supplement the text, and eight pages of color photographs are included in the center of each volume. Appendixes include a listing of "Organizations and Related Web Sites" and "Suggested Resources in the Study of Animal Behavior." Detailed cross-references to related essays appear at the end of each essay. A 26-page index provides subject access to the contents. A useful "Guide to Related Contents" groups entries by type of animal, type of behavior, animal-behavior careers, and other topics.

The *Encyclopedia of Animal Behavior* provides current, authoritative, comprehensive, original articles on animal behavior. The well-written, user-friendly essays are a pleasure to read. Recommended for public and academic libraries. —*Nancy Cannon*

World of Animals: Insects and Other Invertebrates. 10v. 2004. illus. index. Grolier, $419 (0-7172-5894-7). 595.7.

These volumes compose the third cluster of the five-set World of Animals collection, so far joining *Mammals* (2003) and *Birds* [RBB Mr 1 04]. *Insects* continues set numbering where *Birds* left off and is numbered volumes 21–30. Libraries that shelve by Dewey decimal number will find that this new set is shelved prior to both previously released clusters, even though the volume numbers indicate a continuing set.

Geared to middle- through high-school students, the set groups species that share similar characteristics or have similar lifestyles, such as simple and wormlike animals, crustaceans, arachnids, mollusks, and echinoderms. Six of the ten volumes are devoted to insects. Because the set contains a huge diversity of animal types, a "Find the Animal" guide is included in each volume. Much like *Birds* and *Mammals,* each 128-page volume presents information in two types of articles. The first introduces and provides a general overview of major groups (mollusks, insects, flies, jelly animals). The second type, which constitutes the majority of the text, concentrates on describing important groups in detail (jellyfish, sea anemones, corals).

Well-written entries range in length from two to six pages and include numerous full-color photographs and illustrations. These detailed, vivid, and captioned pictures enhance the highly appealing and browsable layout. Many entries have highlighted boxes that offer interesting side notes, for example, the deadly effectiveness of the Australian Box Jellyfish toxin. Cross-referencing in the bottom margin includes related animal or topic, with volume and page number. Each volume concludes with a volume-specific glossary, lists of further reading and Web sites, and a set index.

An additional noteworthy feature is the "data panel" found at the beginning of each entry. Data found here include common name, phylum, number of species, size, key features, habits, diet, breeding, habitat, and distribution. School and public libraries alike will find that this set contains sufficient information to serve the needs of a variety of student users and will appeal to the casual browser as well. —*Shauna Yusko*

Grzimek's Student Animal Life Resource: Birds. 5v. 2005. 1,410p. illus. index. UXL, $260 (0-7876-9235-2). 598.
Grzimek's Student Animal Life Resource: Mammals. 5v. 2005. 1,228p. illus. index. UXL, $260 (0-7876-9183-6). 599.

These two new student reference sources are an offshoot of Gale's *Grzimek's Animal Life Encyclopedia* (2d. ed, Gale, 2002). Upcoming entries in the series are Corals, Jellyfishes, Sponges, and Other Simple Animals; Crustaceans, Mollusks, and Segmented Worms; Insects and Spiders; Fishes; Amphibians; and Reptiles.

In both of the sets under review, each volume begins with a "Reader's Guide," a "Pronunciation Guide for Scientific Names," a "Words to Know" section, and a section on "Getting to Know Birds" or "Getting to Know Mammals." Each of the volumes concludes with a "Species List by Biome" as well as a "Species List by Geographic Range." Each volume also includes a comprehensive index.

Birds treats 166 families and 316 species from around the world, while Mammals offers coverage of 141 families and 265 species. Entries are arranged by taxonomy. Order entries offer an overview of a group of families, and family entries provide an overview of a particular family. Each entry includes sections on physical characteristics, geographic range, habitat, diet, behavior and reproduction, animals and people, and conservation status. The family entries are followed by one or more species accounts, which include the same information, in addition to a map indicating range and a photograph or illustration for each species. Conservation is emphasized, and the sets make use of the IUCN (International Union for Conservation of Nature and Natural Resources, now the World Conservation Union)

Red List categories for each species. Each entry concludes with a list of books, periodicals, and Web sites (including a note of the date when they were last accessed) for further research. Each set includes more than 500 colorful photographs, illustrations, and charts. Colorful sidebars provide supplemental information. Layout is open and appealing, and the writing is clear and easily understood.

These sets would be useful additions for middle-school, high-school, and public libraries. —*Maren Ostergard*

Science Full Text Select. 2004. [Online database]. Wilson, contact for pricing [http://www.hwwilson.com]. (Last accessed December 5, 2004).

One does not usually start a database review with comments about the online thesaurus. However, this well-designed function is one of the shining features of Wilson's *Science Full Text Select*. Keying in a word produces a list of suggested subject headings, even if that word returns no results. For example, *heliotrope* was not found, but seven subject headings were suggested, including *color of flowers* and *color in gardens*. Another positive feature is the WilsonLink function, which, when activated, integrates the Wilson indexes with other vendors' databases (depending on a library's subscriptions) and with the library OPAC. This maximizes opportunities for accessing full text without multiple searches.

The database covers 287 journals (320, with name changes) in science and technology and is geared for public, community college, and high-school libraries. It contains all the content from Wilson's *Applied Science and Technology Full Text, Biological and Agricultural Index Plus,* and *General Science Full Text,* along with related full-text science titles indexed by other Wilson databases, including *Readers' Guide Full Text* and *Wilson OmniFile Full Text.*

Since *Science Full Text Select* is part of WilsonWeb, librarians who subscribe to other WilsonWeb databases will be familiar with the search protocols. While there are several ways to approach a search, the Advanced Search function will meet most users' needs. One may select Boolean operators across several fields, such as keyword, author, or subject, limited by date and document type. Some articles are available in PDF format as well as in HTML if they have graphical content, and users can choose to limit a search to those in PDF as well as those published in peer-reviewed journals. Hits can be sorted by a wide variety of criteria, with relevance (the default), date, title, and author the most useful. There are also a basic search with Boolean possibilities and a Browse function, where one can look for a term within a particular field. The term requested needs to be appropriate to the field for this to be useful. Results can be displayed as brief or full records, with the full records including abstracts of 150–500 words.

In Advanced Search, All-SmartSearch, which searches for documents that have all of the words in a query, is the default. It may not be apparent to students when this kind of search is appropriate, and librarians and media specialists will need to demonstrate the search functions so users will not be overwhelmed.

This database is an eclectic mix of scientific, agricultural, technology, environmental, and medical science titles. The selection should be useful in secondary schools and many public and academic libraries, especially since many of the mainstream science publications are included. —*Linda Scarth*

Science Resource Center. [Online database]. Gale, pricing from $2,610 for two users. [http://gale.com]. (Last accessed September 9, 2004).

Gale's newest resource center focuses on the sciences, from anatomy to zoology. To perform a Basic search, a patron may enter a search term and select Subject (the default), Keyword, or Full-Text from a pull-down menu. Alternately, a patron may search by selecting one from a list of 80 of the most heavily researched technology or life, Earth, physical, and space sciences topics. A patron may also explore the topic highlighted in the Spotlight section (this topic was Physics in September). A search can return up to six different types of materials via tabbed result pages: Reference, Magazines, Academic Journals, Newspapers, Multimedia, and Websites. The results may be sorted by Relevance, Title, Reverse Chronological Order, Chronological Order, Document Type, and Source. Approximate reading levels are indicated by a circle, square, and triangle denoting basic, intermediate, and advanced reading levels, respectively.

Different kinds of searches can yield very different results. When *anatomy* is entered as a basic search term, results include 200 reference documents and 389 magazine articles. But selecting *anatomy* from the topic list returns 28 reference documents and 66 magazines articles. In both cases, a sidebar on the results screen offers ways to narrow a search by listing subtopics, such as *animal anatomy* and *plant anatomy*.

Buttons at the top of the page provide additional search options: Advanced, Person, Publication, and Science Standards searches. The Advanced Search allows Boolean searching. The default setting is Title/Headline AND Source AND Document Number, but patrons may also choose Author, Subject, Full-text, and Keyword from the pull-down menus to mix and match as desired. Other Advanced strategies include Date of Publication, Document Type (e.g., Audio, Experiment, Image, Topic Overview, and Website), Content Type (e.g., Basic, Intermediate, Limit To (e.g., Full-Text Documents, Documents with Images, and Peer-Reviewed Journals), and Number of Results per page. In a Person Search, a patron may enter a name and then choose Biographies only or All results. Or, as in Gale's *Biography Resource Center,* a patron may conduct a Biographical Facts search utilizing criteria such as occupation, gender, nationality, ethnicity, and date and place of birth. Despite a claim that a search can be limited to the biographies of the most studied people, we found no directions for how to accomplish this. The Publication Search offers the choice between Title Starts With and Title Contains searches. The Science Standards search offers the National Science Education Standards, Project 2061 Benchmark for Science Literacy, and State Standards plus the District of Columbia. Unfortunately, not all the states have allowed Gale to link topics to their content standards within the *Science Resource Center*. Also, only the science standards for grades 9–12, rather than grades 6–12, are presented.

As of August 13, 2004, the *Science Resource Center* contained 1,748,734 documents. Journals range from *AIDS Alert* and *Annual Review of Microbiology* to *Popular Mechanics* and *Ranger Rick.* Among the 41 reference titles are Gale's *Gale Encyclopedia of Medicine* and *Notable Women Scientists; Genetics,* from the Macmillan imprint; and *Experiment Central* and *Sick!* from the UXL imprint. *Grzimek's Animal Life Encyclopedia* would make an excellent addition. Other resources include a dictionary, a time line, and a toolbox, which offers learning aids. In Help, examples of how to cite a resource show both the MLA and APA styles.

This is an outstanding addition to young adult and school library digital databases, filling a need for grade- and age-appropriate online science resources. The multitude of information provided in the Toolbox and Help areas offers many ideas for lesson plans. The database may also prove valuable for general audience and basic undergraduate science research. Now if only Gale would automatically cross-reference *Science Resource Center* with *Opposing Viewpoints* and the various Student Resource Centers! —*Esther Sinofsky*

Medicine, Health, Technology, Management

Human Body Systems. 10v. Ed. by Michael Windelspecht. 2004. 2,000p. illus. index. Greenwood, $399.95 (0-313-33119-7). 612.

Written to provide "a one-stop reference source for anyone with an interest in the human body," each of these volumes covers a body system—circulatory, digestive, endocrine, lymphatic, muscular, nervous, reproductive, respiratory, skeletal, and urinary. Approximately 200 pages in length, the volumes are arranged in a similar format. Following a brief introduction, one or two pages are devoted to a listing of "Interesting Facts" (for example, "Babies in the womb dream, which contributes to brain development"), which should be a popular feature for researchers. The main body of each volume expands concepts in several ways. A number of chapters are devoted to a detailed physiological description of the system, its parts, its function, and its link to general health. Additional chapters provide a historical summary of what new insights have been generated by early discoveries and current medical research. Dozens of noted doctors, scientists, and researchers credited with significant discoveries are identified in these chapters, and the relevancy of their work is included. Closing chapters offer an examination of pertinent diseases and disorders, including causes, symptoms, diagnosis, treatment (conventional or alternative), prognosis, and recommended prevention measures. Although there are some black-and-white illustrations, diagrams, and charts, the material is primarily textual. Color illustrations are limited and inserted in the middle of each volume. Completing each volume are a list of acronyms, a glossary, a list of organizations and Web sites, and a bibliography.

Although *Human Body Systems* would make a nice reference set, it is published as a series. There is no comprehensive indexing, and since volumes are catalogued separately, they might not be shelved together. The series foreword defines the audience as "secondary school and introductory college libraries" as well as public libraries. The covers seem designed to appeal to the high-school level, but high-schoolers may find some of the writing too technical. Overall, this reference would be a valuable addition to any high-school and undergraduate library with strong physiology and anatomy programs. General readers in public libraries should also find it accessible and informative. —*Cheryl Ward*

The Encyclopedia of Cancer. By Carol Turkington and William Lipera. 2005. 448p. index. Facts On File, $71.50 (0-8160-5029-5). 616.99.

Thanks to continuing research and medical advances, mortality rates for many of the more common types of cancer are decreasing. The overall steady mortality decline is also attributed to public-awareness campaigns, prevention education, and cancer screenings. The purpose of this encyclopedia is to dispel myths and misconceptions and clarify and reinforce concepts and available options in an effort to create more positive attitudes for patients and caregivers.

More than 400 cancer-related topics are arranged alphabetically in dictionary format. Acronyms, specific cancers, medical procedures, and organizations are interfiled. The entries range in size from only a brief sentence to several pages of description. The longest and most detailed entries usually describe specific forms of cancer (*Brain cancer, Lung cancer*); surgical procedures (*Mastectomy*); screening techniques (*Mammography*); and relevant topics such as *African Americans and cancer, Cell phones, Diet,* and *Pain control*. Most cancer descriptions include causes or risk factors, symptoms, diagnoses, staging, treatment, and, where applicable, prognosis. Three appendixes, a glossary, an extensive bibliography, and a general index complete the volume.

The list of associations in appendix 1 is arranged by subject, with contact information included for grass-roots advocacy groups, national nonprofit and profit organizations, clearinghouses, foundations, and information networks. A national selection of cancer treatment centers, arranged by state, is found in appendix 2. Two lists of human carcinogens—the known and the "reasonably anticipated"—comprise appendix 3.

All in all, the encyclopedia is an excellent resource for its designated audience of general readers, caregivers, and cancer patients. By no means comprehensive, it is a factual and thorough introduction to an extremely complex disease family. Those seeking more in-depth information should consult sources such as the *The Gale Encyclopedia of Cancer: A Guide to Cancer and Its Treatments* (2001). —*Ann Cohen*

The Encyclopedia of Men's Reproductive Cancer. By Carol Turkington and Charles R. Pound. 2004. 304p. index. Facts On File, $65 (0-8160-5030-9). 616.99.

The Encyclopedia of Women's Reproductive Cancer. By Carol Turkington and Mitchell Edelson. 2004. 306p. index. Facts On File, $65 (0-8160-5031-7). 616.99.

Cancers of the reproductive organs are diagnosed in more than 300,000 American men and 80,000 women each year. *The Encyclopedia of Men's Reproductive Cancer* and *The Encyclopedia of Women's Reproductive Cancer* provide basic medical information written at a level accessible to the layperson. Each volume, written by a medical writer and a physician, contains about 400 alphabetically arranged entries that range in length from a sentence to several pages.

Topics covered include risk factors (*Alcohol, Smoking*); types of cancer (*Embryonal carcinoma, Ovarian cancer, Prostate cancer*); medical terminology (*Klinefelter syndrome, Salpingectomy*); treatment (*Biological therapy, Chemotherapy, Medical castration*); dietary options (*Antioxidants, Coenzyme Q10, Phytochemicals*); screening tests (*Lymphangiography, Ultrasound*); drugs (*Compazine, Marinol, Muse*); organizations (*Gynecologic Cancer Foundation, Hospice Foundation of America*); and support groups (*Gilda's Clubs, Man to Man*). Both volumes have lengthy appendixes that list clinical trials as of the publication date. (Current clinical trials are available on the National Cancer Institute Web site [http://www.cancer.gov/clinicaltrials], which can be searched by zip code as well as type of cancer.) Other appendixes are "Helpful Organizations" (including Web addresses and telephone numbers), "Cancer Centers," and "Drugs Used to Treat Reproductive Cancers." A glossary and a four-page bibliography (the most recent articles date from 2003) are also included.

The two-volume, proportionately more expensive *Gale Encyclopedia of Cancer* (2001) is more comprehensive and contains more than 200 illustrations, photographs, and charts. Although the facts in the volumes under review are available elsewhere, these books are well organized and provide reliable general information. The lack of any illustrations may be a drawback for some users. Part of the Facts On File Library of Health and Living, both volumes are worthy of consideration for general medical reference sections in public and academic libraries. —*Nancy Cannon*

The Encyclopedia of the Digestive System and Digestive Disorders. By Anil Minocha and Christine Adamec. 2004. 350p. index. Facts On File, $65 (0-8160-4993-9). 616.3.

The human digestive system is a complicated, elegant network of tubes and organs. This encyclopedia does a wonderful job of offering insight as to how it functions when healthy, as well as when things go terribly wrong. In addition to the entries, the reader will find very helpful appendixes, including contact information for U.S. and Canadian health departments and organizations, U.S. and Canadian poison-control centers, and reliable Web sites for information regarding digestive diseases.

The entries, however, are where the real value is. There are more than 300 of them, ranging in length from just a paragraph or two to multiple pages. They cover topics such as *Acid blocking agents, Contaminated food or water, Crohn's disease, Obesity, Steroids,* and *Vitamin deficiencies*. The discussion of various cancers related to the digestive system is 21 pages long and includes entries on diseases such as anal, colorectal, esophageal, and stomach cancer. Causes, risk factors, symptoms, diagnoses, and courses of treatment are discussed.

Many entries include bibliographic information, and cross-references are appropriately placed throughout the text. The index is very well developed and detailed.

Public libraries of all sizes and academic libraries with consumer-health collections would benefit from having this volume. Densely packed with dependable information, it will be of value not only to the student but also to individuals who are taking steps toward a healthier lifestyle, as well as patients struggling to understand diagnoses and medicalspeak. —*Scottie Wallace*

Enfermedades y trastornos de la salud. 3v. 2004. 1,200p. illus. index. Scribner, $325 (0-684-31273-5). 616.

Hispanics are the fastest-growing segment of the American population. As a result, libraries have many Spanish speakers as patrons. The need for health information is great in any language, but having a source with current, accurate, accessible information in Spanish will help librarians serve those who are more comfortable reading in their native language.

This Spanish-language version of *Human Diseases and Conditions* (1999) covers 280 diseases and conditions. The editorial staff, headed by Neil Izenberg, a physician and director of the Nemours Center for Health Media, are the same people who produced the English-language source. Experienced medical translators translated the text, and Spanish-speaking physicians reviewed the work. They used standard American Spanish to present basic information about human anatomy and physiology as well as common diseases and conditions. The book is attractive, with color illustrations and shaded sidebars that contain definitions of medical terms and useful supplementary information.

Each article begins with a definition of the disease or condition, followed by symptoms, diagnosis, and treatment. Some also have case histories to show that working with health-care professionals will lead to improvement or cure. All have lists of organizations and Web sites (*Fuentes*) at the end for further information. Many of these Web sites have information in English, with no Spanish links. A bibliography of works at the end of the set cites Spanish-language medical texts at a professional level. The inside covers of each volume contain a list of generic drug names in English and Spanish.

With information on common disorders such as *Acné, Enfermedades del corazón* (heart disease), and *Intoxicación alimentaria* (food poisoning), as well as *Raquitismo* (rickets), *Sida y VIH* (AIDS and HIV), and *Síndrome de estrés por repetición* (repetitive stress syndrome), this set belongs in all public, consumer-health, and medical libraries that serve Spanish speakers. —*Barbara Bibel*

ConsumerLab.com. [Online database]. Contact for pricing [http://www.consumerlab.com/]. (Last accessed February 23, 2005).

The growing popularity of herbal preparations, nutritional supplements, and vitamins has increased the demand for information about them. The Food and Drug Administration does not regulate these products, so manufacturers are responsible for ensuring that they are safe and truthfully labeled. One out of four supplements or nutritional products does not contain the designated amount of the active ingredient. Some are contaminated with lead, mercury, or other impurities. How can consumers find out what they are really buying?

ConsumerLab is an independent testing laboratory for health and nutrition products created by a physician and a Ph.D. chemist who specializes in natural products. They test selected samples of products commonly sold in the U.S. to see whether they meet recognized quality standards, have the amount of active ingredients claimed on the label, and break apart for proper absorption. Manufacturers may pay to get their products tested, but the lab will not accept samples directly from them.

The subscription database contains the results of tests on herbs, vitamins, nutritional supplements, and foods, such as nutrition bars and orange juice with calcium, as well as pet products. Users may search by product from a menu or enter terms in the search box. They can compare products and, in some cases, use a price checklist to find vendors or an additional link to get more information from a manufacturer. These extra services are clearly labeled as paid advertisements. The site also has current news about new tests, lists of warnings and product recalls, and an explanation of the criteria for awarding the ConsumerLab seal of approval. The Natural Products Encyclopedia area of the site offers information about substances, conditions, and alternative therapies. Healthsearch provides links to online journals, Medline, and organizations (many of the citations here are old). Technical reports explaining ConsumerLab's methodologies are available for for $950 each.

ConsumerLab.com fills a gap by providing quality-control information for unregulated products that are widely used. Medical, consumer health, and large public libraries with sufficient funds will find this resource very useful. Smaller libraries will want to purchase the book, *ConsumerLab. com's Guide to Buying Vitamins and Supplements: What's Really in the Bottle?* (ConsumerLab, 2003). —*Barbara Bibel*

Encyclopedia of Twentieth Century Technology. 2v. Ed. by Colin S. Hempstead and William E. Worthington. 2004. 933p. illus. index. Routledge, $325 (1-57958-386-5). 603.

In this encyclopedia on the technology that significantly affected people in industrial societies in the twentieth century, entries fall within six broad areas: food, leisure, homes, health, work, and interrelations. The emphasis is on technologies that influenced people's lives rather than twentieth-century technological inventions; often technology exists for decades before evolving into something serviceable. Thus, expect to find entries on things like *Dishwashers,* for which patents were first filed in the mid-nineteenth century but that became devices with widespread use in the mid-twentieth century.

Written by scholars, the 400 alphabetically arranged entries are objective, 1,000-word narratives on individual technologies, objects, systems, or products. Coverage is heaviest in the areas of computers (*Computers, analog; Global Positioning System; World Wide Web*); health and medicine (*Antibiotics, use after 1945; Dentistry; Intensive care and life support*); and transportation (*Air traffic control systems; Automobiles; Transport, foodstuffs*). A further reading list of monographs, periodicals, and Internet sites follows each entry, as do *see also* references. There are 30 longer survey entries that explore broader questions of technological systems, such as *Agriculture and food* and *Energy and power.*

The scope is international, and the language, while sophisticated, is generally free enough of technical jargon for the serious student. Occasional black-and-white illustrations help to clarify the text. The index, however, is too broad. Names are largely excluded, as in the case of Dolly, the cloned sheep. *Dolly* is not indexed at all, and the closest subject in the index, *cloning—animals,* only references one of multiple relevant entries.

Topics such as artificial intelligence, mass spectrometry, and nanotechnology are also covered in any standard science and technology encyclopedia, including, for example, the *McGraw-Hill Encyclopedia of Science and Technology* (9th ed., McGraw-Hill, 2002) and *Van Nostrand's Scientific Encyclopedia* (9th ed., Wiley, 2003). Still, this set offers some unique content and emphasizes the humanistic element of technology. It is probably closest in scope to *The Cutting Edge: An Encyclopedia of Advanced Technologies* (Oxford, 2000), which features only 102 less-detailed entries on newsworthy technology and its impact on everyday life but at a much cheaper price. The *Facts On File Encyclopedia of Science, Technology, and Society* (1999) is also somewhat similar, but it lacks satisfactory further reading lists. Recommended for academic and large public libraries. —*Susan Gardner*

America's Top Doctors. 4th ed. 2004. 1,160p. indexes. Castle Connolly, $79.95 (1-883769-47-7); paper, $29.95 (1- 883769-46-9). 610.69.

When serious illness strikes patients, their families want the best medical care available. This guide helps identify the "best" physicians in 25 specialties and 90 subspecialties recognized by the American Board of Medical Specialties.

The guide, published annually since 2001, is arranged alphabetically by specialty and then by broad geographic region. Physicians' entries, like those in the *Official ABMS Directory of Board Certified Medical Specialists* (Elsevier, annual), contain professionally relevant information including medical schools attended, place of residency, faculty appointments, and fellowships. Each specialty section includes a description of the specialty and the training and education required.

Physicians were nominated by their peers, nurses, or other health-care professionals. Biographical forms were sent to each physician. The editors then reviewed each doctor's professional background, licensing, and disciplinary history. The editors are careful to state (in very fine print) that the nominations are subjective and accuracy of information cannot be ensured. Health-care consumers might be put off by the paid promotional hospital ads interspersed throughout the book and the "for fee" ads for the publisher's Doctor- Patient Advisor and Doctor Select services. The most useful parts of the directory are found in the introductory section, which contains excellent guidance on how to choose a specialist and how to access clinical trials as a treatment option.

Among the appendixes are specialty board organization information, contact details for hospitals listed in individual entries, and a resources list covering databases, clinical trial clearinghouses, and consumer-health organizations. The "Special Expertise Index" lists a physician's area of expertise within a specialty (e.g., Parkinson's disease, ovarian cancer).

Given the public's natural desire to want the best when the need arises, the directory serves as a starting point, and public libraries will find it useful. It should be provided to patrons along with a suggestion to consult the local medical society, the ABMS directory, and their primary-care physicians. —*Marlene Kuhl*

Encyclopedia of Family Health. 18v. 3d. ed. 2005. 2,581p. illus. indexes. Marshall Cavendish, $499.95 (0-7614-7486-2). 610.

This third edition furnishes up-to-date specifics on medical conditions and related health issues. Several variations from the previous (1998) edition are obvious at initial examination. Great attention has been paid to the general aesthetics of the set, which now features eye-catching cover images of diversified people in the act of giving or receiving health care. The layout of pages has been redesigned with more color sidebars and contemporary photographs, resulting in a fresh, more appealing, user-friendly format. Volume 18, the revamped index volume, is in itself a plethora of information, offering a "First Aid Handbook" that integrates diagrams and other visuals with a step-by-step guide to treating 18 common emergencies (a credit card—not a knife or a fingernail—is now suggested for the removal of a bee stinger), a glossary, and a directory of health organizations in addition to a variety of thematic indexes. The "Further Reading and Research" section, also found in volume 18, offers an array of publications and Web sites. Some of the cited books are scholarly and might be difficult for the lay reader to procure.

The alphabetically arranged entries vary in length from one to several pages. New topics have been added, among them *Abstinence, Cell phones, Managed health care, SARS,* and *West Nile virus.* Most indicative of the times is a new, erudite entry on *Weight* that furnishes directions for calculating one's body mass index (BMI) and separate comparison graphs of BMI for girls and boys. Modifications to existing topics have been made when warranted by new data. For example, the risks of hormone-replacement treatment are mentioned in the entry *Menopause.* The newly marketed diabetic pump has been included as a treatment option in *Diabetes. Immunization* now includes the new chicken-pox vaccine. *Marijuana* mentions legal use of the drug for medicinal purposes in California and Hawaii.

Standard in each article are a brief summary giving a general overview of the topic and a sidebar of relevant questions and answers. These and other sidebars are color coded to relate them to one of five broad topic areas, such as diseases or treatments. Photographs—some published previously—and other visuals such as diagrams, graphs, and charts are detailed and vivid. In addition to the thematic and general indexes in volume 18, each volume includes its own index.

Although no book can be substituted for trained medical care, the general information furnished in this set offers a good foundation for understanding medical terms and diseases. Recommended for public libraries, the set's strong visuals and ease of use make it a good choice for young adults as well as adults. —*Cheryl Ward*

Encyclopedia of Health & Behavior. 2v. Ed. by Norman B. Anderson. 2004. 968p. appendixes. bibliogs. indexes. Sage, $350 (0-7619-2360-8). 610.

"Designed to provide an introduction to the many topics in health and behavior for diverse audiences," this *A–Z* work is an important development for the field of public health. Topics cut across all of the fields that compose health and behavior, including theories and methods in health and behavior, biopsychosocial interactions and basic behavioral and social processes, epidemiology of risk and protective factors, health promotion and disease prevention, treatment and rehabilitation, and policy and organizational issues. Social and cultural factors are also covered, including, for example, *Crowding and health, Health disparities, Latino health and behavior,* and *Social or status incongruence.* More than 200 signed entries by credentialed contributors range in length from 1 to 9 pages and are followed by bibliographies for further reading. Two appendixes, repeated in both volumes, are particularly helpful—an annotated 15-page directory of online resources and predominantly national health and behavior organizations and a 67-page general bibliography. Author and subject indexes conclude the set. Access is facilitated also by a list of entries and a reader's guide at the beginning of volume 1.

Jargon and technical terms are difficult to avoid in a work such as this, and despite the fact that it is intended to be an introductory tool, undergraduate and graduate students in the behavioral and social sciences, medical students, and those in the biomedical sciences will have an easier time with this resource than the general public. But although Macmillan's four-volume *Encyclopedia of Public Health* (2001) offers a more comprehensive survey, this work fills a niche and does so very well. Academic and large public libraries that are growing reference collections in the fields of psychology, epidemiology and public health, sociology, nursing, medicine, and anthropology will want to add this to their shelves. —*Sarah Watstein*

Magill's Medical Guide. 4v. 3d. ed. Ed. by Anne Chang and others. 2004. 3,200p. illus. index. Salem, $341 (1-58765-159-9). 610.

Authoritative, up-to-date sources for medical information are a must for any general reference collection. First published in 1995, this is the third revised edition of *Magill's Medical Guide.* Expanded to four volumes and written at a level appropriate for the general reader, the set is "intended for broad informational and educational purposes." The 960 alphabetically arranged articles, signed by subject experts, range in length from 500 words (a half page) to 3,500 words.

The majority of articles relate to diseases and disorders and include information on causes, symptoms, and treatment. Entries begin with standardized ready-reference summaries: the type of topic being covered (e.g., "Disease/Disorder," "Procedure," "Treatment"), the part of the anatomy or system affected, the medical specialties involved, and a brief definition of the topic. All articles conclude with a bibliography. In addition to diseases and disorders, coverage encompasses the basics of anatomy and physiology (*Digestion, Gray hair, Heart*); procedures (*Chemotherapy, Jaw wiring, Pap smear*); medical specialties (*Dermatology, Holistic medicine, Orthopedics*); and common surgical and nonsurgical procedures (*Acupuncture, Circumcision, Xenotransplantation*). This edition contains new articles on such topics as *Biological and chemical weapons, Botox, SARS,* and *Seasonal affective disorder.*

Black-and-white line drawings and photographs supplement the text. Extensive appendixes include a 60-page glossary of medical terms, a 25-page listing of diseases and other medical conditions, types of health-care providers, a listing of medical journals, a general bibliography, organizations and other resources, and an annotated Web site directory. A comprehensive 45-page index provides subject access to the contents. Lists of entries by body part or system and by medical specialty offer additional access points.

Magill's Medical Guide is well-organized, easy to use, and fills the need for accurate general medical information. It is recommended for public, special, and academic libraries. A useful supplement to this and other print sources is the free *Medline Plus Medical Encyclopedia,* from the National Institutes of Health [http://www.nlm.nih.gov/medlineplus/encyclopedia.html], which contains approximately 4,000 reputable, illustrated articles about diseases, tests, symptoms, injuries, and surgeries. —*Nancy Cannon*

The Encyclopedia of the Heart and Heart Disease. By Deborah S. Romaine and Otelio S. Randall. 2004. 382p. illus. index. Facts On File, $65 (0-8160-5087-2). 612.1.

This title is an excellent addition to the Facts On File Library of Health and Living providing a brief foundation for laypersons to understand health and disease of the heart. As heart disease is the cause of more than one-third of all deaths in this country, the title is a must in most libraries. It provides easy-to-understand information on symptoms, treatments, and causes.

More than 900 entries cover prescription and nonprescription drugs used for heart health, important figures in heart research, and illnesses of the heart and surrounding areas. There are articles on smoking, alcohol, physical fitness, biofeedback, nutrition, and other human activities that affect heart health. Articles on eating disorders, diabetes, AIDS, and stroke discuss the effect various conditions and illnesses have on the heart. People from Rene Laënnec, inventor of the stethoscope, to Robert Jarvik, inventor of the artificial heart, are profiled.

Articles are brief, and medical terminology is either explained thoroughly or simplified to increase understanding by the lay reader. Cross-references and *see also* references are used liberally to direct the reader to appropriate articles. Appendixes provide a list of organizations, common abbreviations, and a series of diagrams from the publisher's *Human Body on File: Physiology.* The bibliography is divided into clinical texts, books for general readers, and articles. Overall, this title adds to the well-received series and stands on its own as a solid tool for consumer medical collections. —*Steve Stratton*

The Encyclopedia of Vitamins, Minerals, and Supplements. 2d ed. index. 2004. 353p. Facts On File, $65 (0-8160-4998-X). 612.3.

Interest in vitamins, minerals, food supplements, and herbs is growing. This book provides nonjudgmental coverage of nutritional options without advocating any particular ones. Mainly for the layman, it is presented in easy-to-read A–Z format and updates the 1996 first edition with 100 new entries, including *Bee pollen, Chondroitin, Fen-phen, Golden rice, Green drinks and superfoods, Green tea, Mediterranean diet, Nutraceuticals, Quinoa, Reishi mushroom, Stevia leaf powder,* and *Tempeh.* The more than 900 entries focus on how to use the substances safely, their effects on nutrition, their uses as treatment for assorted health concerns, and common misconceptions about them. Articles on individual vitamins and minerals are detailed. The entry on vitamin E, for example, has sections on history, deficiency, dosage, RDA, and toxicity, along with three charts.

The book ends with 11 appendixes. Some new information appears in the nutrition chronology and the bibliography. Completely new appendixes are "Position of the American Dietetic Association: Food and Nutrition Misinformation," which gives extensive discussion of vegetarian diets; "Health and Human Services Acts to Reduce Potential Risks of Dietary Supplements Containing Ephedra"; and "NCCAM Consumer Advisory on Ephedra— Revised February 28, 2003."

The author is a registered nurse who writes about alternative medicine and other health topics. As part of the Facts On File Library of Health and Living, this work is recommended, for high- school, public, and community college libraries. —*Carole Deily.*

The Encyclopedia of Men's Health. By Glen S. Rothfield and Deborah S. Romaine. 2005. 391p. index. Facts On File, $75 (0-8160-5177-1). 613.

Numerous texts provide information on men's health, among them *The Harvard Medical School Guide to Men's Health* (Free Press, 2002) and *The American Medical Association Complete Guide to Men's Health* (Wiley, 2001). Together with these titles, this offering from Facts On File would provide a reasonable coverage of men's health in easy-to-understand language. Standing on its own, it is not enough for reference collections.

The authors succeed in providing brief, readable entries on any number of men's health topics. *See* and *see also* references direct readers to the appropriate main entries or related entries. Several appendixes provide information on vitamins and minerals necessary for men, preventative health-care recommendations, a glossary of health-care specialties, and a listing of health organizations and agencies. A selected bibliography provides a few other sources of information, and a relatively straightforward index directs readers to specific articles.

One missing component is any article discussing the health issues of minority men—there are no articles on African American, Hispanic, or Native American men. Nor are there articles on the health issues of gay men. The only discussions of men of African, Native, Asian, or Hispanic descent are in articles on *Hypertension* and *Kidney disease*. Brief mentions in the *Sexual orientation* and *HIV/AIDS* entries constitute the only discussion of health issues of gay men.

One area of increasing concern in men's health is the rising incidence of anal cancer found in all men. African American men in particular have a high incidence and low survival rate with this form of malignancy. The number of men diagnosed annually with this particularly virulent cancer is four times the rate of diagnosis of penile cancer, which received nearly a full-page entry in the book. In contrast, a small reference to anal cancer is found under the entry for *Human papillomavirus (HPV)*, which is the known cause of anal cancers, but anal cancer is not listed in the index.

Although the text is easily understandable and will be useful for some patrons, it is not recommended unless the library already owns or can afford other materials to fill the vacuum of information in certain areas. —*Stephen Stratton*

The Merck Manual of Health and Aging. Ed. by Mark H. Beers. 2004. 961p. appendixes. illus. index. Merck, $29.95 (0-911910-36-0). 613.

As our population ages, information about the aging process and caring for the elderly is a necessity. *The Merck Manual of Health and Aging*, a lay version of *The Merck Manual of Geriatrics* (3d ed., Wiley, 2000), provides it in a very accessible format.

The book has four sections. The first, "Fundamentals of Aging," covers such questions as when does a person become old, why does the body change, and how aging affects the organs and systems. Related issues, such as finances, living arrangements, and coping with chronic disease and disability, appear also. Section 2, "Caring for Self and Others," deals with preventive medical care, nutrition, continuity of care, long-term care, and palliative and end-of-life care. Section 3 covers specific medical conditions that are more common in the elderly: falls, sleep problems, movement disorders, heart disorders, cancers, etc. A chapter on the importance of exercise with recommendations for those with specific diseases is very useful. The last section, "Social, Legal, and Ethical Issues," provides vital information on the decision to stop driving, intimacy, mistreatment of the elderly, and health care costs. A chapter explaining informed consent, confidentiality, capacity and competency, and advance directives will help people prepare for medical treatment. Two appendixes cover the generic and trade names of drugs commonly prescribed for seniors and a referral list of organizations. Charts and sidebars offer useful supplemental information. Twenty-five essays in which people share their feelings and insights about aging are scattered throughout the book.

The Merck Manual of Health and Aging is unique because it focuses on how disorders are different in older adults rather than discussing all aspects of a disease. It also emphasizes adapting to the bodily changes of aging and finding effective ways to cope. It is reasonably priced and belongs in all public, medical, and consumer health libraries. —*Barbara Bibel*

Nutrition and Well-Being A to Z. Ed. by Delores C. S. James. 2v. 2004. illus. index. Macmillan, $175 (0-02-865707-1); E-book, contact Gale for pricing (0-02-865990-2). 613.2.

The 250 signed entries that fill these volumes range between a paragraph and four pages in length and contain bibliographies. The outside margins of the text are very wide, allowing terms and phrases used in individual entries to be defined. In the entry *Fast foods*, for example, the reader will find the following terms in bold: *fast food, Americanized, fat, fiber, vitamin, mineral, calorie*. In the adjacent margin all terms are briefly defined—just enough for the entry to become understandable. *See also* references point to other related topics, such as *Convenience foods; Dietary trends, American;* and *Dietary trends, international*.

Black-and-white illustrations are liberally dispersed throughout the pages. They include well-labeled graphs and charts as well as photographs and diagrams. Entries such as *Famine, Food insecurity, Malnutrition,* and *Refugee Nutrition Information System (RNIS)* include disturbing but most appropriate photographs. Haunting images of the faces of starving youngsters carry information to the reader in ways that words cannot.

To keep volume juggling at a minimum, each of the two volumes contains an identical table of contents, topical outline, index, and glossary. Also repeated is the reference section, which includes such information as a metric conversion table, the age-type Food Guide Pyramids, and the Body Mass Index (BMI) Table.

Although the emphasis is on North America, the scope is international, including dietary descriptions, histories, and challenges for Africans, Asians, and Scandinavians, among others. This is a good overview tool for personalities associated with nutrition, such as early vitamin researcher Casimir Funk and "King of the Road" Howard Deering Johnson. It is also a good source for information on current topics, such as *Glycemic index,* the potentially deadly *Female athlete triad,* and *Omega-3 and Omega-6 fatty acids* (although information on trans fats is curiously difficult to find).

The set would be valuable as an introductory or overview tool in public libraries. In high-school libraries, it will serve as a source of solid information as well as a reliable antidote for report-writers' block. —*Scottie Wallace*

The Gale Encyclopedia of Alternative Medicine. 4v. 2d. ed. Ed. by Jacqueline L. Longe. 2005. 2,411p. illus. index. Gale, $425 (0-7876-7424-9). 615.5.

The fact that some alternative health treatments are now covered by health insurance is proof that they have entered the mainstream. The second edition of this set is "a one-stop source for alternative medical information" containing more than 800 articles covering 150 therapies, 275 diseases and conditions, and 300 herbs and other remedies. Alternative health practitioners, educators, pharmacists, and medical writers wrote the alphabetical, signed articles. All entries have resource lists of books, articles, and organizations, and many are illustrated with black-and-white photographs. Sidebars with biographies of leaders in the field, such as Edward Bach, Deepak Chopra, and David Palmer, are a new feature. A photo gallery of color plates of medicinal plants appears in each volume. Many entries have sidebars containing glossaries of key terms.

The entries for therapies (*Acupuncture, Rolfing*) discuss origins, benefits, precautions, side effects, and research and general acceptance. Those covering herbs and other remedies (*Gotu kola, Saw palmetto*) describe general use, preparations, precautions, side effects, and interactions. Information about diseases and conditions covers definitions, descriptions, causes and symptoms, diagnosis, treatment, allopathic treatment, expected results, and prevention. Cross-references make locating relevant material easy. The articles are written in lay language, so they are easy to read and understand.

The second edition has a glossary and an expanded organization list that includes mainstream organizations such as the American Medical Association. It also has information about the efficacy of the various treatments based on research conducted at institutions such as the National Center for Complementary and Alternative Medicine at the National Institutes of Health. Controversial topics, such as the link between childhood vaccines and autism, are covered, but the article on vaccines does not include a citation for the information on the Centers for Disease Control and Prevention's Web site citing studies that show no evidence for this.

Although this edition has only 50 new articles, the expanded coverage and inclusion of evidence-based study data make it a valuable addition to collections in health-science, consumer health, and large public libraries. —*Barbara Bibel*

The Encyclopedia of Breast Cancer. By Carol Turkington and Karen Krag. 2004. 308p. index. Facts On File, $65 (0-8160-5028-7). 616.99.

Few libraries will want to be without this all-in-one volume for the layperson. The authors, one a medical writer and the other an oncologist, have organized a tremendous amount of up-to-date information on every aspect of breast cancer. Included are more than 500 alphabetically arranged entries ranging from *Accessory breast tissue* to *Y-ME* and including risk factors, prevention, treatments, legislation, studies, and more. Many entries are at least one-quarter page and include in-text cross-references (*Isoflavones* includes *Soy products, Estrogen,* and *Tamoxifen; Ductal papillomas* cross-references to *Nipple discharge*). The thorough index at the end helps users, too. Only a few headings are awkwardly phrased (for example, *Childhood events and breast cancer*).

Information is current, with several 2004 studies cited in the text and hundreds of journal articles from 1993 to 2003 listed in the bibliography. There are five appendixes at the end of the text: related associations and agencies by topic (financial aid, hospice, support groups); cancer centers by state; 31 pages of ongoing clinical trials; drugs used; and products for people with breast cancer. These are followed by a brief glossary (*cytokines*

57

and *metastasis* are defined but not *etiology*). One of the well-received entries in Facts On File's Library of Health and Living (others titles cover topics such as obesity and phobias), this is essential for public and college library collections. —*Susan Gooden*

The Encyclopedia of Endocrine Diseases and Disorders. By William A. Petit Jr. and Christine Adamec. 2005. 326p. index. Facts On File, $75 (0-8160-5135-6). 616.4.

Diseases and disorders of the endocrine system, such as diabetes and hypothyroidism, affect millions of Americans. The endocrine system (adrenal glands, hypothalamus, ovaries, pancreas, parathyroid, pineal gland, pituitary, testicles, and thyroid) helps regulate basic functions such as heart rate, blood pressure, energy storage, fertility, tissue growth, and overall body metabolism. Written at a level accessible to the layperson by a well-known endocrinologist and a medical writer, this authoritative volume contains more than 250 alphabetically arranged entries that range in length from a few sentences to several pages.

The goal of this reference is to give a broad overview of the normal and abnormal function of the endocrine system. A useful 13-page introduction provides general information on the functioning of the endocrine system over the human life span as well as a summary of the function of each of the glands. Specific entries in the encyclopedia include *AIDS, Amenorrhea, Blood pressure/hypertension, Diabetes insipidus, Goiter, Graves' disease, Infertility, Melatonin, Obesity, Oral glucose tolerance test, Osteoporosis,* and *Testosterone.* Supplemental information is provided in 16 appendixes, among them "Chart of Thyroid Medications to Treat Hypothyroidism," "Medications to Treat Diabetes," "10 Little-Know Facts about Diabetes Mellitus," and "Web Sites with Information on Endocrine Diseases and Disorders." A 14-page bibliography and a well-done 24-page subject index are provided. Brief bibliographies and relevant Web sites are included at the end of some articles.

This encyclopedia is a good source for basic, reliable medical information. The lack of illustrations may be a drawback for some users. Part of the Facts On File Library of Health and Living, the volume is worthy of consideration for general medical reference sections in public and academic libraries. —*Nancy Cannon*

Encyclopedia of Sexually Transmitted Diseases. By Elaine M. Moore. 2005. 280p. index. illus. McFarland, $65 (0-7864-1794-3). 616.95.

All sorts of maladies may be found in this encyclopedia. Included are those diseases that are covered under the umbrella we've come to identify as STDs—sexually transmitted diseases—but the reader may find some other conditions that are not usually thought of as being in the same company. Examples of these are hepatitis A through E and scabies. Each disease entry includes helpful subsections for etiology, epidemiology, symptoms, complications, diagnosis, treatment, risk factors, and, where appropriate, issues regarding pregnancy. Infections transmitted through means other than sexual contact are also described. In this category, *Body piercing, Needle sharing,* and *Pregnancy* each have their own entries.

The horror resulting from the gross misuse of sexual power may be found in the entries *Child sexual abuse* and *Sexual assault.* Oddly missing, however, is an entry for *Rape,* a term that might have helped steer readers to either of the above as a *see also* reference, if not a full definition.

Names associated with discovery, diagnosis, and healing are found in abundance. Although most are contemporary, the scope includes centuries past. Immunologist Paul Ehrlich, AIDS researcher Robert Gallo, and nineteenth-century French physician Phillipe Ricord are examples. Also defined are programs such as the *Health Disparities Initiative, Healthy Life Choices Project,* and *Healthy People 2010.*

In addition to an index, this work includes lists of books, journals, reports, Web sites; hotlines, and organizations. The *Encyclopedia* would be of value in both public and high-school libraries in which a quick reference on STDs is sought. —*Scottie Wallace*

The Encyclopedia of the Muscle and Skeletal Systems and Disorders. By Mary Harwell Sayler. 2005. 389p. index. Facts On File, $75 (0-8160-5447-9). 616.7.

Yet another addition to the Facts on File Library of Health and Living series, this volume addresses the important and frequently neglected musculoskeletal system—the 206 bones and 600-plus muscles in the human body that define our size, shape, strength, and physical mobility.

The encyclopedia explores and explains why, by midlife, the body visibly complains of overuse and abuse through its aches, pains, stiffness, muscle weakness, and other symptoms of aging. Approximately 500 entries relating to muscle and skeletal disorders, arranged alphabetically, are presented in clear, concise fashion. Although greater emphasis appears to be placed on topics affecting the aging population, subjects do run the full gamut from *Birth defects* to *Hip replacement surgery* and *Osteoarthritis. Cleft lip and palate, Growth hormones, Huntington's disease, Juvenile rheumatoid arthritis, Massage therapy, Pressure points,* and *Scoliosis* are just a sampling of the topics covered. In some cases, generally following longer entries, a few bibliographic references are listed. In appendixes, tables identify the bones, muscles, and bursas; tendons; and joints. Readers will also find advice on finding quality health care and locating credible information on the Internet and contact information for appropriate medical organizations.

The Encyclopedia of the Muscle and Skeletal Systems and Disorders is a valuable addition to popular medical collections. It is rare to find a single source for the general public that encompasses the entire realm of the musculoskeletal system. —*Ann Cohen*

The Gale Encyclopedia of Neurological Disorders. 2v. Ed. by Stacey L. Chamberlin and Brigham Narins. 2004. 1,011p. illus. index. Gale, $300 (0-7876-9150-X); e-book, call 800-877-4253 for pricing (0-7876-9160-7). 616.8.

Gale's addition to its stable of health resources fills a gap in consumer health collections by providing much-needed current information about disorders of one of the most complex systems of the human body.

The two consecutively paged volumes contain approximately 400 signed, alphabetical entries. The authors are health-care professionals and medical writers. The articles cover diseases (*Batten disease, Rasmussen's encephalitis*); syndromes (*Lennox-Gastaut syndrome, Tourette syndrome*); drugs (*Antimigraine medications, Valporic acid and divalproex sodium*); treatments (*Acupuncture, Radiation*); therapies (*Craniotomy, Bodywork therapies*); and diagnostic equipment and devices (*Electronic personal assistive mobility devices, CT scan*). There are also entries for anatomical and physiological topics such as *Cerebral circulation* and common symptoms such as *Dizziness.*

The articles are one to four pages long. All have shaded boxes with definitions of key terms and resource lists, and many have color illustrations. An alphabetical list of all articles appears at the beginning of each volume. The lack of *see* references in this list and in the text is a minor inconvenience. There is a glossary at the end of volume 2. The reading level is fairly high, so public and consumer health collections will also need resources at a lower literacy level.

There is some duplication and overlap with other Gale medical encyclopedias. The article *Amyotrophic lateral sclerosis* is identical to that in *The Gale Encyclopedia of Medicine* (1999). Some material from the *The Gale Encyclopedia of Mental Disorders* (2002) appears here because of the role of neurotransmitters in mental illness. Since many genetic diseases affect the nervous system, there is some overlap with *The Gale Encyclopedia of Genetic Disorders* (2001) also. The article on *Canavan disease* is almost identical. Nevertheless, most public and consumer health libraries will want *The Gale Encyclopedia of Neurological Disorders* because of its focus on complex conditions that are not well covered in other lay medical encyclopedias. —*Barbara Bibel*

The New Harvard Guide to Women's Health. Rev. ed. By Karen J. Carlson and others. 2004. 688p. illus. index. Harvard, $55 (0-674-01282-8); paper, $24.95 (0-674-01343-3). 616.

Librarians will breathe a sigh of relief at the release of this new edition. There is so much good information in the 1996 version, but eight years is a long time in the area of medical guides, and many of us have likely withdrawn the previous edition.

As before, the guide's major focus is on diseases and disorders of the female reproductive system and how diseases common to both sexes may manifest themselves differently in women. The most important change is the updated information on estrogen replacement therapy. In 1996 ERT was viewed as an ideal treatment for women. The 2002 findings of the Women's Health Initiative changed that thinking completely. The research results and the current position of medical professionals are reflected in this edition. Medical advances in the treatment of other diseases and disorders are also covered. The growing acceptance of alternative medicine is reflected in revised articles on the topic. Among the new entries are *Airbags, Dissociative identity disorder, Lyme disease,* and *Lymphedema.*

This edition is 30 pages shorter than the previous one but contains more entries and a center "blue pages" section with bodily systems diagrams, nutrition charts, and more. The page reduction has been accomplished by the use of smaller type. Information on diseases and disorders is presented as questions and answers addressing definitions, symptoms, treatments, and prevention. A topical resource list gives organizations to be contacted for additional information. Many labeled medical drawings appear throughout the book.

The guide is an outstanding source for public and professional libraries. It is aimed at an educated readership. Given the recent publicity on the literacy problem in consumer health information materials (most of which are written at a tenth-grade reading level and above), libraries should be sure to provide other sources on the topic. —*Marlene Kuhl*

The Encyclopedia of Sports Medicine. By Elizabeth H. Oakes. 2004. 322p. illus. index. Facts On File, $65 (0-8160-5334-0). 617.1.

This volume, part of the well-reviewed Facts On File Library of Health and Living, is similar to others in the series. It provides clearly written, alphabetically arranged information on topics of interest to the public and health professionals.

More than 150 entries (*Abrasions* to *Youth participation in sports*) describe causes, diagnosis, prevention, and treatment of sports injuries for amateur and professional athletes. The articles, usually about a page or two each, are clearly written and are generally listed under the common name with a medical term in parentheses: *Shoulder separation (acromioclavicular joint injury), Swimmer's ear (otitis).*

Thorough indexing and cross-references add to the volume's usefulness. The bibliography lists sports-medicine journals and texts as well as a few more popular titles, many dated 2003. Appendixes include safety tips and nutrition for particular sports; common sports injuries; training tips for runners and cyclists; international associations of trainers; and sports-medicine schools, journals, and Web sites. These are somewhat less organized than the rest of the work—why nutrition for golfers but not gymnasts? Why safety tips for skiing but not tennis? Still, there's nothing comparable except the more clinical *Rehabilitation of Sports Injuries* (Blackwell, 2003). This is sure to be used in high-school, college, and public libraries. —*Susan Gooden*

Baby and Child Health. Ed. by Jennifer Shu. 2004. 352p. illus. index. DK, $30 (0-7566-0454-0). 618.92.

Published in association with the American Academy of Pediatrics (AAP), this guide provides information for parents of children up to the age of 11 years. It includes all aspects of physical growth and health as well as emotional and intellectual development. The color-coded sections make it easy to find specific information, and the illustrations demonstrate both symptoms and proper techniques for care and treatment.

The book starts out with sections for infants and young children. Each includes information about growth and development and diagnosis charts for common symptoms. There are also sections on diseases and disorders by organ system and on first aid. "Making Sense of Health Care Information" is a useful essay that tells readers how to evaluate what they find in books, online, and in advertisements. A resource list provides contact information for government and nonprofit agencies offering information about children's health, but there is no bibliography.

Although the fourth edition of AAP's *Caring for Your Baby and Child: Birth to Age 5* was published in 2004, the new DK title is more recent than AAP's *Caring for Your School-Age Child: Ages 5–12* (1999) and *Guide to Your Child's Symptoms* (1997). It is a useful addition to public and consumer-health library collections and priced so that those with sufficient funds could purchase both reference and circulating copies. It is also a good choice for the home. —*Barbara Bibel*

The Encyclopedia of Children's Heath and Wellness. 2v. By Carol Turkington and Albert Tzeel. 2004. 682p. index. Facts On File, $130 (0-8160-4821-5). 618.92.

This title in the Facts on File Library of Health and Living series has more than 600 entries covering pediatric health from the prenatal state through 18 years of age. From serious illnesses, such as Tay-Sachs disease, to simple problems, such as a nosebleed, the encyclopedia offers a discussion of the illness, then provides separate paragraphs on the cause, treatment, symptoms, and prevention for each problem discussed. Particularly helpful are the articles on common conditions such as ADHD, lice, and roseola. The articles are, on the whole, easy to understand and provide good basic information. There are numerous *see* references within the text that will direct the reader to the proper article to answer his or her questions. A table in the entry *Immunization* provides a time line showing when children should be vaccinated against common illnesses.

In addition to entries on diseases and conditions, there are brief articles on medical specialists, vaccinations, associations, even insects that can cause and spread disease. The book focuses on children in the U.S. almost exclusively, and several diseases that effect children in other parts of the world, such as Chagas disease and leishmaniasis, are not discussed. Given the recent spread of West Nile virus, monkeypox, and other illnesses to the U.S., perhaps prominent global children's illnesses should be included in future editions.

An extensive appendix section in volume 2 offers addresses and URLs for support groups and patient-information groups, a list of camps for kids with cancer, toll-free hotlines for information, poison hotlines around the country, children's hospitals, and a guide to handling health emergencies. A thorough index and an extensive bibliography round out the work, which is a recommended title for public libraries and consumer-health collections. —*Stephen Stratton*

Encyclopedia of Military Technology and Innovation. By Stephen Bull. 2004. 331p. illus. index. Greenwood, $75 (1-57356-557-1). 623.

In more than 700 entries, this volume attempts to provide the lay reader with definitions of military technology that are easy to read and understand. At the beginning of the book are an alphabetical list of entries along with a "Guide to Related Terms," in which each entry is grouped under broader topics such as "Armor (personal protection)," "Fortifications and Obstacles," and "Tanks."

The majority of entries deal with military technology from the U.S., United Kingdom, Germany, and Russia, since these countries have made the largest contribution to military technology and innovation. English-language names and NATO designations are used for all terms. Examples of entries are *Gliders, Line of battle (ship), Satellites,* and *Torpedo.* Certain names and terms have often been used in military history to designate types of equipment, as an aircraft or naval vessel name or as a class of naval vessel or armament, and this work makes an effort to give attention to each use. For example, there are separate definitions for *Typhoon* (*Eurofighter*), *Typhoon* (*Hawker*), and *Typhoon class.* In each entry, the relevant topic area (e.g., "Tanks") is noted. Definitions are generally brief, although a few (*Gas masks, Sea mine*) cover more than a page. Boldfaced words in the text indicate terms that have their own separate entries, and *see* references are used to direct the reader to correct entry headings. Many of the entries list additional readings.

A "Chronology of Crucial Advances in Military Technology" lists approximate dates of introduction of particular technologies into military use (e.g., *Shrapnel c. 1790, Computer c. 1943*). The author has produced a work that will be useful to the inquisitive reader wanting brief information, and the bibliography and list of Webs sites found at the end of the volume can serve as springboards for further research. This book would be useful for college and large public libraries. —*Kaye Talley*

American Cars, 1960 to 1972: Every Model Year by Year. By J. Kelly Flory Jr. 2004. 938p. illus. index. McFarland, $65 (0-7864-1273-9). 629.222.

When one thinks of cars from the 1960s, the first thing that comes to mind is muscle cars. This unique book covers the muscle cars of that period. It is arranged by year and includes all of the cars that were offered for sale by U.S. automobile manufacturers. For each model year there is an overview of the cars followed by extensive data about each, including production numbers, pricing, specifications and dimensions, standard equipment and major options, paint color choices, running changes from the previous model year, and other information. The information is presented in standardized form so that comparisons can easily be made from one model to another. The small black-and-white pictures of each model are not of much use since they are so small that the detail cannot be seen. Trucks are not included, and neither are those imports such as the Dodge Colt, Plymouth Cricket, Ford Cortina, and the Opels sold by Buick. A two-page index of car models concludes the book. There is no bibliography, but it appears from the author's acknowledgments that much of the information was gleaned from NADA's *Used Car Guide, Motor* magazine, and the *NATB Motor Vehicle Identification Manual.*

Flory covers an enormous amount of information, and his friendly writing style makes interesting reading. A nice feature is the use of advertising quotes used by the automobile industry, such as "It's the car to arrive in when you've arrived" for the Buick Electra 225 or "Go pert, peppy and proud . . . in a Falcon" for the Ford Falcon or "Sports car action with a luxury look" for the Mercury Marauder. With the interest in trivia, an index of these quotes and the automobiles to which they refer would be extremely valuable. Public libraries will find this a useful reference source. —*H. Robert Malinowsky*

Frontiers of Space Exploration. 2d ed. By Roger D. Launius. 2004. 245p. appendix. bibliog. illus. index. Greenwood, $45 (0-313- 32524-3). 629.45.

Here is an updated and expanded second edition. The first edition, also edited by Launius (chair of the Division of Space History of the National Air and Space Museum) was published in 1998 as part of the Greenwood Guide to Historic Events in the Twentieth Century series. The text includes a chronology, a general historical overview of space flight, 3 lengthy essays on space exploration, and 21 biographical essays. In addition, 26 primary documents trace U.S. space flight history, and there is an up-to-date listing of all U.S. space flights up to and including the *Columbia* disaster of January 2003. A fine annotated bibliography rounds out the volume. The differences between this and the first edition are the expansion to include documents, people, and events that came after the first edition's publication. This is a worthwhile update for libraries that need a good overview of the history of manned space flight in one source, particularly useful for public and high-school libraries. —*Jeff Kosokoff*

National Geographic Encyclopedia of Space. Ed. by Linda K. Glover. 2004. 400p. illus. National Geographic, $40 (0-7922-7319-2). 629.4.

Glover, the primary author and editor of this exceptional book, explains its concept: "I couldn't find a 'SPACE 101' book anywhere that covered all the subjects I needed at an entry level." This is the book she wanted—arranged by concepts, not alphabetically. It is organized in six chapters: "Deep Space," "Our Solar System," "Reaching and Maneuvering in Space," "Human Spaceflight," "Earth Science and Commerce from Space," and "Military and Intelligence Uses of Space." Each chapter is written and edited by a specialist in the field and divided into subchapters that average five pages in length and are in turn broken down into smaller entries. Special essays provide more in-depth information. For example, "The Great Crash of 1994," addressing a huge asteroid that crashed into Jupiter, appears in the section on comets in the "Deep Space" chapter. Explanations are clear and basic, written for the popular audience. There are numerous charts, graphs, and time lines throughout. All measurements use the metric system. Words in bold type cross-reference other entries and subentries.

The appendix consists of double-page maps of the northern sky and the southern sky star charts with constellations, the moon, Mars, the solar system, the Milky Way, and the universe. In addition, the encyclopedia has more than 200 wonderful color pictures from NASA, the Hubble telescope, and satellite images, many of them covering a full page or a double-page spread. The captions clarify concepts in the text, rather than merely repeat it.

We have come to expect the spectacular from National Geographic, and this new encyclopedia reaffirms our faith. Libraries and homes will both want this breathtaking book. —*Robin Hoelle*

Space Exploration Reference Library. 4v. By Peggy Saari. 2005. illus. indexes. UXL, $215 (0-7876-9208-5). 629.4.

In its now familiar Reference Library format, UXL presents a middle-school resource on space exploration. The two-volume *Space Exploration: Almanac* component has 14 chapters averaging 22 pages in length and covering topics such as "Rocketry in Warfare," "Manned Spaceflight Begins," "Space Shuttles," and "Ground-Based Observatories." The third volume, *Space Exploration: Biographies,* profiles individuals (Buzz Aldrin, Mae Jemison, H. G. Wells), but readers will also find articles on the Hubble Space Telescope and the International Space Station. *Space Exploration: Primary Sources* has 15 chapters that extract and explain content from materials ranging from Jules Verne's *From Earth to the Moon* to George W. Bush's January 14, 2004, remarks on space exploration. Chapters in all four volumes conclude with a list of print and Internet resources to consult for additional information.

Like other titles in the Reference Library line, *Space Exploration* is filled with aids for the student. A time line, glossary, list of "Research and Activity Ideas," and general bibliography are repeated in each volume. Chapters in the *Almanac* have their own lists of "Words to Know," and in *Primary Sources,* terms that may be unfamiliar are defined in the page margins. Sidebars and black-and-white photographs provide additional information and break up the text. In addition to volume indexing, there is a separate cumulative index.

Another student-friendly resource, Macmillan's four-volume *Space Sciences* (2002) has much broader coverage and is designed for an older age group. Its selective and synthesizing approach makes *Space Exploration* ideal for the targeted audience, and it is recommended for school and public libraries. —*Mary Ellen Quinn*

The Kingfisher Illustrated Horse & Pony Encyclopedia. By Sandy Ransford. 2004. 224p. illus. index. Kingfisher, $24.95 (0-7534-5781-4). 636.1.

Author Ransford is a full-time writer who has written more than 30 books for children. An expert horsewoman, she owns a horse and two ponies.

This volume has suggested grade levels of three through eight. The opening sections contain general information on horses and then describe various breeds—hotblood horses, coldblood horses, warmblood horses, and pony breeds. The remainder of the volume covers keeping, feeding, grooming, health care, and riding in chapters that are detailed and precise and convey the serious level of commitment necessary to all aspects of care and riding. The lavish color photographs, some of which are taken from the author's *The Kingfisher Illustrated Encyclopedia of Horse and Pony Breeds* (2003), are indispensable visual aids to descriptions of housing, saddling, mounting, and so on. Photographs of youngsters handling animals will appeal to the targeted age group. The text is supported by a clear table of contents, a glossary, and an index. Younger children may have difficulties with some of the text. Terms, such as *gymkhana,* are not defined in context, although they may appear in the glossary.

An attractive, thorough book such as this one should satisfy horse lovers. It is a good choice for both school and public libraries. —*Sharon Cohen*

Encyclopedia of Aquarium & Pond Fish. By David Alderton. 2005. 400p. illus. indexes. DK, $35 (0-7566-0941-0). 639.3403.

In the fine tradition of its excellent how-to guides for raising houseplants, DK here offers a practical and visually appealing manual for all who would keep fish. The author has written various natural history titles and is a consultant to the pet industry. More than 800 individual fish, invertebrate, and plant species are described.

The book begins with a short introduction to the natural history of fish, their classification, and the history of fish keeping. The first major section covers the most popular kind of fish, those that live in fresh water. It begins with the practicalities of setting up and maintaining a tank, including descriptions of common problems and how to address them. Next is a very rich directory of fish organized by family or genus, with commonly available strains (including a few well-known rarities) discussed in terms of their size, temperament, and required conditions for culture. A brief directory of freshwater plants rounds out this section.

For those who like more of a challenge, marine fish are treated next. Following the same general structure as the freshwater fish section, Alderton divides marine fish into parts on culture and fish by family or genus, then finishes with a section on marine invertebrates. A shorter but still very useful section on the basics of keeping pond fish, again with sections on setup, fish by family or genus, and plants, finishes up the body of this volume. A glossary of terms, a handy list of Web sites, and indexes (one by common and scientific names, the other of more general terms) round things out.

This book is a fun read for fish keepers and voyeurs alike. The well-organized and authoritative content lives happily next to beautiful photographs. School and public libraries should strongly consider this volume for their reference shelves. A few circulating copies are a good bet to get heavy circulation in recreational collections at all levels. —*Jeff Kosokoff*

★**The Oxford Encyclopedia of Food and Drink in America.** 2v. Ed. by Andrew F. Smith. 2004. 1,550p. illus. index. Oxford, $250 (0-19-515437-1). 641.3.

Following *The Oxford Companion to Food* (1999) and *The Oxford Companion to Wine* (1999), here is another reference title to feed our fascination with the things we eat and drink. The goal is to pull together "the best scholarship on the history of American food" and make it available to a wider audience. General editor Smith teaches culinary history at the New School University and has written several food-related books. In addition to academicians, the nearly 200 contributors include chefs, cookbook authors, and food writers.

In 770 A–Z entries, readers will find discussions of particular foods and drinks, such as *Brandy, Club sandwich, Orange juice,* and *Potatoes;* more general food categories, such as *Airplane food* and *Cocktails;* and brands, such as *Jell-o, Snapple,* and *Twinkies.* There are also entries for people (Clarence Birdseye, Julia Child [with her 2004 death date noted], Wolfgang Puck); appliances and gadgets (*Bread machines, Frying baskets, Pot holders*); businesses and companies (*Dairy industry, Delicatessens, Nabisco, Pizza Hut*); and iconic marketing images such as the *Pillsbury Doughboy* and the *Quaker Oats Man.* Entries such as *Southeast Asian American food* and *Southwestern regional cooking* treat the contributions of ethnic groups or geographic areas. The long article *Historical overview* offers a detailed chronological survey from the colonial period to the present. Finally, a host of entries address food-related scientific, social, and cultural issues: *Celebrity chefs, Chemical additives, Food stamps, Etiquette books, Jewish dietary laws, Temperance,* and more. Entries on particular foods or gadgets are generally just two or three paragraphs long, but some entries cover many pages. *Native American foods* and its subentries, for example, extend for almost 40 pages and include numerous sidebars, quotes from primary sources, a chart detailing foods of the Columbian exchange, and a recipe for Navajo fry bread. Most entries conclude with a bibliography, and separate general bibliographies for food and drink follow the *A–Z* portion of the text. Also appended are a list of food periodicals; an extensive list of food Web sites; directories of major food-related library collections, museums, organizations, and festivals; and a topical list of entries. Navigation is aided by a detailed index and ample cross- referencing. The 350 black-and-white illustrations add to the set's appeal.

The encyclopedia is not intended to be comprehensive, and readers are bound to find omissions—no entries for the Food Network and Weight Watchers, for example, although the index points to entries in which they are discussed. There is some overlap with *The Oxford Companion to Food* and *The Oxford Companion to Wine,* though these titles have a more technical slant. The *Encyclopedia of Food and Culture* (Scribner, 2002) shares *The Oxford Encyclopedia*'s historical and cultural context, but Scribner's 600 entries are stretched across the globe. *The Oxford Encyclopedia of Food and Drink in America* is highly recommended for all academic and large public libraries and any smaller public libraries that can afford it. —*Mary Ellen Quinn*

Encyclopedia of Kitchen History. By Mary Ellen Snodgrass. 2004. 704p. illus. index. Fitzroy Dearborn, $175 (1-57958-380-6). 643.

This tribute to the history of the kitchen is a wonderful addition to reference material on domestic life. The breadth of topics, including the evolution of the chimney, the uses of fruit from the Pleistocene to the present, cutlery as a status symbol, salt, weights and measures, canisters, and cannibalism, offers more than a glimpse into the social and scientific aspects of the center of family and community life. The term *kitchen* is used in the broadest sense, encompassing campfires, galleys, and mess tents, among other variations.

There are 300 entries, most with further reading lists. Length varies from around half a page for *Manioc* and *Hines, Duncan* to more than eight pages for *Pottery.* Coverage is global; however, *Amanite kitchens; Colonial kitchens, American; Pennsylvania Dutch kitchens;* and similar entries help tip the balance toward the U.S.

A bibliography of sources, including books, articles, databases, and Web sites, is a useful resource for those seeking more information on particular topics. Many of the older resources used in developing this encyclopedia are out of print, making this work more valuable as it carries the information forward. Fuller indexing would have enhanced the volume as a reference tool.

Domestic history is every bit as important as political history, and this work is a synthesis of histories of people, mechanisms, implements, foodstuffs, and processes that developed in and about the kitchen and its activities. It occupies a unique niche among books on food, cooking, homemaking, and history of everyday life and is a recommended addition to most public and academic libraries. —*Linda Scarth*

★**Encyclopedia of Leadership.** 4v. Ed. by George R. Goethals and others. 2004. 1,927p. appendixes. bibliogs. illus. index. Sage, $595 (0-7619-2597-X). 658.4.

People are fascinated by the stories of leaders, but not much has been written about the forces that shape them. This set brings together "what truly matters about leadership" to map an emerging discipline that draws from history, philosophy, sociology, anthropology, political science, and psychology. It seeks to answer questions such as what is leadership? What is a great leader? What is a great follower? What are the types of leadership? And how does someone become a leader?

The set was designed with the needs of several user communities in mind, including students, scholars, and professionals who want to know who the real leaders are and how they got that way. One of the general editors, George J. Goethals, is the founder of the leadership program at Williams College, and the senior editor, James MacGregor Burns, is the Woodrow Wilson Professor of Government emeritus at Williams and senior fellow at the University of Richmond's Jepson School of Leadership, the nation's first undergraduate school of leadership studies. The remaining 17 associate editors and editorial board members represent the mainstream of educational programs and professional leadership academies internationally.

The four volumes contain 373 entries of 1,000–6,000 words each, 150 photos, 300 sidebars from primary and secondary sources, and four appendixes. Entries are arranged alphabetically, but the "Reader's Guide" in the front matter organizes them into 19 broad categories, such as "Biographies," "Followership," "Leadership Styles," "Religion." and "Women and Gender." Entries cover such diverse topics as *Achievement motivation; Activism; Alexander the Great; Alinsky, Saul; Apartheid in South Africa, demise of;* and *Attribution processes.* Each article is signed and provides suggestions for further reading plus cross-references. More than 100 sidebars add dimension to the set by providing texts of or excerpts from speeches, mission statements, journal articles, Web sites, and other sources. Appendixes include a bibliography of significant books on leadership; a directory of leadership programs; presidential speeches on foreign policy and war; and excerpts from the Bible, the Bhagavad Gita, the Analects, and the Qur'an that illustrate leadership concepts. In addition to the "Reader's Guide," a list of sidebars and a detailed and extensive index facilitate navigation.

Because there really is nothing available like this encyclopedia, it is a must buy for academic libraries, particularly where leadership is taught as an academic topic. In addition, it is recommended for any academic and large public library that can afford the rather hefty price tag. Extremely well done, with good quality print and illustrations, this work should become an important resource for active citizens as well as for managers and scholars. —*Diana Shonrock*

Encyclopedia of Public Relations. 2v. Ed. by Robert L. Heath. 2004. 1,067p. illus. index. Sage, $295 (0-7619-2733-6). 659.2.

Some may view public relations as the manipulation of public opinion, while others see it as the conduit for successful communication between organizations and their clients. Regardless of one's opinion, the *Encyclopedia of Public Relations* provides the facts, opinions, and data for a thoughtful analysis of the profession. According to the editor, "this work intends to provide an honest but positively biased treatment of public relations." And so it does.

Nearly 500 articles cover topics in the fields of communication, advertising, marketing, and politics. Articles are arranged alphabetically, each is signed, and many come with a bibliography and *see also* references. The primary focus is on public relations in the U.S.; however, some entries highlight the practice of public relations abroad. Terminology (*Logo, Market share, Press kit*) and theories and models (*Game theory, Health belief model*) get substantial attention. Also treated are individuals (Roger Ailes, P. T. Barnum); organizations (*Federal Communications Commission, PR Newswire*); and historical aspects (*Exxon and the Valdez crisis, Railroad industry in the 19th century*). Illustrations consist of a few black-and-white photographs and tables.

Several appendixes offer additional content, among them "The Public Relations Society of America Code of Ethics," "Milestones in the History of Public Relations," and "Public Relations Online Resources." The "Reader's Guide" that precedes the entries groups entry headings under recurring public relations themes such as *Ethics, Jargon,* and *Management.*

The *Encyclopedia of Public Relations* will complement titles such as *The Encyclopedia of Communication and Information* (Macmillan, 2001). Recommended for academic and large public libraries. —*Sue Polanka*

The Encyclopedia of Wood: A Tree-by-Tree Guide to the World's Most Versatile Resource. Ed. by Aidan Walker. 2005. 192p. illus. index. Facts On File, $35 (0-8160-6181-5). 674.03.

Anyone who likes to tramp through the woods, reads the Arbor Day Foundation newsletter, or shops at home-and-garden centers can probably identify a fair number of common trees: maples, oaks, pines, and the like. Some folks can even tell a red maple from a sugar maple, a black oak from a pin oak, and a southern yellow pine from a Norway pine. However, there's a tremendous difference between identifying a living tree and identifying a piece of wood. Living trees offer lots of helpful hints: bark color, bark texture, foliage, seedpods, height, and overall shape. Seasoned, board-cut pieces of wood offer none of these hints, and that's why this specialized identification guide is so useful.

Thirty pages of introductory material, richly enhanced with outstanding maps, photos, and illustrations, explain tree anatomy, tree growth, wood grain, logging practices, conservation, and the various processes for seasoning and preservation of wood. This material is well written and beautifully presented. The real treasure, however, is the "Directory of Wood" section, which contains entries on 150 "top commercial timbers" arranged alphabetically by scientific name. Each one-page entry begins with a four-by-eight-inch photographic reproduction of the specific type of wood. The quality of the color photographs is so high that readers will be tempted to run their fingers over them to feel the wood's texture. Along with these photos are brief descriptions of growth patterns, appearance (the wood, not the living tree), properties, and uses. Closing out each entry are a small world map showing growth location and a small chart indicating structural features, such as impact resistance, bending strength, and crushing strength.

The Encyclopedia of Wood is a beautifully crafted identification guide for practicing woodworkers and others whose professions depend on wood. Libraries whose constituencies include such individuals should give it serious consideration for purchase. —*Art A. Lichtenstein*

Fine Arts, Decorative Arts, Music

Arts and Humanities through the Eras. 5v. Ed. by Philip M. Soergel and others. 2005. 2,250p. illus. indexes. Gale, $450 (0-7876-5695-X); e-book, call Gale for pricing (0-7876-9384-7). 700.

Over the last two decades the historical focus has shifted from viewing events in a simple historical context to a more integrative perspective. This set offers a multidimensional picture of primarily Western civilization, covering *Ancient Egypt* (2675–332 B.C.E.), *Ancient Greece and Rome* (1200 B.C.E.–476 C.E.), *Medieval Europe* (814–1450 C.E.), *Renaissance Europe* (1300–1600 C.E.), and *The Age of the Baroque and Enlightenment* (1600–1800 C.E.). Similar in organization to Gale's American Eras and World Eras lines, the work exposes readers to each historical period through the study of nine different arts and humanities topics: "Architecture and Design," "Dance," "Fashion," "Literature," "Music," "Philosophy," "Religion," "Theater," and "Visual Arts." Each topic area is treated in a different chapter, but the connections between topics are highlighted both in the text and through cross-referencing. The result is a broader and more inclusive picture of the culture of each period, emphasizing connections between, for example, religion, dance, and literature or between the visual arts and architecture.

Each chapter is structured in the same way, containing a chronology; an overview of the development of the field under scrutiny; a "Topics" section, which discusses various movements, schools of thought, and masterworks that characterize the discipline during that era; a handful of biographies of significant people; and a list of documentary sources. Each of the subsections within "Topics" includes a list of sources. The writing, produced by subject experts, is uniformly clear and informative but quite pedantic. It is certainly not leisure-interest reading but does impart information in an admirably direct style.

Sidebars offer primary source material (letters, poems, essays, songs, epitaphs, etc.). Numerous black-and-white photographs, maps, and reproductions extend the text well. Technical terms and definitions appear both in the text and in the glossary, and lists of works for further reference, as well as media and online sources, are listed at the back of each volume. Although there is not a cumulative index, each volume does have its own accurate index. Aimed at college and university students with or without historical background, this set provides a solid picture of western European history through the arts. —*Ann Welton*

Encyclopedia of the Harlem Renaissance. 2v. By Cary D. Wintz and Paul Finkelman. 2004. 1,408p. illus. index. Routledge, $325 (1-57958-389-X). 700.89.

The Harlem Renaissance continues to attract academic interest across disciplines, and this set reflects that interest as well as the diversity in scholarship devoted to the topic. Debate still rages among critics about the origins, scope, and legacy of the Harlem Renaissance. In 639 entries, this encyclopedia not only covers these and other expected aesthetic issues—literature, art, and music—but also the historical, political, and socioeconomic environment in which the movement took place.

Almost half of the entries are biographical, encompassing actors, politicians, musicians, writers, patrons, and more. Other entries cover specific literary or theatrical works or productions; places (*Apollo Theater, 135th Street Library*); organizations (*Black Star Line, Harlem Globetrotters, Negro Art Theater*); and periodicals (*Chicago Defender, The Nation*). Also discussed are topics such as *Blues, Federal Writer's Project,* and *White patronage.* The series of entries headed *Harlem Renaissance in the United States* deals with the movement in Boston, California, and Chicago, among other places. The encyclopedia's more than 250 contributors range from academics to artists. Entries are alphabetically arranged and individually authored, and each one is followed by a list of "Further Reading." Many also contain *see also* references, and for artists, a list of major works (books, movies, recordings, etc.). Most entries are less than a page long, though substantive essays of about three to five pages are provided on some of the more influential artists, performers, or works. Other longer entries include topics like *Art criticism and the Harlem Renaissance, Civil rights and law, Europe and the Harlem Renaissance* (with subentries on Berlin, London, Paris, and the Soviet Union), and *Riots.* There are even entries devoted to artists or works inspired *by* the Harlem Renaissance movement (for example, Sherwood Anderson's novel *Dark Laughter*). The entries are well written and cogent, particularly on sensitive or emotional topics like lynching and passing.

The volumes also include 180 black-and-white photographs and a street map of Harlem, 1913–1930. This map highlights landmarks like the Apollo Theater and the Cotton Club as well as the residences of famous denizens like Langston Hughes and Marcus Garvey. There is also a very helpful thematic list of entries, with headings like "Nightlife," "Publishers," "Singers," and "Theater Companies."

Overall, this is a significant and useful addition to reference works on the Harlem Renaissance, appealing to users seeking general outlines and summaries as well as to those needing specifics and references. It is accessible to readers on multiple levels and recommended for high-school, college, and public libraries. —*Michael Tosko.*

Atlas of World Art. Ed. by John Onians. 2004. 352p. bibliog. illus. index. maps. Oxford, $150 (0-19-521583-4). 702.2.

With approximately 150 large-format double-page spreads, *Atlas of World Art* is, claims the press release, "the first geographical reference to treat the art of the whole world from prehistory to the present day and to show the importance of natural as well as social factors in shaping artistic activity." Each spread integrates full-color maps (more than 300 in all), attractive photographs of significant art or architecture, and text summarizing artistic activity during the relevant era and locale.

Arrangement is broadly chronological and then regional. A sampling of topics includes "North Africa, A.D. 300–600," "Scandinavia and the Baltic, 1500–1800," and "Japan and Korea, 1900–2000." The subject matter of maps varies greatly. The three maps for "China and Tibet, 1300–1500" show important visual production sites, routes tracing China's global contacts, and city boundaries (color coded by date) and religious sites in Quanzhou. Given the necessary brevity of text, the bibliography at the end of the volume is essential for further reading. A comprehensive index puts page numbers in bold for map references and extrabold for illustration captions. Captions may be less reliable than text information: China's famed terra-cotta warriors are said to have been discovered in the 1960s in a caption and in the 1970s in adjacent text; the caption describing Juan O'Gorman's huge mosaic mural on the University Library in Mexico City attributes the work to José Clemente Orozco.

In size and format, *Atlas of World Art* is very similar to *Atlas of Western Art History* (Facts On File, 1994). The latter's maps are less colorful but are generally larger, often full-page size; the differences in what the maps portray and in choice of illustrations (there is little overlap) are reason enough to have both volumes on hand. *Atlas of Western Art History* limits its coverage to the Western world, including colonial Latin America, from 700 B.C.E. to C.E. 1950, while *Atlas of World Art* takes the whole world, from 40,000 B.C.E. to C.E. 2000, as its domain.

Despite occasional inaccuracies, the atlas is highly recommended for high-school, public, academic, and art libraries. —*Craig Bunch*

The Oxford Dictionary of Art. 3d ed. Ed. by Ian Chilvers. 2004. 816p. index. Oxford, $45 (0-19-860476-9). 703.

This new edition expands by some 200 pages the 1997 second edition, adding more than 200 entries and a very helpful classified list of entries. The chronology and index of museums and galleries have been updated, while "A Selection of Christian and Classical Themes in Painting and Sculpture" has been dropped. The annotated index of museums and galleries contains complete contact information and focuses on "150 of the world's leading collections of Western art." As in previous editions, the focus is Western art beginning with classical Greece.

According to the editor, "almost every entry has been amended in some way and many have been expanded or substantially rewritten." Of the 3,000 entries, about two-thirds are for artists, and the number of entries for people grows to around three-fourths of the total when patrons, collectors, administrators, dealers, and writers are added. Architects, designers, photographers, and practitioners of the applied arts are not the subjects of main entries unless they were also significant as painters, sculptors, printmakers, or draftsmen. There are 28 entries for artists of Mexico, Central and South America, and the Caribbean; most spent significant parts of their careers in Europe or the U.S. Wherever possible, all biographical entries now include places and exact dates of birth and death. Nonbiographical entries cover museums and galleries; academies, schools, and other institutions; exhibitions and prizes; styles, groups, and movements; materials, tools, and techniques; and miscellaneous terms.

Other recent one-volume dictionaries of similar scope, size, and readability and with an emphasis on Western art include *The Penguin Concise Dictionary of Art History* (Penguin, 2000) and *The Yale Dictionary of Art and Artists* (Yale, 2000). The former includes brief quotations by or about the artist for each artist entry. Neither these nor *The Oxford Dictionary of Art* is illustrated. *The Thames and Hudson Dictionary of Art and Artists* (Thames and Hudson, 1994), though shorter and less recent, includes 426 black-and-white illustrations and ventures more into non-Western cultures. All of these volumes are recommended for high-school, public, and academic libraries, though none is as up-to-date as *The Oxford Dictionary of Art*. —*Craig Bunch*

The Queer Encyclopedia of the Visual Arts. Ed. by Claude J. Summers. 2004. 373p. bibliogs. illus. indexes. Cleis, paper, $29.95 (1-57344-191-0). 704.

As stated in the introduction, this encyclopedia "offers a revisionist art history, one that places the achievements of gay, lesbian, bisexual, transgender, and queer artists in historical contexts and that privileges the representation of subjects that have traditionally been censored or marginalized." The first book from the online encyclopedia http://www.glbtq.com attempts to accomplish this through 200 signed entries that are accompanied by bibliographic information and cross-references. Like any well-executed encyclopedia, it provides a sound overview of the topic at hand while encouraging and supporting further exploration.

The introduction further states that "there is real value in seeing queer art in its own terms as an expression of a queer artistic impulse and as a documentation of queer experience." The value to a gay, lesbian, bisexual, or transgender reader seeking context for her or his own sexuality may be profound. Works such as this can be very helpful as sources of reliable information for readers trying to understand the complexities of identity as well as cultural and historical invisibility.

The scope is international, and most entries are several paragraphs in length; many extend over multiple pages. Photographer and jewelry sculptor Laurie Toby Edison, transsexual artist Lili Elbe (formerly Einar Wegener), and architect Philip Johnson are a few examples of artists found in this rich text. Several broad topics are included, among them *Erotic and pornographic art: gay male; Erotic and pornographic art: lesbian; Photography: gay male, post-Stonewall; Photography: lesbian, post-Stonewall*. Entries concerning images such as the rainbow flag and the covers of pulp paperbacks are a nice addition. However, one curiously omitted image is the labrys, a goddess symbol that has significance for lesbians. There are also geographically tied subjects such as *Canadian art, Japanese art*, and *Native American art*. Approximately 80 black-and-white illustrations accompany the text.

The reader can look forward to friendly navigation through the text, facilitated by an index of names, an *A–Z* list of entries, and a topical index. Recommended for public, high-school, and college libraries. —*Scottie Wallace*

Renaissance Art and Architecture. By Gordon Campbell. 2005. 278p. illus. index. Oxford, $45 (0-19-860985-X). 709.

Some 1,400 entries in dictionary format pack this relatively slim but information-rich volume by Campbell, professor of Renaissance studies at the University of Leicester and author of nearly 4,000 entries in *The Oxford Dictionary of the Renaissance* (2003). The great majority of entries in *Renaissance Art and Architecture* are drawn, with little or no change, from that work. Each entry has been reviewed by a specialist and in some cases revised or newly drafted. Uniquely perhaps, Campbell gives equal weight in his 30-page introduction to Renaissance art, architecture, and gardens. More than a third of all entries relate to painters and painting, while roughly equal numbers of entries relate to sculpture, trades and crafts, publishing and printing, and architecture. Bringing up the rear—but dear to Campbell's heart—are 53 entries relating to gardens and garden design.

Preceding the dictionary section is a helpful and heavily subdivided thematic index; following the dictionary section are a one-page guide to further reading and a chronology that lists significant events in art and architecture and, in the facing column, contemporary events. Dictionary entries range from several sentences (e.g., *Eulenkrug, Faience*) to a page or more (*Arms and armour, Botanical gardens, Michelangelo*). Biographical entries are generally much shorter than in the 34-volume *Dictionary of Art* (Grove, 1996), but some, such as those for German printer Johann Mentelin and Swiss glass-stainer Lucas Zeiner, are not found even in the index of the larger work. The great majority of individual works of art and architecture are treated not as main entries but are incorporated into entries on artists and architects. Cross-references between entries and all caps for main-entry terms within entries supplement the thematic index as finding aids. Sixteen color plates and numerous black-and-white illustrations (all well captioned) add visual impact. Updating is recent enough to note the theft of Benvenuto Cellini's golden salt cellar in 2003.

Campbell is thorough and rarely uninteresting, and *Renaissance Art and Architecture* is recommended for academic, museum, and larger public libraries. —*Craig Bunch*

Understanding Architecture. 2v. By Marco Bussagli. 2004. 384p. illus. index. Sharpe, $199 (0-7656-8071-8). 720.

This beautifully illustrated English translation of *Capire l'architettura* was produced in Italy. Volume 1, *What Is Architecture?* has four parts: "People and Space," "Buildings and Typologies," "Techniques, Materials, and Structures," and "Styles." Each is divided into numerous spreads of roughly two to four pages, such as "Music and Architecture," "Religious Buildings," "The Arch," and "Chinese Architecture." The section on styles runs the full gamut of well-known styles from antiquity to contemporary architecture in roughly chronological order. Volume 2, *Civilizations, Architectural Achievements, Outstanding Figures*, features 95 two-page spreads ranging from "Neolithic Populations and Ethnographic Cultures" to "Santiago Calatrava." Along the way are entries on Persepolis, Angkor, Canterbury, Raphael, Thomas Jefferson, the Katsura Imperial Villa, and Brasilia.

Although the set is given juvenile literature subject headings by the Library of Congress, the mostly color illustrations (two or three photos per page on average) will appeal to all ages and aptitudes. The text, however, though clear and well-organized, abounds in technical architectural terms that will be unfamiliar to readers of any age who are not architecture aficionados. The second paragraph of the entry on domes, for instance, includes the terms *calotte, pendentives,* and *squinches,* among others. Although many such terms are identified in nearby diagrams, a glossary would have been helpful. Moreover, while the table of contents makes finding Hagia Sophia or Chartres Cathedral easy enough, the index is limited to personal names and a small number of architects' studios and movements.

With photos that may inspire some to travel and others to careers as architects, the set is suitable for high-school and public libraries. A highly recommended lower-cost alternative is Jonathan Glancey's *The Story of Architecture* (DK, 2000); at about two-thirds the length of *Understanding Architecture*, its pictures will also inspire, and its glossary and index make it more useful as a reference source. —*Craig Bunch*

The DC Comics Encyclopedia: The Definitive Guide to the Characters of the DC Universe. By Phil Jimenez and others. 2004. 351p. illus. index. DK, $40 (0-7566-0592-X). 741.5.

This copiously illustrated encyclopedia chronicles more than 1,000 DC Comics characters from the 1930s to the present. Arranged alphabetically, each entry gives the first appearance, status (hero, villain, etc.), real name, occupation, height, weight, and eye and hair color of the superheroes or supervillains. Special abilities and superpowers are also listed along with ample cross-references to other comic characters or superleague affiliations, such as the L.E.G.I.O.N. cosmic peacekeeping force.

The biographical entries make fascinating reading in alternative history. For example, the Crimson Avenger served in a league called the Seven Soldiers of Victory during World War II. Afterward, he was sent backward in time. He came forward in time and discovered that he was struck with a terminal disease. After his death, an unknown woman purchased two guns that had belonged to him. These guns transformed her into Crimson Avenger II, who became an agent of vengeance and execution. Of course, famous characters such as Wonder Woman or Batman are included. But lesser-known characters, such as Superman's college flame, Lori Lemaris (a mermaid), are also listed.

The colorful design makes this book a pleasure to browse. Special two-page features, such as "Amazing Weapons" and "Romantic Moments," are interspersed with the biographies. Recommended for public libraries with active comic readership. —*Jack O'Gorman*

A Dictionary of Modern Design. By Jonathan M. Woodham. 2005. 520p. illus. index. Oxford, $45 (0-19-280097-3). 745.4.2

Sometimes a book's cover, or in this case, the book jacket, is an indication of what is between the boards. The stylish use of the ISBN number and large colorful bar code are emblematic of good modern design. As well as being a dictionary of modern design, this book is also a concise history. It is filled with biographies of individuals, such as Laura Ashley, Charles Eames, and Robert Venturi, as well as entries for styles (*Art deco, Danish modern*); materials (*Bakelite, Chrome, Formica*); companies (*IKEA, Tupperware, Prada*); and more. Each alphabet letter section, from *A* through *XYZ*, is introduced by a classic example of modern design. For example, *F* is illustrated with a photograph of Fiskars scissors; *N* with a Nokia mobile phone; *R* with a Rubik's Cube. There are no other illustrations.

More than 2,000 entries cover world design from the middle of the nineteenth century through 2004. Occasional boxed entries discuss important concepts such as *Arts and Crafts movement, Green design, Kitsch,* and *Modernism*. If an entry heading is mentioned within the text of another entry, it is preceded by an asterisk. The dictionary portion of the volume is followed by a topically organized bibliography, time lines, and an index of names.

A wealth of information in a well-designed book makes this a required purchase for libraries supporting design programs and for most academic libraries and large public libraries. —*Linda Scarth*

Dictionary of American Classical Composers. 2d ed. By Neil Butterworth. 2004. 548p. illus. index. Routledge, $150 (0-415-93848-1). 780.

This second edition follows the first (called *A Dictionary of American Composers* and published by Garland) by 20 years and includes updated lists of works by the composers who are covered as well as entries that have been rewritten as appropriate. Though aiming for an informative and readable tone, the *Dictionary* tends toward the drily pedantic. It does, however, give a wealth of information on selected composers and their significant works and dates as well as biographical background.

Alphabetically arranged entries cover approximately 650 composers from the eighteenth century to the present. The first edition had more than 1,000 entries, and it is not clear why people were dropped. All of the composers are either American-born or naturalized citizens, in which case music written abroad is also discussed. All have had their music performed widely. Composers of light music, jazz, and popular songs are omitted, with the exception of Stephen Foster, included because of his historical significance. More than 200 black-and-white photographs satisfy curiosity as to how a composer looks.

An appendix listing American composers and their students is followed by a bibliography arranged by composer. There is no cross-referencing, but the index lists all "substantial" references to a composer. Musical compositions and other topics are all listed under composers' names in the index, however, so there is no way to find a piece of music without knowing the composer, or to link composers who share common traits.

The volume is unique among current music reference sources in its focus on Americans. Given the two decades between the first and second editions, this is a worthwhile addition to any college or university library supporting a music program. —*Ann Welton*

The Facts On File Dictionary of Music. By Christine Ammer. 2004. 495p. illus. indexes. Facts On File, $50 (0-8160-5266-2). 780.

Ammer is the author of three earlier editions (1972, 1987, 1995) that all have different titles, the most recent being *The HarperCollins Dictionary of Music*. This edition has a new publisher and has been expanded and updated. The majority of entries pertain to classical music, but there are long definitions of jazz and rock and a few terms (*Vamp, Riff*) that apply to these styles of music.

The definitions are clear and readable, with most less than a page long. All aspects of music are included: instruments, composers, musicians, types of music, music theory, and names of compositions and titles of operas. Line drawings of instruments and examples of music theory accompany the text.

There are tables listing important operas; piano, cello and violin concertos; twentieth-century composers; notable symphonies; and more. Indexes of composers and instruments complete the volume. The indexes refer only to "principal information" on a composer or instrument, whether this be a main entry or a mention within another entry. Up-to-date entries include *Digital recording, DVD,* and *MIDI*. New compositions by John Harbison (*Requiem Mass,* 2003) and Mark Adamo (*Little Women,* 2000) are noted. Topics that readers won't find in this volume include demotic music, pantonality, and the famous harpsichordist, Igor Kipnis.

The Facts On File Dictionary of Music is not as comprehensive as *Baker's Dictionary of Music* (Schirmer, 1997) and not as scholarly as the fourth edition of the *Harvard Dictionary of Music* [RBB My 1 04]. However, it would be a very appropriate purchase for high-school or small public libraries. —*Christine Bulson*

Free Jazz and Free Improvisation. 2v. By Todd S. Jenkins. 2004. 468p. index. Greenwood, $175 (0-313-29881-5). 781.65.

Author Jenkins is editor of the Web site All About Jazz and an active author of jazz-album liner notes, musician obituaries, and jazz-related Web logs. This encyclopedia attempts to cover the relevant history and seminal artists. In his introduction, Jenkins describes the beginnings of free jazz in the late 1950s as "an exploration of all the sounds that could be drawn out of instruments" with "an emphasis on group improvisation that offered a fresh, spontaneous flow of ideas." Two subsequent chapters help set the context for the rest of the encyclopedia. "Controlled Chaos: The Nature of Free Music" attempts to define jazz music and then distinguishes between free jazz and free improvisation. Jenkins quotes guitarist Derek Bailey to explain the difference: "'free jazz is a form of music, while free improvisation is an approach to making music.'" Next, "The Path to Freedom" provides a complete narrative history of these musical forms and details the social and musical milieu out of which they grew. A "Chronology of Events" listing landmark recordings, concerts, label beginnings, and deaths of prominent performers further enhances the encyclopedia.

Encyclopedia entries are alphabetical and range from a short paragraph to 15 pages. Most focus on individual musicians and groups, but record labels and performance venues are also covered A nice feature of many entries for both jazz fan and music librarian is the author's willingness to recommend particular recordings or releases as seminal or emblematic of an artist's oeuvre. Also included in the encyclopedia are a topical list of entries and a "Suggested Readings" section, which includes biographies, reference books, and periodical articles.

Overall, this is an informative and comprehensive reference work on a little-known jazz subgenre and is recommended for comprehensive jazz collections. —*Michael Tosko*

Satchmo: The Louis Armstrong Encyclopedia. By Michael Meckna. 2004. 432p. appendixes. bibliog. illus. index. Greenwood, $65 (0-313-30137-9). 781.65.

This encyclopedia is a comprehensive compendium of the life and work of one of the most influential and pervasive jazz entertainers of the twentieth century. Meckna, professor of music history at Texas Christian University, has compiled the only reference source focused solely on the legendary jazz trumpeter. Biographies on Armstrong abound, but *Satchmo* should become the premier quick-access source for information on his style, legacy, critical reception, films, writings, and recordings.

The encyclopedia is very user-friendly yet exhaustive and detailed. Entries are alphabetical, and most are a short paragraph in length, with a few stretching to a half page long. Cross-references are plentiful, and black-

and-white photos are interspersed throughout the text. A short preface summarizes Armstrong's life, while four appendixes usefully complement the A–Z entries. One appendix is an exhaustive chronology with detailed paragraph summaries of nearly every year of Armstrong's life. Even posthumous recognition is covered, like the 2001 dedication of the Louis Armstrong New Orleans International Airport, the first to be named after a musician. Other appendixes list his recordings on compact disc, movies in which he appeared, and the best Web sites for Armstrong research. The appendixes are followed by a 10-page selected bibliography listing books, journal articles, and sources intended for a juvenile audience as well as more arcane sources like transcribed trumpet solos.

The level of detail in this volume is impressive—and often amusing and entertaining as well. The entry on "When the Saints Go Marching In" informs the reader that the song was formerly a spiritual mainly played at funerals. When his sister objected to Armstrong's sacrilegious jazzy version, he pointed out that she, after all, played bingo in church. Such was his popularity that he often received mail addressed no more specifically than "'Ole Satchmo' Himself/Where ever he is." We even learn that "Satchmo" is derived from "Satchelmouth." Other entries cover theaters in which Armstrong played, musicians with whom he associated, and, of course, his songs and recordings. Overall, this is an excellent resource for academic and large public libraries. —*Michael Tosko*

Woodstock: An Encyclopedia of the Music and Art Fair. By James E. Perowne. 2005. 230p. illus. index. Greenwood, $69.95 (0-313-33057-3). 781.66.

A symbol of the hippie movement and the 1960s counterculture, Woodstock was actually just one of several music festivals of the time. This volume describes and contextualizes the famous 1969 event and notes its legacy. The author teaches music and has written other historical music reference works.

The book opens with a chapter containing two- to three-page descriptions of other music events, from the first rock music festival in the U.S., the Monterey International Pop Music Festival, to the 1971 Concert for Bangla Desh. The production, performers, and impact of each are noted. The next chapter is devoted to the classic Woodstock happening—its organizers, the days' events, the attendees and the cultures they represented (including the drug scene), and the fair's legacy. A separate chapter details people, places, and topics in A–Z format. There, the author explains the role of the New York State Thruway, helicopters, technical crews, the local hospital, nudity, and the 1970 documentary film as well as all the performers. Entries range in length from a paragraph to a page (for *Hendrix, Jimi* and *Hippies,* for example).

Two chapters cover Woodstock '94 and Woodstock 1999, contrasting the planning and outcome of those efforts to relive a time of relative innocence. The latter event was particularly violent. About 50 black-and-white photos (from the Photofest collection) intersperse the text. Most show performers, but several provide a picture of the audience and culture during that period. Appendixes offer "Woodstock Set Lists" and information on recordings and films. An extensive annotated bibliography provides evidence of thorough research.

The spirit of Woodstock appeals to several generations. This volume provides useful information about the event, the actions leading to it, and its aftermath and is recommended for high-school, college, and public libraries. —*Lesley Farmer*

Performing Arts, Recreation

Encyclopedia of Recreation and Leisure in America. 2v. Ed. by Gary Cross. 2004. 800p. illus. index. Scribner, $270 (0-684-31265-4); E-book, contact Gale for pricing (0-684-31450-9). 790.

As more leisure time became available, Americans developed an increasing number of recreational opportunities—and became more ambivalent about those opportunities. There was growing tension between adhering to the work ethic and enjoying the by-products of efficient work. This encyclopedia captures the range of recreational possibilities, as well as many of the consequences arising from it in American culture. To get an idea of the scope of the encyclopedia, one can consult the "Systematic Outline of Contents," found near the end of volume 2, which presents the conceptual framework for the wealth of information contained in the work. Entries are grouped under seven broad categories: "Social Development of Leisure in America"; "Processes: Impact of Technologies"; "Trends"; "People—Identities, Interactions, and Institutions"; "Ceremonial Occasions"; "Leisure Sites"; and "Leisure Activities, Past and Present." Most of these categories are divided further; "Leisure Sites," for example, encompasses "Fairs," "Parks," and other subcategories.

The 271 A–Z entries are signed and include bibliographies and *see also* references. They make very interesting reading. One can explore the history of *Garage and yard sales* and *Playgrounds* and learn about *Puritans at leisure.* There are entries for *Dining out, Religious holidays, Rock-climbing, Stock car racing,* and just about any leisure activity or venue imaginable, including *Brothels.* Some of the essays deal with issues such as the *Globalization of American leisure* and *Work and leisure ethics.* The detailed index found at the end of volume 2 guides users to the depth and breadth of information included. The few photographs break up the text slightly and are sometimes interesting but are not necessary to the information, nor to the audience who will use the encyclopedia.

This encyclopedia is a complement to *The Encyclopedia of Leisure and Outdoor Recreation* (Routledge, 2003), which deals more with the concepts, theories, and models used in the study of leisure by a wide variety of disciplines. *Encyclopedia of Recreation and Leisure in America* is highly recommended to all libraries developing their collections in American history, popular culture, and social issues. High-school and college students will find it useful for assignments, and the general reader interested in culture and leisure can enjoy reading well-written entries on a variety of topics. —*Linda Scarth*

American Frontiersmen on Film and Television: Boone, Crockett, Bowie, Houston, Bridger and Carson. By Ed Andreychuk. 2005. 270p. illus. index. McFarland, $45 (0-7864-2132-0). 791.43.

The exploration of the western frontier has been a cornerstone of movies and television, and the names of six major figures—Daniel Boone, Davy Crockett, Jim Bowie, Sam Houston, Jim Bridger, and Kit Carson—are recognizable to people mainly through these media. This work combines biographical information with extensive filmographies to cover 100 years of American history as reflected in the lives of these men.

The work has one chapter devoted to each individual, with a 14- to 17-page biography followed by a comprehensive filmography. The biographies cover the life and career of each man from birth to death. The filmographies include both silent films and talking pictures, serials, and television series and made-for-television movies. Each program or movie listing starts with brief information on the production, generally followed by credits and cast, a synopsis, and "Notes," which may discuss production history, performances, and the accuracy of the portrayal. The numerous films and programs in which more than one of the six men appear as characters are listed in each relevant chapter and cross-referenced. The chapters are illustrated primarily by movie posters and black-and-white movie and television stills.

The appendix lists 14 documentaries, dominated by films on the Alamo. The lengthy bibliography contains both biographical information and film and television sources. The index lists titles of films and television series, actors, and more.

American Frontiersmen on Film and Television is a useful work on several levels. It provides accurate, basic biographical information on the six individuals covered and also helps the user to assess how these individuals have been portrayed. This work would be useful in library collections covering American history, film, and television. —*Abbie Landry*

American Plays and Musicals on Screen: 650 Stage Productions and Their Film and Television Adaptations. By Thomas S. Hischak. 2005. 343p. index. McFarland, $55 (0-7684-2003-0). 791.43.

Hischak has compiled information on 650 plays and musicals from the "pre-Civil War years to the end of the twentieth century" that have been made into films, from *East Lynne,* the 1863 melodrama that spawned several film versions from 1916 to 1982, to the 2002 movie *Chicago,* the latest adaptation of a comedy first staged in 1926. He tried to be comprehensive but notes in his preface that it is not possible to list every play that has been made into a movie or television production. The plays represented here are American, though foreign films made from these plays are noted.

Each play has an entry that begins with its original New York production date and theater. There is a brief cast list, with the names of the producer, director, and playwright. Each movie developed from the play is listed with production date and studio, major actors, director, producer, and screenwriter. This information is followed by a critique of the play and subsequent movie or television productions. Each critique provides a bit of the plot but not a full synopsis because that is not the purpose of this work. Rather, the critique is meant to discuss whether or not the play transitioned well into film or television. Hischak says in the preface that each critique is meant to be a "consensus of opinions" rather than his own personal opinion.

Entries are listed alphabetically by title. Each takes up less than a page, with about three entries per page. Cross-references help steer the reader when the movie titles and play titles vary. For example, the cross-reference to the movie title *About Last Night* refers to the play title *Sexual Perversity in Chicago.*

The volume contains a bibliography as well as a very detailed name index and title index. This would be a worthy addition to the performing arts collection in an academic or large public library. —*Jennifer Dawson*

Encyclopedia of Early Cinema. Ed. by Richard Abel. 2005. 791p. illus. index. Routledge, $225 (0-415-23440-9). 791.43.

Covering the 1890s to the mid-1910s, this work focuses on the period during which filmmaking progressed from the early flickering moving images that lasted only a matter of seconds to multiple-reel, feature films running more than an hour. By offering an international perspective and encompassing not only the production aspects of early motion pictures but also their distribution, exhibition, and reception, this work fills a gap in the reference literature on film.

Contributed by Abel, a film professor at the University of Michigan, and a team of nearly 140 scholars, the alphabetically arranged entries include key figures; technical innovations; film companies; kinds of films (*Comedy, Newsreels, Polar expedition films*); aspects of film production (*Costume, Lighting, Sound effects*); historical overviews of early cinema in specific countries; film publications; and related social and cultural institutions, practices, and concerns. Of the more than 950 entries, approximately 560 treat inventors, directors, producers, scriptwriters, actors and actresses, and other people involved in filmmaking. Most entries for individuals are relatively brief (between 100 to 200 words), but particularly significant figures, such as Charles Chaplin and Thomas Edison, receive treatments ranging from 450 to 1,000 words. Articles in other categories, for instance, those on specific film genres and national cinemas, often span several pages. Especially notable are the essays on individual countries, which reflect how quickly the technologies for making and showing motion pictures spread to diverse locations throughout the world, such as Cuba, New Zealand, and Vietnam. All entries are signed, and many provide bibliographic references.

Additional features include an extensive general bibliography of sources pertaining to early cinema and 132 black-and-white photographs and other illustrations. Liberal use of cross-references, a thematic guide that arranges article headings into broad subject categories, and a commendably detailed index (which is essential for locating information on individual films since there are no entries for film titles) facilitate access.

Scholarly but not pedantic, this encyclopedia will be a valuable resource in larger academic and public libraries and other institutions that are developing comprehensive collections related to film studies. Unfortunately, its substantial price may prohibit its purchase in many instances. —*Marie Ellis*

The Encyclopedia of Hollywood. 2d ed. By Barbara Siegel and others. 2004. 548p. illus. index. Facts On File, $75 (0-8160-4622-0). 791.43.

Sixteen years after the publication of the first edition, this encyclopedia offers representative entries on the American film industry, from the early, pre-Hollywood days to the present. Entries cover people, including actors, directors, producers, editors, cinematographers, and more; films; studios; genres (for example, *Beach party movies, Screwball comedy*); jobs (*Best boy, Editor*); and terms (*Montage, Rough cut*). Some entries feature a photograph, and many include *see also* references. The A–Z portion of the volume is followed by a selected bibliography. The index is the preferred approach to a name or group since many people are discussed within a category or theme, such as *Child stars* and *Sheen family dynasty.*

In their introduction, the authors note that genuine stardom seldom lasts for more than five years, and in adding newer stars to this edition, they have chosen those who seem to have lasting appeal, among them Julianne Moore, Brad Pitt, and Will Smith. The standard of lasting appeal has also resulted in the addition of some early major figures who may be forgotten (the director Allen Dwan, for example).

Although libraries that have both the first edition and other film titles may not consider this a necessary purchase, this up-to-date edition is easy to use and could be a welcome addition to the circulating as well as the reference collection. With the expansion of library video and DVD collections, it could also be used as a collection development tool. —*Patricia Hogan*

The Encyclopedia of Novels into Film. 2d ed. Ed. by John C. Tibbetts and James M. Welsh. 2005. 586p. illus. indexes. Facts On File, $75 (0-8160-5449-5). 791.43.

The new edition of an encyclopedia first published in 1998 provides an introduction to "significant" film adaptations of more than 300 novels. Arranged alphabetically by novel's title, each entry contains the author's name; brief film credits (director, adaptor[s], producers); and comments on the novel and on the film. Entries are accompanied by brief lists of references and occasional black-and-white photographs. Following the A–Z entries are an essay on the novelist as screenwriter, a selected bibliography, an index by film title, and a general index.

The audience for the work is the general reader, not the film specialist, so the selection is more eclectic than exhaustive. This second edition adds approximately 30 new adaptations, among them *The Bourne Identity, Cold Mountain,* and *Mystic River.* Some older adaptations that were left out of the 1998 edition have also been added, as have remakes of *The Manchurian Candidate* and *The Quiet American,* to name a few. Made-for-TV adaptations are generally not covered. Entry length ranges from a page to more than eight pages for *The Lord of the Rings.* A foreword by Robert Wise discussing the nature of film adaptations is followed by an essay on why film adaptations should be studied.

Enser's Filmed Books and Plays (6th ed., 2003) is far more comprehensive, listing approximately 8,000 adaptations of novels, plays, and nonfiction works, but it is primarily an index and does not provide comparative analysis. *The Encyclopedia of Novels into Film* has a place in both academic and popular collections and should definitely be considered by libraries in which the first edition was heavily used. —*Patricia Hogan*

Encyclopedia of Opera on Screen: A Guide to More Than 100 Years of Opera Films, Videos, and DVDs. By Ken Wlaschin. 2004. 872p. illus. index. Yale, $60 (0-300-10263-1). 791.43.

The enjoyment of reviewing this book took a downward spiral after it was discovered that portions of the book were published earlier by the author in *Opera on Screen* (Sunburst, 1997), even though the introduction to the new volume states "There is no other guide like it."

Entries have been revised from the earlier title, and there are also new entries. The arrangement remains the same, with singers, cities, operas, halls, composers, etc., interfiled in a letter-by-letter alphabetization. Wlaschin also provides subjective entries, such as *Best opera on video* and *Worst opera on film.*

Within entries, films are listed chronologically, with a short summary, the cast, timing, format, and distributor included. The breadth of opera is illustrated in entries for Walt Disney and Maurice Sendak. A smattering of musicals, operettas, and even requiems are also mentioned. There are a few black-and-white photos interspersed in the text. Some typographical errors are annoying—Colin Davis (not David), Albert Coates also referred to as Eric Coates (another English composer).

The index cites only people and works. Consequently, one cannot find productions of small opera companies such as the Santa Fe Opera or the Glimmerglass Opera unless the name of the opera is known. A selective bibliography and addresses of DVD and VHS distributors complete the volume.

Academic and public libraries with a strong opera collection should consider this comprehensive, readable encyclopedia, although they may not want to purchase it if they own *Opera on Screen.* —*Christine Bulson*

The John Wayne Filmography. By Fred Landesman. 2004. 440p. appendixes. bibliog. illus. index. McFarland, $75 (0-7864-1779-X). 791.4302.

John Wayne endures, and a filmography of this celluloid hero not only traces his career but reflects much of the U.S. ideology of rugged independence and down-to-earth practicality that he projected onscreen.

Landesman's introduction reviews Wayne's career, noting the mentality of the studios and the critics along the way. It should be noted that the rest of the book does not focus on Wayne per se but rather discusses each movie as a separate entity. The nearly 200 films are arranged alphabetically; one of the appendixes lists them chronologically from 1926 to 1976. Wayne started as a production crew member and extra during his University of Southern California college football days, so the earliest film entries note his role as a stand-in or prop boy (e.g., *Brown of Harvard,* 1926). Entries vary in length from a half page to four pages. Each one includes the film's date and length, cast, crew, review excerpts, plot synopsis (often taken directly from contemporaneous newsletters and press releases), and notes. Notes vary in content and length but usually include production cost, Wayne's salary, opening venue, minibiographies of directors or selected cast members, and other films released at the same time. It is not clear how the author chose whom to cover in these notes, which is a weakness. Furthermore, the notes are printed as one long paragraph, so the different subject matter cannot be easily distinguished; boldface type for the minibiography names also would have helped readability.

Besides the chronological appendix, there are appendixes of box- office hits, most popular Wayne films shown on TV, an extensive bibliography, and unreleased movies featuring Wayne as well as released movies where someone else took over Wayne's role. This latter appendix is probably the most intriguing; imagine Wayne in *High Noon* or *Patton.* An index of people and movies concludes the volume.

This filmography covers all of Wayne's movies and shows his range from sports to comedy, from westerns to war. Recommended for large motion-picture collections. —*Lesley Farmer*

The Queer Encyclopedia of Music, Dance, & Musical Theater. Ed. by Claude J. Summers. 2004. 303p. illus. indexes. Cleis, paper, $29.95 (1-57344-198-8). 791.

Readers will find it difficult to put this book down. The editor clearly states that it "has no pretensions to comprehensiveness" but is intended to be "an important beginning, not an end"—and what a wonderful beginning it is!

The volume covers primarily the nineteenth, twentieth, and twenty-first centuries, and the subjects included are predominately, though certainly not exclusively, North American and Western European. Little Richard and Tchaikovsky, Dusty Springfield and Dame Ethel Smyth, Hildegard of Bingen and Cris Williamson, Maud Allan and Rudolf Nureyev, disco and vaudeville, divas and directors: all may be found here. It's easy to negotiate the more than 200 alphabetically organized, signed entries and essays throughout the text. An *A–Z* list of entries is provided, as are two very helpful indexes. A topical index will prove extremely useful to people searching for broad categories, such as *AIDS,* and *Drag shows and performers.* Also, the well-developed index of names, located at the end of the book, assists in locating all sorts of diverse individuals who do not have separate entries: Condoleezza Rice (in the entry *Van Cliburn*) is an example.

Entries average half to three-quarters of a page, sometimes longer. The essays may extend for multiple pages and flesh out larger topics, such as *Conductors* and *Set and costume design.* For example, the subtopics "Composers and Lyricists," "The Broadway Diva," "Representations of Gay Characters," "Musicals Written for Gay Audiences," "The Revue," and "Musical Films" are all found within the entry *Musical theater and film.*

The *Encyclopedia* belongs in public libraries of all sizes, and it will be welcomed by students in high-school libraries, where it will be quietly, if not openly, read. —*Scottie Wallace*

The Oxford Companion to American Theatre. 3d ed. By Gerald Bordman and Thomas S. Hischak. 2004. 681p. Oxford, $75 (0-19-516986-7). 792.

Like a well-crafted revival of a beloved play, this new edition of a favorite reference book retains the flavor of the original production while significantly updating its content. The cast here is large and includes actors, choreographers, composers, dancers, designers, directors, lyricists, plays, playwrights, producers, theaters, and theater companies.

The text covers the American stage from its inception to the present, and the alphabetically arranged entries range in length from a few lines to a quarter of a double-columned page. Among the articles new to this edition are *AIDS and the American theatre, Asian-American theatre and drama, Feminist theatre, 42nd Street redevelopment, Performance art,* and *Road tours.* The authors note that to retain all the historical information of previous editions, individual articles have been condensed rather than eliminated. There is more variety here than on a vaudeville bill: *Hair* and *Hairspray; Urinetown* and *Uncle Tom's Cabin;* and *Tony 'n Tina's Wedding* and *The Tale of the Allergist's Wife* are among the plays represented. Articles on individual theater artists often mention a biography or autobiography, a welcome enhancement to a ready-reference source such as this. To present as complete a picture of American theater as possible, entries on theaters beyond the Great White Way, such as the Arena Stage, the Goodman Theatre, La Jolla Playhouse, American Conservatory Theatre, and the Steppenwolf Theatre Company, are included. Capsule histories of every Broadway theater as well as several Off-Broadway houses are another new and notable feature. The volume is recommended for all public and academic libraries and would be useful in high-school libraries with theater and drama collections. —*Carolyn Mulac*

Diamonds around the Globe: The Encyclopedia of International Baseball. By Peter C. Bjarkman. 2005. 607p. illus. index. Greenwood, $75 (0-313-32268-6). 796.357.

Though baseball is popularly viewed as the quintessential American game, this encyclopedia challenges that notion. Author Bjarkman, who has written several other books on baseball, aims "to present the rest of the world of baseball to U.S. fans." He provides a thorough discussion of the tradition of baseball around the globe and effectively shows that the sport is indeed an international one.

The encyclopedia begins with a detailed discussion of the development of baseball as an international sport. In this section of the work, Bjarkman convincingly makes the case that baseball is not "exclusively an American game." For example, he notes that baseball evolved from the English games of cricket and rounders. Furthermore, he states that in Cuba, baseball has been historically connected to nationhood and identity. The introduction is followed by the main text, which is divided into 11 chapters, including 2 on the Olympics and the Caribbean World Series. The remaining chapters are devoted to the history of baseball in particular countries or regions of the world. Countries covered include prominent baseball nations—such as Cuba, Japan, Mexico, Puerto Rico, and Venezuela—and regions not immediately known for baseball—such as Europe and Africa. Each country chapter contains detailed statistics and brief but informative biographies of notable players.

In addition to the main text, the encyclopedia has several other useful features. For example, there is an appendix of the "greatest moments" in the history of international baseball. An excellent annotated bibliography lists major monographs and periodical articles. Finally, black-and-white photographs, including a picture of Fidel Castro pitching, are dispersed throughout the volume.

Diamonds around the Globe will appeal to baseball followers who are interested in discovering the global dimension of the game. It is recommended for public and college libraries. —*Michelle Hendley*

Sports in America: Decade by Decade. 8v. 2004. illus. indexes. Facts On File, $240 (0-8160-5233-6). 796.

Volumes in this sociohistorical treatment of professional and amateur athletics in America and its influence on American culture are organized by time period. Volumes 1 and 2 each cover 20 years (1900–1919 and 1920–1939); volumes 3 through 7, 10 years; and the final volume goes from 1990 to 2003.

Each thin volume—none more than 110 pages—has the same series foreword and an introduction that sets sports-related events within the social and historical context of the period. For instance, volume 1 (1900–1919) discusses the shift from an agrarian society with a long workday to a more urban society with a shorter workday that begins to leave leisure time for spectator sports. Volume 8 (1990–2003) discusses the expansion of women in professional sports and the billions of dollars of revenue going to sports franchises and players.

The volumes are divided into chapters, one for each year. The sporting events and personalities are discussed, and sidebars highlight important milestones. A number of black-and-white photos break up the text, and the essays themselves are well written and accessible. Each volume includes a volume-specific index and several pages of resources as well as identical lists of American sports history resources and sports history Web sites. There is no set index. Through no fault of anyone involved in the set's creation, one fact is already out of date: in volume 1 it is noted that the 1918 World Series has gained immortality "because neither of its contestants, the Cubs or the Red Sox, have won a World Series since."

At first glance the format and size of the volumes give the impression of a younger children's set, but the narrative is written for grades 6 through

12. The set is suitable for school and public library collections and could be cataloged for the circulating collection. —*Jerry Carbone*

Total Baseball: The Ultimate Baseball Encyclopedia. 8th ed. Ed. by John Thorn and others. 2004. 2,676p. glossary. illus. tables. Sport Classic, $59.95 (1-894963-27-X). 796.357.

The eighth edition of *Total Baseball* lives up to even the highest expectations. By continuing to supplement, amend, and expand, this publication reminds us how hard work and dedication can result in a reference book that significantly improves with each edition. John Thorn, chief editor, has masterfully integrated previous editions with much new content from many new and old contributors. Covering major league baseball in wondrous detail, this is, as the new subtitle proclaims, truly the ultimate baseball encyclopedia.

Improvements and enhancements since the seventh edition include the introduction of new statistical measures, a new organizational structure, and detailed table of contents. The important and well-written essays (many new to this edition, others revised from previous editions) that appear here set this volume apart from other comprehensive baseball reference works. These essays are sprinkled throughout the volume and cover ideas such as a discussion of the secret behind the recent success of the Oakland Athletics ("Moneyball"), a ranking of the greatest teams of all time (the '39 Yankees rank first), and an overview of recent research that uncovered the appearance of William Edward White in an 1879 Providence Grays game. White was the first black man, and only former slave, ever to appear in major league game, predating Jackie Robinson's breaking of the color barrier by a full 68 years.

Sections 2 through 5 highlight another new feature in this edition, year-by-year essays covering every single year of major league baseball from 1873 to 2003. As in previous editions and other sections of the encyclopedia, statistics supplement the knowledgeable prose. The reader will also find some wonderful historical essays that originally appeared in the pages of SPORT magazine.

About half of the volume is made up of detailed statistics for every player ever to appear in a major league game. Other statistical sections, including records, awards, and MVP and Hall of Fame voting results, help round out this tribute to the statistical minutiae that fascinates many baseball fans. For anyone who wants to know all about baseball statistics, the detailed "Glossary of Statistical Terms" will delight (and perhaps overwhelm).

If your library can only afford one book about baseball, this is it. Supercedes the seventh and all previous editions. —*Jeff Kosokoff*

Literature

Encyclopedia of Catholic Literature. 2v. Ed. by Mary R. Reichardt. 2004. 842p. Greenwood, $199.95 (0-313-32289-9). 809.

This work is not an encyclopedia in the strict sense, providing entries for authors, literary concepts, historical periods, etc. Rather, it is a collection of lengthy essays on 77 representative literary works, each "informed in a substantial and meaningful way by the structures, tradition, history, spirituality, and/or culture of Catholicism." Essays are written by noted scholars and include a biography of the author, a plot summary for narrative works, a critical discussion with emphasis on Catholic themes and content, critical reception history, and often a supplemental bibliography. Arrangement of essays is by the author's last name. The set concludes with a selected general bibliography. There is no index.

The encyclopedia builds on an earlier title by the same editor, *Catholic Women Writers: A Bio-Bibliographical Sourcebook* (Greenwood, 2001). Besides covering works by both men and women authors, the newer title is diverse in several respects. The works that are discussed represent many literary genres, range in chronology from the fourth to the twentieth centuries, have their origins in different countries and cultures, and are not necessarily all by Catholic authors. Augustine's *Confessions,* Dante's *Divine Comedy,* and Chaucer's *Canterbury Tales* are, not surprisingly, included. So too are such works as Willa Cather's *Death Comes for the Archbishop,* James Joyce's *A Portrait of the Artist as a Young Man,* and Isak Dinesen's *Babette's Feast.* More recent works are Kathleen Norris' *The Cloister Walk* and Sandra Cisneros' *The House on Mango Street.*

The *Encyclopedia of Catholic Literature* will serve readers from such disciplines as history, women's studies, and religion. Recommended for academic and large public library collections. —*Christopher McConnell*

Encyclopedia of Feminist Literature. By Kathy J. Whitson. 2004. 300p. index. Greenwood, $65 (0-313-32731-9). 809.

As stated in the introduction, this volume is not meant to be an all-inclusive list of authors, literary terms, and genres. Instead, the purpose is to provide undergraduate, high-school, and general readers with an entry point to feminist literature. In her introduction, Whitson, a professor of English, tackles the "problematic term *feminist*" with a short history of the concept and finally defines it as the "call for the social, political and economic equality of women."

The authors are predominantly American and British, but significant authors from elsewhere who have been published in English are included. All of the nearly 70 authors are creative writers and not theorists, selected because their works have challenged traditional gender roles, explored female oppression, or critiqued patriarchal social structures. Among them are Isabel Allende, Elizabeth Gaskell, Toni Morrison, Amy Tan, and Virginia Woolf. Each author entry includes biographical information, a thorough interpretative summary of at least one major work, a list of her other writings, internal cross-references, and a list of "References and Suggested Readings." The purpose of the summary section is to entice students and general readers to explore each author's works further. In addition to the author entries, there are 20 articles covering related topics such as *Abolition, Marriage,* and *Pseudonyms.* The volume closes with a list of all works cited.

Although most of the women discussed here are covered extensively in other encyclopedias of literature, this is a handy introduction to some key feminist writers. Readable and accessible, *Encyclopedia of Feminist Literature* is a worthwhile purchase for public, high-school, and undergraduate collections. —*Lisa Johnston*

Encyclopedia of Gothic Literature. By Mary Ellen Snodgrass. 2004. 480p. index. Facts On File, $65 (0-8160-5528-9). 809.

Gothic literature is a perennial favorite with students and readers, and now Facts On File has published a new encyclopedia in its Literary Movements series that covers this popular genre from its origins in the eighteenth century to its uses in contemporary literature. This A–Z encyclopedia has more than 400 entries on authors, books and stories, and related topics such as *Freudian themes, Mad scientists,* and *Melancholy.* The entries range from one or two paragraphs to a full page in length. Each entry includes numerous cross-references to related articles and ends with a short bibliography of books and articles. The encyclopedia also has a list of major gothic works by title and then by author, a time line of gothic literature, a list of film noir and gothic films, and bibliographies of primary and secondary sources.

The strengths of the volume are its coverage of little-known authors, contemporary authors, and short stories that are often read in literature courses in high school and college. While information is readily available on authors such as Edgar Allan Poe and Ann Radcliffe, lesser-known writers, among them Edward Bulwer-Lytton, Margaret Oliphant, and Charlotte Smith, are given short biographical sketches, and their best works are briefly analyzed for gothic themes. More contemporary authors such as Dan Brown, Victoria Holt, and Stephen King are also covered. There are excellent essays on often-studied short stories, for example, "The Lottery," "Gimpel the Fool," and "Rappaccini's Daughter." Also useful to students are the entries on topics, such as *Atmosphere, Disguise motif, Gothic novel,* and *Monsters.*

The major problem with the book is that the author never explains what criteria were used in deciding what writers and works should be included. It often seems that an author or work is here because one or two gothic literary devices are used, and the analysis of what makes them gothic is not always convincing. Despite this drawback, the *Encyclopedia of Gothic Literature* is a well-written reference book that will be very helpful for literature students and is recommended for high-school, college, and public libraries that support research in literature. —*Merle Jacob*

Feminism in Literature: A Gale Critical Companion. 6v. 2004. 3,720p. illus. index. Gale, $795 (0-7876-7573-3). 809.

This is the third in the Gale Critical Companion (GCC) series, joining *The Harlem Renaissance* (2002) and *The Beat Generation* (2003). The series is aimed at upper high-schoolers and undergraduates, with this set taking an in-depth look at the history of women and feminism throughout literature. Feminism is defined here as "a loose confederation of social, political, spiritual, and intellectual movements that places women and gender at the center of inquiry with the goal of social justice."

Overall arrangement is chronological, with volumes 1 and 2 covering the period from antiquity through the eighteenth century; volumes 3 and 4 the nineteenth century; and volumes 5 and 6 the twentieth century. Eleven topical entries averaging 90 pages in length discuss feminism within a specific time period or elaborate on subjects like misogyny, devotional literature, and lesbian literature. These are supplemented by 62 shorter (generally ranging between 20 and 50 pages) entries on major figures associated with feminist literature, such as Margaret Atwood, Jane Austen, Margery Kempe, Christina Rossetti, and Mary Wollstonecraft. Entries follow the same format as the other GCC series: a brief introduction, a list of representative works, reprinted primary source documents (such as excerpts from a literary work or an author's personal letters), reprinted critical essays that are overviews or title specific, a list of annotated further readings, and citations to other Gale sources. Also included in the set are author, title, and subject indexes; a chronology of key events from women's history; black-and-white photographs; and informative sidebars.

Author entries are mostly focused on -nineteenth- and twentieth-century American and English writers, although a little more than 10 percent are international. All of the authors covered can be found elsewhere in other Gale series, but there is only a direct overlap of about 15 percent in content. Furthermore, the reprinted primary and secondary source material and blanket social perspective give students a wealth of information beyond a standard treatment of these "canon" figures. Not found is the breadth of coverage of more contemporary authors that sources like Greenwood's *Encyclopedia of Feminist Literature* (2004) or *Feminist Writers* (St. James, 1996) offer; those titles, for example, include such authors as Dorothy Allison, Ana Castillo, and Jeanette Winterson.

The question for libraries is whether this valuable new set is worth the $795. Will the students who would most benefit from the expanded treatment given be able to find their way to this resource? Recommended for libraries serving women's studies programs and with thorough literary criticism collections. —*Susan Gardner*

Historical Dictionary of Science Fiction Literature. By Brian Stableford. 2004. 451p. bibliog. Scarecrow, $70 (0-8108-4938-0). 809.3.

As the inaugural volume in the Historical Dictionaries of Literature and the Arts series, this work is unfortunately somewhat redundant. Although there is worth in being current (the volume does update many other reference works, albeit in brief), this is an expensive addition to an already crowded market served by the likes of *Trillion Year Spree: The History of Science Fiction* (Atheneum, 1986), *The Encyclopedia of Science Fiction* (St. Martin's, 1993), and *The Cambridge Companion to Science Fiction* (2003).

However, as noted in the introduction, dictionaries are by their nature concise, and this one may supplement resources such as those mentioned above that examine similar topics at greater length. Following an excellent introduction by Stableford, described as an sf practitioner and an academic, the dictionary portion of the volume is arranged alphabetically and discusses some of the important names, themes, magazines, genres, and so on that comprise the history of science fiction. For example, there is a good cross-referenced entry on John W. Campbell and the magazines he edited, the genres he wrote in and influenced, and the authors he unquestionably helped. As the entry says, Campbell, with H. G. Wells, was directly responsible for the evolution of sf.

Also included here are an eclectic time line that traces key events in sf history from 1726 to 2003 and a substantial bibliography of secondary studies (from broad treatments to authors and themes). As previously mentioned, however, this is not a necessary purchase for libraries with similar titles. Unless a library owns no other reference sources on science fiction or has a very large science fiction collection, there is nothing new to justify the expense in this time of lean budgets. —*John Doherty*

Masterplots 2: Short Story Series. 8v. Rev. ed. Ed. by Charles May. bibliog. glossary. indexes. Salem, $499 (1-58765-140-8). 809.3.

This revised edition of *Masterplots 2: Short Story Series* (Salem, 1986) incorporates all the articles from the original set and the 4-volume supplement (1996), adding an additional 250 new essays for a total of 1,490 articles. Each signed entry is arranged alphabetically by short story title and averages 1,500 words in length. Entries begin with the following background facts about the story: author name, type of plot, time period of the story, location, original publication date, and a list of principal characters. This is followed by a plot summary, a discussion of themes and meanings, and a discussion of style and technique. Coverage focuses heavily on North American authors, although there is also representation from other regions, including Europe, Africa, Asia, Latin America, and New Zealand. Coverage of stories by modern authors originally appearing in publications like the *New Yorker*, such as Matthew Klam and David Schickler, is sometimes surprisingly included along with the expected classics. Every volume has a comprehensive title index, and the final volume has a bibliography of monographs and periodicals for both general short story studies and individual authors represented by at least five stories. New to the revised edition is a glossary with 135 terms, a chronological list of titles, a geographical index, and a type of plot index.

As with all *Masterplots* series, coverage is uneven depending on the contributor and can at times seem simplistic or one-dimensional. Still, because there are so few short story aids available, this update is a welcome thing. Editor May discusses the short story's struggle for survival in the modern publishing world in his introduction, and this is certainly reflected in the paucity of reference sources on the form. Gale's *Short Story Criticism* (serial) offers a more comprehensive biocritical survey of its included authors, along with excerpts from serious criticism, but is often limited in its amount of information about an individual title. Likewise, the *Critical Survey of Short Fiction* (2d ed., Salem, 2001) places each author in a broader context and seldom devotes as much attention to individual stories. Readers who want merely, as May suggests in his introduction, an "overview, a context, and a perspective" with which to read an individual short story will find *Masterplots 2: Short Story Series* extremely helpful. Recommended for public, high-school, and undergraduate libraries; libraries already owning the previous set will want to update. —*Susan Gardner*

Multicultural Writers since 1945: An A-to-Z Guide. Ed. by Alba Amoia and Bettina L. Knapp. 2004. 610p. bibliogs. index. Greenwood, $119.95 (0-313-30688-5). 809.

Following up on their *Multicultural Writers from Antiquity to 1945: A Bio-Bibliographical Sourcebook* (Greenwood, 2001), Amoia and Knapp now offer *Multicultural Writers since 1945: An A-to-Z Guide*, which presents signed, brief biocritical essays of 102 authors. Not only have the editors expanded the number of covered authors but they have also included in the present work a table of contents, allowing users to find authors more quickly. Drawn from across the world, the field of authors ranges from critically regarded fiction writers like J. M. Coetzee and Gao Xingjian to writers in the fields of religion (Mircea Eliade) and political and cultural criticism (Frantz Fanon). The editors state that the majority of authors have lived in a culture "other than their own" either voluntarily or by force; a few are included who, though native, have been estranged by a differing dominant culture.

The introduction discusses literature development in various places in the world, including country-specific information in some instances, the effects of postcolonial multiculturalism on literature in general, and particular themes associated with these changes in literature—exile, escape, and distance (not only geographical). Individual entries begin with a short biography, followed by multicultural themes and then a survey of criticism. Entries end with bibliographies of selected primary and secondary sources. Articles average about five pages. The volume ends with a selected bibliography; an index of authors, works, and topics; and information about the editors and contributors.

Similar biocritical information about these authors may be found in Gale's Contemporary Authors series, Salem's *Cyclopedia of World Authors* [RBB Je 1 & 15 04], or Wilson's World Authors series. While the larger sources allow greater detail and a greater number of authors, the single-volume coverage offered by *Multicultural Writers since 1945* sets these "authors who crossed borders" in a particular context. Highly recommended for academic and larger public libraries. —*William Thomas*

Ninth Book of Junior Authors and Illustrators. Ed. by Connie C. Rockman. 2005. 583p. illus. index. Wilson, $105 (0-8242-1043-3). 809.

This latest addition to the *Book of Junior Authors and Illustrators*, first published in 1934 and last revised in 2000, offers solid and appealing information for students, librarians, and educators. Close to 200 authors and illustrators are profiled in this update. Although the focus of the text is on new contributors, 18 profiles from previous editions have been brought up-to-date, including those for Barbara Cooney, Virginia Hamilton, and William Steig.

Each entry begins with a statement in the author's or artist's own words. This is followed by an editorial piece that presents information about the individual's life and work that was not mentioned in the autobiography.

Each entry concludes with a bibliography of selected works of the individual. Also, new to this edition, Web site addresses for some authors have been included.

The book offers an attractive format that features portraits and autographs of each person as well as cover-art illustrations. The collection concludes with a listing of awards and honors cited within the volume and a comprehensive index to all of the volumes of the series. School and public libraries would be well served by this informative and easy-to-read text. —*Maren Ostergard*

Notable Playwrights. 3v. Ed. by Carl Rollyson. 2004. 1,230p. illus. index. Salem, $188 (1-58765-195-5). 809.2.

Part of the Magill's Choice series, this set covers "106 of the most important and best-known dramatists from antiquity to the present day." Entries are taken from *Critical Survey of Drama, Revised Edition* (2003) with some added content. For this leaner version, care was taken to include the dramatists that would be of most interest to students in high school and undergraduate English and drama courses, among them Aeschylus, Bertolt Brecht, Tony Kushner, Christopher Marlowe, Eugene O'Neill, and Wendy Wasserstein.

Entries are arranged alphabetically. Each begins with birth and death dates and locations and a list of principal dramatic works, followed by sections on "Other Literary Forms," "Achievements," Biography," and "Analysis" (including subsections on major plays), a list of other important works, and a bibliography. Average entry length is about 12 pages. Most entries contain an illustration of the playwright. The set concludes with a glossary and a time line for the playwrights by birth. Geographical, categorized, and subject indexes provide multiple access points.

This work has approximately one-sixth of the entries in *Critical Survey of Drama, Revised Edition,* and libraries that already own the larger set probably don't need the spin-off, especially since *Critical Survey* is itself fairly new. It would be a good choice for high-school, public, and undergraduate libraries that haven't acquired the larger set because of space and budget considerations. —*Jennifer Dawson*

American Writers. By Elizabeth H. Oakes. 2004. 430p. bibliogs. illus. indexes. Facts On File, $65 (0-8160-5158-5). 810.9.

American Writers is the newest title in the five-volume Facts On File series American Biographies. The other titles in the series are: *American Religious Leaders* (2003); *American Inventors, Entrepreneurs, and Business Visionaries* (2002); *American Political Leaders* (2002); and *American Political Activists* (2002). Like its predecessors, *American Writers* is geared toward high-school and undergraduate students seeking basic background information.

The volume has alphabetically arranged entries for approximately 260 authors from a variety of genres—poetry, fiction, drama, essay, and autobiography. Each straightforward, easily digested entry contains a short biography, critical analysis, and a bibliography of works about the author in both printed and Web formats. To demonstrate the diversity of American authors, emphasis is placed not only on the literary importance of the writers included but also on their ethnic and cultural backgrounds. For example, the article on nineteenth-century writer Mary Wilkins Freeman discusses not only her published works but also the conflict she experienced as an early feminist with a Puritan religious background. Ha Jin, one of the contemporary writers Oakes describes, has only been writing in English for a decade, yet he has been recognized with many awards, such as the PEN/Hemingway Award and the National Book Award. His entry describes his life in China during the Cultural Revolution and his life as a student immigrant to the U.S. Other features of the volume include a list of entries by literary genre; a list of entries by literary movement, region, subject, and style; a list of entries by decade of the authors' birth; and a general index.

Oakes states in her author's note that she aimed "to include writers who have not often been represented in major reference works of this kind" and that the volume stands out for its "coverage of multiethnic writers and its attention to contemporary writers." Although not innovative or flashy, *American Writers* offers a convenient introduction and is a worthwhile purchase for public, high- school, and undergraduate library collections. —*Lisa Johnston*

Cyclopedia of Young Adult Authors. 3v. 2005. 770p. illus. indexes. Salem, $225 (1-58765-206-4). 810.9.

Salem Press has published an alphabetically arranged set containing 251 author profiles for young adult readers. Though emphasis is on writers within the young adult tradition, authors such as Jane Austen, Daniel Defoe, and William Faulkner are also covered. *Cyclopedia of Young Adult Authors* originated as a resource on authors for the subscription database NoveList.

Each volume begins with a table of contents, which lists the names of the authors included only in that particular volume. A detailed subject index is found at the end of each volume, which includes the authors' book titles as well as sidebar topics and terms. For each included author, from *Joan Abelove* to *Paul Zindel*, ready-reference information includes birth date and place and, where appropriate, death date and place; official Web site; and a list of major works. An opening paragraph provides a brief description of the author's impact on young adult literature, followed by a discussion of the author's life, awards, works, and the themes that flow through the writings. There are no lists of resources for further reading.

Each three-page entry has at least two full-color illustrations and two sidebars, which elaborate on terms (*Apartheid, Protagonist, Samurai*); historical events; film adaptations; individuals; literary topics (*Historical fiction, Local-color writing, Phoenix Award*); aspects of the writers' lives; and more. Sometimes the relevance of the sidebar topics seems slight. For example, the entry for Nancy Werlin includes a sidebar for computer engineer, her father's profession. Words, phrases, and names within an entry that are sidebar topics are highlighted in colored type, with page-number references provided in flags of corresponding colors in the margins. The use of color to indicate cross-references is just one example of the set's strong graphic elements.

Cyclopedia of Young Adult Authors is a worthwhile resource for upper-elementary and middle-school through ninth-grade libraries. Its concise coverage of the included authors' lives and works makes for easy access for the novice researcher. However, the price may be a drawback for smaller libraries. —*Carol Sue Harless*

Encyclopedia of the Chicago Literary Renaissance. By Jan Pinkerton and Randolph H. Hudson. 2004. 426p. bibliog. illus. index. Facts On File, $65 (0-8160-4898-3). 810.9.

Covering the Chicago literary scene from 1880 to 1930, this is the second volume in Facts On File's series on various American literary movements and the writers, books, events, people, and places associated with them.

Most entries are one paragraph in length, but major writers have two- or three-page articles. Important books, such as *Sister Carrie,* also have longer articles that analyze and summarize the work. All of the articles include cross-references to related entries and, where appropriate, recommended books for further reading. Scattered throughout are black-and-white drawings and photographs, but since many of the included authors are little known today, more photographs would have been helpful. At the end of the book is a list of the major authors and their works, a chronology of events in Chicago, and a detailed index.

Besides authors and works, coverage is given to places, buildings, and events that are of "primary or ancillary importance to students of the Chicago Renaissance," but the explanation of why they have been included is not always clear. The article on the Rookery Building explains why it is one of the finest examples of modern architecture, and it also points out that Frank Norris set part of his novel *The Pit* in the building. Yet the entry on Quinn Chapel A.M.E. Church says only that it was the first African American church in Chicago. How or why it relates to the Chicago literary renaissance is never explained. Similarly, post–Chicago renaissance writers such as Gwendolyn Brooks, James T. Farrell, and Saul Bellow are covered in short entries, but these entries do not explain how such writers were influenced by the renaissance writers.

Despite this caveat, the book is an excellent source that introduces students to an important literary movement. This is a major new reference title that academic and public libraries with literature collections will want to purchase. High-school libraries in the Midwest will also find it very helpful to their students. —*Merle Jacob*

Extraordinary American Writers. By John Tessitore. 2004. 288p. illus. index. Children's Press, $39 (0-516-22656-8). 810.9.
Extraordinary People in Jazz. By Marvin Martin. 2004. 288p. illus. index. Children's Press, $39 (0-516-22275-9). 781.65.

Employing similar formats, these two volumes from the Extraordinary Peoples series each contain 60 brief profiles of people with major accomplishments in literature and jazz. The profiles, arranged chronologically and ranging from three to five pages, are accompanied by black-and-white illustrations or photographs of each subject. Under the full name of the person being profiled is a listing of his or her achievements, date of birth and death (if applicable), and a noteworthy quote either by or about the person.

In *Extraordinary American Writers* the choices of people to cover are logical, considering most school curriculums. Kate Chopin, F. Scott Fitzgerald, Allen Ginsberg, Zora Neale Hurston, Eugene O'Neill, and Mark Twain are part of a diverse selection of 45 men and 15 women. The literary forms that are represented encompass fiction, drama, essays, and poetry. The volume concludes with a "For Further Reading" list that includes Web sites. *Extraordinary People in Jazz* chronicles personalities significant in the development of jazz—from its beginnings, with the likes of Duke Ellington and Louis Armstrong, to newcomers, such as Diana Krall and Christian McBride. Following the main entries, the volume offers shorter profiles of 32 additional jazz musicians, a glossary, and a "To Find Out More" section, which includes a selected discography as well as books and online resources.

Both volumes would be a welcome addition to any middle- and high-school collection, particularly because of the reasonable price. —*Cheryl Ward*

The Facts On File Companion to 20th-Century American Poetry. Ed. by Burt Kimmelman. 572p. index. Facts On File, $65 (0-8160-4698-0). 811.

This A–Z compendium of 500-plus signed entries presents an eclectic approach to the study of twentieth-century American poetry, reflecting the wide variety of poetic styles, schools, and movements of the century. Kimmelman, a professor of English at the New Jersey Institute of Technology and himself a poet, draws upon the expertise of 244 academic contributors from all parts of the country and abroad. Analysis by contributors from academic institutions in Australia, Canada, Germany, Guatemala, Israel, Singapore, Spain, Taiwan, and the U.K. lends unique cross-cultural perspectives.

Entries range in length from 500 to 2,000 words, and each has a bibliography. In addition to individual poets, coverage encompasses important poems and collections as well as topics such as *Caribbean poetic influences, Deep image poetry, Fugitive/Agrarian school,* and *Poetry journals*. Of note is the book's expert inclusion of African American poets and poetry. Entries offer extensive, authoritative interpretations of well-known poets Maya Angelou, Rita Dove, and Langston Hughes, to name three, and entries for lesser-known writers like the late modernist African American poet Melvin Tolson.

A work that attempts to offer an encyclopedic treatment of such a broad topic in one volume will no doubt contain omissions, but this does not detract from the overall quality, relevance, and caliber of the book. A valuable companion to standard reference sources like Gale's Contemporary Poets series or Poetry for Students series, it is recommended for all public libraries and undergraduate collections and is sure to be a handy reference guide during National Poetry Month and Black History Month. —*Diana Kirby*

African American Dramatists: An A-to-Z Guide. Ed. by Emmanuel S. Nelson. 2004. 527p. index. Greenwood, $85 (0-313-32233-3). 812.009.

In addition to offering biocritical sketches for 61 writers from the last 150 years, this title has a selected bibliography for further research and an index (primarily author and title). Signed entries follow a general format: biographical information, overview of major works and themes, description of the critical reception, and bibliographies of dramatic works by the artist and studies of those dramatic works. The average length of each entry is about 8 pages, but the length ranges from 4 to 21 pages. The usual names are present—James Baldwin, Lorraine Hansberry, Langston Hughes, Zora Neale Hurston, and Richard Wright—as well as writers who are commanding more attention, among them Pearl Cleage, Angelina Weld Grimké, and Suzan Lori-Parks. The essays are generally clear and readable.

Although there are other competing sets, *African American Dramatists* includes some writers who are seldom covered elsewhere. Among other sources for African American dramatists are *Early Black American Playwrights and Dramatic Writers* (Greenwood, 1990) and its companion, *Contemporary Black American Playwrights and Their Plays* (Greenwood, 1988); this pair has the greatest overlap with *African American Dramatists,* with 54 shared entries. The *Dictionary of Literary Biography* (Gale, 2005) and *Contemporary Authors* (Gale, 2005) combine to provide 49 shared entries. Greenwood's set *American Playwrights, 1880–1945* (1994) and its companion, *American Playwrights since 1945* (1989), though, share only 8 persons with *African American Dramatists.*

Nelson has edited and written several other books that include African American, American, and multicultural writers. This one does have significant overlap with standard sources, but because of its inclusion of harder-to-find writers and its single-volume convenience, it is recommended for academic and public libraries. —*William Thomas*

Dictionary of American Young Adult Fiction, 1997-2001: Books of Recognized Merit. By Alethea K. Helbig and Agnes Regan Perkins. 2004. 558p. index. Greenwood, $75 (0-313-32430-1). 813.

The authors, both professors of English language and literature, have added another dictionary of American fiction to their previously published dictionaries covering children's literature from 1859 to 1999 (also published by Greenwood). By turning their attention to young adult fiction, they have created a volume that will serve middle- and high-school and public librarians. This collection of 741 alphabetically arranged title, author, and character entries covers 290 books and 242 authors. The included books are recipients of the Printz or Alex awards or appeared on the ALA Best Books for Young Adults, New York Public Library Books for the Teen Age, or *Booklist* Adult Books for Young Adults lists between 1997 and 2001.

All entries are written in narrative format, which makes quick reference for bibliographic or other information difficult. Title entries note the subgenre and give a plot summary that is usually very detailed and comprises most of the entry. A brief critical assessment is provided, as are abbreviations for the award list or lists on which the book appears. Author entries are usually much shorter and focus on the aspects of the person's life most relevant to literature. Character entries include physical or personality traits, how the character functions in the story, and how he or she relates to other characters. These entries are often long and convoluted, as are some plot summaries, requiring familiarity with the book being discussed. Characters are listed the way in which they are most often referred to, sometimes listed alphabetically under *Mr., Mrs.,* or *Miss*. Asterisks serve to indicate cross-references within the volume.

The index is extremely detailed and runs more than 140 pages, with main entries in capital letters and book titles in italics. There is also a listing of included titles by the awards they received. Although the dictionary may include more information than is needed on a daily basis, the capability to cross-reference a title with its author and characters is a positive feature. Recommended for school and public libraries. —*Rochelle Glantz*

Encyclopedia of British Writers: 16th, 17th, and 18th Centuries. 2v. Ed. by Alan Hager. 2005. 816p. indexes. Facts On File, $150 (0-8160-5132-1). 820.9.

These two volumes, one covering the sixteenth and seventeenth centuries and the other covering the eighteenth, take a remarkably broad view of their subject, including entries on poets, playwrights, novelists, translators, and a wide range of nonfiction writers (some of whom were not British and some of whom "wrote exclusively in Latin"). The two guiding principles of selection, state the editor, are "that literature is simply the best writing and that an era of culture must be taken as a whole." Thus, there are entries on the influential printer William Caxton, who died in 1491; the French philosophers-writers Descartes, Pascal, and Voltaire; historians, painters, and composers; staples of British literature courses such as Shakespeare and Milton; and hundreds of lesser-known figures. A much smaller number of entries cover topics such as *Celtic revival movement, Conduct books,* and *Reformation.* The downside to such inclusiveness is that William Blake, for example, is summarized in just two pages. Yet even the most obscure individuals are rarely given fewer than 300 words.

The writing is uniformly clear and jargon free. Possibly unfamiliar literary terms, such as *domestic tragedy* or *soliloquy,* are generally defined at the point of use. Each biographical entry begins with birth and death dates and writing genre, such as *essayist* or *translator*. A biographical narrative is combined with (for shorter entries) or followed by (for longer entries) a critical analysis. The great majority of biographical entries are followed by lists of works about and by the author; these books will be most easily found in a university library. Each volume ends with a selected bibliography and an index specific to the volume. The series also includes the well-received *Encyclopedia of British Writers: Nineteenth and Twentieth Centuries* (2003).

Recommended for high-school and university libraries, these volumes will be of most use to students of British literature seeking a level of detail somewhere between entries in a general encyclopedia and those in Scribner's British Writers series. —*Craig Bunch*

South Asian Literature in English: An Encyclopedia. Ed. by Jaina C. Sanga. 2004. 360p. illus. index. Greenwood, $85 (0-313-32700-9). 820.9.

Focusing on Bangladesh, India, Pakistan, and Sri Lanka, this encyclopedia covers the region's English-language literature, its English-language writers (born in South Asia or identified with the region), and related topics (for example, *East India Company, Nationalism*). The 136 entries are arranged alphabetically. "Entries by Topic" groups articles under eight categories, including "Literary Theorists," "Novel/Film Adaptations," "Novelists," and "Short Story Collections." Coverage is weighted toward novels and novelists, with less attention paid to drama, poetry, and short stories. The 31 entries on "Literary and Historical Terms and Issues" help round out this resource and make it somewhat unique.

Articles are the work of 64 international contributors and average one to two pages in length. Cross-references are not included. Each article ends with a list of further readings, which can include books, articles, and Web pages. Illustrations comprise 4 maps (Bangladesh, Kashmir, South Asia, and Sri Lanka) and 37 black-and-white photographs depicting authors, South Asian culture (e.g., a Hindu festival), and film stills. A chronology beginning with 2,500 B.C.E. (Indus Valley civilization) and ending in 2003 (relations between India and Pakistan) precedes the entries. Following the entries, a four-page selected bibliography lists anthologies of South Asian literature, secondary sources, and relevant periodical titles. The encyclopedia ends with an index and list of contributors with affiliations. A few articles assume some prior knowledge of South Asian literature and culture. For example, one article refers to the practice of sati without an accompanying definition.

This volume supplements and expands on editor Sanga's prior publication *South Asian Novelists in English: An A-to-Z Guide* (Greenwood, 2003) and is recommended for academic and large public libraries. —*Stephen Fadel*

Encyclopedia of Post-Colonial Literatures in English. 3v. 2d ed. Ed. by Eugene Benson and L. W. Connolly. 2005. 1,892p. index. Routledge, $450 (0-415-27885-6). 820.9917

This second edition provides a timely update to the 1994 version, expanding from two volumes with about 1,600 entries to three volumes with about 1,800 entries. The majority of entries focus on individuals writing in English, from countries affected by British colonization. New material on Cyprus and its writers adds to attention already given to literatures from Bangladesh, India, Malaysia, Pakistan, and other countries, plus regions of Africa. Biographical entries—many updated from the first edition—provide a brief statement on the writer's life and major works, sometimes including quotations. Updates are more likely to have occurred for still-living writers and range from an added paragraph (e.g., *Singh, Kirpal*) to a more significant rewrite (e.g., *Simpson, Louis*).

Topical entries have an overview followed by separate treatments discussing how that topic is approached within the literature of specified countries. *Criticism (Overview)*, for example, introduces the most relevant postcolonial theorists and is followed by 13 entries on criticism from Australia, Canada, the Caribbean, India, and so on. Although not every country included in the encyclopedia is treated within each topical entry, the second edition often has new national entries for various topics: *Travel Literature* has added entries for Bangladesh, Cyprus, and India. Entries on the countries themselves generally provide an introduction to the geography and natural history, pre-European culture, post-European history, political institutions, and current political and economic status.

Signed entries range from half a page to two pages in length; many have suggestions for further reading appended. Ninety-six new contributors lend their expertise to this second edition. Lists of topics begin each volume, with extensive indexing (more than 100 pages) at the end of volume 3. Access in the index is by author, title, and topic.

Some of the authors and topics may appear in scattered publications like *The Encyclopedia of Literature in Canada* (Univ. of Toronto, 2002) or *World Writers in English* (Scribner, 2003), but no other source has this depth or range. This work is highly recommended for academic and large public libraries. —*Joseph Thomas*

Everyone and Everything in Trollope. 4v. Ed. by George Newlin. 2004. 3,911p. illus. indexes. Sharpe, $499.95 (0-7656-1320-4). 823.

The reputation of the most prolific Victorian novelist underwent an eclipse after his death but has recovered in recent years, and several of his novels have made the leap from graduate-seminar fare to slick adaptations for *Masterpiece Theatre*. In this set, Newlin, who also compiled *Everyone in Dickens* (Greenwood, 1995), covers Trollope's work in exhaustive detail. The first two volumes treat the novels, the third is devoted to short fiction and sketches, and the fourth covers nonfiction.

The 47 novels are arranged by Trollope's principal themes, such as "Bartsetshire" (the fictional English county where several of the books are set) and "Family Law." For each novel, Newlin provides a chapter-by-chapter plot summary and excerpts passages describing each character, major and minor. Some of the descriptions for principal characters cover more than 10 pages. In volumes 3 and 4, Trollope's shorter works and nonfiction writings are similarly treated but arranged by type—short stories, sketches, plays, or, in the case of nonfiction, by subject or locale. Each volume has an index that is specific to it and lists all the fictional characters and real people who are mentioned, including those with no names (*bailiff, in a decent coat*). Volume 3 also contains a variety of set indexes through which one can track down, for example, all of the horses or lady's maids that inhabit Trollope's world. Volume 4 includes the "Topicon," a Trollope concordance with his words on everything from good and evil to central heating.

This is not a resource for the faint of heart. The organization is hard to decipher, and the amount of detail is almost overwhelming. Even devoted fans will probably be happier with the *Oxford Reader's Companion to Trollope* (1999). Newlin has done a service for the advanced reader and the scholar, however, and *Everyone and Everything in Trollope* belongs in collections supporting Trollope research or Victorian studies. —*Mary Ellen Quinn*

The Oxford Companion to the Brontës. By Christine Alexander and Margaret Smith. 2004. 586p. bibliogs. illus. Oxford, $95 (0-19-866218-1). 823.

For almost two centuries both general readers and scholars have been intrigued by the writings that sprang from the fertile imaginations of a curate's children raised on the moors of Yorkshire. Covering not only the three Brontë sisters who have attracted the most attention (Anne, Charlotte, and Emily) but also their brother, Branwell, and their father, Patrick, this guide provides a wealth of information about their lives and works and the society in which they lived, as well as historical and critical perspectives on their writings. The more than 1,000 alphabetically arranged entries include lengthy articles on each Brontë and his or her individual works and shorter entries on characters and places in the writings and real people, places, and other entities associated with them. In addition, numerous substantive thematic and topical entries (for example, *Art of the Brontës, Health and medicine, Psychoanalytic approaches*) help to elucidate the Brontës' world and their creative output. Bibliographical references generally accompany longer entries, and a selective bibliography appears at the end of the volume. The latter provides no references to relevant Internet sites, an unfortunate omission, since useful tools for studying the Brontës are available on the Web. Additional features include a generous network of cross-references, a number of black-and-white illustrations, a chronology, and a section that identifies dialect and obsolete words in the Brontës' writings. Providing an overview of the entire work is a classified index that arranges entries into topical categories, enabling users to find, for example, all entries relating to adaptations of the Brontës' works or to places where they traveled.

As Brontë scholars, Alexander and Smith are highly qualified to have undertaken this project, and they and the seven other contributors have created a valuable compendium of impeccable scholarship. Containing more than twice as many entries as *The Brontës: A to Z* (Facts On File, 2003), this excellent guide is the most comprehensive and scholarly reference companion to the Brontës now available. It is highly recommended for all academic libraries and larger public libraries. —*Marie Ellis*

Literary Cultures of Latin America: A Comparative History. 3v. Ed. by Mario J. Valdes and Djelal Kadir. 2004. 2,240p. illus. index. Oxford, $395 (0-19-512621-1). 860.9.

This ambitious set features 205 signed articles from 242 scholars in 22 countries and claims to be "the largest comparative history project in the world." It covers five centuries of various multidisciplinary aspects (including historical, political, social, economical, and geographical) of Latin American culture on the grounds that literature responds to and enriches the culture from which it derives. The scope of Latin American literature here is extremely broad and expands on the traditional canon to include marginal authors and Brazilian literature, although English-, French-, and Dutch-speaking cultures of the Caribbean are mostly excluded.

The three volumes have separate, broad motifs. Volume 1, *Configurations of Literary Culture,* gives a framework for cultural production, including exclusionary barriers, and an overview of popular culture. Volume 2, *Institutional Modes and Cultural Modalities,* maps out the cultural concentrations of the production of literature (including literary forms and geographic cultural centers). Volume 3 is titled *Latin American Literary Culture: Subject to History.* Within volumes, articles are grouped in thematic sections such as "Linguistic Diversity of Latin American Cultures," "The Novel," and "Amerindian Literary Cultures." Article length generally ranges from 5 to 30 pages, and each article has its own bibliography.

More than 251 black-and-white illustrations (including maps and charts) accompany the text. The set concludes with a list of contributors and a broad subject index. Also, there is a list of included people with birth and death dates, but since this gives no page references and some people listed aren't in the subject index, it isn't very helpful.

The essays are somewhat arcane and not traditionally organized, so it will be difficult for people without advanced background knowledge of Latin American studies to find what they need. There is some overlap, though not a lot, with *The Cambridge History of Latin American Literature* (Cambridge, 1996), but that work is more traditionally arranged. The editors of the present work strived to make it complementary to, rather than a rival of, the *Cambridge* resource. Because of the advanced language and subject matter, this title is only recommended for large research libraries and those with Latin American studies programs. —*Susan Gardner*

Latin American Mystery Writers: An A-to-Z Guide. Ed. by Darrell B. Lockhart. 2004. 225p. bibliogs. index. Greenwood, $89.95 (0-313-30554-4). 863.

Latin American Science Fiction Writers: An A-to-Z Guide. Ed. by Darrell B. Lockhart. 2004. 230p. bibliogs. index. Greenwood, $89.95 (0-313-30553-6). 863.

Lockhart, an assistant professor of Spanish at the University of Nevada, Reno, has edited two new companion volumes on popular Latin American literature. Both volumes trace the development of their genres over roughly the past 100 years, with selective biocritical coverage of 54 writers in *Mystery* and 70 writers in *Science Fiction.* The scope is broadly defined in both cases: *Mystery* encompasses both the classic detective fiction model and contemporary hard-boiled literature, while *Science Fiction* includes authors who only incorporate partial elements of the conventional model in their texts. Both genres, being popular, reflect contemporary Latin American cultural and societal concerns. *Latin America* spans countries of the Americas that are Spanish- or Portuguese-speaking but excludes Hispanic, Latino, or Chicano authors from the U.S. The majority of authors are associated with Argentina, Mexico, and Cuba.

The format is identical for each volume: alphabetically arranged author entries written by scholars feature the country of association, a narrative with biographical information that summarizes the author's literary contribution and impact on the genre, and a bibliography of primary and critical sources. Length of the narrative varies and can be anywhere from a couple of paragraphs to seven pages. All titles include English translations. Both volumes feature introductory essays on the genre and information on the contributors, many of whom are affiliated with Latin American universities. The volumes conclude with an index (mostly authors and titles) and a bibliography of literary anthologies and criticism by country.

Despite the occasional inclusion of a well-known name like Jorge Luis Borges, authors are more often little known, for example, as in the case of Alvaro Abós and Sauli Lostal in *Mystery* and Héctor G. Oesterheld and Irving Roffé in *Science Fiction*. Names like this are often not found in standard English-language literary sources such as Gale's *Literature Resource Center* database, nor are they in specialized sources such as *Latin American Writers* (Scribner, 1989). Occasionally, a well-known name associated with the genre is excluded, for example, Macedonio Fernandez, missing from the science fiction volume.

Although brief overviews can sometimes be gleaned from genre-specific titles like *Encyclopedia of Science Fiction* (St. Martins, 1993), these two new titles fill a void. Both genres are relatively fledgling, and furthermore, the notion of "popular culture" in Latin America is a recent phenomenon. Recommended for libraries serving Latin American studies programs. —*Susan Gardner*

The Dostoevsky Encyclopedia. By Kenneth Lantz. index. 2004. 499p. Greenwood, $99.95 (0-313-30384-3). 891.7.

In 248 entries, this "brief survey of existing knowledge and opinion" covers Fyodor Dostoevsky's fictional writings, selections of nonfiction works (e.g., *Letters, Polemical articles*), people (family members, writers, and others), places, key periodicals, literary groups and movements, and a selection of general but relevant topics such as *Gambling* and *Women*. The "Topical List of Entries" lists eight categories, the largest being for "Russian Writers, Critics, Thinkers, and Historical Figures," with 63 entries.

Arranged alphabetically, articles vary in length from one-half page to five pages. Targeting the general reader on through specialist, Lantz (University of Toronto) describes topics from different perspectives, often using quotes from Dostoevsky's writings and other resources. For example, the article *Crime and criminal justice* summarizes Dostoevsky's views on criminal psychology, the penal system, and other related topics, extracting quotes from a letter by Dostoevsky, from notebooks for *Crime and Punishment,* from drafts of *The Devils,* and from *The Idiot, Notes from the Dead, A Raw Youth,* and *Writer's Diary*. Entries on Dostoevsky's writings go beyond plot summaries, often discussing background and themes.

Within articles, bold type indicates a *see also* reference. Unfortunately, many possible *see also* references are missed (e.g., *Slavophilism* in the article *Westernizers; Gogol, Nikolai Vasilevich* in the article on Mikhail Lermontov). Each article includes a source list, which often contains transcribed Russian language titles, probably more useful for the scholar than the general reader. Internet sources are not included. Additional features include an index, a six-page bibliography (English- and Russian- language books), an alphabetical list of articles, and a very detailed chronology.

Unique in format and scope compared to the 10 essays that make up *The Cambridge Companion to Dostoevskii* (2002), *The Dostoevsky Encyclopedia* makes a handy ready-reference tool for academic and large public libraries. —*Stephen Fadel*

Geography, Biography

Junior Worldmark Encyclopedia of the Nations. 10v. 4th ed. 2004. illus. index. UXL, $315 (0-7876-9215-8); e-book, contact Gale for pricing (0-7876-9363-4). 903.

This fourth edition of what is now a standard work for school libraries follows the format of previous editions. Articles on 193 countries are presented in alphabetical order. Each article begins with a black- and-white illustration of the nation's flag and seal and a summary list that includes capital city, title or beginning line of anthem, monetary unit, weights and measures, holidays, and time. This data is followed by 35 uniform sections of narrative covering topics such as topography, history, government, industry, and health. Each profile ends with names of famous people and a bibliography. The bibliographies list titles, intended for young readers, that will have more complete information about daily life, foods, and plants and animals. No Web sites are cited, an unfortunate omission since students increasingly use the Internet for so much of their information. The next edition should include at least the official Web site of the country. Each volume has a comprehensive glossary, and the last volume has an index to the complete set.

This edition is based on the eleventh edition of the *Worldmark Encyclopedia of the Nations* (2004). The list of advisors to this *Junior* version includes many school library media specialists and social studies teachers. The *Junior Worldmark* has fewer entries because it does not cover dependencies. It also has fewer sections within chapters than the adult version. However, the content is designed to be useful to students, and the maps, charts, sidebars highlighting geographic and biographical information, and photographs that accompany the text are not found in the parent set.

This is an exemplary set for all school and public libraries. Because it is up-to-date, and relatively inexpensive, it should replace earlier editions. —*Robin Hoelle*

Encyclopedia of Modern Jewish Culture. 2v. Ed. by Glenda Abramson. 2005. 1,036p. index. Routledge, $395 (0-415-29813-X). 909.04924.

The Blackwell Companion to Jewish Culture, published in 1989, is a single-volume source that includes biographies and thematic surveys on all aspects of Jewish culture. This new two-volume consecutively paged set from Routledge is its successor. Abramson, editor of *The Blackwell Companion,* continues in that capacity. With a multinational group of contributors, she has updated the existing entries and added more material. Two-thirds of the content in this edition is new. The signed alphabetical entries include biographies, essays on topics related to Jewish culture, and surveys of topics that are more peripheral. All articles have bibliographies.

According to the preface, for the purpose of this work, *modern* is anything after the middle of the eighteenth century, the time of the Haskalah (enlightenment) movement, which began after the emancipation of the Jews in the 1790s. *Jewish* is used broadly to include "involvement in this community" in relation to cultural and creative activity whether or not the person practiced the religion. *Culture* refers to shared experiences and sources. Within these parameters, readers will find biographies of Moses Mendelssohn and the Ba'al Shem Tov as well as of Albert Einstein, Sigmund Freud, and Arnold Schoenberg. There are articles on Arab Jewish culture, modern biblical scholarship, and the Holocaust in American Jewish philosophy. An article on *Jews and Marxism* examines the Jewish passion for social justice as a reinterpretation of messianism. A series of articles examines the Holocaust in art, film and television, and literature. Added coverage of Sephardic culture and of Jewish life in Australia and South Africa shift the work away from being heavily focused on Europe and the U.S.

By concentrating on modern Jewish culture and examining those who challenge or take issue with it (Philip Roth, Karl Marx), this encyclopedia provides a unique point of view. Since it is relatively brief and focused, patrons will still need to consult in-depth sources such as the *Encyclopedia Judaica* (1972) for a broader picture. It is, however, a useful addition to reference collections in academic, synagogue, and large public libraries. —*Barbara Bibel*

Encyclopedia of the Arctic. 3v. Ed. by Mark Nuttall. 2004. 2,380p. illus. index. Routledge, $525 (1-57958-436-5). 909.

Interest in the polar regions has increased in the past few years, as evidenced by the publication of *Antarctica and the Arctic: The Complete Encyclopedia* (Firefly, 2001), *Antarctica: An Encyclopedia from Abbott Ice Shelf to Zooplankton* (Firefly, 2002), *Encyclopedia of Antarctica and the Southern Oceans* (Wiley, 2002), and ABC-CLIO's *Exploring Polar Frontiers: A Historical Encyclopedia* [RBB My 1 04]. This new encyclopedia, concentrating on the entire North Polar region, is a comprehensive examination of the history, geography, geology, natural resources, peoples, cultures, languages, environments, exploration, exploitation, animals, climate, and ecology of this unique and important area. The Arctic polar region encompasses eight countries: Canada, Finland, Greenland/Denmark, Iceland, Norway, Russia, Sweden, and the U.S. It is a place of extremes, of unique and fragile ecosystems, and of numerous groups of indigenous peoples and a wide variety of animals, and it is a major influence on climates throughout the globe.

Each of the encyclopedia's three volumes begins with an A–Z entry list, and a thematic entry list is contained in volume 1. All of the more than 1,200 entries conclude with further reading references, and *see* and *see also* references are included when appropriate. Biographical entries (for example, *Amundsen, Roald; Boas, Franz; Hudson, Henry*) range from a few paragraphs to several pages and give background information, as well as the nature and significance of the subject's work. Some biographical entries include photographs. Place entries provide location, history, status, and climate of the area and are accompanied by maps and photographs. Entries on broader topics, such as *Biodiversity, Climate,* and *Fossils,* are more extensive and include numerous maps, graphs, and small black-and-white photographs.

More than 350 scientists, historians, and scholars contributed to this work, and their writing is clear and consistent in quality. The liberal use of graphs, tables, and schematics helps to make the more technical topics clear to both scholarly and general readers. The only drawback to this outstanding resource is the 29-page index in volume 3. Long strings of undifferentiated page numbers should have been broken out for ease of use, and titles should not have been indexed on their initial articles (e.g., *The History of Greenland*). That, however, is a small fault in an otherwise exceptional reference work that will be an essential addition to academic, scientific, and large public libraries. —*Nora Harris*

The Islamic World: Past and Present. 3v. Ed. by John L. Esposito. 2004. 672p. illus. index. Oxford, $325 (0-19-516520-9). 909.

Oxford has published a series of well-received titles on Islam, including the *Oxford History of Islam* (1999) and the *Oxford Dictionary of Islam* (2003). This current offering, intended for a young adult audience, is based on the four-volume *Oxford Encyclopedia of the Modern Islamic World* (2001). All the articles have been rewritten, updated, and expanded to provide an accessible, comprehensive overview of the fundamental principles, history, and influence of Islam.

Articles are arranged in alphabetical order and run from a few paragraphs to a few pages. Topics include individuals, countries, aspects of Islamic practice and their social implications, historic events, sacred sites, and Islam's impact on art, architecture, technology, science, and more. Numerous black-and-white illustrations and an assortment of charts and maps accompany the articles. Each volume also features a multipage, full-color photo essay (for example, "Daily Life," "Art and Architecture"). These pictures (and their descriptive captions), such as the one of a Bedouin astride his camel, talking on his mobile phone, are extremely effective in portraying current conditions in various Islamic countries.

In addition to the revised entries, the set offers other user-friendly enhancements. Each of the three volumes includes a chronology, a general glossary, and a dictionary-style listing of "People and Places." There are a table of contents in volume 1 and a complete set index in volume 3; numerous *see* and *see also* references provide further guidance. Definitions of technical terms and historic or political references appear in margins, as needed. Numerous sidebars fill in background information. Longer articles, such as *Education* and *Women,* have been broken into manageable subsections. Controversial subjects (Osama Bin Laden, September 11, suicide attacks, terrorism, and so on) are covered objectively. Volume 3 directs researchers to additional information sources (print and online). Materials appropriate for younger readers are indicated with an asterisk.

There are no multivolume student-oriented reference sources on Islam currently in print. Secondary-school collections and public libraries will want to add this balanced, reasoned, and age-appropriate resource. —*Kathleen McBroom*

★**Encyclopedia of Exploration.** 2v. By Carl Waldman and others. 2004. 1,424p. illus. indexes. Facts On File, $200 (0-8160-4678-6). 910.

The search for food, land, precious metals, and scientific knowledge, as well as people to exploit, enslave, or convert, has fueled our drive to explore the unknown. This set provides thorough information about explorers and explorations from 2450 B.C.E. to the present.

Volume 1, *The Explorers,* presents more than 950 biographical entries that begin with birth and death dates, nationality, occupations, and areas of the world explored, followed by an account of the subject's exploration activities. Among the explorers who are covered are the well known, such as Neil Armstrong, Ferdinand Magellan, and Ernest Shackleton, but also the less familiar, such as Ahmad Ibn Fadlan (fl. 920s), whose record of his diplomatic mission from Baghdad to Russia and eastern Europe is the earliest account of that region in pre-Christian times, and Koncordie Dietrich (1821–91), a German naturalist whose travels through the Australian outback resulted in the largest collection of flora and fauna assembled by a woman. Entries range from two or three paragraphs to four pages in length and are accompanied by 144 illustrations and photographs. Appendixes list explorers by occupation, by region of activity, by nationality or sponsoring country, and in chronological order by birth date.

Volume 2, *Places, Technologies, and Cultural Trends,* has more than 260 A–Z entries on such topics as *Aerial photography, Circumnavigation of the world, Drift ice, Fur trade, Native peoples and exploration, Orinoco River, Virginia Company,* and *Women explorers.* Entries range in length from 2 paragraphs to more than 10 pages and are accompanied by 67 photographs and illustrations and 62 maps. An appendix contains maps by region; by ancient routes in the Mediterranean, Europe, and Asia; by new water routes; and by the interior in Asia, the Americas, the Pacific Ocean and Australia, Africa, the Arctic, and the Antarctic. The volume concludes with a very thorough chronology of exploration, a further reading list for the set, a list of volume 2 entries by subject, and a 35-page cumulative index for both volumes. In both volumes, capital letters are used in the text to designate terms that are also entry headings.

This set is well organized and very readable. It will be used by students in high school and college and by anyone who wishes to learn more about explorers and exploration. It is highly recommended for public, school, and undergraduate libraries. —*Nora Harris*

Explorers and Exploration. 11v. 2004. 878p. illus. indexes. Marshall Cavendish, $329.95 (0-7614-7535-4). 910.

In a set designed for grades 4–8, some 177 articles and more than 700 full-color illustrations deliver information on explorers and exploration. Most of the alphabetically arranged entries cover people, from Alexander the Great to early Chinese explorer Zhang Quian, but there is also treatment of places (*Northwest Passage, Portugal, Underwater exploration*);

science and technology (*Aviation, Dead reckoning, Global Positioning System*); and other topics (*Caravan, Native peoples, Smithsonian Institution*). Chronologically, the set extends from about 500 B.C.E. to 2004.

Entry length ranges from three to eight pages, and each entry is color coded to indicate the period of history to which it belongs. A four-color map or other illustration takes up at least a third of every page, giving the set a vibrant look. Also adding visual interest as well as another dimension of text are sidebars that contain information about relevant technology, brief biographical profiles, quotations, or interesting facts and displays of key dates. All entries have cross-references to other related entries.

The indexes in volume 11 offer several ways of accessing the content. There are three thematic indexes ("Biographical Index," "Geographical Index," and "Index of Scientific Technology"); a general index; and a separate index for maps. Volume 11 also contains a time line, a glossary, and four lists of additional resources: a bibliography, a list of museums and other places to visit, Internet sites, and books and other resources aimed at younger readers.

For a similar audience, *The Grolier Student Library of Explorers and Exploration* (1997) provides a more thematic context, with each volume devoted to a specific region or aspect of discovery. UXL's *Explorers and Discoverers* (1994) has information on 200 or so individual explorers. Because these works and the Marshall Cavendish set take different approaches, they complement rather than duplicate each other. Attractive, well organized, and well indexed, *Explorers and Exploration* is recommended for school and public libraries. It will definitely appeal to its designated audience, and its inviting appearance will encourage even older readers to browse. —*Mary Ellen Quinn*

Historical Gazetteer of the United States. By Paul T. Hellman. 2004. 865p. index. Routledge, $150 (0-415-93948-8). 911.

This voluminous reference work provides brief but detailed historical records of U.S. cities and towns. Arrangement is alphabetical by state, including the District of Columbia. Each state chapter contains a brief description of major cities, date of incorporation into the U.S., the number of counties, and a rough breakdown of how the state categorizes municipalities, towns, townships, and cities. This is followed by alphabetical entries for significant places. Inclusion is determined more by historical importance (national or regional) than by population. All county seats are included.

Entries are in paragraph form and typically begin by noting the county and the part of the state in which the place is located as well as its approximate distance from the state's most important city. Events are listed chronologically. The entry on Los Angeles begins in 1542, when the Spanish explorer Juan Rodriguez Cabrillo sailed into the harbor and named the place "Bay of Smokes and Fires" for all of the Native American campfires. It ends with former president Ronald Reagan's death, on June 5, 2004, in suburban Bel Air. Events and people related to politics, entertainment, and sports are included. Other events may include disasters; establishment of colleges, universities, libraries, and other institutions; and construction of railroads, airports, and bridges.

The largest U.S. cities, as expected, warrant longer entries. New York City, for example, occupies more than six pages. These longer entries can be difficult to read, but the dates printed in bold type facilitate scanning. There is also a sweeping index of close to 100 pages where people and places can be referenced.

According to the introduction, the *Historical Gazetteer* attempts to compile in one volume information that previously was available only by consulting a variety of disparate sources—encyclopedias, local historical societies, historical monographs, etc. Overall, this is an excellent counterpart to almanacs and atlases and a solid geographical and historical reference work for users in public and academic libraries. —*Michael Tosko*

State and National Boundaries of the United States. By Gary Alden Smith. 2004. 240p. illus. index. McFarland, $45 (0-7864-1861-3). 911.

Smith has written a readable and well-researched book on how boundaries of U.S. states have been determined. Chapters are arranged by region (New England, Mid-Atlantic, Upper South, etc.) and then by state. The history of a state's boundaries is described, followed by an explanation of the borders of the contiguous states. The preface mentions that most of the boundaries are discussed twice, with each neighboring state. Although the information may be repeated, the exact wording is different.

Boundaries may change because of physical features such as mountains and water, so courts still hear boundary claims of states. The author notes that in 1998 New Jersey claimed and was awarded the landfilled part of Ellis Island. Another interesting fact is that Wyoming, Colorado, and Utah are the only states with boundaries of latitude and longitude.

A number of line-drawn maps accompany the text and are the only illustrations. Two appendixes list state and citizen nicknames and a chronology of boundary dates, from the Virginia Company receiving a grant in 1606 to a Supreme Court decision to award an island in a river to Maine in 2001. An extensive bibliography is arranged by chapter with a number of references to historic government documents and periodical articles from the late nineteenth and early twentieth century. The index appears to include only proper names but still may be useful.

Although there are U.S. Geological Survey bulletins and professional papers on state boundaries, this volume is the first commercially published reference on the topic. It is recommended for academic and large public libraries. —*Christine Bulson*

Atlas of North America. Ed. by H. J. De Blij. Apr. 2005. 320p. illus. index. Oxford, $125 (0-19-516993-X). 912.7.

Oxford has joined Reader's Digest (*Atlas of America*, 1998) and National Geographic (*Atlas of North America*, 1985) in publishing a regional atlas. This new volume stretches the boundaries by including Mexico as well as Canada and the U.S. It is said to replace the second edition of Oxford's *Regional Economic Atlas of the United States and Canada*, published in 1975.

The first section of the source under review contains physical, cultural, economic, political, and geographic maps of the region. Interesting maps include one of women in state legislatures and another of land use by commodity—corn, hogs, soybeans, etc. Regional country maps are included as well as maps of the 50 states of the U.S., 13 provinces of Canada, and 32 states of Mexico. Most of the U.S. states have a full page (eleven inches by fifteen inches), but some, such as New Hampshire and Vermont, and Tennessee and Kentucky, are combined on a page. The majority of the excellent cartography is by Phillips, but MapQuest supplied a number of city maps, which are in separate sections under each country. There are current city-center maps of Boston, Chicago, New Orleans, New York, Washington, Montreal, and Mexico City. For each country, there is a section that provides a page of encyclopedic information for every state or province, including a box of demographic, economic, and geographic statistics—persons with a disability, home-ownership rate, minority-owned firms, persons per square mile, etc.—with comparisons to the country as a whole

Although many of the Mexican maps have more than one state on a page, the maps are more detailed than those in a world atlas. Much of the encyclopedic and statistical information will not be found in the usual reference sources. The Canadian provincial maps are large, with Nunavut, Southern British Columbia, and Southern Alberta each on a two-page spread. The inclusive index lists cities and physical features with a grid location and longitude and latitude.

Since the Internet still does not provide the clarity or depth of a good atlas, the *Atlas of North America* will be a useful source in school, academic, and public libraries. —*Christine Bulson*

Hammond World Travel Atlas. 2004. 413p illus. index. Hammond, $65 (0-8437-1982-6). 912.

Hammond, now a part of Langenscheidt Publishing, has produced an atlas with a new concept. It is billed as a source of geographic knowledge as well as a travel guide. The 300-plus pages of maps are of good quality but are littered with "pictograms," which are icons identifying features and attractions. There are more than 100 of these color-coded symbols. Natural attractions are blue or green; cultural sites are yellow. The subjects of the pictograms are diverse—glaciers, deserts, wildlife reserves, museums, battlefields, markets, festivals, impressive skylines, Aborigine reservations, hill resorts, places of interest for religious cultures, and more. An extreme example of the pictograms is a double-page spread of Hispaniola and Lesser Antilles filled with symbols as well as names of cities, national parks, and airports. The pictograms used on a particular page are listed at the bottom of the page, but on a map it is difficult to distinguish an active volcano from a rock landscape or a memorial from a palace.

The atlas is visually attractive, with many color photographs. Each double-page spread of maps has a border of small photographs with a description of sites or attractions and a grid locator. Descriptive information on countries is very limited. No mention is made of current wars or conflicts.

The index contains about 100,000 entries with pictograms and page and grid locators. It is unfortunate that the example used in the good explanation of how to use the index lists an incorrect page number. The use in the index of international license-plate codes for identifying countries is confusing. Who would guess that ROU is Uruguay or SP is Somalia?

The *Hammond World Travel Atlas* is a -medium-sized atlas with competition from DK's *World Atlas* (2005), Oxford's *Atlas of the World* (2004), and the *Reader's Digest Illustrated World Atlas* (2004). It could be considered by any library that wants a current atlas with a new twist. —*Christine Bulson*

Illustrated World Atlas. 2004. 399p. illus. index. Reader's Digest, $49.95 (0-7621-0536-4). 912.

Reader's Digest has published a new medium-sized atlas with maps from European Map Graphics Ltd. Previous Reader's Digest atlases have used Rand McNally or Bartholomew maps. As is often the case, the title of this atlas is very similar to that of the desk or school atlas published by Reader's Digest: *Illustrated Atlas of the World* (5th ed., 2004). The new atlas appears to replace the *Reader's Digest Illustrated Great World Atlas* (1997).

The atlas under review has 200 pages of maps and a gazetteer of 80,000 place-names. The first 50-plus pages are devoted to weather, migration, resources, communication, and other global topics. These pages are eye-catching, with tables, graphs, pie charts, and full-color photos. Preceding the atlas section are two pages providing instructions for using maps with keys to symbols. The maps are arranged by continent, beginning with Australasia and going west to Europe, Africa, and the Americas. Classic atlases, such as Oxford's *Atlas of the World* (12th ed., 2004), begin with Europe, and some atlases now put the Americas first.

Each continent section starts with three two-page spreads containing a variety of graphics showing the highest, longest, and largest geographic features and data on population, climate, employment, and more along with a political map with capitals of countries underlined. The regional maps that follow are topographical, using lots of color, which makes it difficult to read some small place-names, boundaries, and mountain passes. International airports are clearly indicated with the IATA code (IAD, ORD, LHR), and regional airports just have a plane symbol. On one map, the code for LaGuardia Airport (LGA) appears in Hyannis, Mass., as well as correctly in New York. On the outside margin of each right page, the area being shown is indicated in vertical letters, which is useful for quickly finding a map. Some maps also have the page numbers for continuation maps, another useful feature. There are five foldout maps—of the Caribbean, the Himalayas, the Mediterranean, Rift Valley, and the Yangtze River—that clearly illustrate the formation of these areas. In a check of 10 cities and towns mentioned in a current *New York Times,* eight were listed in the gazetteer and found on a map. However, no specific city maps are included—city maps are a feature found in some but not all medium-sized atlases.

The gazetteer includes cultural, hydrographic, and topographic features as well as place-names, with symbols denoting the different feature types. For countries, a box is inserted in the column where the country is listed, giving the area, population, life expectancy, literacy, languages, and GDP.

Illustrated World Atlas is recommended for libraries that need an additional midsize, current atlas. It is comparable to *The New Concise World Atlas* (Oxford, 2003). The hardcover of the atlas is identical to the attractive dust jacket, so libraries that discard the jacket will still have an eye-catching volume. —*Christine Bulson*

National Geographic Atlas of the World. 8th ed. 2004. 416p. illus. index. National Geographic, $165 (0-7922-7543-8). 912.

The National Geographic Society (NGS) is celebrating its ninetieth year of mapmaking with the eighth edition of the *Atlas of the World*. Promotional material describes some of the differences from the seventh edition. There are 15,000 changes in the text and maps. The section on the "Human World" has new double-page spreads on "Migration," "Conflict and Terror," "Transportation and Communication," and "Health, Nutrition, and Literacy." These and other introductory topics have eye-catching maps, charts, graphs and photographs accompanied by a limited amount of text. "Transportation and Communication" clearly depicts the Internet explosion and the digital divide. Another change is a new "Cities" section with maps, fact boxes, and photographs of 51 world cities. Some maps are of the area (Philadelphia, Shanghai, Tehran); some of just the city center (Buenos Aires); and some of both (Beijing, Cairo, Tokyo). This section replaces the useful city-map section for each continent (which had many more maps of smaller cities) in the seventh edition.

The heart of the atlas, the maps of continents and countries, shows great cartography, the strength of NGS. As in previous editions, the Americas are first, with coverage proceeding eastward around the globe. North America is given additional coverage—22 maps for North America, 13 for Asia—since the primary readership is from the U.S. and Canada. The maps are not as colorful as those in other atlases, but the number of place-names is impressive, rivaling the *Times Atlas of the World* (10th ed., Crown, 1999). All maps are double-page spreads, with the exception of four—Low Countries, Denmark, New Zealand, and New Guinea—that each have a single page. The binding is described as unique in that the atlas will open flat, but it is still tight, so some information will be lost if it is rebound.

An additional change from the previous edition is that the country information follows the map section rather than being included with each continent. The country facts are current, and there is a reference to the plate number for the country map. Other material includes updated geographic comparisons, for example, Mt. Everest increasing in height. Distances by air and temperature and rainfall for major cities are given in the metric system, which is not useful for many U.S. readers, although a conversion chart is provided. The index, with 140,000 entries, provides plate number and grid location with a descriptor for rivers, mountains, etc.

A Web site accompanies the atlas; its useful update section already has a printable patch for the new Great Sand Dunes National Park. Other features of the Web site are less useful, especially the flashy animations. The interactive maps will be of interest to student researchers.

World atlases never contain every town, lake, or mountain that a user may want to find. This atlas does not include my hometown of Worcester, N.Y., or Wahroonga, the suburb of Sydney, Australia, where my niece lived for a year. However, the *National Geographic Atlas of the World* is a major, comprehensive, current atlas that should be considered for high-school, academic, and public libraries as well as for individual purchase. It will be a mainstay of the atlas collection. —*Christine Bulson*

Placenames of France: Over 4,000 Towns, Villages, Natural Features, Regions, and Departments. By Adrian Room. 2004. 334p. McFarland, $49.95 (0-7864-2052-9). 914.4.

Covering historic and current French place-names, both natural and inhabited, this volume lists a vast number of terms reflecting the entire history of the region, from pre-Celtic times to the present. Alphabetically arranged entries provide a brief description of the place that is named, its location (usually the department), and its origin or etymology. Since this area has been ruled by various peoples, entries indicate the influence on place-names from other languages, such as Basque, Breton, Flemish, German, and Spanish.

The appendixes are particularly useful, including the words for inhabitants of particular locations (for example, *Grenoblois,* from Grenoble); renamings after the French Revolution; and Métro stations and major place-names in Paris. The introduction provides a helpful overview, and a short, unannotated bibliography offers other toponymic sources. Since almost all the literature on place-names in France is written in French, this unique work fills a void in the literature and is recommended for academic and large public libraries. Author Room has also compiled *African Placenames* (McFarland, 1994) and *Placenames of the World* (McFarland, 1997), among numerous other reference sources. —*Donald Altschiller*

The American Counties: Origins of County Names, Dates of Creation, and Population Data, 1950–2000. 5th ed. By Joseph Nathan Kane and Charles Curry Aiken. 2004. 529p. Scarecrow, $95 (0-8108-5036-2). 917.3.

Last updated in 1983 by the late Joseph Nathan Kane, this title is a basic collection of information and data about counties. Aiken is a countyphile who has enthusiastically brought the last edition up-to-date by adding the previous two census numbers. He covers all county-level geographic areas as recognized by the U.S. government, including Alaska's boroughs and census areas, Louisiana's parishes, New York's boroughs, and the independent cities of Maryland, Missouri, Nevada, and Virginia. Information is provided in an *A–Z* listing of areas, with population from the 1950 census forward, the county seat, the date of creation, area in square miles, and the origin of the name. Three appendixes list all counties by date of creation, counties by state along with the statutes that created them, and counties by the county seat. A brief bibliographic essay notes the author's sources.

Aiken claims that there is no other book with this data, though there are books that contain some of it, such as *United States Counties* (McFarland, 2003) and *County Name Origins of the United States* (McFarland, 2001). The *County and City Data Book,* by Bernan, also provides extensive demographic data. There are also Web sites that have a good portion of the data. The Census Bureau Web site [http://www.census.gov/prod/www/ccdb.html] makes considerably more demographic data easily available but does not provide information about county names. The National Association of Counties Web site [http://www.naco.org/Template.cfm?Section=Find_a_county] also provides a wealth of detail, including many photographs of county courthouses. *The American Counties* can be a quick way to get a glimpse of these basic geographic regions, but if a library already owns one or more of the other texts, this one is not a necessary purchase. —*Stephen Stratton*

Native American Placenames of the United States. By William Bright. 2004. 600p. Univ. of Oklahoma, $59.95 (0-8061-3576-X). 917.3.

A comprehensive geographic compendium dedicated to librarians, Bright's book supplies linguistic and anthropological data on cities, towns, and geographic landmarks. An impressive list of helpful colleagues from across the U.S. and Canada represents a scholarly background in 20 native languages. A meticulous pronunciation key offers detailed explanation of 46 arcane symbols and sounds suited to the needs of specialists.

Following a 13-page explanation of how and why Bright chose each entry, the text contains entries in a two-column spread with clear typefaces. Entries average three to six lines and generally include the name of the state and county in which each place is located, a pronunciation guide, an etymology, abbreviated citations to sources, occurrences of the name in other states, and cross-references to related names. A sprinkling of slightly longer entries includes those for *Caribou, Horse, Lehigh, Manito, Oregon,* and *Pecan.* Back matter offers 14 pages of references ranging from Frederic Baraga's dictionary of the Ojibwa language, compiled in 1880, and Antonio Peñafiel's *Nomenclatura geográfica de México* (1897) to a 1994 Aleut dictionary and *Making Dictionaries: Preserving Indigenous Languages of the Americas* (Univ. of California, 2002).

This work should find a place in academic libraries supporting Native American studies and American geography programs and in reference collections of large public libraries. —*Mary Ellen Snodgrass*

The Riverside Dictionary of Biography. 2004. 867p. illus. Houghton, $24 (0-618-49337-9). 920.02.

Just as the British *Chambers Biographical Dictionary* (2002) provided the basis for *The Houghton Mifflin Dictionary of Biography* (2003), the *Chambers Concise Biographical Dictionary* (2002) has begotten this volume in Houghton Mifflin's American Heritage Dictionaries line.

Entries are similar to those in *The Houghton Mifflin Dictionary of Biography,* having name, birth and death dates, a brief identifying phrase, and narrative text in which related entries are cross-referenced. Downsizing has been achieved not only by cutting the number of entries from 18,000 to 10,000 but also by lopping off some entry length. Gone are the longer sidebar entries found in the Houghton Mifflin as well as the occasional citations to source material. On the other hand, *The Riverside Dictionary of Biography* adds a few black-and-white portraits at the beginning of every alphabetical section and also scatters quotations here and there throughout the text. A few individuals not found in Houghton Mifflin have been added, among them John Kerry and Ang Lee. In some cases *Riverside* has the advantage of greater currency, noting, for example, Lance Armstrong's sixth Tour de France win and the deaths of Ray Charles, Julia Child, and Ronald Reagan in 2004. Both volumes retain a slight British bias. Nigella Lawson and Richard Branson rate entries but not Martha Stewart or Donald Trump.

Libraries that already own *The Houghton Mifflin Dictionary of Biography* probably don't need to add *Riverside,* even though it is slightly more up-to-date. For other libraries, it is a sound and economical choice. —*Mary Ellen Quinn*

UXL Newsmakers. 4v. Jan. 2005. 835p. illus. index. UXL, $215 (0-7876-9189-5). 920.

Who are the headliners who interest youth? Identifying them is the goal of this set from Gale's middle-school line. One hundred biographies deal with newsworthy figures in art and design, business, entertainment, government, music, science, social issues, sports, and writing. However, the specific criteria for inclusion are not given (although they can be surmised).

Most figures are from the U.S. but other countries are represented (for example, there are entries for Saddam Hussein, Indra Nooyi, and Yao Ming). The broad professional categories overlap, so Beyonce, for example, is found under both entertainment and music; Arnold Schwarzenegger is listed under entertainment and government. Entertainers make up the largest percentage of biographies; only five people are listed under social issues, and eight are government related. Many of the entries cover young newsmakers (e.g., 50 Cent, Hilary Duff, Serena Williams), but older figures, such as Frank Gehry and Walter Dean Myers, are included for their current accomplishments. The ensemble cast of *Queer Eye for the Straight Guy* also has an entry.

Each volume begins with a complete list of biographies and a list by "field of endeavor" and concludes with a set index (with some errors). Articles range from six to eight pages and include personal and professional information and a short bibliography of print and Web sources. Most also have one or two black-and-white photos. Details are not exhaustive (no mention is made of Hugh Jackman's stint in *Oklahoma!* for instance), but the benchmarks are noted, and interesting tidbits, such as Sofia Coppola's venture into fashion designing, keep the reader's attention. Sidebar information also accompanies about a third of the entries. Writing is clear and accessible; the general tone is very supportive.

Other biography resources exist for youth, such as Omnigraphics' Biography Today series. However, this set includes an interesting variety of known faces, which should attract middle-schoolers in particular. —*Lesley Farmer*

Avotaynu Guide to Jewish Genealogy. Ed. by Sallyann Amdur Sack and Gary Mokotoff. 2004. 624p. illus. Avotaynu, $85 (1-886223-17-3). 929.

What a treat for genealogists when two of today's foremost authorities on Jewish genealogical research join forces with more than 60 international experts to create a much-needed reference book. Editors Sack and Mokotoff are the publishers of *Avotaynu: The International Review of Jewish Genealogy.* Designed for "one-stop shopping" assistance, *Avotaynu Guide to Jewish Genealogy* is both a beginning and advanced guide for anyone seriously researching Jewish family lineage.

Information is organized into four primary categories—basic methodology, specific topics, research in the U.S., and researching one's country of ancestry. The first section, "The Essentials of Jewish Genealogical Research," is intended for those new to family research. In addition to general information, it covers shtetl geography, naming practices, Jewish culture and religion, information sources such as JewishGen, and groups such as Jewish genealogical societies. Information on how to research specific topics comprises the second portion of the guide. Here, the sophistication level rises to accommodate the needs of experienced researchers. Where to turn when looking for victims of the Holocaust, following migration routes throughout history, and tracing rabbinical genealogy are just a few items covered. The section on U.S. research leaves no stone unturned. Contributors offer advice on using immigration and census records, archives, historical societies, and draft records, among other sources. Expert researchers will welcome the last section, which provides background information and useful addresses and Web sites for individual countries throughout the world.

Each chapter has an extensive bibliography. Several appendixes, including one that explains the Daitch-Mokotoff Soundex system used by the Jewish genealogical organizations for indexing names, provide additional information. The lack of an index for the volume is a drawback.

Regardless of which aspect of research one enters into, this is the definitive resource to consult. The *Avotaynu Guide to Jewish Genealogy* makes the seemingly impossible possible. —*Ann Cohen*

The Family Tree Resource Book for Genealogists: The Essential Guide to American County and Town Sources. Ed. by Sharon DeBartolo Carmack and Erin Nevius. 2005. 704p. illus. F&W/Family Tree, paper, $29.99 (1-55870-686-0). 929.

Since 1947 professional and amateur genealogists have relied upon *The Handy Book for Genealogists* (10th ed., Everton, 2002) to tell which local records exist and how to access them. It has been revised and updated through 10 editions. Now a team from Family Tree has produced a new, similar source that it feels is more affordable and easier to use, and it corrects previous discrepancies even within the county and municipal sources' own information about what is available.

The introduction includes very basic information, such as the difference between microfilm and microfiche, a sample letter and guidelines for requesting information by mail, suggestions for preparing to visit an archive, and an admonition to preserve and protect the material that is consulted.

Arranged alphabetically by state, the chapters provide the expected information: maps showing current counties; historical overviews, including critical dates; information about special repositories; bibliographies of published sources; and listings for county, parish and town-hall contacts. Each listing provides the date of establishment, address, phone number, Web site, parent county, and types of records kept and dates begun. Also included for each state are unique aspects of available records (for example, Florida's Spanish Land Grants, Georgia's Civil War salt allotments, and Utah's midwives' records) and tips, such as the existence of independent cities and townships whose records might not be in county-based sources.

Libraries owning *The Handy Book for Genealogists* will want to keep it. Its bibliographies are more extensive, information is more precise in some areas, color maps and flags (of the 19 foreign countries included) are more attractive, the hard binding is more durable—and it is a classic in its field. But librarians will want to add this new tool to their collections. The information is more current, the research tips are quite pragmatic, the format for the local records sources is easier on the eyes, and the reasonable price makes it easy to justify the overlapping information. —*Sally Jane*

Oxford Dictionary of Nicknames. By Andrew Delahunty. 2004. 240p. indexes. Oxford, $25 (0-19-860539-0). 929.403.

J-Lo and A-Rod, as they are known to millions of people, are the nicknames of superstar Jennifer Lopez and baseball great Alex Rodriguez. Although they are not listed in this dictionary, the reader will find 1,800 other nicknames of figures in politics, sports, entertainment, and many other fields, along with some organizations and places. Arranged alphabetically by nickname, the dictionary contains useful and occasionally amusing annotations. The general index lists the actual names of the individuals and refers to the single or multiple nicknames cited in the text; a thematic index also provides helpful access.

Although the book somewhat favors British nicknames, including football clubs and British Army regiments, it still provides many useful American monikers, such as *The Man on the Wedding Cake* (Thomas Dewey) and *Mr. Television* (Milton Berle), along with nicknames for the states. The *Dictionary of Nicknames* (Routledge and Kegan Paul, 1984), a thinner book, has some unique features, including a large number of nicknames ending as "the Great" and also "the Good." The *Dictionary of Historic Nicknames: A Treasury of More Than 7,500 Famous and Infamous Nicknames from World History* (Facts On File, 1984) has much longer annotations in a large volume, but the entries are listed by real name. The *Oxford Dictionary* is a worthwhile work that should usefully supplement the other nickname sources found in any good reference collection. —*Donald Altschiller*

Ancestry Library Edition. [Online database]. ProQuest, call 800-521-0600, ext. 3183 or 3452 for pricing [http://www.ancestrylibrary.com]. (Last accessed March 4, 2005).

Ancestry Library Edition (formerly *Ancestry Plus*) has gone through some changes this past year, with My Family not renewing their contract with Gale and instead signing with ProQuest. ProQuest also has another stronghold in the genealogical database department with the *HeritageQuest* database.

The interface for the *Ancestry* collection of databases seems simpler and more intuitive, with global search boxes to place a name; state, province, or county; and year range. If the user wants to search within a specific database, there are census images listed for all the years included in the database, back to the 1790 census, with new years tagged. The home page also has links to a few featured collections, such as the U.S. Immigration Collection; Birth, Marriage & Death Records (SSDI); and the U.K. Census Collection. By way of an All Databases link, users can browse an alphabetical index of the entire *Ancestry* collection of databases or Browse the Entire Collection by region (the U.S., Canada, U.K., Ireland, and Europe) or by state. Browse Records organizes all of the databases that *Ancestry* offers by type, such as Census; Birth, Marriage & Death; Family Facts; Military; Directories & Member Lists; and Court, Land & Probate. Each database in the *Ancestry* collection can be searched individually, and search forms vary depending on the type of record.

At first glance, the global Advanced Search form looks similar to the home page, but it has a few different options. One option allows the user to search different record types, and another to search for names with a certain proximity. A Soundex filter helps with spelling variations.

When a global name search is performed, a list of the databases where the name has occurred in the *Ancestry* records will appear, broken up by type.

Selecting a database leads to a results list showing each person with the name being searched, a database-specific form for refining the search, and information about the particular database. Clicking on a name in the results list leads to a fuller listing for that individual and links to the actual census image. The images are in PDF, and some are difficult to read, but they can be adjusted in various ways to make reading easier. *Ancestry Library Edition* also contains charts and forms that can be printed. These forms include an ancestral chart, research calendar, census forms, correspondence record, family group sheet, and source summary. All forms and charts are in PDF.

All libraries providing genealogical materials should subscribe to *Ancestry Library Edition*. Patrons can find family members but can also find out such interesting facts as the origin of their names, geographical distribution of the last name, and average life spans. —*Jennifer Dawson*

History

World History: Ancient and Medieval Eras. [Online database]. ABC-CLIO, $599 [http://abc-clio.com]. (Last accessed March 4, 2005).

World History: Ancient and Medieval Eras provides primary and secondary sources from the prehistoric era to the end of the Middle Ages. Content is organized under 11 distinct time periods (called Topics), including Prehistory (up to 1000 B.C.), Ancient Rome (1000 B.C.E.–500 C.E.), and Africa (3000 B.C.E.–1,500 C.E.) and concluding with Medieval Europe (500–1500 C.E.). The database coverage is well rounded; it does not focus solely on Europe but instead offers a more worldwide perspective, which is becoming increasingly important in today's world.

The front page immediately grabs the user's attention by offering interesting tidbits such as "Term of the Day" and "Did You Know?" that give quick historical snippets and are used to pique curiosity. The user can find information by doing a quick keyword search, or using the Advanced Search mechanisms. Options in Advanced Search include search by Topic or Subtopic (for example, the Early Aegean Age, the Classical Age, or the Hellenistic Age under Ancient Greece) and filter by type of document, such as maps, essays, biographies, and quotes. Users can choose to have entry title only or title and summary displayed in the Results list, which is relevancy ranked. Content pages offer links to related entries, grouped by type, as well as hyperlinks.

Teachers can use the database to create lesson plans, as there are specific lessons for each of the time periods, with ample opportunity for interactive learning. The Staff version of the database allows teachers to create tests and compile lists of links that can then be uploaded to the Student version. Other features of the database include a dictionary and an e-mail "Ask the Cybrarian" function.

Although some of the content is drawn from the publisher's print reference sources, many of the articles, which are not signed, were commissioned especially for the site. Articles include references so students can search for further information if necessary; it would be helpful if in an updated version users could connect directly with their institution's online catalog from the database to see which of the referenced titles are owned.

This is a very handy tool and fits in well with ABC-CLIO's other online offerings, such as *World History: Modern Era* and *World Geography*. It bridges the gap between print encyclopedias, popular Web sites, and more academic online article indexes and is recommended for high-school and public libraries. —*Susanna Eng*

★**New Dictionary of the History of Ideas.** 6v. Ed. by Maryanne Cline Horowitz. 2004. 2,780p. illus. index. Scribner, $695 (0-684-31377-4). 903.

This long-awaited update to the original *Dictionary of the History of Ideas* is "designed to introduce a general audience to the main ideas and movements of global cultural history from antiquity to the twenty-first century." This is an entirely new work rather than a mere revision, featuring more than twice as many articles as the original (well over 700 as compared to just over 300) as well as a more definite global view of the topics covered when compared to the Eurocentric nature of the older set. There are more than 550 contributors, including such well-known writers as Peter Burke, Nathan Glazer, Arthur Hertzberg, Moshe Idel, Margaret L. King, and Martin E. Marty. Entries include those on the same topics but entirely rewritten from the original (*City, Nationalism, Time*) along with those that could barely have been thought of in the mid-1970s (*Computer science, Sexual harassment, Visual culture*). Just as telling, reflecting the scholarly shift over the past 30 years, are entries that no longer exist, such as *Baconianism; Faith, hope, and charity;* and *Uniformitarianism and catastrophism.*

Although the original edition was not entirely bereft of illustrations, they were sparse. Not so with this edition: black-and-white illustrations are scattered throughout, most notably in entries such as *Architecture, Humanity in the arts, Iconography,* and *Maps and the ideas they express.*

Each volume opens with a "Reader's Guide" that provides a general outline of the articles in the set, divided into four main sections: "Communication of Ideas," "Geographical Areas," "Chronological Periods," and "Liberal Arts Disciplines and Professions." The detailed "Reader's Guide" is a good companion to the index, which occupies more than 200 pages of volume 6. Main entries in the set are often divided by separately authored subentries; examples include *Gender* (divided into *Overview* and *Gender in the Middle East*) and *Motif* (*Motif in literature* and *Motif in music*). The longest main entry of the set, the 30-page *Communication of ideas,* is divided into seven parts. Articles conclude with up-to-date bibliographies (often divided into primary and secondary sources) and *see also* references. The casual reader will likely miss an entry often referred to in various cross-references: the 54-page essay *Historiography,* which is placed just after the preface in volume 1 rather than in the main alphabetic arrangement. It would have been helpful to mention this placement in the *see also* references.

The casual reader may also be caught off guard by the fact that many entries presume that the reader is acquainted with the older edition—or at the very least has some background in the topic. *Law,* for example, begins, "The development of law and jurisprudential ideas since the 1970s" and continues to concentrate on events of the recent past rather than providing the historical concentration seen in the previous edition. The preface affirms that this title "focuses on topics of interest today and features developments in scholarship since 1970." Does this mean libraries must retain the older set? Fortunately, the answer is no. Scribner allowed the first set to be released free of charge online courtesy of a grant authorized by the *Journal of the History of Ideas* for digitization through the University of Virginia Library Electronic Text Center. It is accessible at http://www.historyofideas.org.

This well-written set will appeal to anyone interested in the topic and is highly recommended for large public and academic libraries. In all, worth the 30-year wait. —*Ken Black*

Berkshire Encyclopedia of World History. 5v. Ed. by William H. McNeill and others. 2005. 2,600p. illus. index. Berkshire, $525 (0-9743091-0-9). 903.

A masterful title that weaves together the social, scientific, anthropological, and geographical influences on world history, this set will be the benchmark against which future history encyclopedias are compared. Featuring 538 articles by 330 scholars representing multiple disciplines, the title adroitly pulls together the major societies (*Mongol Empire, Sumerian society*); political movements (*Revolution—Cuba; Women's emancipation movements*); and, indeed, the traditionally studied wars (*World War I*) that have shaped the world we live in, all while remaining cognizant of how each has had an impact on the other. The academic credentials of the editors are impeccable. Senior editor McNeill has written dozens of respected texts and was winner of the National Book Award in 1964 for *The Rise of the West.*

Although attempting to cover as broad a subject as world history in five volumes seems impossible, the editors and their contributors have pulled the feat off with aplomb. No article runs more than approximately 10 pages, but each captures the essence of the topic being addressed, as well as the distinct style of the contributor. Cross-references are noted at the end of most entries, and the lists of further reading contain contemporary works. Primary source material is not left out, however; more than 500 sidebars featuring quoted material often use primary sources. The entry *Babylon,* for example, includes some text from the Code of Hammurabi.

Each volume opens with a "Reader's Guide" listing 34 subject categories, allowing users to concentrate on articles dealing with, for example, topics related to "Communication" or "Health and Disease." The first volume also features "This Fleeting World," a 56-page essay by David Christian covering the foraging, agrarian, and modern eras of history. Oddly, this essay is repeated in volume 5 (and may also be found in its entirety on the publisher's Web site [http://www.berkshirepublishing.com/assets/pdf/ThisFleetingWorld.pdf]).

With relatively few entries, not everyone will agree with what is included. In a set that features but 110 biographical entries, should there really be one devoted to American abolitionist and author Lydia Child? Do *Bullroarers* deserve a separate entry? In keeping with the philosophy of the set, however, there are nine entries in a row on trading—beginning with *Trading patterns, ancient America*—that discuss commerce among the people of various regions. Accompanying the text are numerous black-and-white illustrations and more than 50 maps, most of them excellent line-drawn maps created for the set. There are a few minor errors in cross-referencing and indexing.

As McNeill states in his preface, the encyclopedia is "designed to help both beginners and experts to sample the best contemporary efforts to make sense of the human past by connecting particular and local histories with larger patterns of world history." The encyclopedia succeeds admirably and belongs on the shelves of all high-school, public, and academic libraries. In short: buy it. Now. —*Ken Black*

The Crusades Reference Library. 3v. By J. Sydney Jones. 2005. illus. indexes. UXL, $165 (0-7876-9175-5). 909.07.

Published by UXL, Gale's imprint for reference books written at the reading level of the average seventh-grader and focusing on curriculum topics, *The Crusades Reference Library* covers the First Crusade (1095–99) through the Ninth Crusade (1271–72). Each volume—*Almanac, Biographies,* and *Primary Sources*—begins with a "Reader's Guide" providing a short introduction to the Crusades, a glossary, and a time line. All chapters in the three volumes end with a bibliography of print and online sources for further reading and research and an index. The cumulative index is in a free supplemental volume.

In 13 concise chapters, *Almanac* discusses such topics as the conquering of Jerusalem by the caliph Umar, pilgrimages to the Holy Land, the traditions of chivalry, and territorial expansion and colonization as motivations for the Crusades. Its explanation of the difference and divisions between Sunni and Shiite Islam alone is useful reading for a wider audience. The volume begins with a section on research and activities for students and their teachers.

Biographies includes entries on 25 key figures. Both well-known figures, such as the Muslim leader Saladin and Eleanor of Aquitaine, and those who are maybe less familiar, such as Anna Comnena, the twelfth-century author and Byzantine princess, are covered. Each entry has a boxed quotation by its subject, and most include portraits. The entries are readable and well organized.

Primary Sources consists of 24 full or excerpted documents, first-person accounts, treaties, and speeches; the complete Magna Carta; and a section from the epic poem *The Song of Roland.* This volume is the cornerstone of *The Crusades Reference Library,* as it illustrates the history for the school audience. Sidebars define highlighted words, and grey-boxed paragraphs explain historical figures or events mentioned. All excerpts from the primary sources are followed by text that illuminates the history of the document and poses discussion questions.

Each volume includes more than 40 illustrations—from photographs of churches and towns to pages from illuminated manuscripts. A listing of information on these illustrations would have been a helpful and valuable addition.

The Crusades Reference Library is a recommended purchase for school and public libraries. Each volume can be purchased separately but they work better together. —*Lisa Johnston*

Day by Day: The Nineties. 2v. By Smita Avasthi. 2004. 1,513p. illus. indexes. Facts On File, $214.50 (0-8160-4895-9). 909.82.

This is the latest in a series that began with the 1940s, and as in the earlier volumes, there is coverage of national and international events that occurred on each and every day throughout the decade, in this case from January 1, 1990, to December 31, 1999. Ten categories organize daily events—one titled "World Affairs," four on world regions excluding the U.S., three focusing on the U.S. (e.g., "U.S. Economy & Environment"), one on science, and one on "Culture, Leisure, & Lifestyle." Each spread covers, on average, five to seven days. Dates are listed on the left and right margins, and categories are arranged across the top, with events listed below the appropriate category. The font is small, entries are succinct, and each page is packed with facts and figures. Multiple events under the same day and category are separated by ellipses.

Users seeking events that occurred on a known date need only turn the page to the correct date. For those looking for an event but uncertain of the date, volume 2 contains a name index and a separate subject index.

Instead of page numbers, dates and column letters are given (e.g., *Boutros-Ghali, Boutros 1995 Mar 31A*). For multiple entries on a single subject or name, entries are arranged under various subtopics. For example, subtopics under China include *accidents and disasters in, arms sales by, civil strife in, foreign trade, sports,* and more. Unfortunately, the slight indentation of subtopics hampers quick identification of main topics.

Additional features include a summary of events by year and also by decade. Gale's *American Decades: 1990–1999* (2001) goes into greater depth on selected national events and people but lacks daily coverage and international scope. These features, along with ease of use and the ability to view events in context and identify trends, make *Day by Day: The Nineties* the event chronology tool of choice. Recommended for school, public, and academic libraries. —*Stephen Fadel*

Great Events from History: The Middle Ages, 477–1453. 2v. Ed. by Brian A. Pavlac. 2004. 952p. illus. indexes. Salem, $160 (1-58765-167-X). 909.07.

Great Lives from History: The Middle Ages, 477–1453. 2v. Ed. by Shelley Wolbrink. 2004. 1,198p. illus. indexes. Salem, $160 (1-58765-164-5). 920.

Salem Press continues its revised and expanded Great Events and Great Lives series with sets concentrating on the Middle Ages. Previous sets include *Great Events from History: The Ancient World, Prehistory–476 C.E.* and *Great Lives from History: The Ancient World, Prehistory–476 C.E.* (both 2004). The Middle Ages volumes focus on the people and events throughout the world from after the Fall of Rome, in 476 C.E., to 1453. Coverage is worldwide.

Entries are arranged chronologically in *Events* and alphabetically in *Lives*. Each entry begins with ready-reference information, followed by a summary of the person's life or the event, a paragraph or two on "Significance," a list of further readings, and cross-references to entries both within a set and within the companion set. Each set includes 11 maps of the medieval world and indexes by category, location, personage, and subject.

Events, which is derived from the 12-volume *Great Events from History* (1972–1980), offers 322 essays, beginning with *Confucianism arrives in Japan* (fifth or sixth century) and ending with *Fall of Constantinople* (May 29, 1453). Two hundred of the entries are original, and all bibliographies have been updated. Length averages two to three pages. A "Keyword List of Contents" helps readers locate entries on particular topics. *Lives* is derived from the 10-volume *Dictionary of World Biography* (1998–1999), which was a revision of *Great Lives from History* (1987–1995). Of the 356 essays in *Lives,* a mere 59 are new. The articles range from three to six pages and include such individuals as Thomas Aquinas, Eleanor of Aquitaine, and Muhammad. Bibliographies have been updated, and more than 100 regnal and dynastic tables have been added.

Events has a great deal of new content, and because it has not been updated in quite some time, this revision is welcome and recommended for high-school, undergraduate, and public libraries. Since *Lives* offers less new content, libraries where budgets are tight and *Dictionary of World Biography* is already owned might want to pass it up. —*Susanna Eng*

The Kingfisher History Encyclopedia. 2004. 480p. illus. index. Kingfisher, $24.95 (0-7534-5784-9). 909.

Designed to help students ages 8–14 with homework or a school project, this revised and updated book is also an interesting and enjoyable resource to browse. Organized chronologically and then thematically, the encyclopedia divides history into 10 time periods, from "The Ancient World 40,000–500 B.C." to "The Modern World 1950–Present Day." This last section concludes with the "War on Terror" and has information current to 2003.

Each section begins with a two-page spread showing "The World at a Glance," a map, and brief text highlighting events that were occurring on each continent during the period. This is followed by approximately 20 one- or two-page topical entries. Non-Western cultures are represented. For example, "The Renaissance" includes entries on the Aztecs, Safavid Persia, Japan and China, and the Songhay Empire. In addition to text, entries have boxes showing key dates, a running time line at the top of each page, maps, and numerous illustrations, almost all of them in color. Each large chronological section concludes with a series of pages that give overviews of the arts, architecture, and science and technology. A highly useful ready-reference section at the end of the volume provides the names and dates of a variety of rulers (for example, Roman emperors, popes, kings and queens, presidents, prime ministers) and ancient Egyptian and Chinese dynasties. A list of major wars and a brief listing of Web sites are also provided.

Students will find this tool useful and engaging, and adults will enjoy browsing through it as well. School and public libraries will want to purchase this update and circulate older editions. —*Shauna Yusko*

Great Events from History: The Ancient World, Prehistory–476 C.E. 2v. Ed. by Mark W. Chavalas. 2004. 1,018p. bibliogs. glossary. illus. indexes. maps. Salem, $160 (1-58765-155-6). 930.

Great Lives from History: The Ancient World, Prehistory–476 C.E. 2v. Ed. by Christina A. Salowey. 2004. 998p. bibliogs. illus. indexes. maps. Salem, $160 (1-58765-152-1). 920.03.

Salem Press is publishing two series of reference books, both revisions of previous works. The series start out with these volumes on events and people in the ancient world. The full series will cover prehistory through the twenty-first century. The articles in both the ancient world sets have a similar format—they all start with ready-reference listings and conclude with the significance of the event or person, *see also* references, and further readings. The entries range in length from 1,000 to 3,000 words, and both sets include a section with 19 maps of the ancient world.

Great Events from History, a revision of a series by the same name published from 1972 to 1980, includes some essays from other, more recent works, such as *Chronology of European History: 15,000 B.C. to 1997,* published in 1997. Out of 418 essays, 289 are completely new. The scope is fairly wide, and the articles are in chronological order, starting at 25,000 B.C.E., with the earliest creation of African art, and ending at 476 C.E., with the fall of Rome. To help place the events in context, the work contains a time line, a glossary, a bibliography, and four indexes. To appease our visual senses, the work also includes black-and-white illustrations and the aforementioned maps.

Great Lives is a revision of *Dictionary of World Biography* (Fitzroy Dearborn, 1998), which itself was a revised version of *Great Lives from History* (1987–1995). The new work has 325 essays, of which a mere 65 are new additions; the articles are in alphabetical order and the work contains about 170 illustrations, a chronological list of entries, a bibliography, and three separate indexes. Among the reasons given for the revision of the two series are expanded geographical coverage, more focus on women, and updated bibliographies. The focus on women is not expansive, though it includes such regulars as Mary, Nefertiti and Sappho, but this may have more to do with the era than a lack of research; later volumes in the Lives series may cover more women, as more is known about women's history in later years.

Great Events has not been updated in some time. With a considerable amount of new material, this revision is both justified and welcome and is recommended for high-school, undergraduate, and public libraries. *Great Lives,* on the other hand, offers only a handful of new biographies, and one must question the necessity of publishing a newly revised edition so soon. As a companion to *Great Events,* it is helpful, but if libraries already own the previous edition, they may want to spend their money on something else. —*Susanna Eng*

Encyclopedia of the Enlightenment. By Peter Hanns Reill and Ellen Judy Wilson. 2004. 670p. illus. index. Facts On File, $75 (0-8160-5335-9). 937.25.

A revision of a work originally published in 1996, this volume has "140 new, updated, or expanded articles," according to its preface, giving it just over 800 entries total. Increased emphasis has been placed on "the Enlightenment in a global context," as well as on the "Counter-Enlightenment," or interest in spiritualism and esotericism that emerged in the late eighteenth century. New entries include *Colonialism, Great Awakening,* and *Washington, George,* as well as several that demonstrate greater focus on women—*Behn, Aphra; Fielding, Sarah;* and *Women and the Enlightenment,* to give a few examples. The alphabetically arranged set has more than 120 black-and-white illustrations and extensive cross-references throughout. A chronology opens the work, and a selected bibliography follows the entries. Lengthier entries conclude with a selected reading list. There are no maps, although given the general reading level of the work, maps for such entries as *Holy Roman Empire* or *Prussia* would be a nice addition.

The encyclopedia keeps to its theme of being "conceived and written as a point of departure for anyone . . . who wishes to begin encountering this world in all its complexities." Entries are infused with references to the cultural and philosophical context of the period, plus the volume succeeds admirably in showing the Enlightenment's reach beyond its traditional continental European locale.

Two much more comprehensive works have been published recently: Oxford's four-volume *Encyclopedia of the Enlightenment* (2003) and a two-volume set published by Fitzroy Dearborn in 2001 with the same title that was translated from a 1997 French work. Although libraries with comprehensive collections in this area will likely find the current volume lacking when compared to those two, it is nevertheless a worthwhile and reasonably priced purchase for public and academic libraries of all sizes. —*Ken Black*

Eastern Europe: An Introduction to the People, Lands, and Culture. 3v. Ed. by Richard Frucht. 2004. 928p. illus. index. ABC-CLIO, $285 (1-57607-800-0); E-book, $310 (1-57607-801-9). 940.

According to its preface, this set is designed to work in conjunction with the earlier *Encyclopedia of Eastern Europe: From the Congress of Vienna to the Fall of Communism* (Garland, 2000), by the same editor. This new edition is more expansive than the earlier one-volume text and certainly stands well on its own.

The volumes are divided by region: Northern Tier (Poland, Estonia, Latvia, Lithuania); Central Europe (formerly under the Habsburg Empire—Czech Republic, Slovakia, Hungary, Croatia, Slovenia); and Southeastern Europe (formerly under the Ottoman Empire—Serbia and Montenegro, Macedonia, Bosnia-Hercegovina, Albania, Romania, Bulgaria, Greece). Entries are organized by country and authored by scholars. Each volume begins with the same preface, introduction, and nine black-and-white maps delineating the political, cultural, and territorial changes over the past millennium. Only volume 3 contains an index, which covers all three volumes and is useful for finding references (for example, *Marshall Plan, Roman Catholic Church*) across various countries. Entries are interspersed with black-and-white period photographs as well as informational boxes focusing on topics such as "The Polish Language," "The Holocaust in Latvia," and "Vlad III Dracula."

Each country entry has subsections for "Land and People," "History," "Political Developments," "Cultural Development," "Economic Development," and "Contemporary Challenges," as well as a selective bibliography and a chronology. Average entry length is more than 50 pages. The history sections tend to be by far the longest, while the political sections are often the most obtuse, mainly because of the nebulous nature of the political history of many of these countries. A user is unlikely to find a summary of the history and politics of any of these countries with this much detail without reading a full-length text.

Overall, this is an excellent and informative reference work that subverts many of the myths of a backward and undeveloped region and replaces them with rich, varied portrayals of human achievement and sociopolitical complexity. Recommended for academic and large public libraries. —*Michael Tosko*

Encyclopedia of the Medieval World. 2v. By Edward D. English. 2005. 920p. illus. index. Facts On File, $150 (0-8160-4690-5). 940.1.

Having already published *Encyclopedia of the Middle Ages*, by Matthew Bunson, in 1995 (now out of print), Facts On File offers this new work by a professor of medieval history at the University of California–Santa Barbara. It covers the time period from the late antique world to about 1500 C.E. and includes events, people, institutions, and culture in western and eastern Europe, Scandinavia, North Africa, Byzantium, and the Near East. The 2,000 entries discuss significant people, art, politics, literature, religion, economics, law, science, and warfare in an *A–Z* format. The articles range in length from a few sentences to one page. All have numerous cross-references and a list of further reading that includes both current and classic articles and books. The articles are aimed at students in high school and college so the language is direct and all concepts are explained. There are also 122 black-and-white illustrations, 19 maps, and 33 genealogical charts of the ruling houses of Europe. The volumes conclude with detailed lists of all the rulers of the various kingdoms, a 50-page bibliography, and a comprehensive index.

Reflecting recent scholarship, topics such as ecology, labor, and women are discussed much more fully than in earlier reference sources. Entries are interdisciplinary and refer to non-European and non-Christian cultures. For example, *Universities and schools* and *Wills and testaments* compare Christian ideas and practices to those in Judaism and Islam. Other articles, such as *Kabbala* and *Kalam,* bring out various aspects of Judaism and Islam. However, there are no overview articles on Christianity or the Catholic Church, or on medieval literature and poetry. Students will have to know the names of individual popes, saints, literary works, and so on. Some articles are curiously missing important *see also* references. For example, the brief *Barbarians and barbarian migrations* has no cross-references to *Franks, Vandals,* and other related entries.

The interdisciplinary nature of the articles and the way they compare Christian, Jewish, and Islamic ideas and practices make them invaluable for students who want to see how medieval cultures contrasted. Librarians will have to weigh this set against other reference sources, such as the *Greenhaven Encyclopedia of the Middle Ages* (2003) or *The Middle Ages: An Encyclopedia for Students* (Scribner, 1996). The former is less expensive but not as comprehensive, while the latter, though based on the scholarly *Dictionary of the Middle Ages* (Scribner, 1982), is written for students from middle school and up. Librarians will also need to consider whether to replace *Encyclopedia of the Middle Ages.* The newer work is recommended to high-school, college, and public libraries that want to update or broaden their history reference collections. —*Merle Jacob*

★**The Encyclopedia of World War II:** A Political, Social, and Military History. Ed. by Spencer C. Tucker. 5v. 2005. 2,251p. illus. index. ABC-CLIO, $485 (1-57607-999-6); e-book, $530 (1-57607-095-6). 940.53.

Intended for grades seven through the adult level, *The Encyclopedia of World War II* is the latest work overseen by Tucker, editor of the award-winning *Encyclopedia of the Vietnam War* (ABC-CLIO, 1998), among other titles. Unlike regionally focused resources, such as *World War II in Europe: An Encyclopedia* (Garland, 1999), and encyclopedias with a U.S. perspective, such as *World War II: The Encyclopedia of the War Years, 1941–1945* (Random House, 1996), this set covers "the entire scope of the Second World War from its earliest roots to its continuing impact on global politics and human society."

The 1,465 alphabetically arranged articles provide an international perspective on people; key battles, campaigns, and events; military equipment and strategy; countries; and other relevant topics. Examples of article titles include *Afrika Korps; Displaced persons; Italy campaign; Jeep; Krebs, Hans; Military medicine; Sport and athletics;* and *Wannsee Conference.* Country entries not only cover the main Allied and Axis powers but also such countries as Afghanistan, Brazil, Estonia, Iraq, Mexico, New Zealand, and Somalia as well as world regions (e.g., *Latin America and the war*). To facilitate use, some articles contain geographic subheadings.

Throughout, the contributors provide equal treatment of both Allied and Axis powers. For example, the article *Propaganda* not only covers propaganda programs in the Axis countries but also propaganda in Britain, the Soviet Union, and the U.S. Besides focusing on events and issues occurring during the war, many articles—such as *Cold War, origins and the early course of* and *Film and the war*—shed light on the war's impact on postwar society.

Length of entries varies from one-fourth of a page (e.g., *Shimada Toyosaku*) to several pages (e.g., the seven-page *Women in World War II*). Entries are signed and end with *see also* references and a reference list of mostly books, both old and new. Text is complemented by 395 black-and-white photographs and 19 tables. Volumes 1 through 4 each provide a complete alphabetical list of all entry titles and an 18-page map section. An additional 55 maps accompany relevant articles. Volume 4 includes a 10-page chronology, a 10-page glossary (mostly abbreviations), a 25-page bibliography (not annotated), and a list of the 248 contributors, most of whom are U.S. academics. Volume 5, edited by Priscilla Roberts (University of Hong Kong), provides the full text of 238 documents arranged chronologically, beginning with an excerpt from Hitler's *Mein Kampf* (1924) and ending with a 1949 document on Soviet espionage during World War II. Volume 5 also contains a cumulative index. Additional features include 13 sidebar articles on controversial issues and turning points in the war (e.g., "A Turning Point? Battle of Stalingrad"). Three general essays reviewing the origins, overview, and legacy of the war begin the set.

More scholarly than the chronologically arranged *History of World War II* (Marshall Cavendish, 2004), *The Encyclopedia of World War II* updates, expands, and provides new material not covered in *The Oxford Companion to World War II* (Oxford, 1995). An excellent resource for high-school, public, and academic libraries. —*Stephen Fadel*

History of World War II. 3v. 2004. 960p. illus. indexes. Marshall Cavendish, $249.95 (0-7614-7482-X). 940.53.

Volume 1 of this set on World War II explores the origins and outbreak of the war, beginning with the legacies of World War I and taking the reader through 1941. The years 1942–1945, which cover the military campaigns in Africa, Asia, and Europe, are the focus of volume 2. Volume 3 discusses victory and the aftermath of war. Chapters in each volume are chronologically arranged. Sidebars throughout each chapter present "Focus Points" with information on key people, technology, political background, events, battles, and tactics as well as extracts from eyewitness accounts.

Although not exhaustive in detail (each chapter covers approximately 20 pages), topics are more than adequately summarized and present a good overview of the war's impact throughout the world. Key people highlighted are from both sides of the conflict (e.g., Dwight Eisenhower, Adolf Hitler, Douglas MacArthur, Erwin Rommel). "Technology Focus Points" discuss such things as radar defense, radio aids to navigation, the M4 Sherman tank, and atomic-bomb technology. Each volume contains a generous amount of primary photographs, which gives the contemporary reader a visual look at war, in addition to more than 90 full-color maps illustrating major battles and campaigns. Attention is given to the home front in different countries and to the economic and social impact of the war on the people.

Volume 3 also contains a bibliography; suggested works for further research; separate indexes of personalities, places, battles, and campaigns; and a comprehensive index. In addition, this volume contains several excellent sections giving information on the armies, naval vessels, and aircraft of both the principal Allied nations and the principal Axis nations. A time line of WWII is another useful tool.

Entries are easy to read and to comprehend, and all three volumes have an attractive appearance. This is an excellent source of WWII information for high-school and public libraries. —*Kaye Talley*

Encyclopedia of Irish History and Culture: 2v. Ed. by James S. Donnelly. 2004. 1,100p. illus. index. Scribner, $270 (0-02-865902-3). 941.5.

In this encyclopedia, designed for "the educated lay public," more than 400 signed articles produced by 205 expert contributors come in three sizes. The largest articles offer more than 2,000 words of in-depth coverage and historical overview. The medium-sized (1,000–2,000 words) and smaller articles (less than 1,000 words) cover historical figures and more discrete events and topics. The A–Z entries are preceded by a chronology and followed by a selection of almost 150 primary documents ranging from the *Confessio* of St. Patrick (c. 450) to the Belfast/Good Friday Agreement (1998)—a real bonus to users. Access is aided by an alphabetical list of entries and a comprehensive index with the main entries in bold type. Twenty-three maps and numerous black-and-white photographs and illustrations accompany the text.

Providing the latest in scholarship, entries are well written and cover the gamut of historical, social, and cultural topics. Long articles, such as *Agriculture, Arts,* and *Home Rule movement and the Irish Parliamentary Party,* are divided into chronological subentries. Biographies are limited to the most important figures, such as Maud Gonne, Daniel O'Connell, Charles Stuart Parnell, and Mary Robinson. Each article concludes with a bibliography of additional resources and may also have *see also* references to other entries and to the primary documents.

For smaller collections, the one-volume *Encyclopedia of Ireland* (Yale, 2003) or *The Encyclopedia of Ireland: An A–Z Guide to Its People, Places, History, and Culture* (Oxford, 2000) may provide sufficient coverage. *Encyclopedia of Irish History and Culture* would make a good purchase for a public library with clients interested in Ireland and is a must purchase for academic libraries serving both graduate and undergraduate students. —*Abbie Landry*

The Illustrated Encyclopedia of Scotland. Ed. by Iseabail Macleod. 2004. 400p. illus. Oyster; dist. by Graphic Arts, $35 (1-932573-03-8). 941.

Those looking for concise information on the history, geography, culture, economy, and politics of Scotland can turn to this volume, which provides entries on a variety of topics. Arranged in alphabetical order, the entries range in size from one or two sentences to a page or more for major topics, such as *Edinburgh, Golf,* and *Scottish Enlightenment*. Historical figures, such as Mary, Queen of Scots and William Wallace, have entries, as do modern figures, such as J. K. Rowling and Rod Stewart. Most of the articles are concise, briefly identifying the subject and cross-referencing related material. Most of the more than 240 illustrations are in vivid color; almost every major castle, town, and geographic feature entry is accompanied by a photograph. The volume ends with maps of current unitary authorities, a calendar of festivals, a list of societies and organizations, and additional readings arranged by subject.

The main problem with the encyclopedia is the superficial coverage found in many of the entries. For example, the entry *Eaglesham* mentions the landing of Rudolf Hess, and on the following page there is a picture of the wreckage of his plane, but the entry does not explain why the event was important. Though this volume is not a resource for in-depth information, attractive design and a reasonable price would make it a good browsing item in public libraries that need a reference volume on Scotland and don't already own the larger *Collins Encyclopedia of Scotland* (rev. ed., 2001). —*Abbie Landry*

London: A Historical Companion. By Kenneth Panton. 2004. 480p. illus. Tempus; dist. by Trafalgar Square, $50 (0-7524-2577-3). 942.1.

This volume is an illustrated and expanded version of Panton's *Historical Dictionary of London* (Scarecrow, 2001). In place of the Web addresses of London agencies and places, bibliography, and other features that have been dropped, the new version adds black-and-white illustrations, maps, and more entries. The book is an A–Z dictionary covering people, events, buildings, and places in the city of London over its 2,000-year history. It opens with an excellent 10-page condensed history of the city and closes with appendixes that list historical events of the last 2,000 years and the Lord Mayors of London.

The heart of the book is the dictionary, with articles that range from one or two paragraphs to one or two pages in length. The diverse entries include articles on the geographic areas of the city such as Paddington, Soho, and Covent Garden that cover how the area got its name, the history of the area, the people who lived or worked there, and its present usage. These articles would have benefited from a small map showing where in London the area is located. Important buildings, bridges, museums, and streets make up the majority of entries. Individuals both real and imaginary—William Shakespeare, Sir Christopher Wren, Prince Albert, Sherlock Holmes—are covered. In addition, there are entries for terms such as *Hackney cabs* and *Sloane Rangers*. All of the entries are very readable and in a few paragraphs give the importance of the person, place, or event in London's history. There are a few glaring omissions—for example, no entry for Roman London, although reference is made to Roman London in entries such as *Bishop's Gate* and *Londinium*. It is unfortunate that the bibliography was dropped; it would have been useful for students.

London: A Historical Companion is an excellent reference source for English-literature and history students as well as for travelers. The book's readability makes it a good ready-reference source for high-school and college students and adults who want to know more about London. Recommended for public and academic libraries.—*Merle Jacob*

France: A Reference Guide from the Renaissance to the Present. By William J. Roberts. 2004. 714p. illus. index. Facts On File, $85 (0-8160-4473-2). 944.

Italy: A Reference Guide from the Renaissance to the Present. By Roland Sarti. 2004. 712p. illus. index. Facts On File, $85 (0-8160-4522-4). 945.

These titles are part of the publisher's European Nations series. A boon for any student of European area studies, the series provides information accessible for grades nine through college.

Each volume begins with a historical survey from the Renaissance to the present. These sections are similar in length in the France and Italy volumes: 100–110 pages. The next section in each volume is a historical dictionary in A–Z format of people, events, and places that figure prominently in the political, social, and cultural history of the country. Other sections include chronologies of major dates, maps, and lists of rulers and statesmen. Each volume also includes a bibliography. While the France volume has just a simple "Selected Bibliography" of books in both French and English arranged alphabetically, the Italy guide goes further by providing a more substantial classified bibliography.

The major portion of every volume is the historical dictionary. Each entry consists of a 300- to 500-word essay. Biographical entries include birth and death dates as well as a summary sentence of the biographee's importance in addition to the narrative. Portraits accompany some of the biographical entries. Numerous *see* references aid navigation.

These and other titles in the European Nations series will be a good first stop for any high-school or college student studying the historical events and ideas that make a nation's modern history. When writing a research paper or preparing for a debate, these volumes should be consulted often for quick facts or for a summary of the grand sweep of history. Recommended for public, high-school, and college libraries. —*Jerry Carbone*

Russia: A Reference Guide from the Renaissance to the Present. By Mauricio Borrero. 2004. 497p. appendixes. bibliog. illus. index. maps. Facts On File, $85 (0-8160-4454-6). 947.

Here, within the bounds of less than 500 pages, readers will find an authoritative reference work distinguished by readability throughout and by wise decision making regarding what information to include and how it might best be presented.

The author, who teaches at St. John's University and oversees Russian reviews for H-Net, has provided five introductory essays offering a concise overview of Russian and Soviet history. These are followed by the main part of the book, the "Historical Dictionary, A–Z," which appears to consist primarily of biographies interspersed with topical entries, such as *Futurism; Leningrad, siege of;* and *Volga River*. There are also a chronology and appendixes containing lists of Russian rulers (1462–2004) and 24 historical maps.

Boldface is used in the index to indicate that a topic or person is the subject of a main entry, while Roman type denotes mention or discussion within an entry or in one of the longer essays at the front of the book. A student interested in the dissidents of the late twentieth century will quickly find that Andrei Amalrik, Petr Grigorenko, and Andrei Sakharov are all subjects of alphabetical entries, as are Vladimir Bukovsky, Lev Kopelev, the Medvedev brothers, Aleksandr Solzhenitsyn, Aleksandr Tvardovsky, and Andrei Sinyavsky—several of whom do not have entries in Macmillan's four-volume *Encyclopedia of Russian History* [RBB My 15 04]. To omit Yuri Daniel and others from the focused attention of individual entries only reflects the limits made necessary by the scope of a general reference and in no way detracts from the overall quality of this volume in Facts On File's European Nations series. It is a splendid resource, which is designed to serve the needs of students (from the ninth grade up) as well as academic specialists and general readers. —*Harold Cordry*

Encyclopedia of the Byzantine Empire. By Jennifer Lawler. 2004. 366p. illus. index. McFarland, $75 (0-7864-1520-7). 949.5.

The Byzantine Empire had an impact that was broad both temporally and geographically. Extant from 476 C.E. to 1453 C. E., when Constantinople fell to the Ottoman Turks, and extending across southeastern Europe, through the Middle East, and into southwestern Asia, the Byzantines influenced the course of a thousand years of history from the political level to that of daily life.

To put the "Greek" Middle Ages defined by the Byzantine Empire in context, this volume's detailed, readable introduction offers a survey of the major cultures of the period. Additional opening material on transliteration from Greek and correct pronunciation is most informative. The body of the alphabetically organized text contains 1,500 entries treating people (*Attila the Hun, Justinian I*), places (*Hagia Sophia, Venice*), and other topics (*Clothing, Crusades, Iconoclasm, Literature, Taxes*) associated with the empire. Entries of greater relative importance are given appropriately greater weight. For example, *Constantinople* is covered in three columns compared to one third of a column for *Court etiquette*. Cross-references are noted in bold within the entry text. The black-and-white illustrations are few in number but are appropriately placed and serve to extend the text. The straightforward prose is clear if a bit dry. The volume concludes with, among other items, maps, genealogical charts of ruling families, a chronology of emperors, a glossary, an eight-page bibliography, and an accurate index.

More concise and to the point than the wide-ranging treatment in Cyril Mango's *The Oxford History of Byzantium* (2002), this is an excellent starting point for information on an empire that did much to form Eastern Europe. It is recommended for academic and large public libraries. —*Ann Welton*

Peoples of Eastern Asia. 11v. 2004. 648p. illus. indexes. Marshall Cavendish, $329.95 (0-7614-7547-8). 950.

This set is a thorough portrait of the countries that comprise the eastern section of Asia, a region of diverse history and heritage. An introduction in volume 1 summarizes the region's history, setting the stage for a better understanding of what follows. Entries are arranged alphabetically by country in volumes 1 through 10; volume 11 contains indexing and other material.

In each country entry, color relief maps indicate the capital, major cities and rivers, and prominent landforms, and a hemisphere map locates the country in its continent. Several color-coded side boxes highlight general information at a glance—geographical and statistical data, average temperatures for January and July, annual precipitation. A time line extends along the bottom of each page. Text for each country captures the past and the present, detailing the pertinent historical dynamics as well as the land and the people (cross-referencing is used when an ethnic group crosses country boundaries). Information on culture abounds, including—but not limited to—religion, clothing, houses, family life, national holidays and festivals, health and education, food and drink, and the arts. Entries range in length from 5 pages for East Timor to more than 80 pages (spread over two volumes) for China. India and Indonesia each have their own volume. Sprinkling the crisp white pages are numerous illustrations, most of them in color.

Individual volumes conclude with a glossary, an index, and a bibliography of useful books and Internet sites. Volume 11 contains the set index along with a plethora of additional reference information: a comprehensive bibliography of general reference works, magazines, regional nonfiction, biography, autobiography and memoirs, Web sites, and fictional sources (a wonderful feature); musical sources; a pronunciation guide; a list of national days; and several thematic indexes.

Best suited for upper-elementary- and middle-school students, this reference set is highly recommended for school and publics libraries. It is user-friendly, interesting to read, concise yet thorough, and visually appealing. —*Cheryl Ward*

Encyclopedia of Mongolia and the Mongol Empire. By Christopher P. Atwood. 2004. 678p. illus. index. Facts On File, $75 (0-8160-4671-9). 951.7.

While most students of world history know of the Mongol Empire created by Chinggis (Genghis) Khan, Mongolia, a country with a long and complex history, remains a bit of a cipher. This detailed account of Mongolian history from 209 B.C.E. to 2003 C.E. does much to fill in the lacuna. Though there is special emphasis on the thirteenth and fourteenth centuries, the time of the expansion of the Mongol Empire, coverage is good for all time periods, and the encyclopedia as a whole makes a sound case for the enormous influence of Mongolian civilization on the history of the Far East, the Indian subcontinent, and Eastern Europe.

The introduction includes a guide to pronunciation, a real necessity. The approximately 1,800 alphabetically arranged entries are well weighted, with longer articles, for example, that on Chinggis Khan, extending for over five pages and shorter entries (e.g., *Falconry*) rating less than a column. Seventeen maps and 78 black- and-white illustrations are well placed and serve to extend and clarify the text. Suggestions for further reading are given at the end of entries for which important works exist. Most entries have *see also* lists appended as well. The volume ends with a list of rulers and leaders of Mongolia and the Mongol Empire; a detailed chronology of events from 209 B.C.E. to 2003 C.E.; a general bibliography; and a comprehensive, accurate index.

Author Atwood, a professor of Mongolian history at Indiana University, clearly knows his material. Communicating it all accessibly is challenging, however, and many entries will be best understood by those with significant background in the culture and social structure. Given this, the encyclopedia is best suited for general university and college collections where it will find use by students of world history. —*Ann Welton*

Dictionary of the Israeli-Palestinian Conflict: Culture, History, and Politics. 2v. 2004. 517p. illus. Macmillan, $270 (0-02-865977-5; e-book, contact Gale for pricing (0-02-865996-1). 956.9405.

This text is based on a French publication, *Shalom, Salam: Dictionnaire pour une meilleure approche du conflit Israélo-Palestinien,* published in 2002. New entries and new information have been added, and the title is now updated through the death of Yasir Arafat. Claude Faure, a member of the French Information Ministry for 30 years, and an analyst on Israeli-Palestinian issues for 10 years, wrote the original book, which *Le Monde* praised for its ease of access and thoroughness.

It is not entirely clear what has been translated and what was created new in the English edition, but, according to the introduction, the set has been "entirely rewritten to answer appropriately the questions of English-reading audiences." The reader may be puzzled by entries for Osama bin Laden and Ayman Muhammad al-Zawahri, or for the war in Iraq. Neither of these individuals has played a role in the Israeli or Palestinian causes, nor does the war involve the Israeli or Palestinian governments, and the entries do not provide an Israeli-Palestinian context. Inserting such entries into the dictionary seems to add a specific political tone that is missing from most of the rest of the text.

Articles are generally brief and well written, and most display no bias. Peace negotiations, warring, and statesmanship are covered in brief biographical sketches of individuals of all nationalities from the last century who have been involved in some way. Major battles are explained and geographically located. Political and revolutionary parties of all variety are defined. Jewish and Islamic holidays, beliefs, and traditions are explained thoroughly. One major mistake is the entry for Baha'i, which refers to the faith as a Muslim sect. A good time line of the conflict is appended along with a glossary of common terms. Each volume concludes with an extensive bibliography of English titles for further reference. There is no index.

Libraries owning the original French work probably have no need for this edition. Likewise, those having the *Encyclopedia of Palestinians* (Facts On File, 2000) or *An Historical Encyclopedia of the Arab-Israeli Conflict* (Greenwood, 1996) will find many of the same topics covered, with only recent events missing. The dictionary is recommended for academic and public libraries that need a current overview. —*Stephen Stratton*

Historical Dictionary of Iraq. By Edmund A. Ghareeb. 2004. 536p. appendixes. bibliog. Scarecrow, $85 (0-8108-4330-7). 956.7.

This entry in the Historical Dictionaries of Asia, Oceania, and the Middle East series is a solid resource that attempts to cover the area currently known as Iraq from the time of ancient Mesopotamia through the current conflicts. It is limited in depth but by far makes up for that in its broad coverage of people, events, culture, organizations, institutions, and more throughout the long history of the region.

One problem with a title like this is that it is out-of-date as soon as it is published, especially given the fast pace of events in Iraq. Some people listed as alive in the dictionary have been killed in the fighting going on in Iraq. Ayatollah Sayed Mohammed Baqir al-Hakim does have a death date listed, but his biography was not updated to include the information of his death by a terrorist bombing during the U.S.-led occupation of Iraq. Izz al-Din Salim, another Ruling Council member who has been killed, is not provided a death date. The book does have biographies of several important people, including Ilad Allawi, the current prime minister, and Ghazi Mashal Ajil al-Yawer, the current president of Iraq, though their roles in the U.S.-appointed government are not included in their biographies. The volume also covers many historic figures, including Hamurabi, Ottoman rulers, numerous scholars, and religious figures. Good entries on Assyrians and Chaldeans as well as Kurds give an idea of the breadth of the Iraqi citizenry that does not get discussed in coverage of the current war. A map of the numerous historic tribes of Iraq is helpful in placing many of the disputes playing out in front of TV news cameras.

The dictionary portion of the volume is supplemented by a helpful chronology of Iraqi history, a collection of United Nations Security Council resolutions of Iraq, and a listing of all members of Iraqi cabinets since 1920 as well as an extensive bibliography for further reading. This work should be a required purchase in academic, public, and even some high-school libraries to ensure that they have a resource that provides a fuller look at a subject that is often portrayed one-dimensionally in today's media. —*Stephen Stratton*

Encyclopedia of Ancient Asian Civilizations. By Charles F. W. Higham. 2004. 440p. bibliogs. illus. index. maps. Facts On File, $75 (0-8160-4640-9). 959.

Beginning with an informative introduction that gives an overview of the major stands of Asian civilization from 5,000 B.C.E. to 1,100 C.E., this alphabetically arranged encyclopedia presents clear information on a wide variety of archaeological sites, significant persons, dynasties, and religious and other cultural practices. More than 900 articles cover Central and East Asia, the Southeastern Asian islands, the Indian subcontinent, and Japan and Korea. The entries are written clearly, though without much verve, and include cross- references in small capitals within the body. Entries for people begin with an italicized summary of the person's status and importance. Some articles include *see also* references at the end, with longer treatments generally terminating with lists of sources (usually two to six) for further reading. Weighting on the entries is appropriate, with shorter treatments for less significant people, places, or concepts (e.g., Chongdi, a Han emperor who ruled briefly) and more in-depth coverage for topics like Buddhism or Harappa (a great city of the Indus Valley Civilization).

More than 50 well-placed black-and-white photographs enhance the presentation. Five maps at the beginning of the volume show the locations of archaeological sites throughout Asia and the Indian subcontinent. All are in black and white, with the elevations indicated only in grey scale, making them a little harder to read than color maps would be. However, they still serve quite ably in terms of locating sites from the text entries. A three-page chronology and extensive bibliography follow the body of the work, as does an accurate index, with main headings indicated by boldface numbers and illustrations by italics.

A sound companion to *Asian History on File* (Facts On File, 1995), this is a good beginning point for research, especially in regard to archaeological excavations. Suitable for most public and academic library collections and for those high schools with a focus on world or ancient history. —*Ann Welton*

Southeast Asia: A Historical Encyclopedia from Angkor Wat to East Timor. Ed. by Keat Gin Ooi. 3v. 2004. 1,791p. illus. index. ABC-CLIO, $285 (1-57607-770-5); e-book $310 (1-57607-771-3). 959.

Southeast Asia is the encyclopedia that will be used for exploring and understanding this geopolitical region for many years. Its pages are packed with well-explained, easily accessible articles. Editor Ooi, a social and economic historian from Malaysia, has assembled a group of writers that represent a wide range of expertise from around the world to focus on Brunei, Cambodia, East Timor, Indonesia, Laos, Malaysia, Myanmar, the Philippines, Singapore, Thailand, and Vietnam. Some articles also cover the influence that China, India, Japan, Sri Lanka, and Taiwan have had on the region.

The introduction is a well-written and concise history of Southeast Asia. It includes bold type cross-references that lead readers to articles within the main text of the encyclopedia. The 800 articles range in length from 300 to 3,000 words, and each has cross-references and a list of bibliographic references. In addition to entries for each country, there are entries on events, organizations, and individuals, and on topics from folklore, geography, war, and religion, among other subject areas. There is strong coverage of the Dutch, British, and Portuguese colonial presence in the region. Economic, social, and political transformations are explained in depth. Each entry is credited, and the contributors are listed in an appendix with their university or corporate affiliation. In the last volume are maps, country fact tables, a topical list of entries, a chronology organized by country, a bibliography of more than 70 pages, and a thorough index.

This set is highly recommended for public, academic, and some high-school libraries for the broad coverage and generally easy-to-understand articles. —*Steve Stratton*

★**Encyclopedia of African History.** Ed. by Kevin Shillington. 3v. 2004. 1,824p. illus. index. Routledge, $495 (1-57958-245-1). 960.

As the editor notes in the introduction, while African societies have long recorded their history as oral tradition, the mature study of African history as an academic discipline developed after World War II and the end of the colonial period. *The Cambridge History of Africa* (1986) and the *UNESCO General History of Africa* (1998) have functioned as standard sources to consult for overviews. *Encyclopedia of African History* is the first multivolume reference set to be devoted to the history of the whole continent. Other fairly recent titles have had either a more limited geographical or chronological scope, such as the excellent *Encyclopedia of Africa South of the Sahara* (Scribner, 1997) or the more focused *Encyclopedia of Twentieth-Century African History* (Routledge, 2002). The *Encyclopedia of African Nations and Civilizations* (Facts On File, 2001) is pitched to a lower student or popular level.

Over 300 authors, more than one-third of them African, have contributed close to 1,100 articles, most of which have further reading suggestions. The majority of the articles are about 1,000 words in length, with longer surveys of regions and broad topics such as *Community in African society* or *Political systems*. About one-third of the matter is devoted to ancient Africa through the eighteenth century, covering topics such as the Iron Age, the Songhay empire, and the Yoruba states. The remainder details the social, economic, and political history of each region and modern state, from the nineteenth century "scramble for Africa" through the colonial period to the postcolonial period to the recent past. There are entries on important modern cities as well as some biographical entries and articles on topics such as clothing and language.

The fore matter of the book includes a list of entries A–Z and also a thematic grouping, which is primarily chronological. Using both the entry lists and the detailed index are essential, as the organization and naming of the entries can be a little confusing. For example, a reader going directly to *Slave trade* will find two entries that begin with those words but that are specific only to the parallels with the ivory and arms trade; most of the entry headings for articles on the slave trade begin with the word *slavery*. In the index, however, one can find well over 100 references to *slave trade* in various entries.

One of the criticisms of both the UNESCO and Cambridge histories was the absence of information on women and gender issues. This set does address some of the issues in the essay on historiography of women on the continent, although the article is only 2 pages plus an extensive reading list. In the index, there are only 17 other references to about 30 pages total of text under *Women* and 3 more topics listed under *Gender*. It seems there is still work to do—there are close to three times as many references to missionary activity as to women.

Newly commissioned maps of countries and regions are crisp and clear. Other illustrations in black and white are rather small and of varying clarity. The level of the individual entries varies—even the educated reader might find some a bit academic in tone and detail. For information that is more general, many nonspecialist readers may find the *Encyclopedia of Africa South of the Sahara* more approachable if northern Africa is not a focus of inquiry. *Encyclopedia of African History* is not very approachable at the high-school level, but most university libraries and large public libraries will want to acquire what is certainly the most in-depth, current reference work on the history of the continent as a whole. —*Margaret Power*

Junior Worldmark Encyclopedia of the Canadian Provinces. 4th ed. 2004. 276p. illus. index. UXL, $58 (0-7876-9196-8); e-book, contact Gale for pricing (0-7876-9360-X). 971.

Junior Worldmark Encyclopedia of the Mexican States. 2004. 336p. illus. index. UXL, $58 (0-7876-9161-5); e-book, contact Gale for pricing (0-7876-9361-8). 972.

Here are two nicely organized, easy-to-use volumes about the closest neighbors to the U.S. Opening with political maps of the respective countries and ending with colorful state and provincial seals and flags, these are sure to be used in elementary- and middle-school libraries, especially where Canada and Mexico are part of the curriculum.

Canadian Provinces, in its fourth edition, includes profiles of the 10 provinces and 3 territories, plus a general article on Canada. Each chapter is about 20 pages long and provides data on the province name and meaning, nickname, motto, flag, and time zone plus 40 numbered sections covering size, climate, plants and animals, population, history, government, industry, health, the arts, education, libraries, tourism, famous people, and more. Chapter bibliographies list recent books as well as travel and provincial Web sites. Many words are defined in context, and a glossary includes terms such as *aboriginal, constant dollars, shoal,* and *protectorate*—but not Neoeskimo or Paleoeskimo. The index is not thorough. The only reference to Alexander Mackenzie points to the *Canada* entry, but he is described more fully in *Northwest Territories*. Confederation Bridge does not appear in the index, although it is mentioned several times in *Prince Edward Island*.

The first edition of *Junior Worldmark Encyclopedia of the Mexican States* has many of the same attractive features. Within state entries, organization is again by uniform numbered headings, and there are pronunciation guides for each state. A map showing the location within the country and important peaks, rivers, and cities is found in every section. Bibliographies typically list National Geographic and Mason Crest titles as well as the Web site *Mexico for Kids* [http://www.elbalero.gob.mx/index_kids.html]. The index seems adequate, except that there are no index entries for Aztecs or Mayas except the *Aztec Stadium* and the *Mayan World Studies Center*. As in the volume on Canada, illustrations are not indexed.

Because the information they contain is so accessible, it's hard to imagine these titles sitting on a shelf. They belong in most school libraries, including high-school libraries, and in public libraries serving students. —*Sue Gooden*

The Oxford Companion to Canadian History. Ed. by Gerald Hallowell. 2004. 748p. index. Oxford, $79.95 (0-19-541559-0). 971.

The purpose of this wide-ranging guide is to provide "the basic details of the main events, institutions, places and people in Canada's past." Editor Hallowell is a former senior editor of Canadian history at the University of Toronto Press.

The *Companion's* impressive 1,654 entries, the work of more than 500 mostly academic subject experts, are arranged alphabetically and range in length from a few sentences to two pages. Cross-referencing is indicated by asterisks within entries. In addition to the A–Z articles, the book contains a precise index; lists of monarchs, governors general, prime ministers, and provincial premiers; and the words of the national anthems. Text is complemented by ten basic maps, five depicting the historical settlement of Canada and five identifying geographic locations.

The entries cover several major subject areas, including politics and the constitution, industry and the economy, education and religion, law, medicine and science, transportation, and social and cultural history and effectively reflect the regional, linguistic, and cultural diversity of Canada. For example, there are several excellent articles devoted to Canada's aboriginal peoples. In addition, there are extensive articles related to the nation's "founding peoples," the French and British. Finally, there are entries discussing other key groups, including Jews and Chinese and African Canadians. Other entries cover common Canadian topics such as *Anne of Green Gables, Fur trade, Hockey,* and *Peacekeeping.*

This is an excellent entry point into Canadian history, although it should be noted that treatment of topics is deliberately brief and, because of space constraints, there are no suggested readings or a bibliography of sources. The volume will be particularly useful as a quick reference for users who are already very familiar with Canadian history. Lower-level undergraduates and general readers may need to refer to *The Canadian Encyclopedia* (McClelland & Stewart, 2000) for further details. Nevertheless, the *Companion* is highly recommended for all Canadian libraries, as well as any U.S. library near the Canadian border or supporting Canadian history or Canadian studies programs. —*Michelle Hendley*

Mexico: An Encyclopedia of Contemporary Culture and History. Ed. by Don M. Coerver and others. 2004. 621p. index. ABC-CLIO, $80 (1-57607-132-4); E-book, $90 (1-85109-517-9). 972.08.

This is primarily a survey of twentieth-century Mexico, with some coverage extending into the twenty-first century or backward into the nineteenth. The arrangement is alphabetical. Some among the more than 160 entries treat people, states, institutions, and political events and developments. There are also entries on popular culture (*Comic books, Popular music, Television*), social issues and trends (*Drug trafficking, Education, Immigration/Emigration*), and a wide range of other topics other topics (*Food, Muralist movement, North American Free Trade Agreement*).

Articles range from a few paragraphs to several double-column pages. All articles have *see also* references and a list of further readings, which do not overlap with the general bibliography. Spanish terms are translated immediately after their use in the text. A chronology of events and simple topographic and political maps are placed at the beginning of the book. There are fairly few references to works published after 2000 in either the bibliography or the further reading lists, although some Web sites are listed.

Encyclopedia of Modern Mexico (Scarecrow, 2002) has a similar chronological scope but is more focused on government and politics. The editors of the ABC-CLIO title do not indicate a definite audience, but, given the cursory nature of many of the articles, the book would probably be best for undergraduates taking a survey course on Mexico or Latin America or high-school students taking similar courses. Public libraries may also find it useful. —*Kathleen Stipek*

Americans at War: Society, Culture, and the Homefront. 4v. Ed. by John P. Resch. 2004. illus. index. Macmillan, $475 (0-02-845806-X); e-book, contact Gale for pricing (0-02-865993-7). 973.

War isn't just about battles or campaigns, victories or defeats, territory gained or lost; it's also about people and the effects that war has upon a society. *Americans at War* focuses on how war shaped (and was shaped by) American society, culture, and national identity from 1500 to the present. Each of the volumes covers a different time period: 1500–1815, 1816–1900, 1901–1945, and 1946 to the present. The 395 articles were written by 234 academic and independent scholars and average around two pages in length.

Each volume contains the same preface, alphabetical list of entries, topical outline, chronology, glossary, and index. Specific to each volume are an introduction summarizing the period of time being covered and an appendix containing a selection of primary documents. Articles are alphabetically arranged and include selected bibliographies and *see also* references. Sidebars appear throughout the text to supplement topics. Illustrations are in black and white.

In addition to events (*Bacon's Rebellion, New York City Draft Riots, 9-11*) and people (Abigail Adams, Tokyo Rose, Colin Powell), entries cover topics related to dissent (*Boston Tea Party: politicizing ordinary people; Nuclear freeze movement*); gender (*Rosie the Riveter, Women integrated into the military*); literature (*Uncle Tom's Cabin, Cold war novels and movies*); politics (*Anti-Federalists, Homestead Act*); ethnicity (*Black Codes; Muslims, stereotypes and fears of*); and more. Among the types of primary source documents found in the appendixes (an average of 22 documents per volume) are acts of Congress, court cases, first-person narratives, letters, speeches, and songs. Examples of these documents are the Stamp Act of 1765, the song "Battle Hymn of the Republic" (1861), "Franklin D. Roosevelt's Fireside Chat on the Bank Crisis" (1933), and "Pardon for Vietnam Draft Evaders" (1977).

Written for general readers, students, and researchers, *Americans at War* delivers well-written articles and would make an excellent addition to high-school, academic, and public libraries. —*Kaye Talley*

Annals of America. 22v. 2003. illus. index. Encyclopaedia Britannica, dist. by World Book, $529 (0-85229-960-5). 973.

World Book is now the distributor for Encyclopaedia Britannica's *Annals of America*. The current edition is the first new edition since 1987.

Annals contains more than 2,500 documents and 5,000 black-and-white photographs. Coverage begins in 1493 with "Christopher Columbus: Discovery of the New World," taken from his letters. Volume 22 is new and extends the set to 2001 with an article on September 11 and its aftermath, taken from *Encyclopaedia Britannica 2001 Year in Review*. Each volume begins with a chronology for the time span it covers, and each entry begins with a brief introduction that provides some context. In some cases, documents have been excerpted and slightly modernized. A volume-by-volume list of contents and an index that lists authors and their selected documents can be found in volume 22.

Annals has not been altered so much as added to. The first edition was published under the guidance of Mortimer Adler, and volumes 1–18 reflect a typically Adlerian plan to present "all the great American documents." Each of these volumes closes with an index of authors, including brief biographical summaries. Subsequent volumes strive to present material that is representative rather than "great"—newspaper and magazine articles, official reports, and the like. The author index found in volumes 1–18 has been replaced in later volumes by a subject index, but subject indexing is not cumulative for these volumes, and there is no subject indexing at all for volumes 1–18.

In 1972, we recommended *Annals* for secondary-school libraries and public libraries, "particularly those serving students where the use of primary materials is emphasized in American history courses." We also recommended it for academic libraries where, although many of the documents might be already be at hand, "the convenience of having such a handy compilation available is obvious." Now, of course, many of the documents that are collected in *Annals* are available on the Web, at sites like Amdocs [http://www.ukans.edu/carrie/docs/amdocs_index.html] and http://www.ourdocuments.gov. Because of the wider availability of historical documents, *Annals* is not a necessary purchase, but it still offers a convenient way to add these materials to the reference collection. —*Mary Ellen Quinn*

Atlas of the Civil War. 2005. 400p. illus. index. Oxford, $85 (0-19-522131-1). 973.7.

This is the latest in a long series of atlases dealing with the American Civil War.

Each of five major chapters is devoted to a single year from 1861 to 1865. In addition to every important battle, there is coverage of nonmilitary topics, such as population, the economy, transportation, elections, and the home front. For example, the chapter "1862: The Struggle for Union" has a section on the Emancipation Proclamation (with a table showing the number of slaves per county in 1862). The chapter "1863: The Turning of the Tide" has a section on Confederate trade. Each chapter covers around 60 pages. The work ends with a list of major battle sites, a chronology, a glossary, a short bibliography, and an index, which provides access to illustrations and maps as well as names.

The most stunning feature of this atlas is the full-color maps that depict not just battles but the value of farmland, the spread of slavery, the construction of railroads, and more. Approximately 40 specially commissioned three-dimensional maps show terrain and troop movements. The western campaigns, such as the invasion of New Mexico by Texas, receive full coverage even though they are not as widely known as the more famous battles in the East. Even smaller battles, such as Pleasant Hill and Mansfield, which are important to Louisiana but not well known outside the state, are included. Illustrations, many of them reproductions of period photographs, add still another dimension to this work.

What sets this atlas apart from others on the Civil War is the inclusion of the social, cultural, economic, and political facets of the war. Its scope and reasonable price recommend it to high-school, public, school, and academic libraries. —*Abbie Landry*

Birth of the Bill of Rights: Encyclopedia of the Antifederalists. 2v. By Jon. L. Wakelyn. 2004. 600p. index. Greenwood, $199.95 (0-313-32922-2). 973.4.

The Antifederalists lost the battle over the ratification of the U.S. Constitution of 1787, but their arguments helped to ensure the creation of the Bill of Rights. This set aims to highlight the significance of the Antifederalists "through a review of their careers, their political values, and their arguments against the Constitution." Author Wakelyn, a history professor, maintains that the encyclopedia represents "the largest and most comprehensive collection of data on the Antifederalists known to date."

Volume 1, *Biographies,* opens with a good overview, followed by alphabetically arranged entries on 140 Antifederalists. These were selected based on several criteria, including being identified as the most significant "in the best histories of the ratification controversy." Among them are Samuel Adams, Patrick Henry, James Monroe, and Mercy Otis Warren. The entries, which range in length from a few paragraphs to several pages, contain information on family, education, career, activities during and after the Revolution, and state and national service. A list of references follows each biographical essay. Other features of the first volume include a detailed bibliographical essay containing a range of resources on the Antifederalists, including works on political theory, biographies, and primary sources.

Volume 2, *Major Writings,* contains more than 100 writings and speeches of the Antifederalists, including addresses to state ratification conventions, letters in newspapers, and private letters. The documents are listed under each of the original 13 states "according to the first date when its ratification convention met," beginning with Pennsylvania and concluding with North Carolina. A brief but helpful description of each document's significance is also included. A precise index for the set is repeated in both volumes.

The *Birth of the Bill of Rights* is a well-written introduction to a group of individuals Wakelyn describes as "often lost to history" and the historical importance of their opposition to the Constitution. It is recommended for academic and large public libraries. —*Michelle Hendley*

The Clinton Years. By Shirley Anne Warshaw. 2004. 524p. illus. index. Fact On File, $85 (0-8160-5333-2). 973.929.

The Kennedy Years. Rev. ed. By Joseph Siracusa. 2004. 616p. illus. index. Facts On File, $85 (0-8160-5444-4). 973.922.

The Clinton Years, a new work, and *The Kennedy Years,* a revision, are part of the publisher's Presidential Profiles series. They contain 350 and 250 biographies, respectively, of people who played an important role in the Clinton and Kennedy administrations, either directly or indirectly. Alphabetically arranged, each profile includes the person's name, date of birth and (where pertinent) death, and offices held or occupation, followed by a detailed account of the person's contribution to the social or political scene. *The Clinton Years* emphasizes members of the administration and of Congress but also covers world leaders, such as Yasser Arafat and Boris Yeltsin, and individuals caught up in various scandals, such as Monica Lewinsky and James and Susan McDougal. *The Kennedy Years* sticks to Americans but encompasses individuals—John Glenn, Frank Sinatra, and Malcolm X, for example—who loomed large in the public eye.

Both volumes follow the same format, with biographical profiles followed by appendixes (a chronology of events during each administration by year, month, and day and a list of U.S. government officials). The Kennedy volume adds lists of members of the Senate and Congress and of governors who served during the time period. Also in the Kennedy volume are cross-references to other volumes in the series in which an individual has an entry. Finally, both volumes have a selection of primary documents and a bibliography.

Like others in the series, these volumes are excellent resources for the high-school researcher and public library user. The biographical focus makes them a good complement to other reference sources on the presidency. —*Carol Harless*

Debatable Issues in U.S. History. 5v. illus. index. June 2004. Greenwood, $200 (0-313-32910-9). 973.

In a chronological arrangement, this set gives an introduction to numerous debatable issues in American history, providing balanced coverage on all sides. Each volume includes 10–12 topics, a glossary, a bibliography, and a cumulative index.

Most of the issues are well-known topics, such as the Salem witch trials, Prohibition, and the Equal Rights Amendment, and involve the power of the national government or balancing personal freedoms with the common good. Many were decided by the Supreme Court. Each entry opens with a brief description of the issue. Historical background is followed by analysis of the pro and con arguments and the outcome of the topic. Mixed into each 8- to 12-page chapter are interesting sidebars that offer additional information or highlight key figures. "In Their Own Words" sidebars provide excerpts from primary sources and give a feel for the selected points of view, but having just two or three quoted sentences, often with no guidance on retrieving the whole document, may be frustrating even for middle-schoolers. Photos are credited but not always identified. For example, where and when was the demonstration shown at the beginning of the chapter "Cold War and Anti-Communism"?

Readability is at the middle-school level, but the topics will also be useful for high-school students. Many terms are defined in the text, and each volume includes a unique glossary of about 20 words. The lists of sources in each book cite about 6–10 books and 6–8 Web sites for further information but not the primary documents from which the excerpts are extracted. Indexing is cumulative for the whole set but is barely adequate. For example, a user finding the index entry *presidential election of 2000* may miss references to other elections, which are cited in the index as *election of 1800, election of 1824,* and *election of 1876.*

Despite some weaknesses, these short introductions to each controversial topic may be enough to spark additional research, and they certainly make difficult issues a little clearer. Suitable for school and public libraries. —*Susan Gooden*

Discover America. 51v. 2005. 1,632p. illus. indexes. Encyclopedia Britannica, $699 (1-59339-183-8). 973.

Buying a set of state books is a pretty big investment these days. Most of us are looking to get the most bang for our money and are always trying to balance information needs, accuracy of the text, reading level(s), and rate of information degradation.

This new offering by Encyclopedia Britannica is loaded with color photographs and is written in a conversational style reminiscent of a travel guide. It would appeal to students in grades 3–8. According the Britannica Web site, the text has a reading level of grades 4–6. There is plenty of white space, and the typeface is fairly large. The format is uniform throughout the 50 state volumes. Short (two to four page) sections cover each state's land and climate, natural resources, plants and animals, tourism, industry, goods and services, natives, explorers and missionaries, early settlers, population, politics and government, cultural groups, arts and entertainment, and sports. A "Brain Teaser" section has fun facts (how big is Lincoln's nose on Mount Rushmore?). Rounding out each volume are a "Facts and Resources" page that includes a list of print and Web resources, a short glossary, and an index. Each volume also has one map with a scale and compass rose.

There are many positive things about this set. *The Fact Book* (volume 51) that is included in the set is full of charts, maps, history, and symbols. The state volumes cover the high points needed by most students, and information is general enough that it does not appear likely to go out of date soon. There are not as many numbers and data as in *Junior Worldmark Encyclopedia of the States* (Gale, 2004), which contains more information from the 2000 census on the same topics but in a less-attractive four-volume set. As with any set of this size, there are some slight deficiencies. The flag, state-bird, and state-seal images are so small that one would need a magnifying glass to see them clearly. The words to the state songs are not included, and there are no lists of famous people or governors. Finally, the maps are not very large, and although they do have the locations of cities and bodies of water, they do not locate the states in relation to the rest of the U.S.

In spite of its shortcomings, this is an impressive set for libraries in the market for information for younger students or reluctant readers. For older students, the material would probably need to be supplemented. Recommended for school and public libraries that serve a student population in grades 3–8. —*Dona Helmer*

The Education of the Presidents of the United States. 3v. Ed. by Fred L. Israel. 2004. 515p. illus. index. Mason Crest, $75 (1-59084-546-3). 973.

At age 12, George Washington laboriously copied in longhand script "Rules of Civility and Decent Behavior and Conversation." FDR, while a student at the Groton School, studied Latin, Greek, algebra, English literature and composition, ancient history, and Bible studies. JFK graduated cum laude from Harvard; Ford graduated with a 1.82 GPA, although he earned an A in American Government. Replete with fascinating tidbits of information, this set, consisting of three chronologically arranged volumes covering presidents from George Washington to George W. Bush, offers an unusual historical retrospective: What was the formal—or informal—educational experience of U.S. leaders? Did it matter?

Each of the 42 signed essays, ranging from 8 to 16 pages, takes the reader from a president's birth to death or to the present time. More than 300 illustrations (many newly published) intersperse the text, including sepia and black-and-white photographs, pages from books, minutes from meetings, engravings, paper cutouts, journal entries, tuition bills, and report cards. A detailed caption appears with each, providing additional information or clarifying difficult-to-read images. Visually, the most interesting chapters are those for later presidents, for whom much memorabilia is available. Volume 3 contains the set index and a useful list of Internet resources for further inquiry. Less useful is the "Selected Guide to Presidential Biographies," since the bibliographic information provided here lacks ISBN and publisher.

Geared for secondary-level students, this title would be of use to a school not locked into a rigid core curriculum or for public libraries serving history buffs. The reasonable price might help to make it an option. —*Cheryl Ward*

Encyclopedia of American Historical Documents. 3v. Ed. by Susan Rosenfeld. 2004. 1,801p. bibliogs. index. Facts On File, $300 (0-8160-4995-5). 973.

In recent years, high-school and college students in history courses have been encouraged, even required, to engage with primary sources. The 1,600-plus documents gathered in this set were selected to correspond to the 10 eras of the national American History Standards for grades 9–12 (http://www.sscnet.ucla.edu/ nchs/standards). Additional selection criteria include a limitation of one document per topic, documents with enduring importance to twenty-first-century readers, documents representing turning points in U.S. history, documents significant in more than one social or cultural realm, and documents that touch on controversial issues. Selected documents also provide insights into five themes important in American history (e.g., diversity, the environment, popular culture). Within each of the 10 chronological eras documents are arranged topically, and chronologically within each topic. This structure complements the structure of the 11-volume *Encyclopedia of American History* (Facts On File, 2003).

Most documents appear in their entirety; however, some (e.g., the *Federalist Papers,* Nathaniel Hawthorne's *The Blithedale Romance,* the USA PATRIOT Act) are represented by key excerpts. Laws, speeches, treaties, political party platforms, and song lyrics mingle with amendments to the U.S. Constitution, presidential statements, and court decisions. Introductory notes explain the origins of each document, place it in its historical context, and comment on its legacy. A concluding note cites the document's source. A list of suggested readings closes the section for each era, and a cumulative index concludes each volume.

From the period of European expeditions to the Americas through the creation of the Homeland Security Department, the documents shed light on conflicts, controversies, principles, ideas, and trends in the world's most ambitious experiment in government of the people, by the people, and for the people. More selective but more affordable than the 10-volume *American Decades Primary Resources* (Gale, 2003), this is very welcome as the new source of choice to succeed Henry Steele Commager's *Documents of American History* (8th ed., Appleton-Century-Crofts, 1968). Commager, however, ought to remain by its side, since it reproduces documents the new compilation omits. For example, the *Encyclopedia*'s one-document-per-topic approach means that, although other Southern states seceded from the union, only South Carolina's ordinance of secession is included. Users of high-school, public, and college libraries will benefit from the convenient access this new set gives to thought-provoking historical documents. —*James Rettig*

Encyclopedia of American National Parks. 2v. Ed. by Hal K. Rothman and Sara Dant Ewert. 2004. 650p. illus. index. Sharpe, $199 (0-7656-8057-2). 973.

Rothman and Ewert, both history professors, have edited an encyclopedia that provides information for all parks, historic sites, recreation areas, monuments, memorials, preserves, battlefields, seashores, and heritage corridors administered by the National Park Service. The entries are alphabetical by park, with one to three pages devoted to each site. The location, acreage, date of establishment, a short history, and visitor information are provided. Each entry concludes with the address, Web site, and a short bibliography. Simple regional maps in the beginning of each volume show the location of the parks. The first volume has a history of NPS and a few short biographies of people known for their work in NPS. The index, found in each volume, is a listing of parks by state.

The reading level of the encyclopedia is appropriate for middle- or high-school students, but the lack of color photographs, sidebars, boxes, etc., will make it unappealing for this age level. If the source had been published 10 years ago, it would have been a popular addition to high-school, public, and possibly academic libraries. However, the Web sites of the parks, developed by NPS, give the same information and more in an eye-catching format. The Web sites also include detailed maps of each park, which are necessary for visitors. The bibliographies for each entry in the encyclopedia (combined into 30 pages in volume 2) and the comprehensive coverage are the only advantages of the encyclopedia over the individual Web sites.

With unexciting prose and black-and-white photographs, this is a possible purchase only for libraries that do not have Internet access or that want the convenience of having information on all the parks in one print source. —*Christine Bulson*

Encyclopedia of Black Studies. Ed. by Molefi Kete Asante and Ama Mazama. 2005. 531p. illus. index. Sage, $150 (0-7619-2762-X). 973.

Just as Sheikh Amadu Bamba, the Senegalese Sufi saint, can be considered the most prolific writer of Africa, Asante must surely be considered the most prolific author and editor in black studies. He and Mazama, both of Temple University, have put together a 250-entry encyclopedia of what they consider the black studies canon. Anyone familiar with Mazama or Asante will recognize the Afrocentric orientation of their text. Afrocentricity is not an anti-European or anti-Caucasian view of the world but a way for Africans and people descended from Africans the world over to view the world from their own vantage point. The encyclopedia's contributors are a who's who of the black studies field today.

The book has an explanatory preface and excellent introduction that summarizes black studies for those unfamiliar with the field. Most of the articles provide a short bibliography of further reading for those seeking more in-depth knowledge. One appendix contains an extensive bibliography that also covers black studies programs at American universities and a list of major black studies journals. A thorough index will easily lead the reader to any topic located within the text. The list of contributors rounds out a solidly put-together title.

For students seeking a good grounding in Afrocentricity, this is an excellent place to start. Articles cover many of the basics of the field, from concepts and theories (*Diaspora, Black nationalism*), to selected books important in laying out Afrocentric ideas (*Black Athena, Mis-Education of the Negro*), to a short article on *Diopian historiography*. One of the most concise and understandable explanations of Ebonics can be found in this text. Those who confuse African American studies with black studies may find some glaring omissions. There are no entries on Martin Luther King or Malcom X (although numerous reference to both can be traced through the index). However, there are a two-page article on Marie Laveau and a page and a half on the Fisk Jubilee Singers.

This is a required text for large public libraries and all academic libraries. It provides a thorough understanding of and easy reference into a growing, dynamic field of study. —*Stephen Stratton*

Encyclopedia of Native American Wars & Warfare. Ed. by William Kessel and Robert Wooster. 2005. 398p. illus. index. Facts On File, $75 (0-8160-3337-4). 973.

More than 600 entries provide access to information about the persons, tribes, treaties, battles, places, weaponry, and concepts related to armed conflicts between Native Americans and those of European descent, for the years between 1599 and 1890 and primarily the geographic locations now within the borders of the U.S. The sharply focused, extensively cross-indexed entries, accompanied by 78 black-and-white illustrations and 36 maps, are intended to introduce the topic to students in grade nine and up. Preceding the entries are five essays, written by the editors: "American Indians Prior to 1492," "Warfare Terminology," "Armies of Empire: Colonial, State, Federal and Imperial Forces in the Indian Wars," "Wars and Warfare," and "Wars and Warfare, Another View." Appendixes include a list of tribes of North America organized by culture area (region), a chronology, and a selected bibliography. The index indicates main entries, entries with photographs or maps, and chronology entries.

The *Encyclopedia of Native American Wars & Warfare* complements other recent reference books by Facts On File related to Native American culture and history, including the *Biographical Dictionary of American Indian History to 1900* (2001) and the *Chronology of American Indian History* (2001). There are few direct competitors to this title, and the limited overlap with the *Encyclopedia of American Indian Wars, 1492–1890* (ABC-CLIO, 1997) encourages complementary use rather than replacement. The entries each encyclopedia has on common topics often show significant differences with respect to context, reporting, and level of detail, even though both encyclopedias generally agree on the basic facts. Given its attention to context and breadth of entries, the *Encyclopedia of Native American Wars & Warfare* may make a better beginning point for novice researchers and is recommended for public, high-school, and academic libraries. —*Joseph Thomas*

Encyclopedia of the American Presidency. By Michael A. Genovese. 2004. 546p. appendixes. bibliogs. illus. index. Facts On File, $85 (0-8160-4699-9). 973.

Heightened interest in a national election year will bring more questions to the reference librarian regarding the office of the U.S. presidency. Facts On File has published a tool to help obtain a historical and comprehensive perspective on these questions.

Encyclopedia of the American Presidency seeks to provide a current and definitive guide to the role of the president throughout history. With 600 entries arranged in an *A–Z* format, *the volume* provides a treasure trove of information regarding elections, court cases, scandals, domestic and foreign policy issues, war and peace, political opponents and running mates, plus a number of other topics. The entries are wide-ranging: *Ashcroft, John; Air Force One; Impeachment; Rating the president; Secret Service;* and *Veto power,* among others. The entries on the individual presidents run from several paragraphs (William Henry Harrison, who died one month after taking office) to four full pages (Franklin Roosevelt); they all include a synopsis of the life and presidency as well as a bibliography of further readings.

Special features in the volume add value. There are four appendixes: sections on the U.S. Constitution dealing with the presidency, an annotated chronology of presidential elections, a selected general bibliography, and a bibliography by president.

This source promises to be a good first stop for students, journalists, history buffs, and general readers looking for information on the American executive branch. It should find a home in any high-school, public, or academic library. —*Jerry Carbone*

Frontier America. 10v. By David M. Brownstone and Irene M. Franck. 2004. illus. index. Grolier, $369 (0-7172-5990-9). 973.

Large, clear type font, abundant color illustrations, and generous column width make this treatment of the American frontier appropriate for the designated audience of grades seven through nine. It covers "the many frontiers that together make up the earliest settled regions of what is now the United States, from the first contacts between Europeans and Native Americans to the closing of the frontier in the late 1800s."

The first two volumes present the overall history of the American frontier, with volume 2 containing a chronology of key events and a map of the lower 48 states. Volumes 3 through 10 offer alphabetically organized articles on events, people, and places. Each state is given a separate entry with a "Quick Frontier Facts" box. State entries are longer than the general entries, which vary in length from one to three columns. Articles are adequately cross-referenced, with related subjects noted in small capitals. There are also longer articles that cover wider subjects, such as "Water on the Frontier" or "The Oregon Trail."

Each volume has its own table of contents, with maps noted, and a full, accurate set index. Volume 10 has a lengthy list of Web sites, current as of early 2004, and a print bibliography of mostly adult works.

The writing style is brisk and engaging enough to hold the attention of younger researchers. Coverage is evenhanded. There is no other student-level resource that covers this aspect of American history in such depth, and the set is a sound addition to school libraries as well as to public libraries with heavy young adult use. —*Ann Welton*

Historical Dictionary of Syria. By David Commins. 2d ed. 2004. 340p. Scarecrow, $70 (0-8108-4934-8). 973.7.

This volume is part of the publisher's Historical Dictionaries of Asia, Oceania, and the Middle East series. Commins, a professor of history at Dickinson College in New Jersey, lived in Syria for two years and has written extensively on the region.

There are more than 350 entries in the second edition of the dictionary, over 100 of them entirely new. A majority of the new entries focus on the cultural institutions of Syria. There are articles explaining the Alawi and Druze faiths, which play a large role in Syrian politics. Other entries cover literature and art, still others the coffeehouses and other aspects of Syrian daily life. Entries are very readable, imparting a respect for the country's history and explaining details with an apolitical view.

The dictionary provides excellent coverage of historical figures as well as people and communities within current-day Syria. Entries are supported by an introduction that surveys Syrian history from ancient times, through the caliphates and Mamluks, to the period of Asad family rule. Other features include a helpful chronology and an extensive bibliography. Two maps show the administrative regions of Syria and land use.

Like other volumes in the series, this one provides an authoritative and succinct overview of the history of a nation about which many Americans are ignorant. It would be a good addition to academic and large public library collections. —*Stephen Stratton*

Historical Dictionary of the Civil War and Reconstruction. By William L. Richter. 2004. 968p. Scarecrow, $100 (0-8108-4584-9). 973.7.

Any event as pivotal as the American Civil War is going to be constantly reviewed, reanalyzed, and reconsidered. This extremely readable volume by a Ph.D. in history from Louisiana State University includes new interpretations of events and individuals. Part of the publisher's Historical Dictionaries of U.S. Historical Eras series, it seeks to place the war in context by encompassing the years 1844–1877.

The dictionary's more than 800 entries are organized alphabetically, with numerous *see* references to main entries. Key personnel, battles, legislation, legal cases, and elections are all covered. The main figures (Lincoln, Davis) are represented with lengthy, multipage biographies, with lesser figures receiving approximately one page. Even minor but notable events, such as the Red River Campaign, Colfax Race Riot (1874), and Coushatta Massacre, are included. Controversial individuals—Lee and Grant, for example—are portrayed in balance, and the work takes a new look at stock characters, such as *Carpetbaggers* and *Scalawags,* who may not have been the total villains as usually portrayed. A selected bibliography, divided by subject headings, covers more than 200 pages. The dictionary concludes with a selection of primary documents.

Some omissions are apparent. There is no entry on the *Hunley,* the first submarine in history to sink a ship, nor on General Leonidas Polk, "the Fighting Bishop." Women who served as nurses, among them Clara Barton, Kate Cumming, and Dorothea Dix, are lumped into one article, *Nurses,* rather than meriting their own entries. Other notable women, such as Belle Boyd, Mary B. Chesnut, and Harriet Tubman, are not mentioned.

The number of reference works on the Civil War grows almost daily. Although not as expansive as ABC-CLIO's *Encyclopedia of the American Civil War: A Political, Social, and Military History* (2000), this book should be added to reference collections of academic and large public libraries. The readable style, balanced coverage, and authoritative scholarship make it an important work. —*Abbie Landry*

Junior Worldmark Encyclopedia of the States. Ed. by Timothy L. Gall and Susan Bevan Gall. 4v. 4th ed. illus. index. 2004. UXL, $185 (0-7876-9197-6); e-book, call 800-877-4253 for pricing (0-7876-9354-2). 973.

Based on the sixth edition of *Worldmark Encyclopedia of the States* (Gale, 2003), this set is designed for students in middle and high school. It contains information on all 50 states, the District of Columbia, Puerto Rico, U.S. Caribbean Dependencies, and U.S. Pacific Dependencies. There is also an entry for *United States of America.*

Using data from the 2000 Census and numerous other sources, each entry begins with an introductory section of about 20 quick facts such as origin of the name, nickname(s), capital, motto, description of the flag, and title of the state song. There are also small black-and-white line drawings of the seal and flag; for color pictures of flags, the user must check the end pages in the back of each volume. Following this introduction is the profile containing 40 numbered subsections with information on topics such as location, topography, population, ethnic groups, religion, arts, communications, and famous people. Rounding out the profile is a short (four to eight items) bibliography and a listing of two Web sites. Each entry has a full-page black-and-white geopolitical map, numerous tables and charts (including presidential vote patterns), a list of all governors since statehood, and small black-and-white photographs of people and places.

The entries have been thoughtfully arranged to make them easy to use. The introductory section contains all those quick facts that students need for reports, and the arrangement of the meatier profile sections facilitates comparison between different states. Each volume has a glossary and a list of abbreviations, and volume 4 contains a simple index to the entire work.

Overall, this is a great buy for the price. The only down side is that there are no color illustrations, but that can be helped by going to the individual state's Web sites listed in the entries. Recommended for school and public libraries that serve a student population in grades 5–12. —*Dona Helmer*

Reconstruction Era Reference Library. 3v. By Roger Matuz. 2004. illus. index. UXL, $165 (0-7876-9216-6); e-book, contact Gale for pricing (1-4144-0454-9). 973.8.

Reconstruction Era Reference Library consists of three volumes: *Almanac, Biographies,* and *Primary Sources,* with a separate cumulative index, covering the period from the end of the American Civil War (April 1865) to the inauguration of President Rutherford B. Hayes (1877).

The *Almanac* volume begins with "Words to Know." A time line (duplicated in each of the volumes) lists important dates and events of the Reconstruction era and is followed by a list of "Research and Activity Ideas." A chronological overview of the era is provided in nine chapters, each having its own "Words to Know" sidebar along with sidebars that describe people, events, and facts of special interest.

The *Biographies* volume covers political and military leaders as well as activists, artists, writers, and more. Among them are Louisa May Alcott, Frederick Douglass, Ulysses S. Grant, and Zebulon Vance. Within each biographical entry are cross-references to other individuals covered in this volume. *Primary Sources* contains 19 complete or partial documents, such as the Fourteenth Amendment of the U.S. Constitution and Rutherford B. Hayes' inaugural address. Each document is accompanied by an introduction, keys to reading the document, a discussion of subsequent events related to the document, and other material. Here and throughout the set, every chapter concludes with a list of further reading, often including Web sites.

Like other UXL Reference Library titles, *Reconstruction Era* is an excellent resource set for middle-school and high-school libraries and public libraries that cater to a school clientele. —*Carol Harless*

U.S.A. Twenties. 6v. illus. index. Grolier, $419 (0-7172-6013-5). 973.91

This set offers alphabetically arranged articles addressing social and political aspects of the U.S during the 1920s. The detailed entries range from one full page to several, presume no previous knowledge on the part of the reader, and offer insightful overviews that help researchers connect and understand the impact and influence events, people, trends, and scientific advances had on shaping the decade.

The fairly sophisticated text is presented in a three-column format. The nearly 300 entries range from straightforward biographies to historical case studies to survey articles on artistic and socioeconomic movements. Expected topics appear (*Harlem Renaissance, Prohibition*), as do topics often more difficult to research from the perspective of a particular era (*Astronomy, Civil engineering, Highway network, Opera*). Articles have been written by a team of editors and are complemented by numerous illustrations (period posters, vintage photographs, political cartoons, magazine covers, etc.) accompanied by detailed captions sufficient to satisfy the curiosity of browsers. Boxed inserts, charts, and graphs help summarize data. Numerous cross-references direct researchers to related articles. The article *Real estate,* to take one example, incorporates an ad for a 1928 Sears and Roebuck kit house, an insert on the innovative Better Homes in America mortgage company, a political cartoon on the Florida land boom, and cross-references to entries on *Credit, Florida land boom, Housing, Skyscrapers,* and *Suburbs and suburbanization,* among others.

There are several entries on media (*Movie industry, National Broadcasting Company, News and current affairs*); literature (*Newbery Award and children's literature, Pulp magazines, Science fiction*); and the arts (*Chrysler Building, Modernism, Painting*). These are in addition to numerous biographical entries on luminaries from every field—athletes, entrepreneurs, politicians, newsmakers, and so on. Time lines, a detailed set index, and a bibliography of books (adult level, primarily academic-press titles) and Web sites are included in each volume.

Surface information and definitions for many of these subjects can be accessed readily through Internet search engines and standard encyclopedias. However, this set's appeal lies in its comprehensiveness and thoroughness. Aimed at student researchers but sure to attract browsers, this engaging set is recommended for high-school, community college, and public library collections. —*Kathleen McBroom*

Encyclopedia of New Jersey. Ed. by Maxine N. Lurie and Marc Mappen. 2004. 927p. bibliogs. illus. maps. Rutgers, $49.95 (0-8135-3325-2). 974.9.

Few entities have endured a negative reputation to the extent that the state of New Jersey has. Because of its association with toxic waste and organized crime, many neglect to give the state the regard that its early and recent history and accomplishments would warrant. Mappen, a former vice chairman of the Task Force on New Jersey History and executive director of the New Jersey Historical Commission, was inspired by the *Encyclopedia of New York City* (Yale Univ., 1995) to produce a similar work that would define and illuminate what New Jersey is. His coeditor, Lurie, is chair of the history department of Seton Hall University.

In size and appearance, this volume closely resembles the *Encyclopedia of New York City.* According to the preface, it contains 2,900 entries written by more than 600 authors. Biographies of the contributors are given at the end of the volume. Among the areas covered are architecture, folklore, geography, literature, and transportation. The length and depth of the entries varies from a short paragraph to two-plus pages. All are signed, and many contain bibliographies, though much of the cited material would be difficult to obtain outside of the area. Although some of this information is likely to be duplicated in sources specific to single disciplines, there is nothing else that offers the expansive coverage of this state. Information on small geographic areas and minor political and historical figures might not easily be found anywhere else. The black-and-white illustrations enhance the text, as does the midvolume section of colored plates.

The front matter begins with a list of donors who helped defray the cost of production and development, leaving this sizable volume with a bargain price. Certainly all New Jersey libraries would need to buy this work, as should most libraries in the Northeast. Academic and large public libraries everywhere should find it useful. —*Danise Hoover*

★**The Encyclopedia of Chicago.** Ed. by James R. Grossman and others. 2004. 1,117p. illus. index. Univ. of Chicago, $65 (0-226-31015-9). 977.3.

Developed over the last 10 years by the Newberry Library with the cooperation of the Chicago Historical Society, the monumental *Encyclopedia of Chicago* will be the definitive historical reference source on Chicago for years to come. Funding from the National Endowment for the Humanities, the John D. and Catherine T. MacArthur Foundation, the City of Chicago, the state of Illinois, and three major Chicago corporations helped ensure a very reasonable price. Some 633 experts from across the U.S. wrote the more than 1,400 entries. The encyclopedia is enhanced with numerous photos, engravings, and maps.

Entries treat such topics as *Acting, ensemble; Agrarian movements; Annexation; Chicago Symphony Orchestra; Literary images of Chicago; Machine politics;* and much, much more. Besides encompassing Chicago history, ethnic groups, businesses, cultural institutions, sports, crime, architecture, religions, and other topics, the editors wanted to have the broadest geographic coverage. In addition to the 77 recognized Chicago neighborhoods, 298 suburban municipalities in the six surrounding counties in northern Illinois and two in northern Indiana are covered. Biographical entries of prominent Chicagoans are not included since these would duplicate information in such readily available sources as the *American National Biography* (Oxford, 1999) and *Woman Building Chicago, 1790–1990* (Indiana Univ., 2001). Instead there is a "Biographical Dictionary" at the end of the book that lists 2,000 deceased Chicagoans with short entries noting birth, death, and occupation. There is also a separate "Dictionary of Leading Chicago Businesses, 1820–2000" that offers brief historical summaries for 236 for-profit companies. Important companies are also discussed in entries on significant industry sectors such as *Clothing and garment manufacturing, Department stores, Iron and steel,* and *Transportation.* These entries are very detailed and give a complete history of each industry and its place in Chicago.

The encyclopedia is set up in an *A–Z* format with three types of entries—broad essays of 1,000 to 4,000 words, midlevel entries of 200 to 1,000 words, and basic entries of 200 words. The broad essays give an overview and synthesize scholarship on a subject, while the basic entries focus on a specific event or institution and give brief information to identify what it is and why it is important. The midlevel entries are meant to fill in the gaps left by the broad essays and give more analysis than is found in the basic entries. All entries are signed and cross-referenced and list a bibliography of related books and articles for further reading. The work also features 21 long interpretative essays that reflect recent scholarship in urban history (for example, *Racism, ethnicity, and white identity; Street life*); numerous sidebars that offer varying viewpoints on different topics; a time line of Chicago history; a list of Chicago mayors; historical population statistics for all municipalities; several inserts with color photos and maps; and a comprehensive 60-page index. Fifty-six maps cover topics such as blues clubs in Chicago, Chicago's Deep Tunnel system, Indian settlement patterns in 1830, street railways in 1890, and movie theaters in Chicago in 1926, 1937, and 2002. A notable feature of the volume is the 400 thumbnail maps that show where each municipality and neighborhood is located in the Chicagoland region.

The scope of entries and their readability make the encyclopedia outstanding. All ideas, facts, people, and places are explained fully and in terms high-school and general readers can understand. This is a superb ready-reference work on Chicago, a good starting point for students doing research, and just a wonderful book to browse through. There is no other source that contains the breadth and depth of information found here. *The Encyclopedia of Chicago* is a must purchase for every academic, public, and school library in Illinois. Academic and large public libraries across the U.S. will want it as well. —*Merle Jacob*

Encyclopedia of the Great Plains. Ed. by David J. Wishart. 2004. 940p. illus. index. Univ. of Nebraska, $75 (0-8032-4787-7). 978.

Here is a unique reference book with a lot to offer for relatively little money. Its goal is "to give definition to a region that has traditionally been poorly defined." The area of the Great Plains is delineated more by characteristics such as climate and topography than by political boundaries and encompasses all or parts of Texas, New Mexico, Oklahoma, Kansas, Colorado, Nebraska, Wyoming, South Dakota, North Dakota, Montana, Alberta, Sasketchewan, and Manitoba.

The volume is composed of 27 major topic sections, including "African Americans," "Agriculture," "Architecture," "Education," "Film," "Industry," "Transportation," and "War." Each section begins with an interpretive essay and a synthesis of the topic, followed by 20 to 60 alphabetically arranged entries. For example, "Media" has entries on *Brokaw, Tom; Denver Post; Immigrant newspapers; Radio;* and *Telegraph,* to name a few. The entries include extensive cross-referencing plus a multitude of black-and-white illustrations and maps. All entries are signed by their contributors, and most contain a reference or two for further information.

The overarching topical arrangement makes good indexing essential. Readers looking for information on individual Great Plains states, for example, will need to turn to the index to find that there are brief state entries in the "Politics and Government" section. Fortunately, the indexing is detailed enough to pull together content from across the encyclopedia.

This volume is valuable for a wide variety of user groups, including high-school students, undergraduates, and researchers. It is highly recommended for most libraries in the heartland as well as for all academic and large public libraries. —*Diana Shonrock*

Greenwood Encyclopedia of American Regional Cultures. 8v. 2004. 3,200p. illus. index. Greenwood, $699.95 (0-313-33266-5). 979.

The most recent presidential election showed clearly that the U.S. is very different from one region to the next. These differences have never been thoroughly explored from a cultural point of view. Certainly there is coverage of individual states and regions, but this multivolume work is the first to offer the uniform coverage of the entire U.S. It divides the country into eight regions: the Great Plains, the mid-Atlantic, the Midwest, New England, the Pacific, the Rocky Mountains, the South, and the Southwest. The work, though called an encyclopedia, has volumes that stand alone, each with its own editor or editors, each with its own call number. Arrangement is the same in each volume, however, with uniform sections that deal with cultural topics such as "Architecture," "Art," "Ethnicity," "Food," "Religion," and more. Each of the chapters offers coverage that begins with the Native Americans who inhabited the area before colonization, so the discussion of architecture is likely to begin with native "earthworks" rather than a discussion of buildings.

Each of the sections has an extensive "Resource Guide" that may include a list of organizations, museums, and special collections as well as print resources and Web sites. Sidebars and highlighted pages emphasize some information, such as biographical profiles. Photographs and other illustrations enhance the text. There is, however, a remarkable lack of maps for a reference work with a focus such as this; the only maps are small locator maps repeated at the head of each section. Each volume concludes with a time line, a bibliography, and an index.

The scholarly tone of this encyclopedia makes it appropriate for academic and large public libraries. Since it was designed in coordination with the National Standards for United States History and the Curriculum Standards for Social Studies, it can be assumed that the publisher has intended this for the high-school market as well. These volumes are both informative and entertaining, useful to the researcher and the pleasure reader as well. —*Danise Hoover*

Historic Documents Series: Online Edition. [Internet database]. 2005. CQ, pricing starting at $150 [http://www.cqpress.com]. (Last accessed May 2, 2005).

Historic Documents Series: Online Edition will be familiar to users and librarians in two ways. First, it uses the same interface as the *CQ Electronic Library*, and second, it is identical in content to the 32-volume print Historic Documents series.

The search engine is fairly simple. The basic search searches the full text. Advanced search allows the user to select which segment of the database to search and whether to search the full text or titles only; it also offers a way to specify the date of the document or the event that the document describes. There is no obvious way to navigate back to the basic search page from the advanced search page, though using the browser's back button works fine. It is possible to browse by topic or by title or view and search the entire cumulative index from the basic screen. Phrase searching is enabled by binding the phrase with quotation marks, and the page suggests Boolean operators are the way to build a strategy. If one is more adventurous (*Medicaid w/10 abortion*), the strategy works just fine, though there is nothing in the limited documentation that might lead a user to try this search grammar.

The results of the search are displayed in order by the number of times the search terms appear in the document, though it is fairly easy to resort the documents either by date or alphabetically by title by clicking on arrows on the top of the list.

Currently the database contains documents for the years 1972–2003. Other years will be added as they become available. There is no content added to the electronic version beyond what is in the print series. The documents themselves come from a wide range of sources within government publications and are selected by the series' editorial board each year. Whether or not the documents selected will be the most important to future researchers is yet to be determined, but the attempt is to cover the major topics of the year. Each document is preceded by an introduction in italics that puts the document in its context. The different typeface of the introduction is not as obvious on the screen as it is in print, but it is an important feature nonetheless. A major asset of this series is the Citenow feature, which provides the proper citation in a variety of formats with a click.

There is nothing fancy here, not a lot of bells and whistles, but if the print series is an important feature of your collection, it is likely that the electronic version will be worth the cost. The search capability and the potential for remote access should be enhancement enough. —*Danise Hoover*

History Reference Center. [Online database]. EBSCO, pricing from $595. (Last accessed December 22, 2004).

When one thinks EBSCO, one often thinks periodicals. But books make up the largest source type in EBSCO's *History Reference Center* (HRC), with 650 titles. Although HRC includes encyclopedias, such as the *Encyclopedia of North American Indians* (Houghton Mifflin, 1996–), most of the books are titles usually found in the circulating section of libraries, such as *Ellis Island* (Compass Point Books, 2003) and *Sudan* (Chelsea House, 2002). Publications from Cambridge University Press, Oxford University Press, and Salem Press are included, but EBSCO defines the HRC audience as primarily secondary schools, and young adult publishers make up a big chunk of the title list.

The database also contains 58,000 primary documents (including 55,000 documents from *American Reference Library* [Western Standard, 2003–]); 12,000 photos and maps; and full text from 57 periodicals (e.g., *American Heritage, Cobblestone*). EBSCO plans to add almost 100 hours of historical audio and video material, although this content was not available at the time of our review.

The familiar EBSCOhost search interface provides users with Basic and Advanced search screens. Search techniques including Boolean operators, proximity, and wildcard/truncation are available but might be too advanced for younger students. HRC includes common search limiters and expanders, such as publication date, and search within full text as well as some unique search limits—Lexile Reading Level and Timeline (for example, World History—Unrest & Revolution [1750–1850]). Users can also browse Subjects, Publications, or Images. Database administrators can tailor search screens to best serve their user population.

A Basic Search on *Stalingrad* found 31 items, including 4 documents (for example, Roosevelt's note of congratulations to Stalin on the Stalingrad victory) as well as 9 reference-book articles and 18 periodical articles. In addition, there were two images—apparently images are not counted in the total results amount. Sort choices for results include Date, Relevancy, and Source. Tabs at the top of the results list enable users to browse items by source type (e.g., Periodicals). The majority of information is full text. Results can include color PDFs as well as text in HTML. Many entries from young adult books include text with illustration captions but no illustrations. Results can be saved to a folder for printing and e-mailing.

One-year unlimited usage with remote access costs $595 for middle schools and $795 for high schools. Pricing for academic and public libraries is based on FTE or population served.

Because so much of the content comes from young adult publishers, *History Reference Center* supports high-school users, more so than such products as Gale's *History Resource Center: U.S.* and Facts on File's suite of history databases, such as *American History Online* [RBB Je 1 & 15 04]. Suitable for school and public libraries. —*Stephen Fadel*

Subject Index

AFRICA
Encyclopedia of African History. 84

AFRICAN AMERICANS
African American Dramatists. 71
Encyclopedia of Black Studies. 88
On the Trail of the Buffalo Soldier 2: New and Revised Biographies of African Americans in the U.S. Army, 1866-1917. 41

ALTERNATIVE MEDICINE
Gale Encyclopedia of Alternative Medicine. 57

ANATOMY
Encyclopedia of the Digestive System and Digestive Disorders. 54
Encyclopedia of the Heart and Heart Disease. 56
Encyclopedia of the Muscle and Skeletal Systems and Disorders. 58
Human Body Systems. 53

ANIMALS
Encyclopedia of Animal Behavior. 52
Encyclopedia of Animals: A Complete Visual Guide. 52
Encyclopedia of Aquarium & Pond Fish. 60
Encyclopedia of Cryptozoology: A Global Guide to Hidden Animals and Their Pursuers. 24
Grzimek's Student Animal Life Resource: Birds. 52
Grzimek's Student Animal Life Resource: Mammals. 52
Kingfisher Illustrated Horse & Pony Encyclopedia. 60
World of Animals: Insects and Other Invertebrates. 52

ARCHITECTURE
Understanding Architecture. 63
Outstanding Art and Architecture Online (Web). 15
Renaissance Art and Architecture. 63

ARCTIC
Encyclopedia of the Arctic. 74

ART
Another Look at . . . Grove Art Online. 7
Arts and Humanities through the Eras. 62
Atlas of World Art. 62
Dictionary of Modern Design. 64
Outstanding Art and Architecture Online (Web). 15
Oxford Dictionary of Art. 63
Queer Encyclopedia of the Visual Arts. 63
Renaissance Art and Architecture. 63
Woodstock: An Encyclopedia of the Music and Art Fair. 65

ASIA
Encyclopedia of Ancient Asian Civilizations. 84
Encyclopedia of Mongolia and the Mongol Empire. 83
Peoples of Eastern Asia. 83
South Asian Literature in English: An Encyclopedia. 72
Southeast Asia: A Historical Encyclopedia from Angkor Wat to East Timor. 84

ASIAN AMERICANS
Asian Databook. 33

ASTRONOMY
A to Z of Scientists in Space and Astronomy. 50
Firefly Encyclopedia of Astronomy. 50

ATLASES
Atlas and Dictionary Update, 2005. 15
Atlas of North America. 75
Hammond World Travel Atlas. 75
Illustrated World Atlas. 76
National Geographic Atlas of the World. 76

BASEBALL
Diamonds around the Globe: The Encyclopedia of International Baseball. 67
Total Baseball: The Ultimate Baseball Encyclopedia. 68

BIOGRAPHY, GENERAL
UXL Newsmakers. 77
Oxford Dictionary of National Biography. 12
Riverside Dictionary of Biography. 77

BIOLOGY
Biology Matters! 49

BUSINESS
Encyclopedia of American Women in Business: From Colonial Times to the Present. 39
Industry Research Using the Economic Census: How to Find It, How to Use It. 39
International Directory of Business Biographies. 39

CANADA
Junior Worldmark Encyclopedia of the Canadian Provinces. 85
Oxford Companion to Canadian History. 85

CAPITALISM
Encyclopedia of Capitalism. 38

CARS
American Cars, 1960-1972: Every Model Year by Year. 59

CATHOLICISM
Catholic Schools in the United States: An Encyclopedia. 44
Encyclopedia of Catholic Literature. 68

CHEMISTRY
Chemistry: Foundations and Applications. 51

CHICAGO
Encyclopedia of Chicago. 90
Encyclopedia of the Chicago Literary Renaissance. 70

CHINA
Discovering World Cultures: The Middle East. 35

CIVIL WAR
Atlas of the Civil War. 86
Historical Dictionary of the Civil War and Reconstruction. 89

CLOTHING
Encyclopedia of Clothing and Fashion. 46

COMICS
DC Comics Encyclopedia: The Definitive Guide to the Characters of the DC Universe. 63

COMPOSERS
Dictionary of American Classical Composers. 64

COMPUTER SCIENCE
Berkshire Encyclopedia of Human Computer Interaction. 24

COUNTIES
American Counties: Origins of County Names, Dates of Creation, and Population Data, 1950-2000. 76

COUNTRIES
Discover America. 87
Junior Worldmark Encyclopedia of the Nations. 73

CRIME
American Dictionary of Criminal Justice: Key Terms and Major Court Cases. 43
Crime and Punishment in America Reference Library. 43
Encyclopedia of Criminology. 44
Encyclopedia of Prisons & Correctional Facilities. 44
Encyclopedia of White-Collar and Corporate Crime. 44

CUBA
Encyclopedia of Cuban-United States Relations. 37

CULTURE
Discovering World Cultures: The Middle East. 35
Antebellum Period. 35
Encyclopedia of Contemporary Chinese Culture. 35
Encyclopedia of Latino Popular Culture. 33
Encyclopedia of Modern Jewish Culture. 73
Gilded Age. 35
Greenwood Daily Life Online. 13
Pop Culture Latin America! Media, Arts, and Lifestyle. 35
The Greenwood Encyclopedia of Daily Life. 13

DATABASES
Ancestry Library Edition. 78
Another Look at . . . Grove Art Online. 7
ConsumerLab.com. 54
CQ Voting and Elections Collection. 38
Early American Imprints, 1639-1800. 25
Encyclopedia Americana Online. 3
Encyclopedia Britannica Online. 2
Encyclopedia Britannica Online School Edition. 2
Greenwood Encyclopedia of Daily Life. 13
Grolier Multimedia Encyclopedia. 3
Grolier Online. 3
Historic Documents Series: Online Edition. 91
History Reference Center. 91
Kids InfoBits. 27
La nueva encyclopedia cumbre. 27
New Book of Knowledge Online. 3
Oxford Digital Reference Shelf. 28
Science Full Text Select. 53
Science Resource Center. 53
World Book Online Reference Center. 4
World History: Ancient and Medieval Eras. 78

DEATH
Encyclopedia of Death and Dying. 35

DECADES
Day by Day: The Nineties. 79
U.S.A. Twenties. 89

DICTIONARIES
Atlas and Dictionary Update, 2005. 15
Cambridge Guide to English Usage. 48
Canadian Oxford Dictionary. 47
Descriptionary. 48
Firefly Five Language Visual Dictionary. 47
Hatchet Jobs and Hardball: The Oxford Dictionary of American Political Slang. 48
Oxford American Writer's Thesaurus. 48
Oxford Rhyming Dictionary. 48

DISEASE
Encyclopedia of Breast Cancer. 57
Encyclopedia of Cancer. 54
Encyclopedia of Endocrine Diseases and Disorders. 58
Encyclopedia of Men's Reproductive Cancer. 54
Encyclopedia of Sexually Transmitted Diseases. 58
Encyclopedia of the Digestive System and Digestive Disorders. 54
Encyclopedia of the Heart and Heart Disease. 56
Encyclopedia of Women's Reproductive Cancer. 54
Enfermedades y trastornos de la salud. 54
Gale Encyclopedia of Neurological Disorders. 58

DOCUMENTS
Annals of America. 86
Encyclopedia of American Historical Documents. 87
Historic Documents Series: Online Edition. 91

DRAMA
Notable Playwrights. 70

EARTH SCIENCE
UXL Encyclopedia of Water Science. 51
Encyclopedia of Earth Science. 51
Student's Guide to Earth Science. 51

EASTERN EUROPE
Eastern Europe: An Introduction to the People, Lands, and Culture. 81

ECONOMICS
Encyclopedia of World Trade: From Ancient Times to the Present. 45
Value of a Dollar: Prices and Incomes in the United States, 1860-2004. 39

EDUCATION
Catholic Schools in the United States: An Encyclopedia. 44

ELECTIONS
CQ Voting and Elections Collection. 38
Countdown to November (Web). 14
Reference Sources on the Presidency and Presidential Elections. 20

ENCYCLOPEDIAS
Compton's Encyclopedia and Fact-Finder. 1
Encyclopedia Americana. 1
Encyclopedia Americana Online. 3
Encyclopedia Britannica Online. 2
Encyclopedia Britannica Online School

Edition. 2
Grolier Multimedia Encyclopedia. 3
Grolier Online. 3
Kingfisher Children's Encyclopedia. 27
New Book of Knowledge. 2
New Book of Knowledge Online. 3
Scholastic Children's Encyclopedia. 27
World Book Encyclopedia. 2
World Book Online Reference Center. 4

ENVIRONMENT
Teen Guides to Environmental Science. 38

ESPIONAGE
Encyclopedia of Cold War Espionage, Spies, and Secret Operations. 37
Encyclopedia of Intelligence and Counterintelligence. 37

EVALUATION
Encyclopedia of Evaluation. 24

EXPLORATION
Explorers and Exploration. 74
Encyclopedia of Exploration. 74
Read-alikes: Exploring Exploration. 18

EXTREMISTS
Encyclopedia of Modern Worldwide Extremists and Extremist Groups. 36

FESTIVALS
Encyclopedia of Religious Rites, Rituals, and Festivals. 30
Holidays, Festivals, and Celebrations of the World. 46

FILM
American Frontiersmen on Film and Television. 65
American Plays and Musicals on Screen: 650 Stage Productions and Their Film and Television Adaptations. 65
Encyclopedia of Early Cinema. 66
Encyclopedia of Hollywood. 66
Encyclopedia of Novels into Film. 66
Encyclopedia of Opera on Screen: A Guide to More Than 100 Years of Opera Films. 66
Holocaust Film Sourcebook. 25
John Wayne Filmography. 66
Movieland Directory: Nearly 30,000 Addresses of Celebrity Homes, Film Locations, and Historical Sites in the Los Angeles Area, 1900-Present. 46

FOOD
Encyclopedia of Kitchen History. 61
Oxford Encyclopedia of Food and Drink in America. 60

FRANCE
Placenames of France: Over 4,000 Towns, Villages, Natural Features, Regions, and Departments. 76
France: A Reference Guide from the Renaissance to the Present. 82

GAZETTEERS
Historical Gazetteer of the United States. 75

GENEALOGY
Ancestors in German Archives: A Guide to Family History Sources. 26
Ancestry Library Edition. 78
Avotaynu Guide to Jewish Genealogy. 77
Family Tree Resource Book for Genealogists: The Essential Guide to American County and Town Sources. 77
Some Key Reference Works for Genealogists. 21

GENETICS
Encyclopedia of Genetics. 51

GENOCIDE
Encyclopedia of Genocide and Crimes Against Humanity. 33

GOTHIC STUDIES
Encyclopedia of Gothic Literature. 68
Guide to the Gothic III: An Annotated Bibliography of Criticism, 1993-2000. 25

GOVERNMENT AND POLITICS
American Statesmen: Secretaries of State from John Jay to Colin Powell. 37
Encyclopedia of Civil Liberties in America. 36
Encyclopedia of Cuban-United States Relations. 37
Encyclopedia of Federal Agencies and Commissions. 40
International Government Information and Country Information: A Subject Guide. 26
Local and Regional Government Information: How to Find It, How to Use It. 24

HARLEM RENAISSANCE
America's Top Doctors. 55

HEALTH
Baby and Child Health. 59
Encyclopedia of Children's Health and Wellness. 59
Encyclopedia of Family Health. 55
Encyclopedia of Health and Behavior. 56
Encyclopedia of Men's Health. 56
Encyclopedia of Sports Medicine. 59
Encyclopedia of the Harlem Renaissance. 62
Magill's Medical Guide. 56
Merck Manual of Health and Aging. 57
New Harvard Guide to Women's Health. 58

HISPANIC AMERICANS
Encyclopedia of Latino Popular Culture. 33

HISTORY
Reference Sources in History: An Introductory Guide. 26

HISTORY, AMERICAN
Atlas of the Civil War. 86
Birth of the Bill of Rights: Encyclopedia of the Antifederalists. 86
Debatable Issues in U.S. History. 87
Frontier America. 88
Uniting States: The Story of Statehood for the Fifty United States. 36

HISTORY, ANCIENT
Encyclopedia of Ancient Asian Civilizations. 84
Great Events from History: The Ancient World, Prehistory-476 C.E. 80
Great Lives from History: The Ancient World, Prehistory-476 C.E. 80

HISTORY, WORLD
World History: Ancient and Medieval Eras. 78
Berkshire Encyclopedia of World History. 79
Encyclopedia of the Enlightenment. 80
Kingfisher History Encyclopedia. 80
New Dictionary of the History of Ideas. 78

IMMIGRATION
U.S. Immigration and Migration Reference Library. 33

IRELAND
Encyclopedia of Irish History and Culture. 82

ISLAM
Islamic World: Past and Present. 74

ITALY
Italy: A Reference Guide from the Renaissance to the Present. 82

JAZZ
Free Jazz and Free Improvisation. 64
Satchmo: The Louis Armstrong Encyclopedia. 64

JEWS AND JUDAISM
Avotaynu Guide to Jewish Genealogy. 77

JUDAISM
Encyclopedia of Modern Jewish Culture. 73
JPS Guide to Jewish Traditions. 31
Student's Encyclopedia of Judaism. 31

LATIN AMERICA
Pop Culture Latin America! Media, Arts, and Lifestyle. 35
Latin American Mystery Writers: An A-to-Z Guide. 73
Latin American Science Fiction Writers: An A-to-Z Guide. 73
Literary Cultures of Latin America: A Comparative History. 72

LAW
Encyclopedia of Law Enforcement. 43
Landmark Supreme Court Cases: The Most Influential Decisions of the Supreme Court of the United States. 40
U.S. Legal System. 40
West's Encyclopedia of American Law. 40

LEADERSHIP
Encyclopedia of Leadership. 61

LIBRARIES
Encyclopedia of the Library of Congress: For Congress, the Nation, & the World. 26

LINGUISTICS
Encyclopedia of Linguistics. 47

LITERATURE
Arthurian Annals: The Tradition in English from 1250-2000. 24
Encyclopedia of Post-Colonial Literatures in English. 72
Encyclopedia of the Chicago Literary Renaissance. 70
Literary Cultures of Latin America: A Comparative History. 72
Masterplots 2: Short Story Series. 69

LITERATURE, CHILDREN'S
Ninth Book of Junior Authors and Illustrators. 69
Popular Series Fiction for Middle School and Teen Readers: A Reading and Selection Guide. 26

LITERATURE, YA
Popular Series Fiction for Middle School and Teen Readers: A Reading and Selection Guide. 26
Dictionary of American Young Adult Fiction, 1997-2001. 71
Encyclopedia of Young Adult Authors. 70

LONDON
London: A Historical Companion. 82

MATHEMATICS
A to Z of Mathematicians. 50
Universal Book of Mathematics: From Abracadabra to Zeno's Paradoxes. 50

MEXICO
Junior Worldmark Encyclopedia of the Mexican States. 85

Mexico: An Encyclopedia of Contemporary Culture and History. 85

MIDDLE AGES
Crusades Reference Library. 79
Encyclopedia of the Byzantine Empire. 83
Encyclopedia of the Medieval World. 81
Great Events from History: The Middle Ages. 80
Great Lives from History: The Middle Ages. 80
Women in the Middle Ages: An Encyclopedia. 34
World History: Ancient and Medieval Eras. 78

MIDDLE EAST
Dictionary of the Israeli-Palestinian Conflict: Culture, History, and Politics. 83
Historical Dictionary of Iraq. 84
Historical Dictionary of Syria. 89

MINORITIES
Encyclopedia of the World's Minorities. 34

MUSIC
Facts On File Dictionary of Music. 64
Queer Encyclopedia of Music, Dance, & Musical Theater. 67
Woodstock: An Encyclopedia of the Music and Art Fair. 65

MUSICIANS
Extraordinary People in Jazz. 70

MYTHOLOGY
African Mythology A to Z. 31
Celtic Mythology A to Z. 31
Dictionary of Gods and Goddesses. 30
Gods, Goddesses, and Mythology. 30
Handbook of Classical Mythology. 31
Handbook of Inca Mythology. 32
Native American Mythology A to Z. 31
South and Meso-American Mythology A to Z. 31

NATIVE AMERICANS
Encyclopedia of Native American Wars & Warfare. 88

NICKNAMES
Oxford Dictionary of Nicknames. 78

NUTRITION
ConsumerLab.com. 54
Encyclopedia of Vitamins, Minerals, and Supplements. 56
Nutrition and Well-Being A to Z. 57

PARKS
Encyclopedia of American National Parks. 88

PHILANTHROPY
Philanthropy in America: A Comprehensive Historical Encyclopedia. 42

PHILOSOPHY
Ethics. 29
Oxford Companion to the Mind. 28

PHYSICS
Encyclopedia of Physics. 50

PLACENAMES
Native American Placenames of the United States. 77
Placenames of France: Over 4,000 Towns, Villages, Natural Features, Regions, and Departments. 76

POETRY
Facts On File Companion to 20th-Century

American Poetry. 71

PRESIDENTS
Clinton Years. 86
Education of the Presidents of the United States. 87
Encyclopedia of the American Presidency. 88
Kennedy Years. 86

PROVERBS
Oxford Dictionary of Proverbs. 47

PSYCHOLOGY
Popular Psychology: An Encyclopedia. 29
Psychology Basics. 29

PUBLIC RELATIONS
Encyclopedia of Public Relations. 61

QUOTATIONS
Oxford Dictionary of Quotations. 28

RECONSTRUCTION
Historical Dictionary of the Civil War and Reconstruction. 89
Reconstruction Era Reference Library. 89

RECREATION
Encyclopedia of Recreation and Leisure in America. 65

REGIONS, U.S.
Encyclopedia of the Great Plains. 90
Greenwood Encyclopedia of American Regional Cultures. 90

RELIGION
Encyclopedia of Religious Rites, Rituals, and Festivals. 30
Encyclopedia of Christian Theology. 31
Holy People of the World. 29
Shamanism: An Encyclopedia of World Beliefs, Practices, and Culture. 30

RUSSIA
e.encyclopedia science. 49

SCIENCE
Russia: A Reference Guide from the Renaissance to the Present. 83
Science Full Text Select. 53
Science Resource Center. 53
Science, Technology, and Society. 36
World Book's Science & Nature Guides. 49

SCIENCE FICTION
Latin American Science Fiction Writers: An A-to-Z Guide. 73
Historical Dictionary of Science Fiction Literature. 69

SCIENCE HISTORY
Science in the Ancient World: An Encyclopedia. 49
Science in the Contemporary World: An Encyclopedia. 49
Science in the Early Twentieth Century: An Encyclopedia. 49

SCIENTISTS
A to Z of Mathematicians. 50
A to Z of Scientists in Space and Astronomy. 50

SCOTLAND
Illustrated Encyclopedia of Scotland. 82

SHAMANISM
Shamanism: An Encyclopedia of World Beliefs, Practices, and Culture. 30

SOCIAL ISSUES
Affirmative Action: An Encyclopedia. 38
Encyclopedia of American Social Movements. 32
Encyclopedia of Homelessness. 42
Encyclopedia of Rape. 43
Encyclopedia of Social Theory. 32
Encyclopedia of Social Welfare History in North America. 42
Exploring Gun Use in America. 43
Poverty in the United States: An Encyclopedia of History, Politics, and Policy. 40
Public Opinion and Polling around the World: A Historical Encyclopedia. 32

SPACE
Frontiers of Space Exploration. 60
National Geographic Encyclopedia of Space. 60
Space Exploration Reference Library. 60

SPANISH LANGUAGE
Enfermedades y trastornos de la salud. 54
La nueva enciclopedia cumbre. 27
Reference Books in Spanish for Children and Adolescents. 19

SPORTS
Encyclopedia of Sports Medicine. 59
Sport in American Culture: From Ali to X-Games. 36
Sports in America: Decade by Decade. 67
Sports Market Place Directory, 2004. 45

STATES
Encyclopedia of New Jersey. 90
Junior Worldmark Encyclopedia of the States. 89
State and National Boundaries of the United States. 75
Uniting States: The Story of Statehood for the Fifty United States. 36

TECHNOLOGY
Science, Technology, and Society. 36
Encyclopedia of Military Technology and Innovation. 59
Encyclopedia of Recorded Sound. 45
Encyclopedia of Twentieth Century Technology. 55

TELEVISION
Alone Together (Web). 14
American Frontiersmen on Film and Television. 65
Encyclopedia of Television. 45

TERRORISM
Terrorism: A Guide to Events and Documents. 32

THEATER
Queer Encyclopedia of Music, Dance, & Musical Theater. 67
Oxford Companion to American Theater. 67

TOBACCO
Tobacco in History and Culture: An Encyclopedia. 46

WAR
Encyclopedia of Native American Wars & Warfare. 88
Americans at War: Society, Culture, and the Homefront. 85
Empires at War: A Chronological Encyclopedia from Sumer to the Persian Empire. 41
Encyclopedia of Wars. 41
Encyclopedia of World War II: A Political, Social, and Military History. 81
History of World War II. 81
Victorians at War, 1815-1914. 41
Weapons of Mass Destruction: An Encyclopedia of Worldwide Policy, Technology, and History. 42

WOMEN'S STUDIES
Encyclopedia of American Women in Business: From Colonial Times to the Present. 39
Encyclopedia of Feminist Literature. 68
Feminism in Literature. 68
Women in Early America: Struggle, Survival, and Freedom in a New World. 34
Women in the Middle Ages: An Encyclopedia. 34
Working Americans, 1880-2005: Volume 6, Women at Work. 34

WOOD
Encyclopedia of Wood: A Tree-by-Tree Guide to the World's Most Versatile Resource. 61

WRITERS
African American Dramatists. 71
American Writers. 70
Dostoevsky Encyclopedia. 73
Encyclopedia of British Writers: 16th, 17th, and 18th Centuries. 71
Encyclopedia of Young Adult Authors. 70
Everyone and Everything in Trollope. 72
Extraordinary American Writers. 70
Latin American Mystery Writers: An A-to-Z Guide. 73
Latin American Science Fiction Writers: An A-to-Z Guide. 73
Multicultural Writers since 1945: An A-to-Z Guide. 69
Ninth Book of Junior Authors and Illustrators. 69
Notable Playwrights. 70
Oxford Companion to the Brontes. 72

YOUTH REFERENCE
Biology Matters! 49
Children's Reference Sources. 16
Crime and Punishment in America Reference Library. 43
Crusades Reference Library. 79
Debatable Issues in U.S. History. 87
Discover America. 87
e.encyclopedia science. 49
Encyclopedia of Young Adult Authors. 70
Explorers and Exploration. 74
Exploring Gun Use in America. 43
Extraordinary People in Jazz. 70
Frontier America. 88
Grzimek's Student Animal Life Resource: Birds. 52
Grzimek's Student Animal Life Resource: Mammals. 52
Junior Worldmark Encyclopedia of the Canadian Provinces. 85
Junior Worldmark Encyclopedia of the Mexican States. 85
Junior Worldmark Encyclopedia of the Nations. 73
Junior Worldmark Encyclopedia of the States. 89
Kids InfoBits. 27
Kingfisher Children's Encyclopedia. 27
Kingfisher History Encyclopedia. 80
Kingfisher Illustrated Horse & Pony Encyclopedia. 60
My First Britannica. 28
Ninth Book of Junior Authors and Illustrators. 69
Peoples of Eastern Asia. 83
Reconstruction Era Reference Library. 89
Reference Books in Spanish for Children and Adolescents. 19
Scholastic Children's Encyclopedia. 27
Science Resource Center. 53
Space Exploration Reference Library. 60
Student's Guide to Earth Science. 51
Teen Guides to Environmental Science. 38
Twenty Best Bets for Student Researchers. 22
UXL Encyclopedia of Water Science. 51
UXL Newsmakers. 77
World Book's Science & Nature Guides. 49
World of Animals: Insects and Other Invertebrates. 52

Title Index

A to Z of Mathematicians. 50
A to Z of Scientists in Space and Astronomy. 50
Affirmative Action: An Encyclopedia. 38
African American Dramatists. 71
African Mythology A to Z. 31
Alone Together (Web). 14
American Cars, 1960-1972: Every Model Year by Year. 59
American Counties: Origins of County Names, Dates of Creation, and Population Data, 1950-2000. 76
American Dictionary of Criminal Justice: Key Terms and Major Court Cases. 43
American Frontiersmen on Film and Television. 65
American Plays and Musicals on Screen: 650 Stage Productions and Their Film and Television Adaptations. 65
American Statesmen: Secretaries of State from John Jay to Colin Powell. 37
American Writers. 70
Americans at War: Society, Culture, and the Homefront. 85
America's Top Doctors. 55
Ancestors in German Archives: A Guide to Family History Sources. 26
Ancestry Library Edition. 78
Annals of America. 86
Another Look at . . . Annals of America. 6
Another Look at . . . Grove Art Online. 7
Antebellum Period. 35
Arthurian Annals: The Tradition in English from 1250-2000. 24
Arts and Humanities through the Eras. 62
Asian Databook. 33
Atlas and Dictionary Update, 2005. 15
Atlas of North America. 75
Atlas of the Civil War. 86
Atlas of World Art. 62
Avotaynu Guide to Jewish Genealogy. 77

Baby and Child Health. 59
Berkshire Encyclopedia of Human Computer Interaction. 24
Berkshire Encyclopedia of World History. 79
Biology Matters! 49
Birth of the Bill of Rights: Encyclopedia of the Antifederalists. 86

Cambridge Guide to English Usage. 48
Canadian Oxford Dictionary. 47
Catholic Schools in the United States: An Encyclopedia. 44
Celtic Mythology A to Z. 31
Chemistry: Foundations and Applications. 51
Children's Reference Sources. 16
Clinton Years. 86
Compton's Encyclopedia and Fact-Finder. 1
ConsumerLab.com. 54
Countdown to November (Web). 14
CQ Voting and Elections Collection. 38
Crime and Punishment in America Reference Library. 43
Crusades Reference Library. 79

Day by Day: The Nineties. 79
DC Comics Encyclopedia: The Definitive Guide to the Characters of the DC Universe. 63
Debatable Issues in U.S. History. 87
Descriptionary. 48
Diamonds around the Globe: The Encyclopedia of International Baseball. 67

Dictionary of American Classical Composers. 64
Dictionary of American Young Adult Fiction, 1997-2001. 71
Dictionary of Gods and Goddesses. 30
Dictionary of Modern Design. 64
Dictionary of the Israeli-Palestinian Conflict: Culture, History, and Politics. 83
Did You Hear about the Reference Book That . . . ? 18
Discover America. 87
Discovering World Cultures: The Middle East. 35
Dostoevsky Encyclopedia. 73

e.encyclopedia science. 49
Early American Imprints, 1639-1800. 25
Eastern Europe: An Introduction to the People, Lands, and Culture. 81
Education of the Presidents of the United States. 87
Empires at War: A Chronological Encyclopedia from Sumer to the Persian Empire. 41
Encyclopedia Americana. 1
Encyclopedia Americana Online. 3
Encyclopedia Britannica Online. 2
Encyclopedia Britannica Online School Edition. 2
Encyclopedia of African History. 84
Encyclopedia of American Historical Documents. 87
Encyclopedia of American National Parks. 88
Encyclopedia of American Social Movements. 32
Encyclopedia of American Women in Business: From Colonial Times to the Present. 39
Encyclopedia of Ancient Asian Civilizations. 84
Encyclopedia of Animal Behavior. 52
Encyclopedia of Animals: A Complete Visual Guide. 52
Encyclopedia of Aquarium & Pond Fish. 60
Encyclopedia of Black Studies. 88
Encyclopedia of Breast Cancer. 57
Encyclopedia of British Writers: 16th, 17th, and 18th Centuries. 71
Encyclopedia of Cancer. 54
Encyclopedia of Capitalism. 38
Encyclopedia of Catholic Literature. 68
Encyclopedia of Chicago. 90
Encyclopedia of Children's Health and Wellness. 59
Encyclopedia of Christian Theology. 31
Encyclopedia of Civil Liberties in America. 36
Encyclopedia of Clothing and Fashion. 46
Encyclopedia of Cold War Espionage, Spies, and Secret Operations. 37
Encyclopedia of Contemporary Chinese Culture. 35
Encyclopedia of Criminology. 44
Encyclopedia of Cryptozoology: A Global Guide to Hidden Animals and Their Pursuers. 24
Encyclopedia of Cuban-United States Relations. 37
Encyclopedia of Death and Dying. 35
Encyclopedia of Early Cinema. 66
Encyclopedia of Earth Science. 51
Encyclopedia of Endocrine Diseases and Disorders. 58
Encyclopedia of Evaluation. 24
Encyclopedia of Exploration. 74
Encyclopedia of Family Health. 55

Encyclopedia of Federal Agencies and Commissions. 40
Encyclopedia of Feminist Literature. 68
Encyclopedia of Genetics. 51
Encyclopedia of Genocide and Crimes Against Humanity. 33
Encyclopedia of Gothic Literature. 68
Encyclopedia of Health and Behavior. 56
Encyclopedia of Hollywood. 66
Encyclopedia of Homelessness. 42
Encyclopedia of Intelligence and Counterintelligence. 37
Encyclopedia of Irish History and Culture. 82
Encyclopedia of Kitchen History. 61
Encyclopedia of Latino Popular Culture. 33
Encyclopedia of Law Enforcement. 43
Encyclopedia of Leadership. 61
Encyclopedia of Linguistics. 47
Encyclopedia of Men's Health. 56
Encyclopedia of Men's Reproductive Cancer. 54
Encyclopedia of Military Technology and Innovation. 59
Encyclopedia of Modern Jewish Culture. 73
Encyclopedia of Modern Worldwide Extremists and Extremist Groups. 36
Encyclopedia of Mongolia and the Mongol Empire. 83
Encyclopedia of Native American Wars & Warfare. 88
Encyclopedia of New Jersey. 90
Encyclopedia of Novels into Film. 66
Encyclopedia of Opera on Screen: A Guide to More Than 100 Years of Opera Films. 66
Encyclopedia of Physics. 50
Encyclopedia of Post-Colonial Literatures in English. 72
Encyclopedia of Prisons & Correctional Facilities. 44
Encyclopedia of Public Relations. 61
Encyclopedia of Rape. 43
Encyclopedia of Recorded Sound. 45
Encyclopedia of Recreation and Leisure in America. 65
Encyclopedia of Religious Rites, Rituals, and Festivals. 30
Encyclopedia of Sexually Transmitted Diseases. 58
Encyclopedia of Social Theory. 32
Encyclopedia of Social Welfare History in North America. 42
Encyclopedia of Sports Medicine. 59
Encyclopedia of Television. 45
Encyclopedia of the American Presidency. 88
Encyclopedia of the Arctic. 74
Encyclopedia of the Byzantine Empire. 83
Encyclopedia of the Chicago Literary Renaissance. 70
Encyclopedia of the Digestive System and Digestive Disorders. 54
Encyclopedia of the Enlightenment. 80
Encyclopedia of the Great Plains. 90
Encyclopedia of the Harlem Renaissance. 62
Encyclopedia of the Heart and Heart Disease. 56
Encyclopedia of the Library of Congress: For Congress, the Nation, & the World. 26
Encyclopedia of the Medieval World. 81
Encyclopedia of the Muscle and Skeletal Systems and Disorders. 58
Encyclopedia of the World's Minorities. 34
Encyclopedia of Twentieth Century Technology. 55

Encyclopedia of Vitamins, Minerals, and Supplements. 56
Encyclopedia of Wars. 41
Encyclopedia of White-Collar and Corporate Crime. 44
Encyclopedia of Women's Reproductive Cancer. 54
Encyclopedia of Wood: A Tree-by-Tree Guide to the World's Most Versatile Resource. 61
Encyclopedia of World Trade: From Ancient Times to the Present. 45
Encyclopedia of World War II: A Political, Social, and Military History. 81
Encyclopedia of Young Adult Authors. 70
Enfermedades y trastornos de la salud. 54
Ethics. 29
Everyone and Everything in Trollope. 72
Explorers and Exploration. 74
Exploring Gun Use in America. 43
Extraordinary American Writers. 70
Extraordinary People in Jazz. 70

Facts On File Companion to 20th-Century American Poetry. 71
Facts On File Dictionary of Music. 64
Family Tree Resource Book for Genealogists: The Essential Guide to American County and Town Sources. 77
Feminism in Literature. 68
Firefly Encyclopedia of Astronomy. 50
Firefly Five Language Visual Dictionary. 47
France: A Reference Guide from the Renaissance to the Present. 82
Free Jazz and Free Improvisation. 64
Frontier America. 88
Frontiers of Space Exploration. 60

Gale Encyclopedia of Alternative Medicine. 57
Gale Encyclopedia of Neurological Disorders. 58
Gilded Age. 35
Gods, Goddesses, and Mythology. 30
Great Events from History: The Ancient World, Prehistory-476 C.E. 80
Great Events from History: The Middle Ages. 80
Great Lives from History: The Ancient World, Prehistory-476 C.E. 80
Great Lives from History: The Middle Ages. 80
Greenwood Daily Life Online. 13
Greenwood Encyclopedia of American Regional Cultures. 90
Greenwood Encyclopedia of Daily Life. 13
Grolier Multimedia Encyclopedia. 3
Grolier Online. 3
Grzimek's Student Animal Life Resource: Birds. 52
Grzimek's Student Animal Life Resource: Mammals. 52
Guide to the Gothic III: An Annotated Bibliography of Criticism, 1993-2000. 25

Hammond World Travel Atlas. 75
Handbook of Classical Mythology. 31
Handbook of Inca Mythology. 32
Hatchet Jobs and Hardball: The Oxford Dictionary of American Political Slang. 48
Historic Documents Series: Online Edition. 91
Historical Dictionary of Iraq. 84
Historical Dictionary of Science Fiction Literature. 69
Historical Dictionary of Syria. 89

Historical Dictionary of the Civil War and Reconstruction. 89
Historical Gazetteer of the United States. 75
History of World War II. 81
History Reference Center. 91
Holidays, Festivals, and Celebrations of the World. 46
Holocaust Film Sourcebook. 25
Holy People of the World. 29
Human Body Systems. 53

Illustrated Encyclopedia of Scotland. 82
Illustrated World Atlas. 76
Industry Research Using the Economic Census: How to Find It, How to Use It. 39
International Directory of Business Biographies. 39
International Government Information and Country Information: A Subject Guide. 26
Islamic World: Past and Present. 74
Italy: A Reference Guide from the Renaissance to the Present. 82

John Wayne Filmography. 66
JPS Guide to Jewish Traditions. 31
Junior Worldmark Encyclopedia of the Canadian Provinces. 85
Junior Worldmark Encyclopedia of the Mexican States. 85
Junior Worldmark Encyclopedia of the Nations. 73
Junior Worldmark Encyclopedia of the States. 89

Kennedy Years. 86
Kids InfoBits. 27
Kingfisher Children's Encyclopedia. 27
Kingfisher History Encyclopedia. 80
Kingfisher Illustrated Horse & Pony Encyclopedia. 60

La nueva encyclopedia cumbre. 27
Landmark Supreme Court Cases: The Most Influential Decisions of the Supreme Court of the United States. 40
Latin American Mystery Writers: An A-to-Z Guide. 73
Latin American Science Fiction Writers: An A-to-Z Guide. 73
Literary Cultures of Latin America: A Comparative History. 72
Local and Regional Government Information: How to Find It, How to Use It. 24
London: A Historical Companion. 82

Magill's Medical Guide. 56
Masterplots 2: Short Story Series. 69
Merck Manual of Health and Aging. 57
Mexico: An Encyclopedia of Contemporary Culture and History. 85
Movieland Directory: Nearly 30,000 Addresses of Celebrity Homes, Film Locations, and Historical Sites in the Los Angeles Area, 1900-Present. 46
Multicultural Writers since 1945: An A-to-Z Guide. 69
My First Britannica. 28

National Geographic Atlas of the World. 76
National Geographic Encyclopedia of Space. 60
Native American Mythology A to Z. 31
Native American Placenames of the United States. 77
New Book of Knowledge. 2
New Book of Knowledge Online. 3
New Dictionary of the History of Ideas. 78
New Harvard Guide to Women's Health. 58
Ninth Book of Junior Authors and Illustrators. 69
Notable Playwrights. 70
Nutrition and Well-Being A to Z. 57

On the Trail of the Buffalo Soldier 2: New and Revised Biographies of African Americans in the U.S. Army, 1866-1917. 41
Outstanding Art and Architecture Online (Web). 15
Oxford American Writer's Thesaurus. 48
Oxford Companion to American Theater. 67
Oxford Companion to Canadian History. 85
Oxford Companion to the Brontes. 72
Oxford Companion to the Mind. 28
Oxford Dictionary of Art. 63
Oxford Dictionary of National Biography. 12
Oxford Dictionary of Nicknames. 78
Oxford Dictionary of Proverbs. 47
Oxford Dictionary of Quotations. 28
Oxford Digital Reference Shelf. 28
Oxford Encyclopedia of Food and Drink in America. 60
Oxford Rhyming Dictionary. 48

Peoples of Eastern Asia. 83
Philanthropy in America: A Comprehensive Historical Encyclopedia. 42
Placenames of France: Over 4,000 Towns, Villages, Natural Features, Regions, and Departments. 76
Pop Culture Latin America! Media, Arts, and Lifestyle. 35
Popular Psychology: An Encyclopedia. 29
Popular Series Fiction for Middle School and Teen Readers: A Reading and Selection Guide. 26
Poverty in the United States: An Encyclopedia of History, Politics, and Policy. 40
Psychology Basics. 29
Public Opinion and Polling around the World: A Historical Encyclopedia. 32

Queer Encyclopedia of Music, Dance, & Musical Theater. 67
Queer Encyclopedia of the Visual Arts. 63

Read-alikes: Exploring Exploration. 18
Reconstruction Era Reference Library. 89
Reference Books in Spanish for Children and Adolescents. 19
Reference Sources in History: An Introductory Guide. 26
Reference Sources on the Presidency and Presidential Elections. 20
Renaissance Art and Architecture. 63
Riverside Dictionary of Biography. 77
Russia: A Reference Guide from the Renaissance to the Present. 83

Satchmo: The Louis Armstrong Encyclopedia. 64
Scholastic Children's Encyclopedia. 27
Science Full Text Select. 53
Science in the Ancient World: An Encyclopedia. 49
Science in the Contemporary World: An Encyclopedia. 49
Science in the Early Twentieth Century: An Encyclopedia. 49
Science Resource Center. 53
Science, Technology, and Society. 36
Shamanism: An Encyclopedia of World Beliefs, Practices, and Culture. 30
Some Key Reference Works for Genealogists. 21
South and Meso-American Mythology A to Z. 31
South Asian Literature in English: An Encyclopedia. 72
Southeast Asia: A Historical Encyclopedia from Angkor Wat to East Timor. 84

Space Exploration Reference Library. 60
Sport in American Culture: From Ali to X-Games. 36
Sports in America: Decade by Decade. 67
Sports Market Place Directory, 2004. 45
State and National Boundaries of the United States. 75
Student's Encyclopedia of Judaism. 31
Student's Guide to Earth Science. 51

Teen Guides to Environmental Science. 38
Terrorism: A Guide to Events and Documents. 32
Tobacco in History and Culture: An Encyclopedia. 46
Total Baseball: The Ultimate Baseball Encyclopedia. 68
Twenty Best Bets for Student Researchers. 22

U.S. Immigration and Migration Reference Library. 33
U.S. Legal System. 40
U.S.A. Twenties. 89
Understanding Architecture. 63
Uniting States: The Story of Statehood for the Fifty United States. 36
Universal Book of Mathematics: From Abracadabra to Zeno's Paradoxes. 50
UXL Encyclopedia of Water Science. 51
UXL Newsmakers. 77

Value of a Dollar: Prices and Incomes in the United States, 1860-2004. 39
Victorians at War, 1815-1914. 41

Weapons of Mass Destruction: An Encyclopedia of Worldwide Policy, Technology, and History. 42
West's Encyclopedia of American Law. 40
Women in Early America: Struggle, Survival, and Freedom in a New World. 34
Women in the Middle Ages: An Encyclopedia. 34
Woodstock: An Encyclopedia of the Music and Art Fair. 65
Working Americans, 1880-2005: Volume 6, Women at Work. 34
World Book Encyclopedia. 2
World Book Online Reference Center. 4
World Book's Science & Nature Guides. 49
World History: Ancient and Medieval Eras. 78
World of Animals: Insects and Other Invertebrates. 52